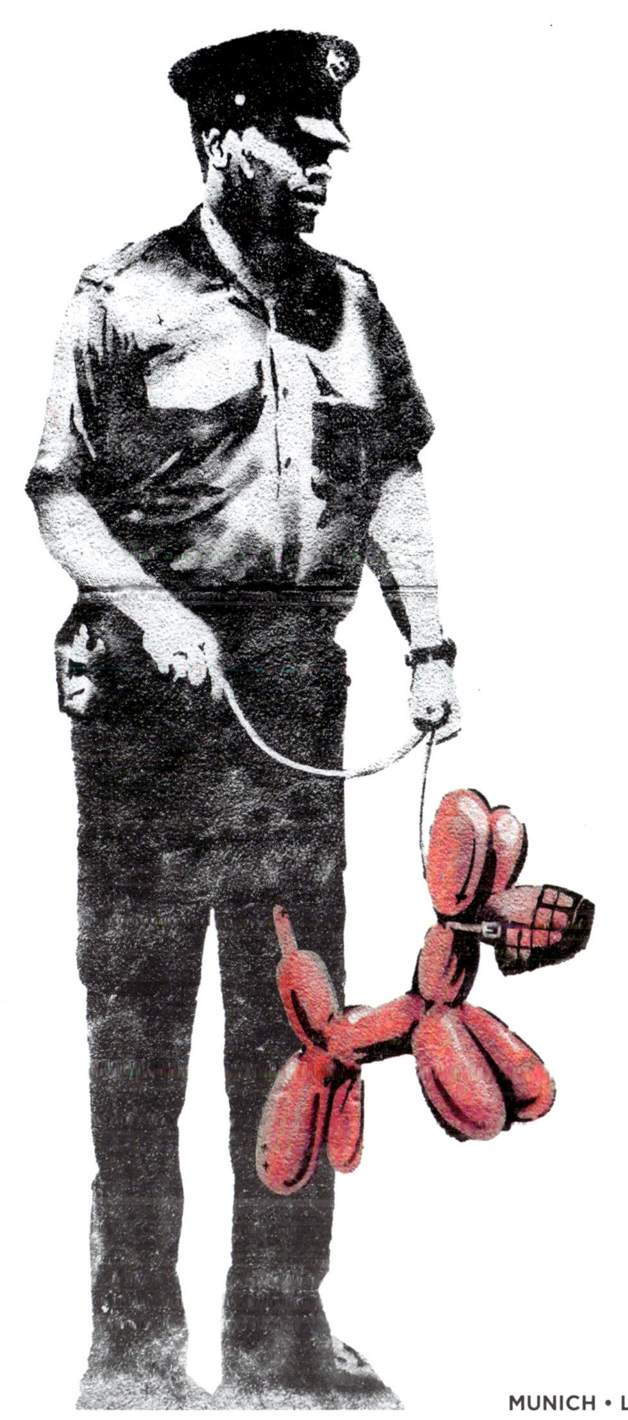

PRESTEL

MUNICH · LONDON · NEW YORK

URBAN JUNGLE

ALESSANDRA MATTANZA

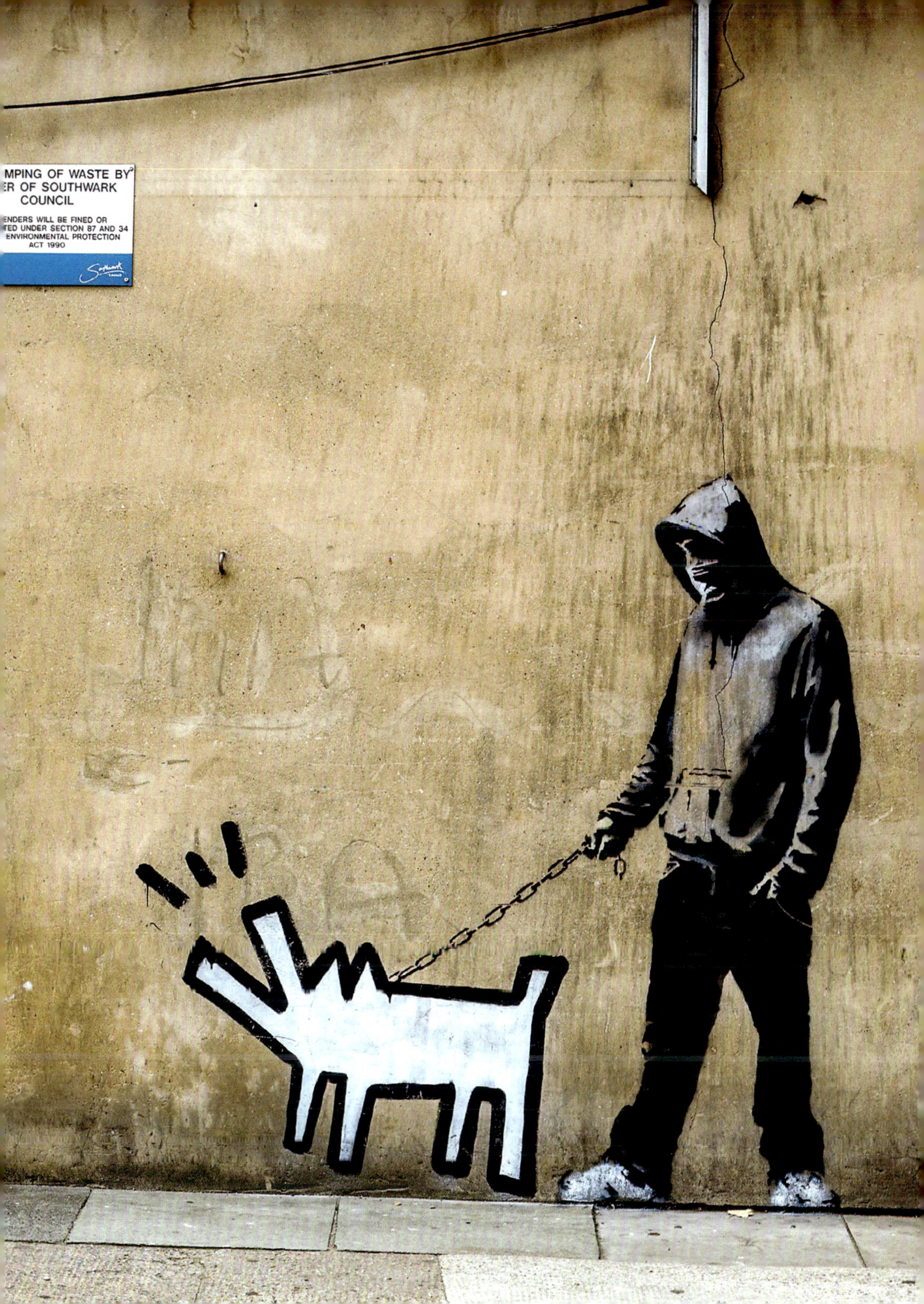
MPING OF WASTE BY
ER OF SOUTHWARK
COUNCIL
ENDERS WILL BE FINED OR
TED UNDER SECTION 87 AND 34
ENVIRONMENTAL PROTECTION
ACT 1990
Southwark
Council

"IMAGINE A CITY WHERE GRAFFITI WASN'T ILLEGAL, A CITY WHERE EVERYBODY COULD DRAW WHATEVER THEY LIKED. WHERE EVERY STREET WAS AWASH WITH A MILLION COLORS AND LITTLE PHRASES. WHERE STANDING AT A BUS STOP WAS NEVER BORING. A CITY THAT FELT LIKE A PARTY WHERE EVERYONE WAS INVITED, NOT JUST THE ESTATE AGENTS AND BARONS OF BIG BUSINESSES. IMAGINE A CITY LIKE THAT AND STOP LEANING AGAINST THE WALL — IT'S WET"

BANKSY

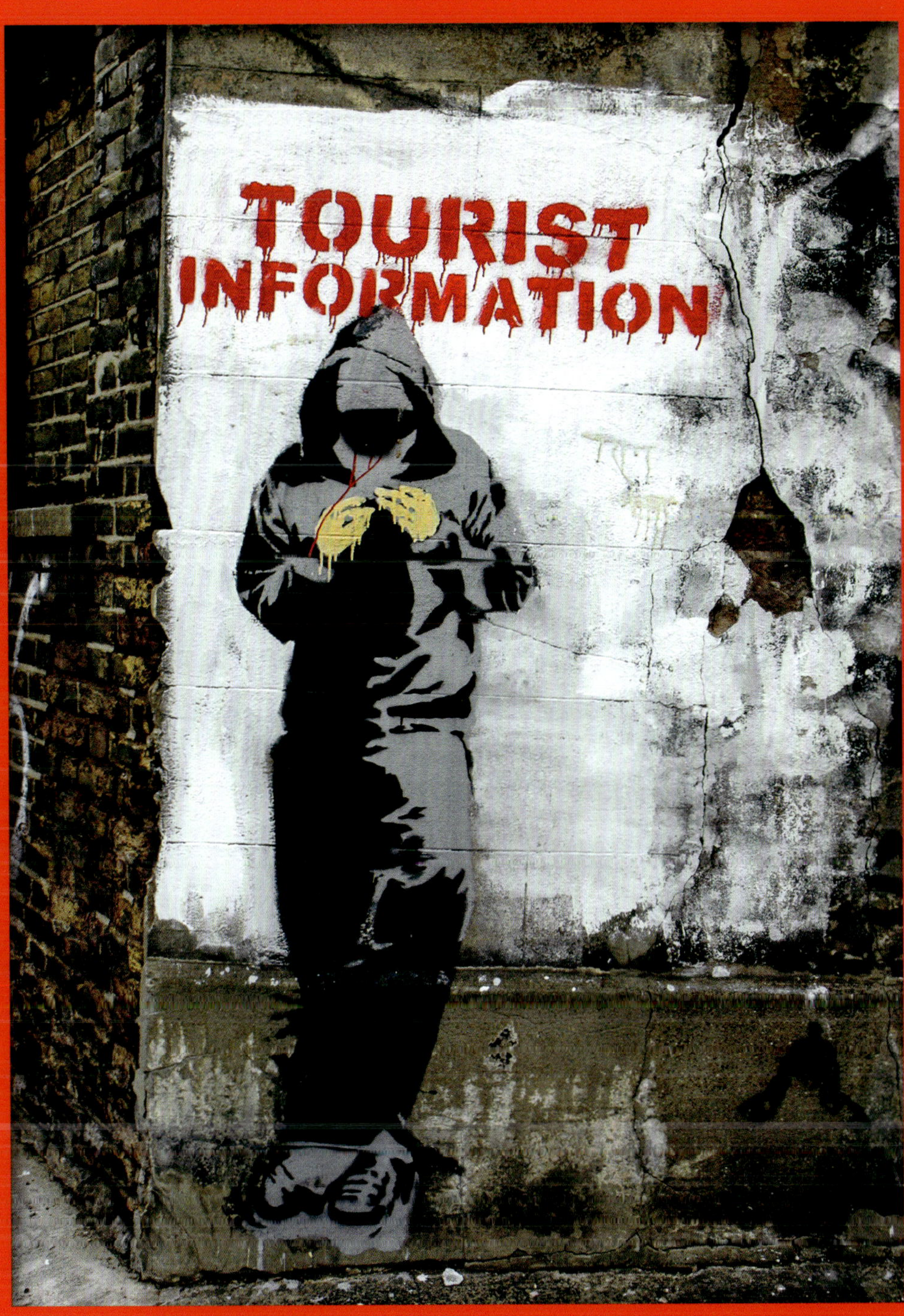

TOURIST
INFORMATION

**BANKSY LOVES COLORS, AS
YOU CAN TELL FROM THE
BRIGHT RED CONTRASTING
WITH BLACK INSCRIPTIONS,
FROM HIS FIERY RED
HEARTS, FROM HIS BLUE
SKIES CRACKING THE WALLS
OF DISCORD LIKE WOUNDS
ON THE SKIN, OR FROM
HIS PINKS AND YELLOWS
CONTRASTING WITH
THE PURE BLACK OF HIS
STENCILS.**

The characters inhabiting Banksy's urban jungle are just as "colorful." With their biting, irreverent, and inquisitive personalities, they are magnetic in their will to act to change the status quo. They are heroes and anti-heroes baring their souls. Banksy plays with colors, giving them a specific purpose throughout all his oeuvre: they are metaphors of blood, protest, and suffering, because everything has a meaning in his creations, and nothing is left to chance. And so, great cities and metropolises are not just mazes of concrete, but they become great canvases on which to spread the colors from a palette and unleash creativity. Banksy fills them with his characters, giving life to a rather varied and insolent asphalt jungle. If, on the one hand, there are humanized animals, on the other, human beings take on pretty wild and instinctive characteristics, as if they lost their self-control and revealed themselves, thus becoming instruments of social protest, messengers spreading the voice of the artist, who vigorously defends his anonymity and lets them speak for him. Sometimes, Banksy's characters almost look like they came straight out of a film. They are eclectic, romantic in their own way, nonconformist, with something of a Fellini movie fading into the complex existentialism of Michelangelo Antonioni and giving a nod to Tim Burton's darkness and the Coen brothers' parody of the absurd. After all, Banksy is an avid reader, as well as a writer and a fan of auteur movies. "Film is incredibly democratic and accessible, it's probably the best option if you actually want to change the world, not just re-decorate it," he said. "I think it's pretty clear that film is the pre-eminent art form of our age. If Michelangelo or Leonardo Da Vinci were alive today, they'd be making *Avatar*, not painting a chapel," he suggested.

Perhaps Banksy expressed some appreciation for digital art? After all, he is the author of books, documentaries, and videos; he surfed the web almost with the talent of a hacker, reaching millions of followers on his official Instagram profile.

What is certain is that Banksy never ceased to take a stand against those values promoted by many tech companies that profess their will to make the world a better place. He made his thoughts on this regard abundantly clear. "There's nothing more dangerous than someone who wants to

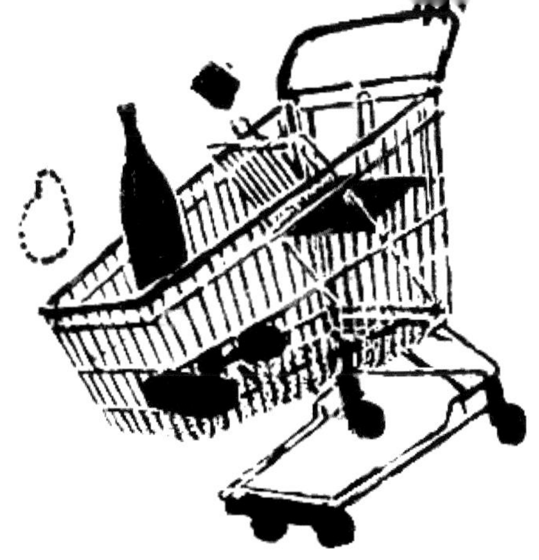

make the world a better place," he said, even though a while ago, talking about graffiti and street art, he also said: "I just wanna make the world a better-looking place. If you don't like it, you can paint over it!" Recalling these words, he recently said with a vein of melancholy: "I originally set out to try and save the world, but now I'm not sure I like it enough." With this series of quotes and words written on the walls or shouted to the wind, Banksy reveals his most intimate self, touching the hearts of people because he mixes with people; like a chameleon he becomes one of them, and after all, his entire oeuvre has always been dedicated to people. That's why his urban jungle welcomes people of all ages and of all social categories and classes, lost souls looking for their identity, tormented and destroyed by the system and the capitalist society. They are figures standing at a crossroads or looking for an alternative route that doesn't lead them to adapt, but to find their own rules of life.

Sometimes, Banksy oscillates from one feeling to another, from one thought to another, or from one idea to another, and often even contradictorily. Artists are typically fickle because they are sensitive and subject to sudden mood changes; they are unpredictable and irrational like an untamed colt, fierce and combative like a tiger, free and independent like a street cat. All this applies perfectly to Banksy, indeed, in him it is amplified and intensified. After all, these same features also describe the characters inhabiting his urban jungle, who make up a kaleidoscope of virtues and vices, contrasts and contradictions. All of this is beautifully reflected in this quote by Banksy: "Some people become cops because they want to make the world a better place. Some people become vandals because they want to make the world a better-looking place."

Banksy often has a difficult relationship with his subjects. For a long time, he has had a particularly conflictual relationship with the police, with which he often had quarrels, especially when he was breaking the law with his graffiti. "My main problem with cops is that they do what they're told. They say, 'Sorry mate, I'm just doing my job' all the fucking time," he once said, exasperated. And then, he also said: "It is a very frustrating feeling you get when the only people with good photos of your work are the police department."

According to an urban legend, it was indeed the police who inspired Banksy to use stencils in his art when he was only eighteen. On a dark night, he hid under a truck to escape the police. He noticed a printed tag placed at the fuel tank base. While taking a closer look, he began to think that using stencils could have significantly reduced the time needed to paint on the walls, thus also minimizing the risk of being caught. "As soon as I cut my first stencil, I could feel the power there. I also like the political edge. All graffiti is low-level dissent, but stencils have an extra history. They've been used to start revolutions and stop wars," he said.

His relationship with the police is one of the most prolific and conflicted in the history of art.

It starts with direct confrontation…

Fuck the Police (2000) speaks for itself: It is a stencil depicting a policeman looking with disappointment at this offensive sentence written in red on the wall when it is already too late to do anything about it.

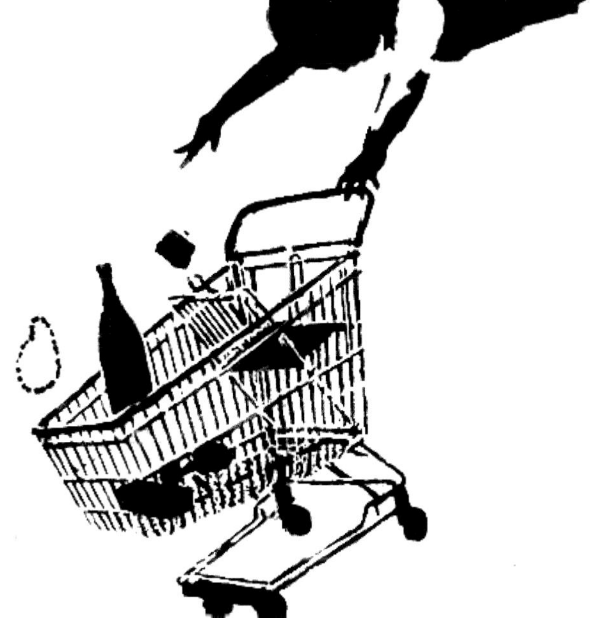

Stop Me Before I Paint Again (2004) is another clear act of defiance against the police serving the powers that be.

Snorting Copper (2005) depicts a policeman sniffing a line of cocaine on a road, a clear example of widespread hypocrisy and corruption.

Banksy might have had fun portraying the police in a thousand irreverent, fun, ironic and sometimes cruel ways. How could we forget the *Rude Copper* (2002) staring at you while raising his middle finger in a gesture of defiance but also intransigence and contempt? And then there's the *Riot Copper* (2002), ready for action with his billy club but with a smiley emoji face. In 2003, it is the turn of *Flying Copper*, with a smiley emoji face and angel wings on his back. And who could forget the 2004 *Kissing Coppers*, a pair of British policemen kissing to promote gender equality.

However, Banksy's urban jungle is mostly inhabited by the *Villains*: the most sinister figures, those who show their worst side and reveal all the sins of a hypocritical and bourgeois society. There's the man offering his dog the paw he has just cut off with a saw he is hiding behind his back, while the poor animal still looks at him grateful and submissive. And it doesn't get better with the wife trying to draw her husband's attention away from her lover who is hanging naked from the windowsill to avoid being discovered. Cruelty, betrayal, and hypocrisy are rampant.

But there are also the *Urban Lovers* who seek love even in a tough and harsh world, like the man with a bunch of flowers waiting at the entrance of a nightclub, or like the two lovers dreamily looking at each other with diving helmets on their heads. And there's also the *Urban Angels*, dark and eerie figures with their faces often hidden by their hoodie. They are like Banksy's alter egos: dark and gloomy, they look like fallen angels.

And then there's the *Invisibles*, those who are normally invisible to the eyes of society, who do not occupy prestigious positions, who fight to survive every day of their lives, and whose rights are trampled on with no one to protect them. Banksy sees them, talks to them, wants to listen to them, seeks to protect them.

Banksy still recalls the strong personality of a maid he ran into in a hotel room in Los Angeles. It is no coincidence that she became the protagonist of one of his most popular stencils, which depicts her while lifting up the wall as you would do with a carpet. The metaphor is clear and the criticism evident.

The workers and waste collectors who are often instructed to wipe off graffiti have become part of Banksy's stencils more than once.

Finally, there are the *Rebels*, those who openly rebel against the system, like the now famous protester who is about to throw a bunch of flowers instead of a bomb.

In any case, the message is clear: dare and don't be scared. To all those who are afraid to venture out onto the streets, Banksy's advice is: "Nothing in the world is more common than unsuccessful people with talent—leave the house before you find something worth staying for."

A POLICE OFFICER IN RIOT GEAR WITH A WEAPON, ANGEL WINGS, AND A SMILEY EMOJI FACE.

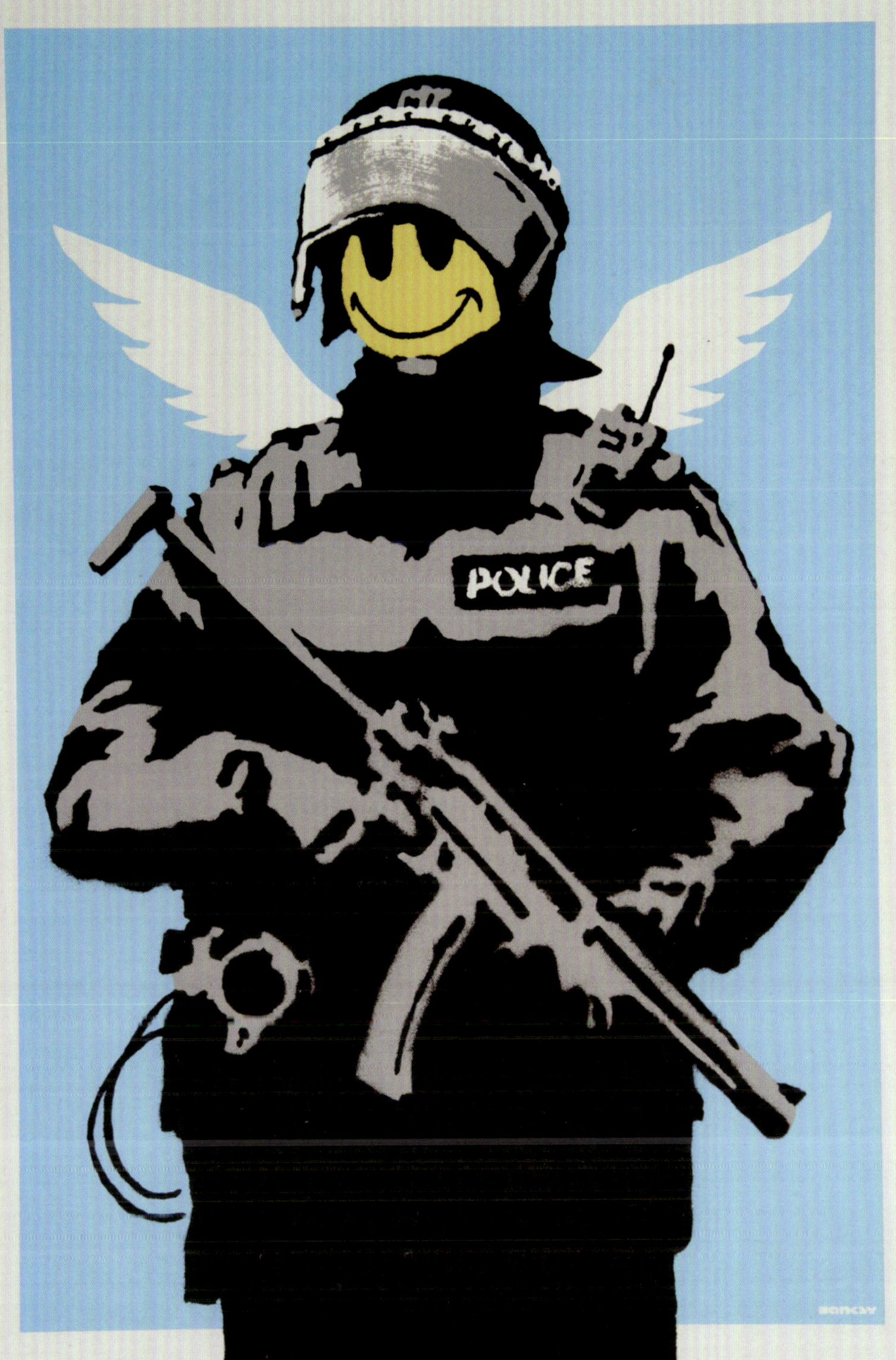

POLICE
Banksy

FLOWER THROWER – ASH SALON STREET, BETHLEHEM, 2003

A MAN THROWS A BUNCH OF FLOWERS INSTEAD OF A FIREBOMB: A STRONG MESSAGE OF PEACE AND RECONCILIATION TO BREAK DOWN THE BARRIERS BETWEEN THE PEOPLES OF ISRAEL AND PALESTINE.

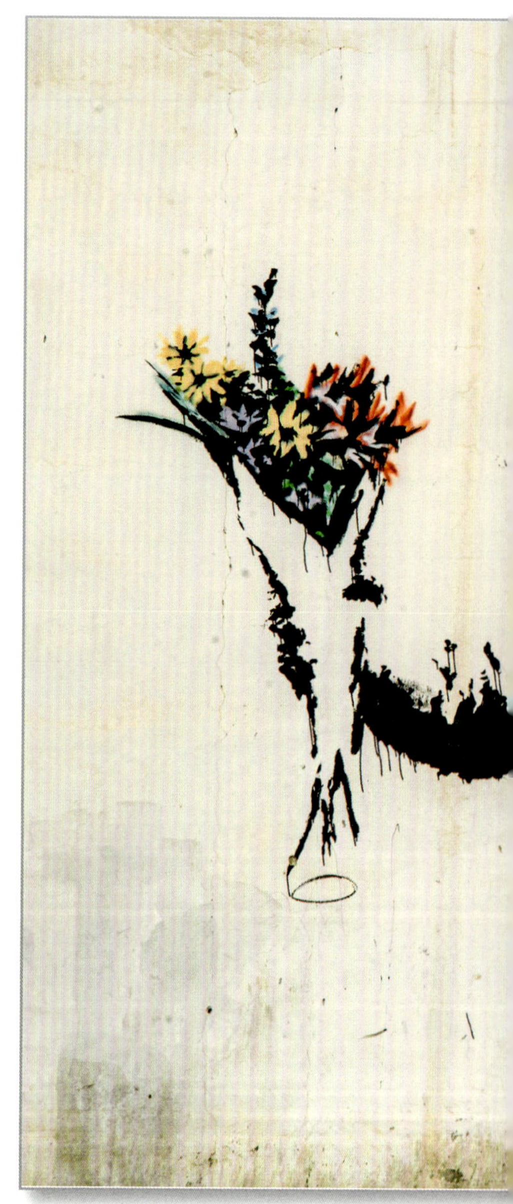

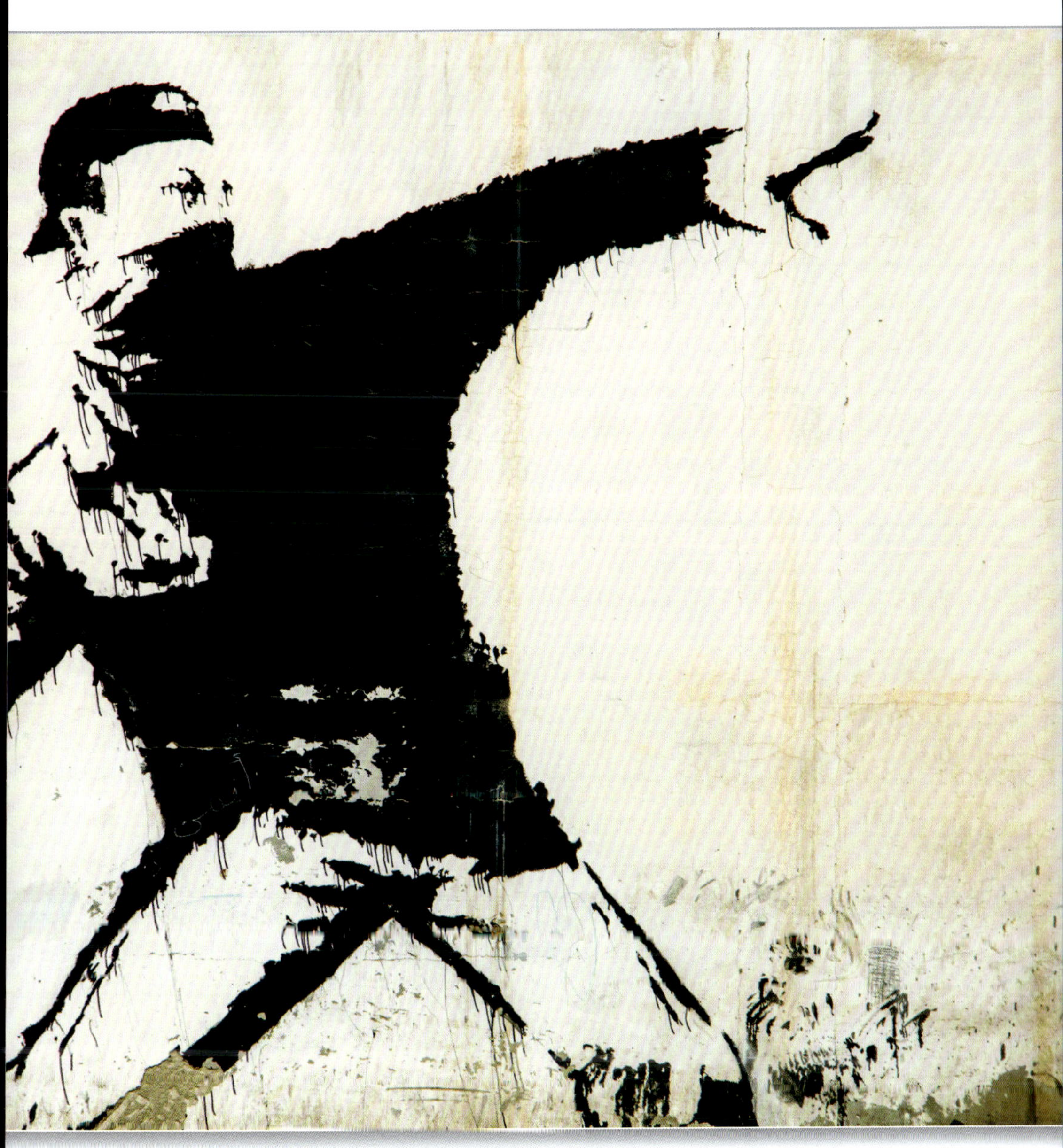

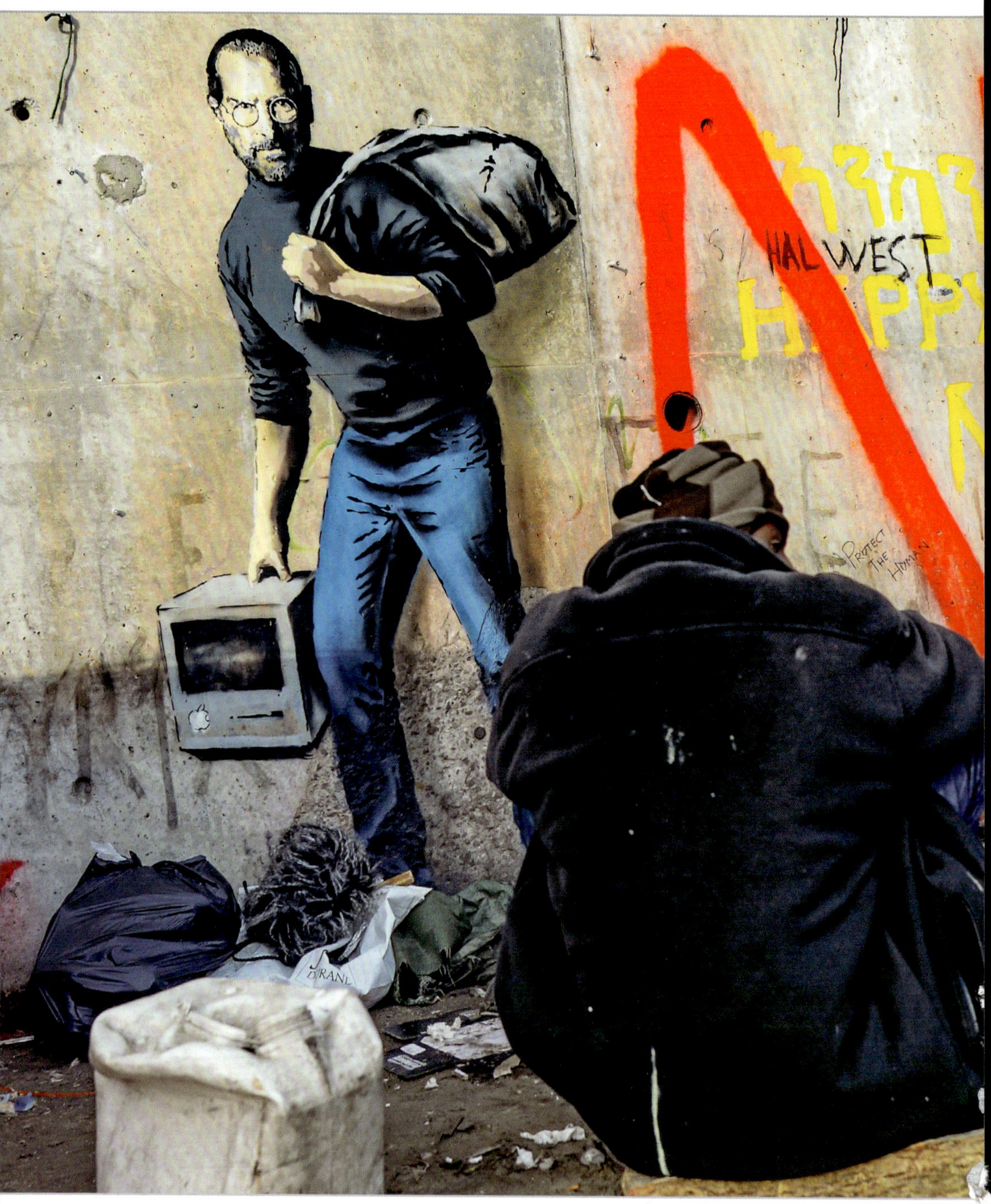
HAL WEST
PROTECT
THE
HUMAN
DURANI

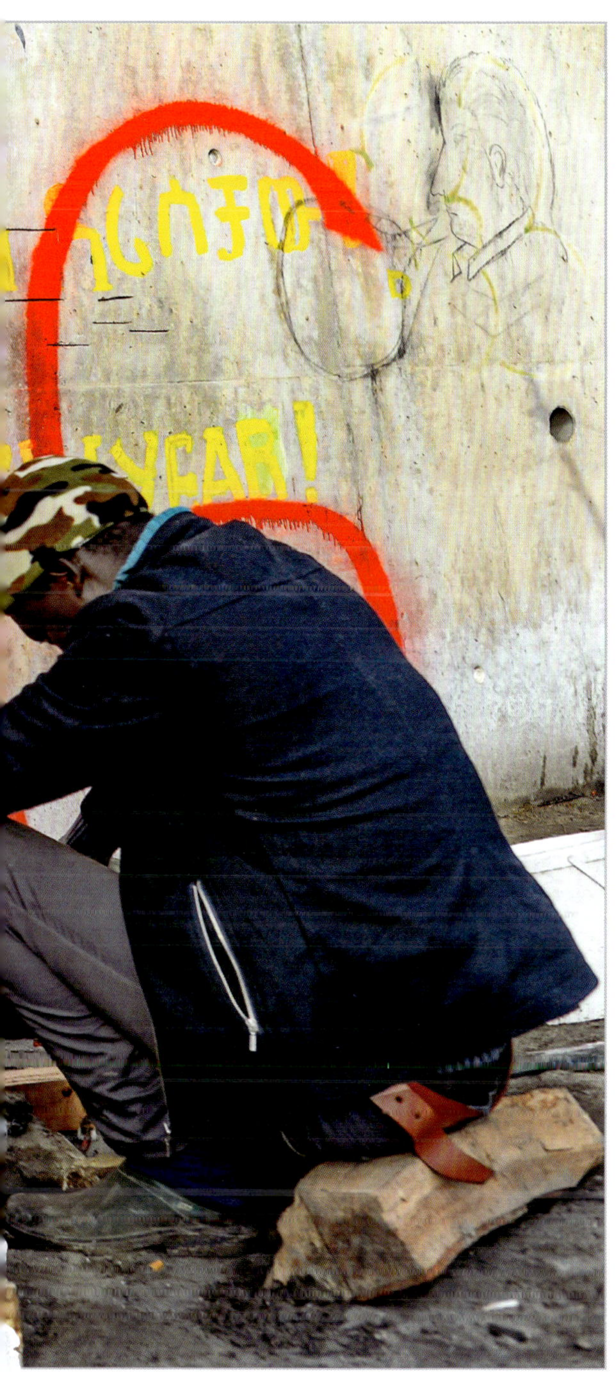

A SON OF A MIGRANT
FROM SYRIA – CALAIS, 2015

STEVE JOBS IN A REFUGEE CAMP IN CALAIS WITH A BAG OVER HIS SHOULDER AND A MACINTOSH REMINDS US OF HIS ORIGINS AS THE SON OF A SYRIAN IMMIGRANT, ADOPTED BY A COUPLE OF ARMENIAN AMERICANS.

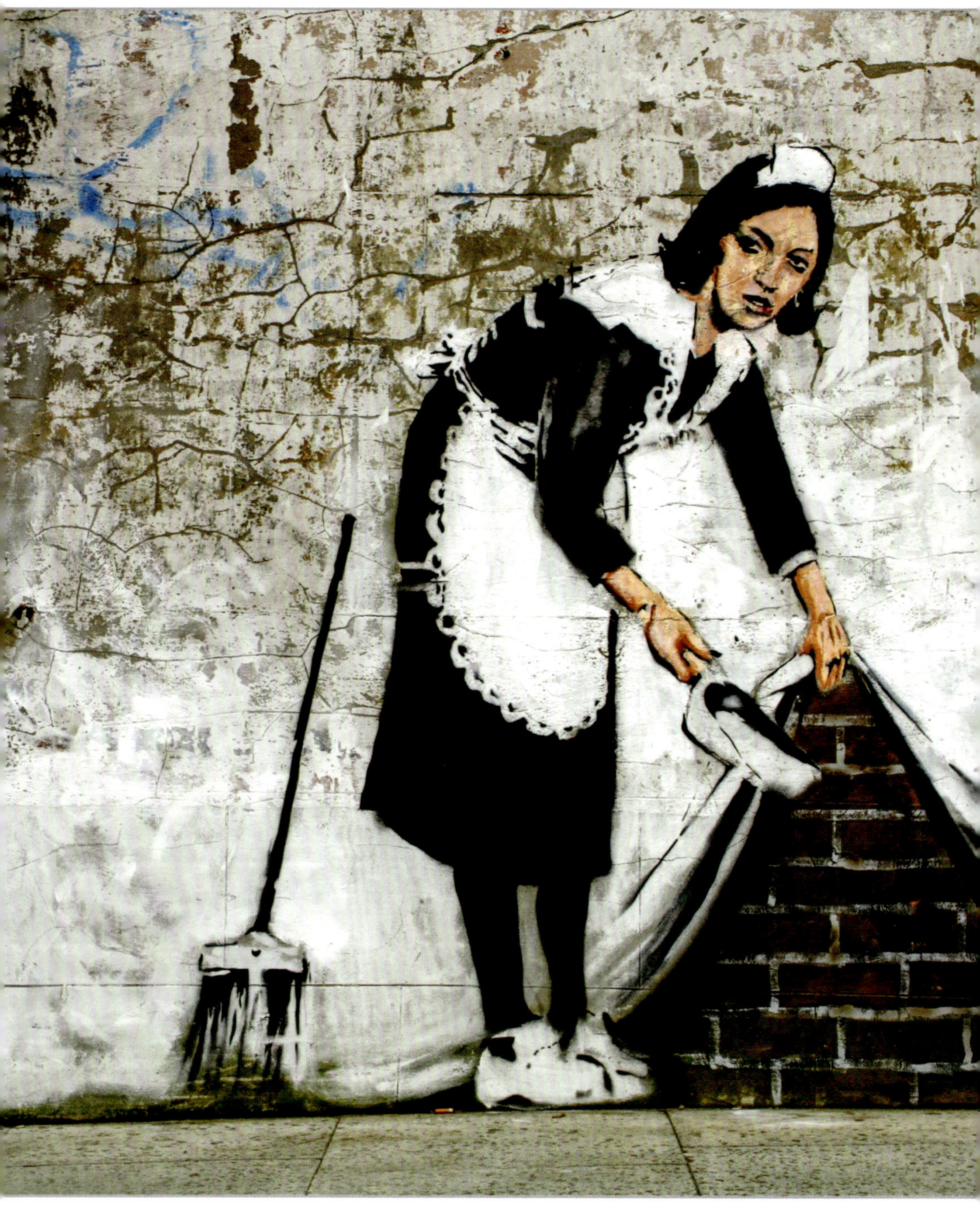

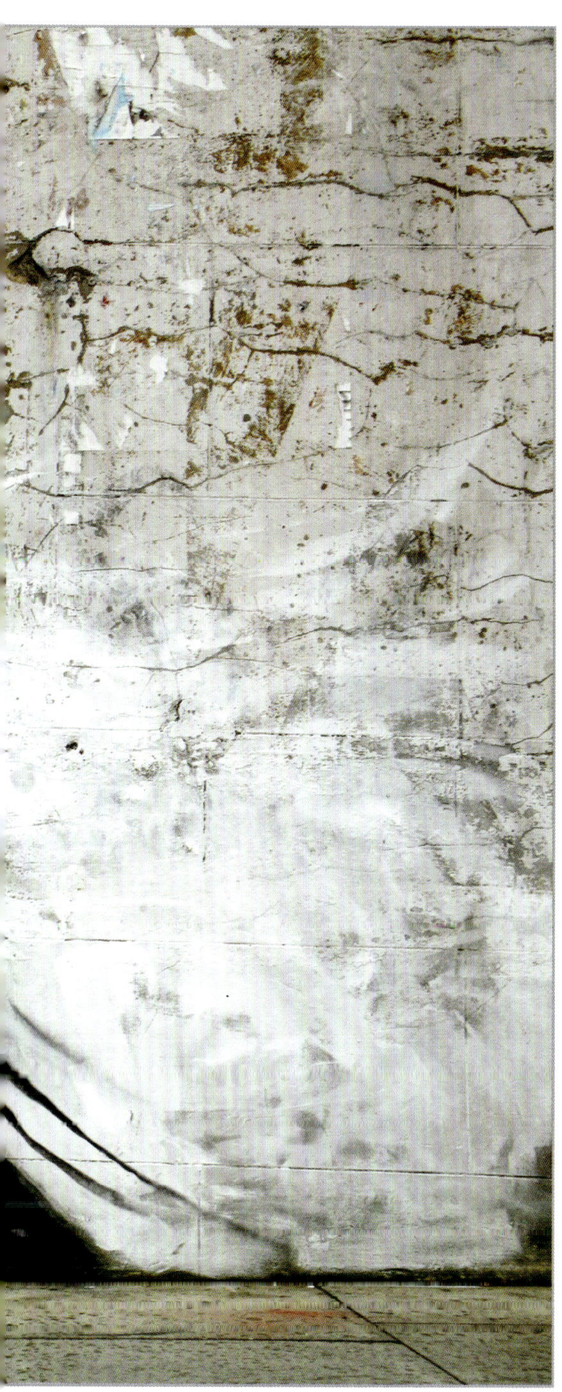

THE WAITRESS LEANNE IS SWEEPING THE DUST UNDER THE CARPET, JUST LIKE GOVERNMENTS OFTEN DO WHEN THEY TRY TO HIDE THE MOST THORNY ISSUES.

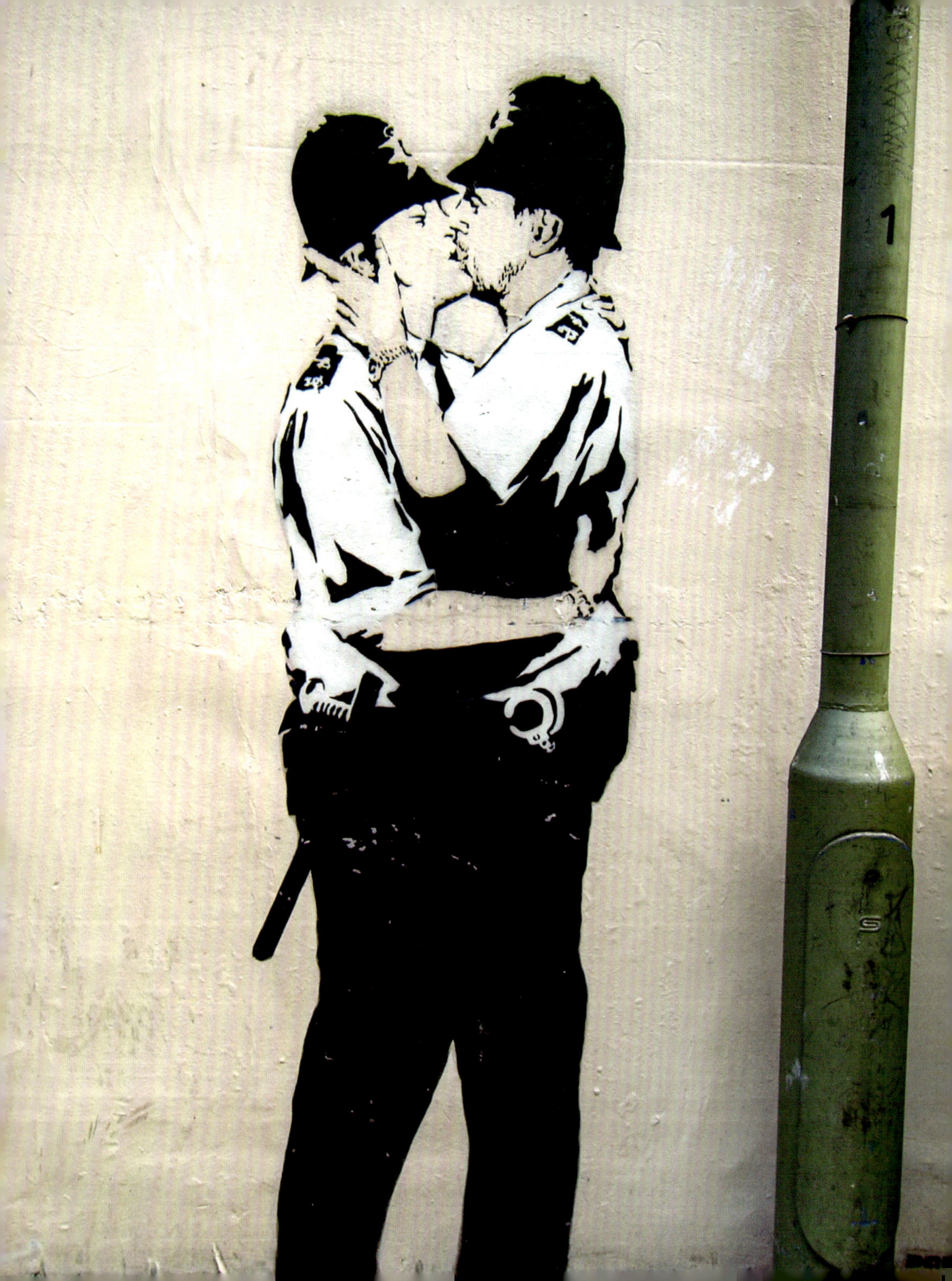

A TRUE ICON FOR THE LGBTQIA+ COMMUNITY, BUT NOT ONLY. THIS GRAFFITI WORK IS BANKSY'S DENUNCIATION OF THE HYPOCRISY OF THE WHOLE BRITISH ESTABLISHMENT.

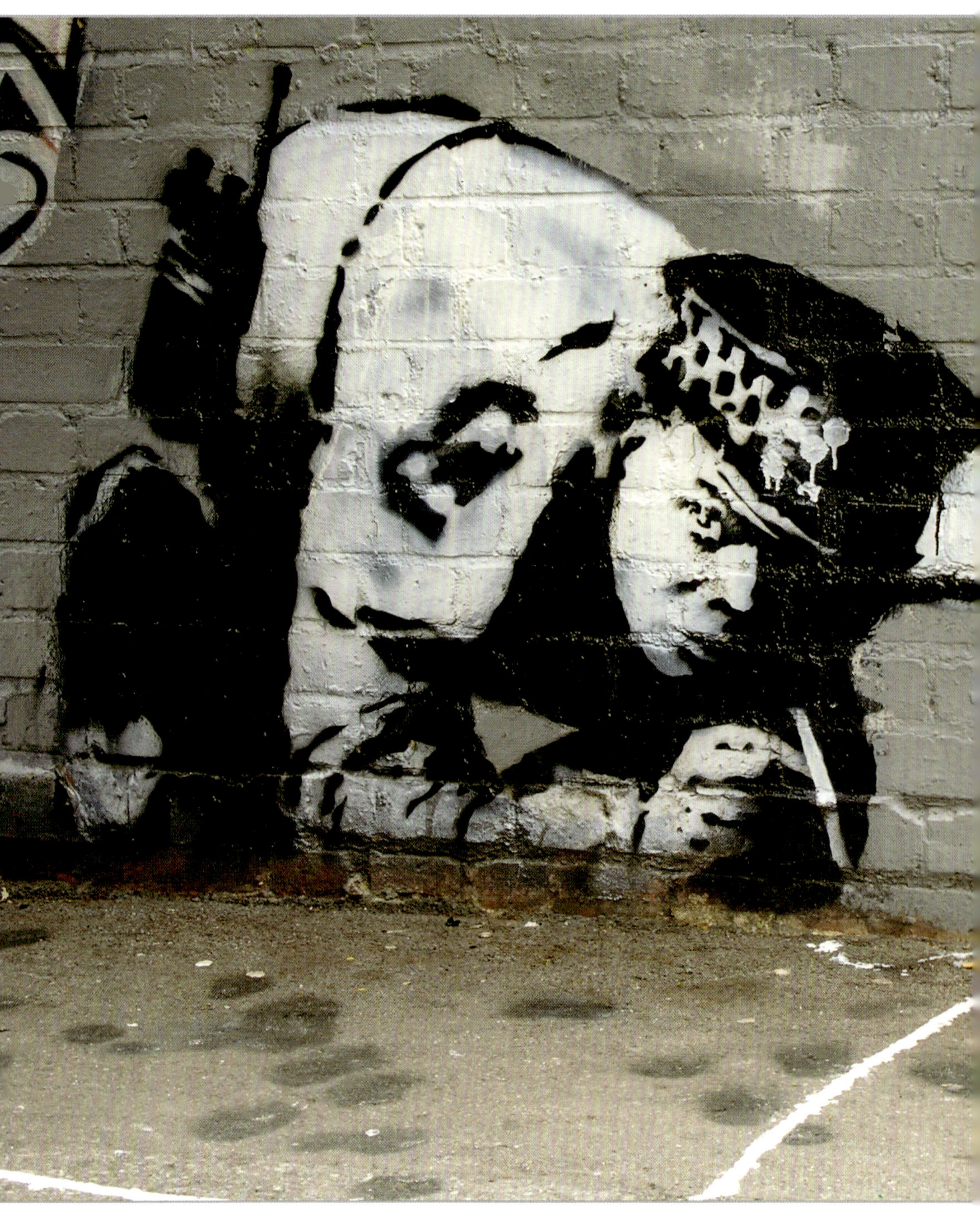

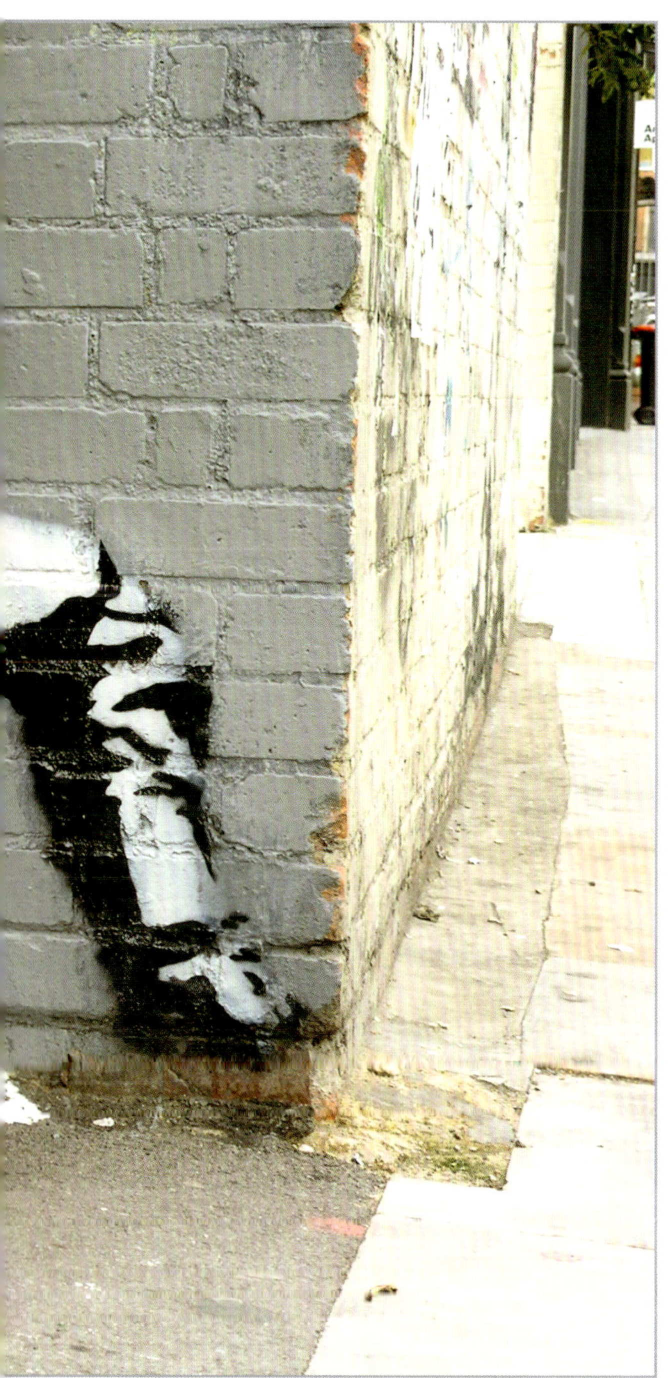

A VERY PECULIAR INVESTIGATION... A POLICE OFFICER IS PORTRAYED AT A CRIME SCENE WHILE SNIFFING COCAINE.

24-25 *HOODIE WITH KNIFE – THE CANS FESTIVAL, LONDON, 2008*

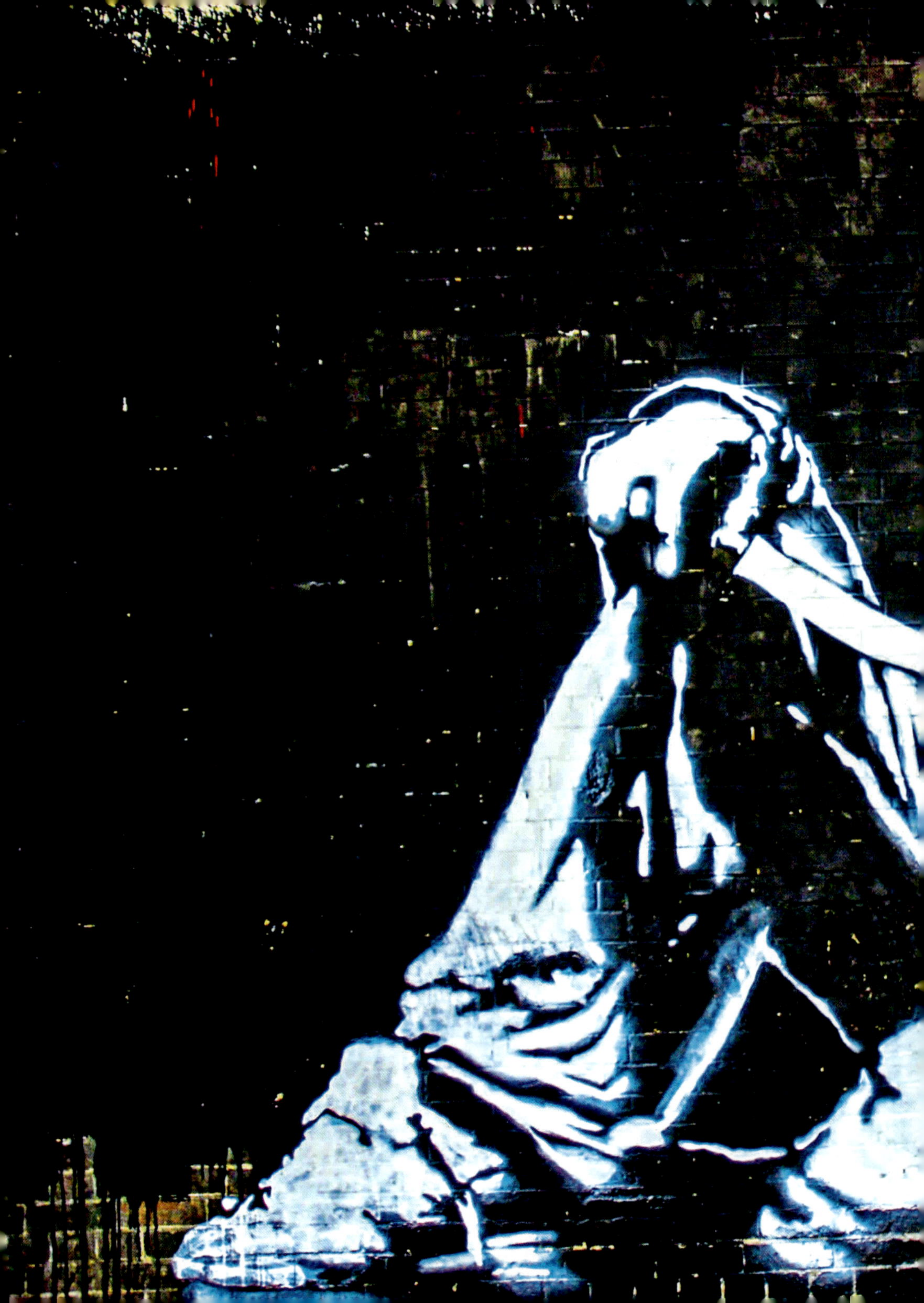

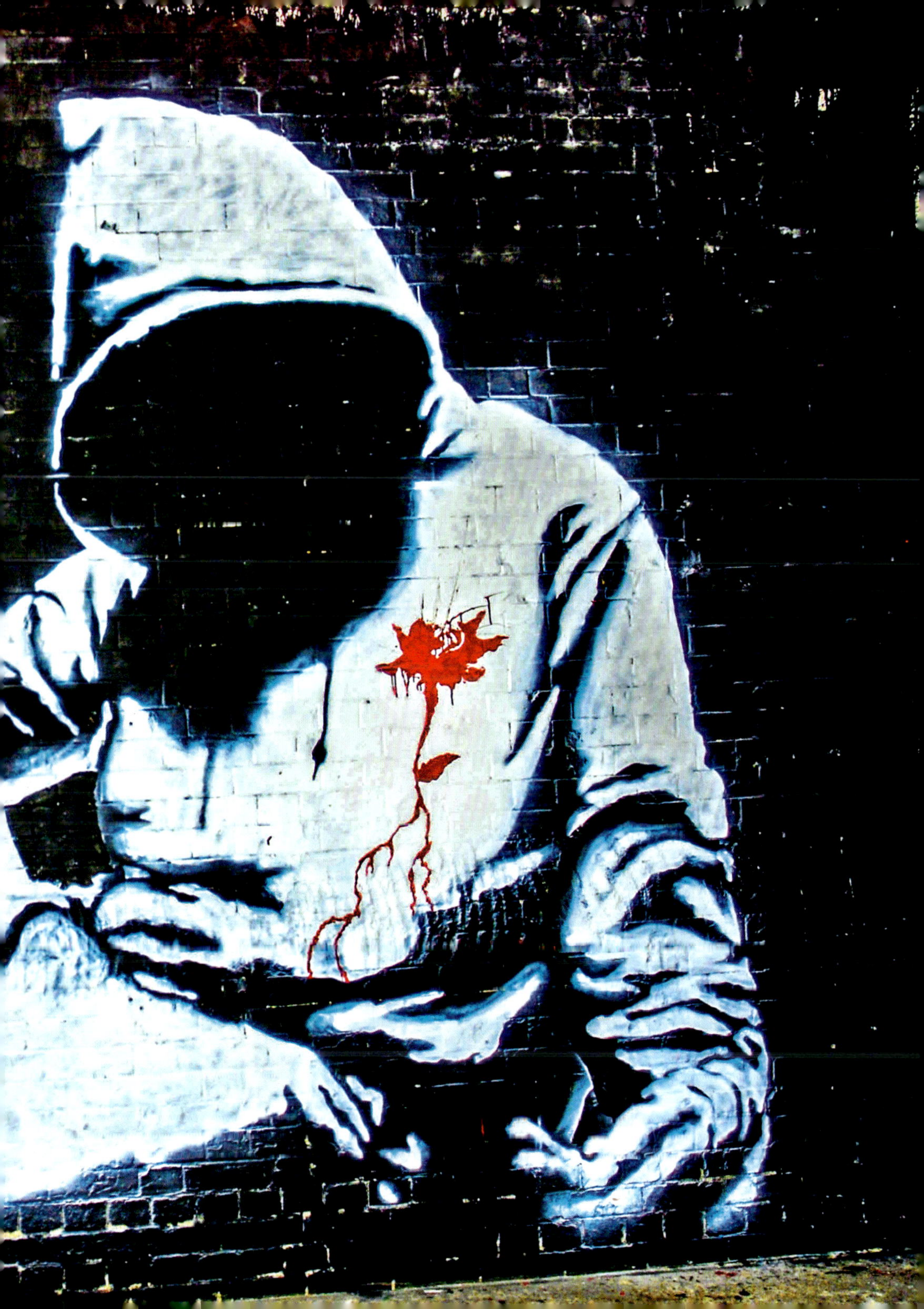

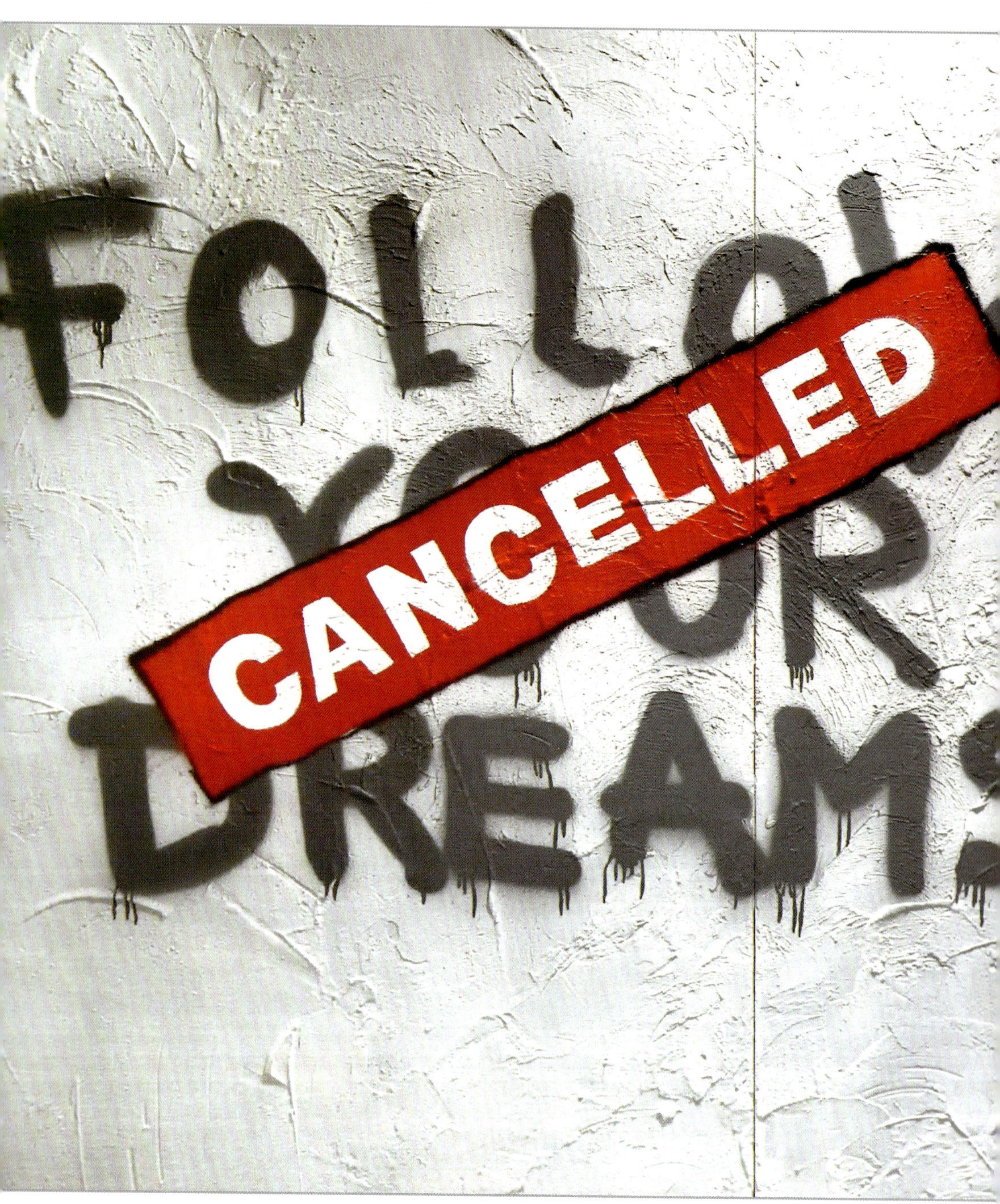
FOLLOW YOUR DREAMS
CANCELLED

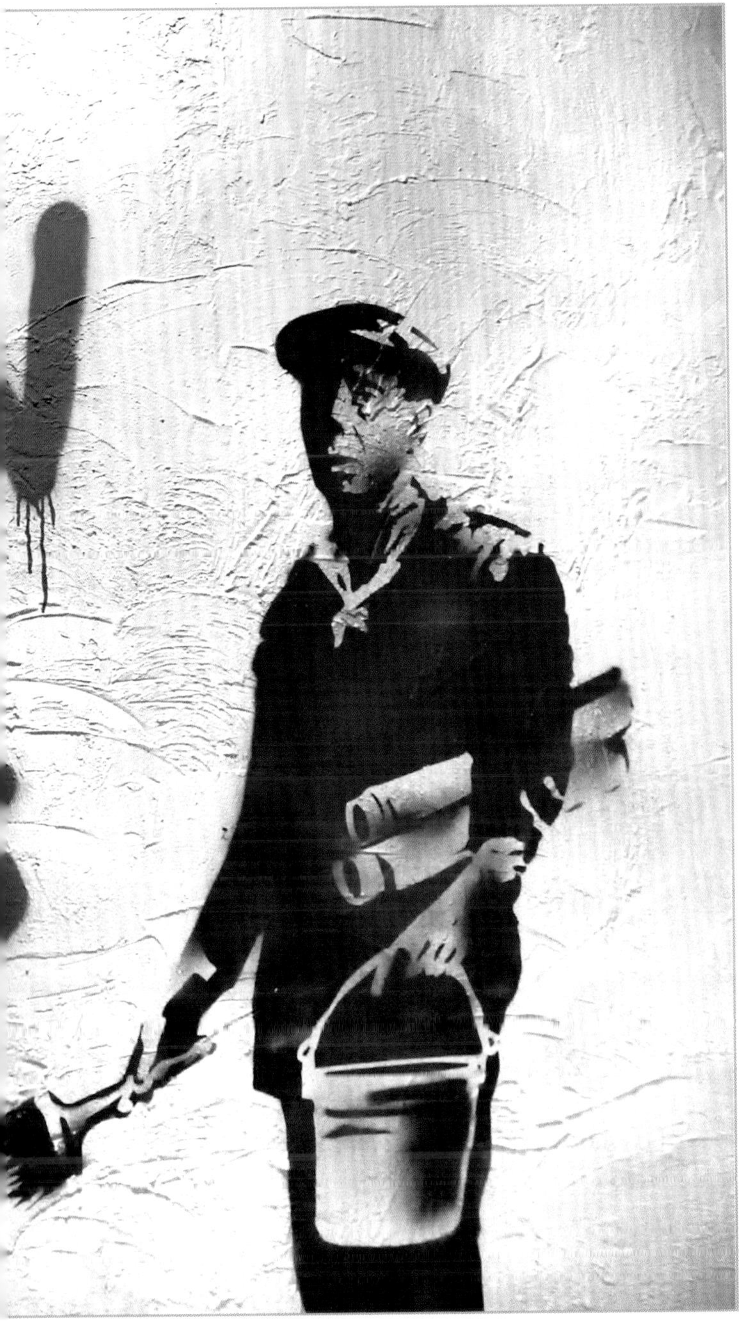

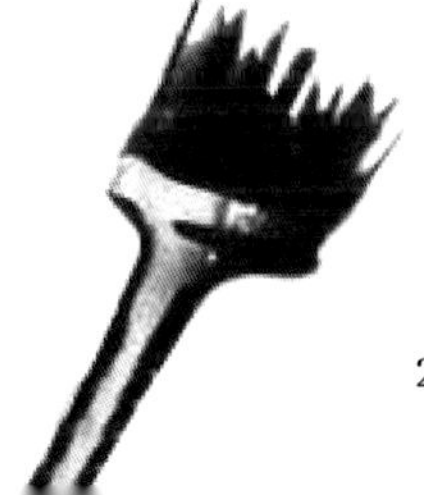

FOLLOW YOUR DREAMS – BOSTON, 2010

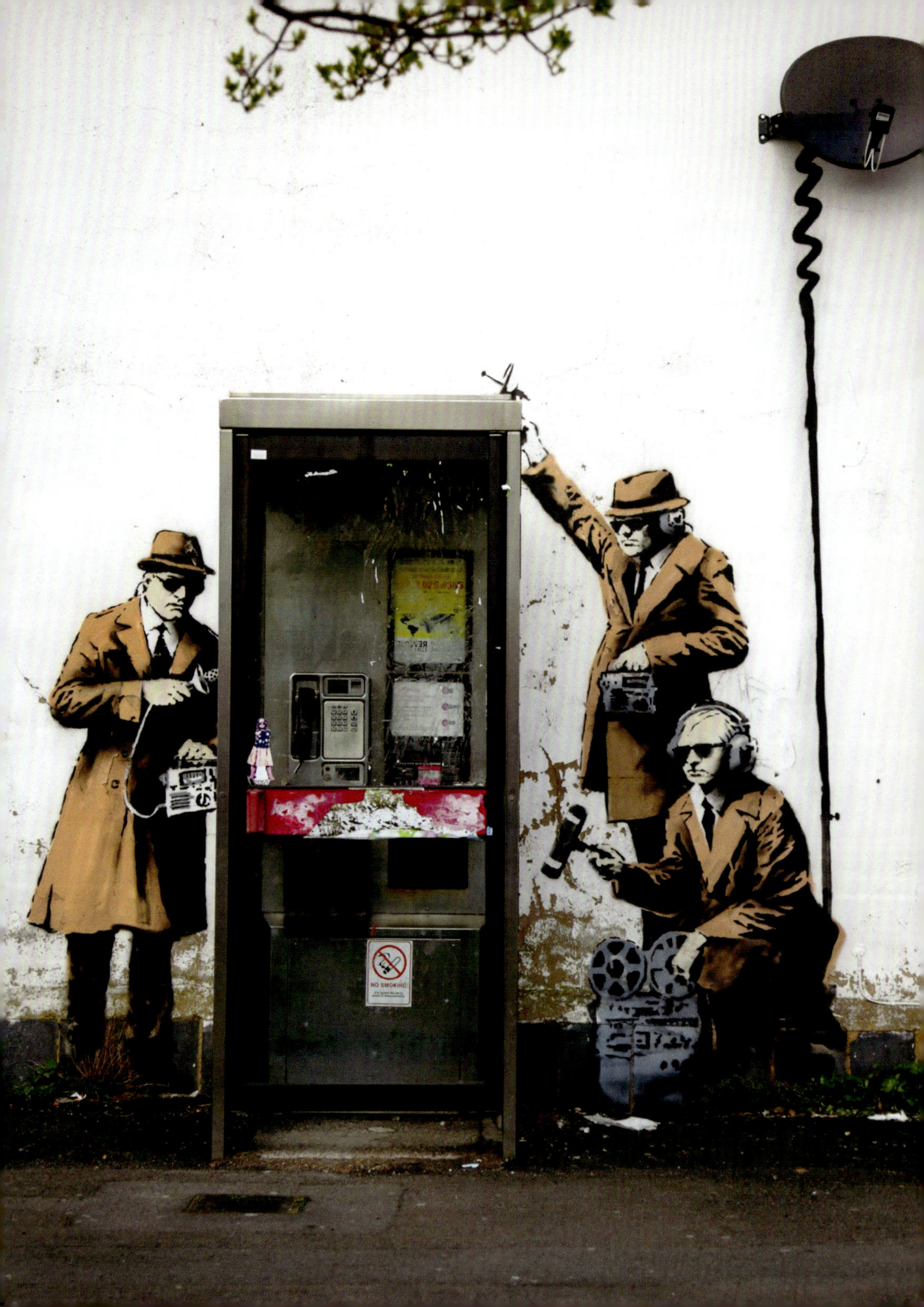

THREE GOVERNMENT SPIES ARE LISTENING TO A CONVERSATION AROUND A PHONE BOOTH A FEW MILES FROM THE GCHQ (GOVERNMENT COMMUNICATIONS HEADQUARTERS).

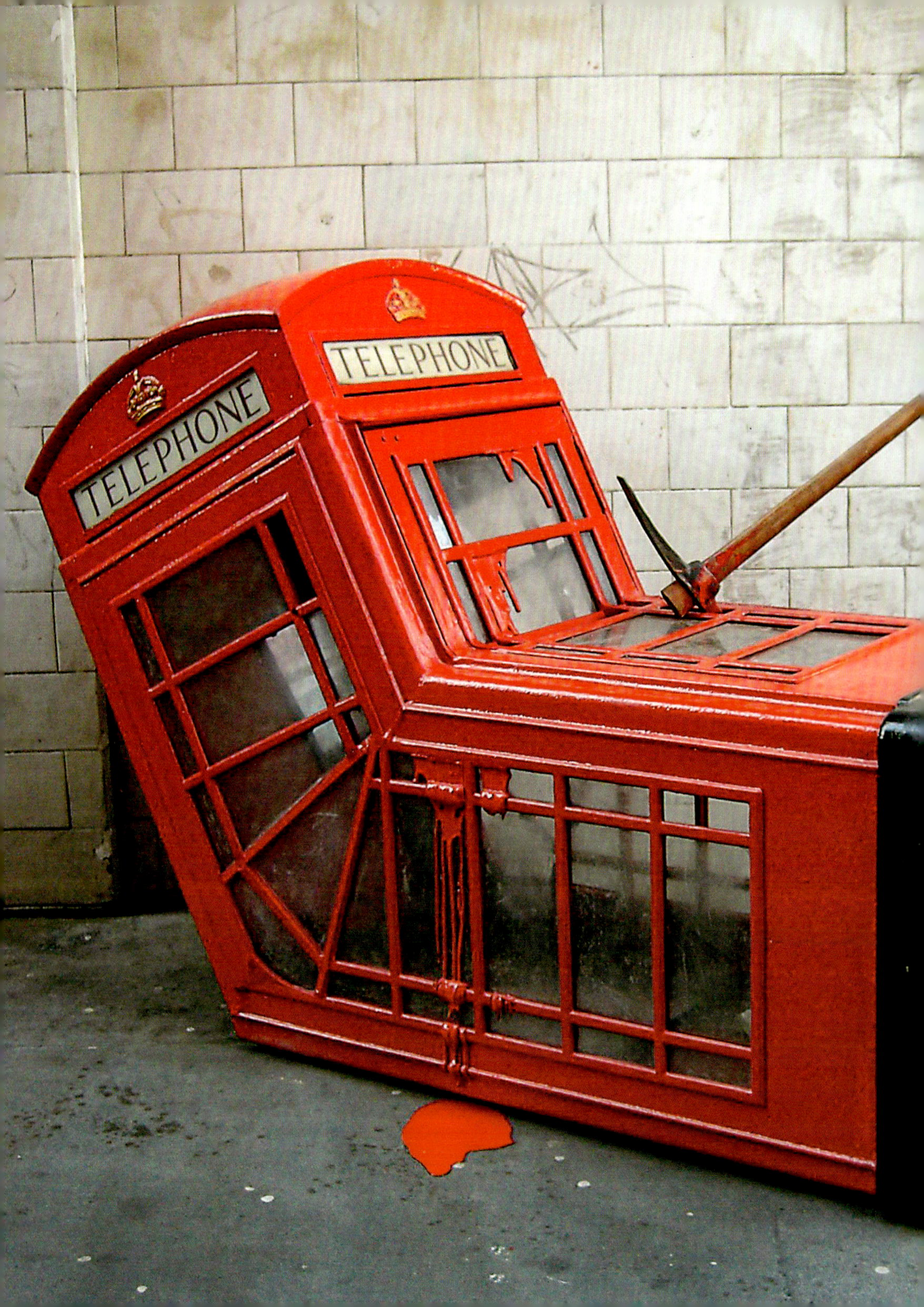

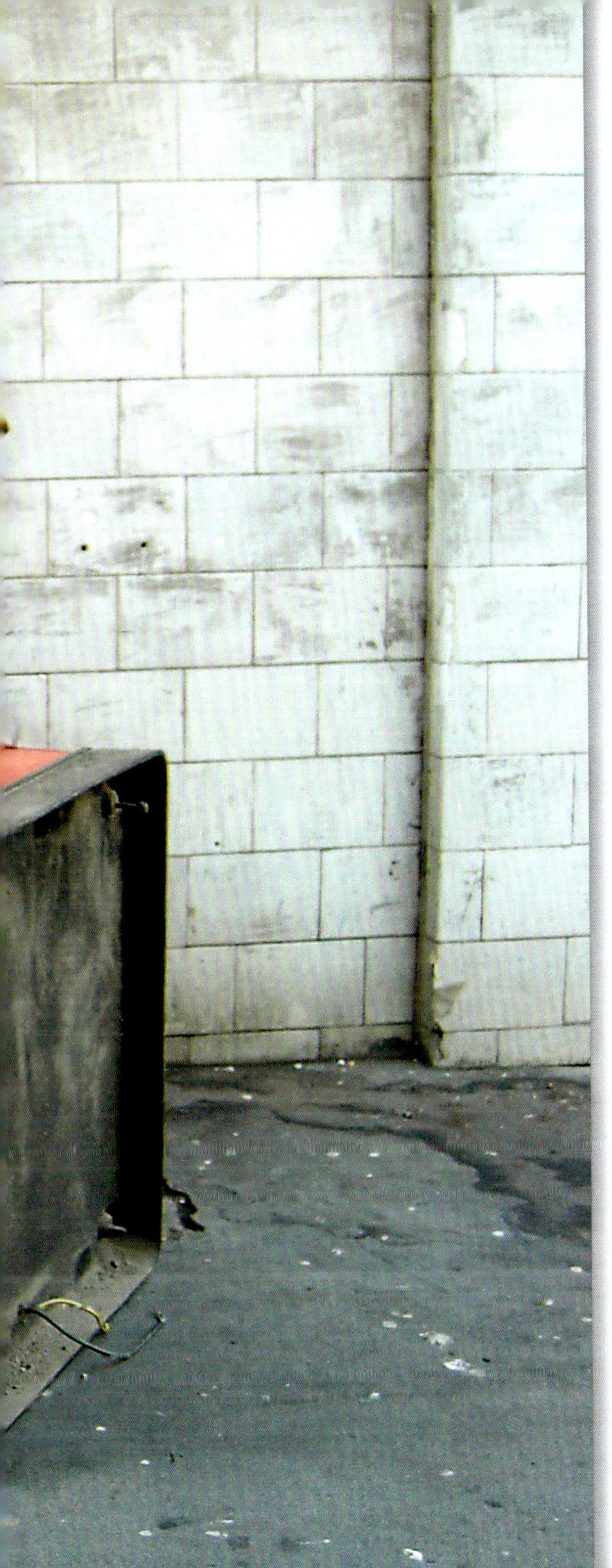

**BANKSY LITERALLY
MURDERED A PHONE BOOTH
WITH A PICKAXE NEAR SOHO
SQUARE.**

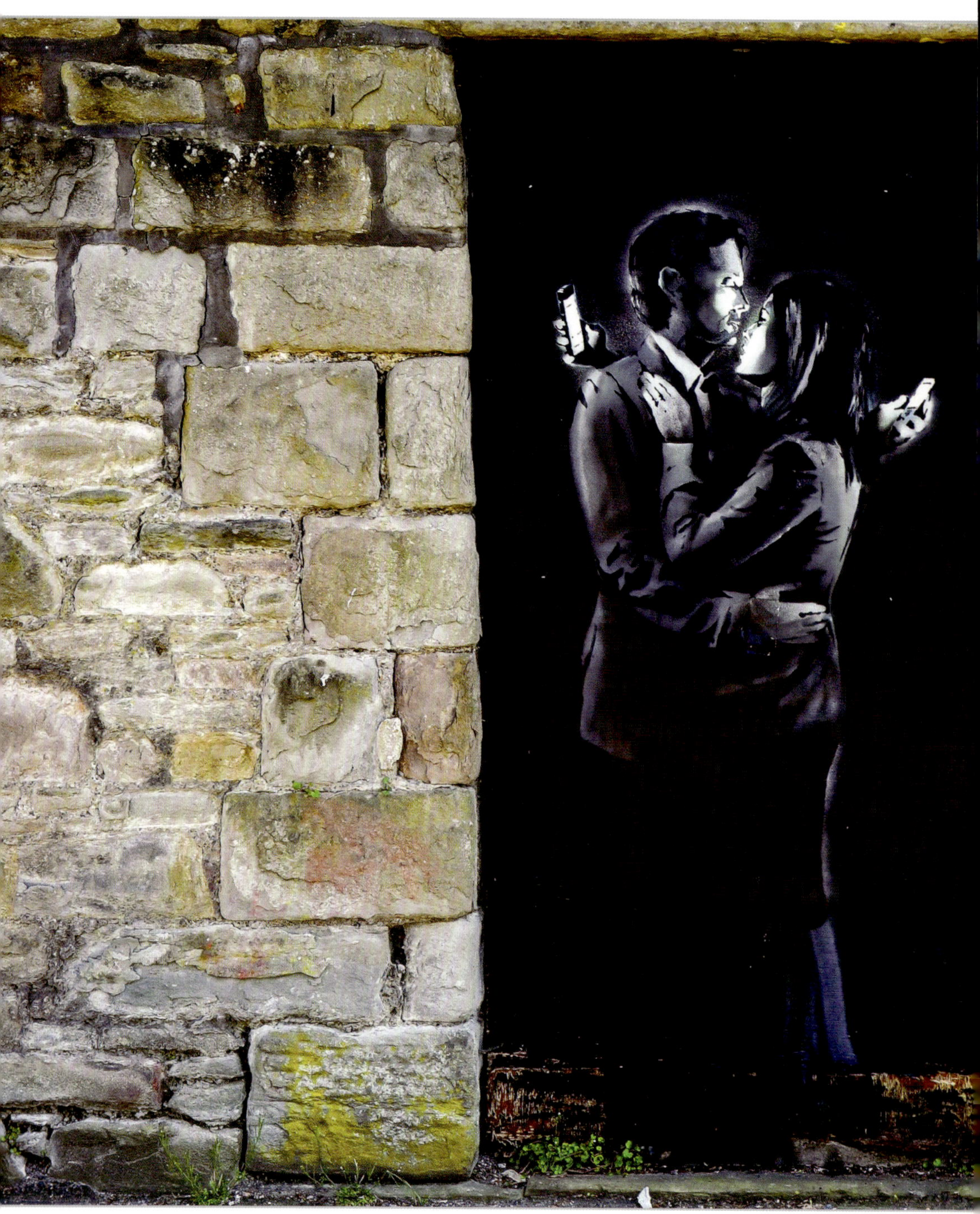

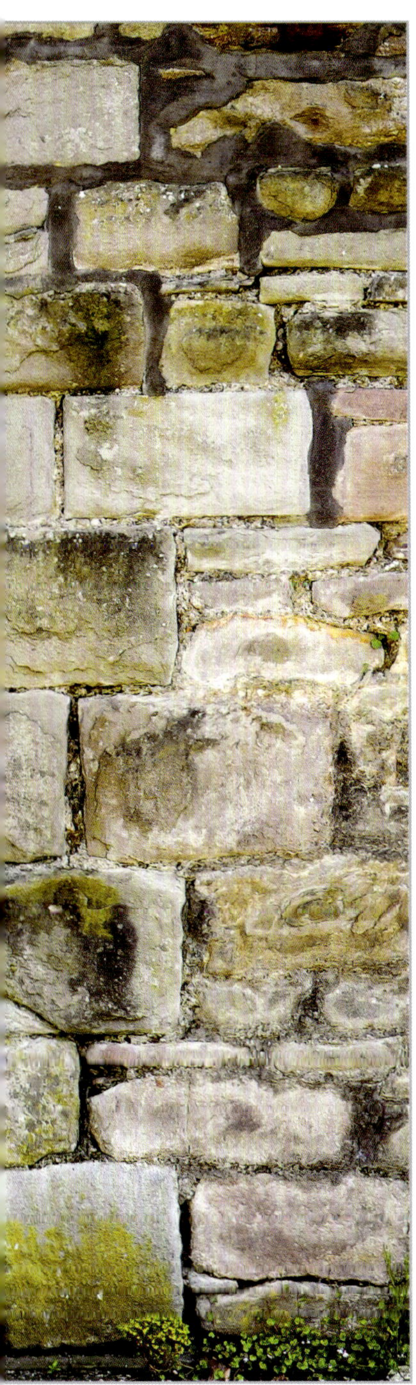

A MAN AND A WOMAN DISTRACTED BY THEIR SMARTPHONES ARE HUGGING EACH OTHER WITH INDIFFERENCE: DEFINITELY RELEVANT NOWADAYS.

34–35 GRAFFITI REPRESENTS THE MOST ANCIENT FORM OF ART. HERE, A MAN IS REMOVING INVALUABLE PREHISTORIC DRAWINGS FROM THE WALLS OF THE LEAKE STREET TUNNEL. IT IS A GESTURE THAT PROMPTS US TO REFLECT ON THE REAL VALUE OF GRAFFITI.

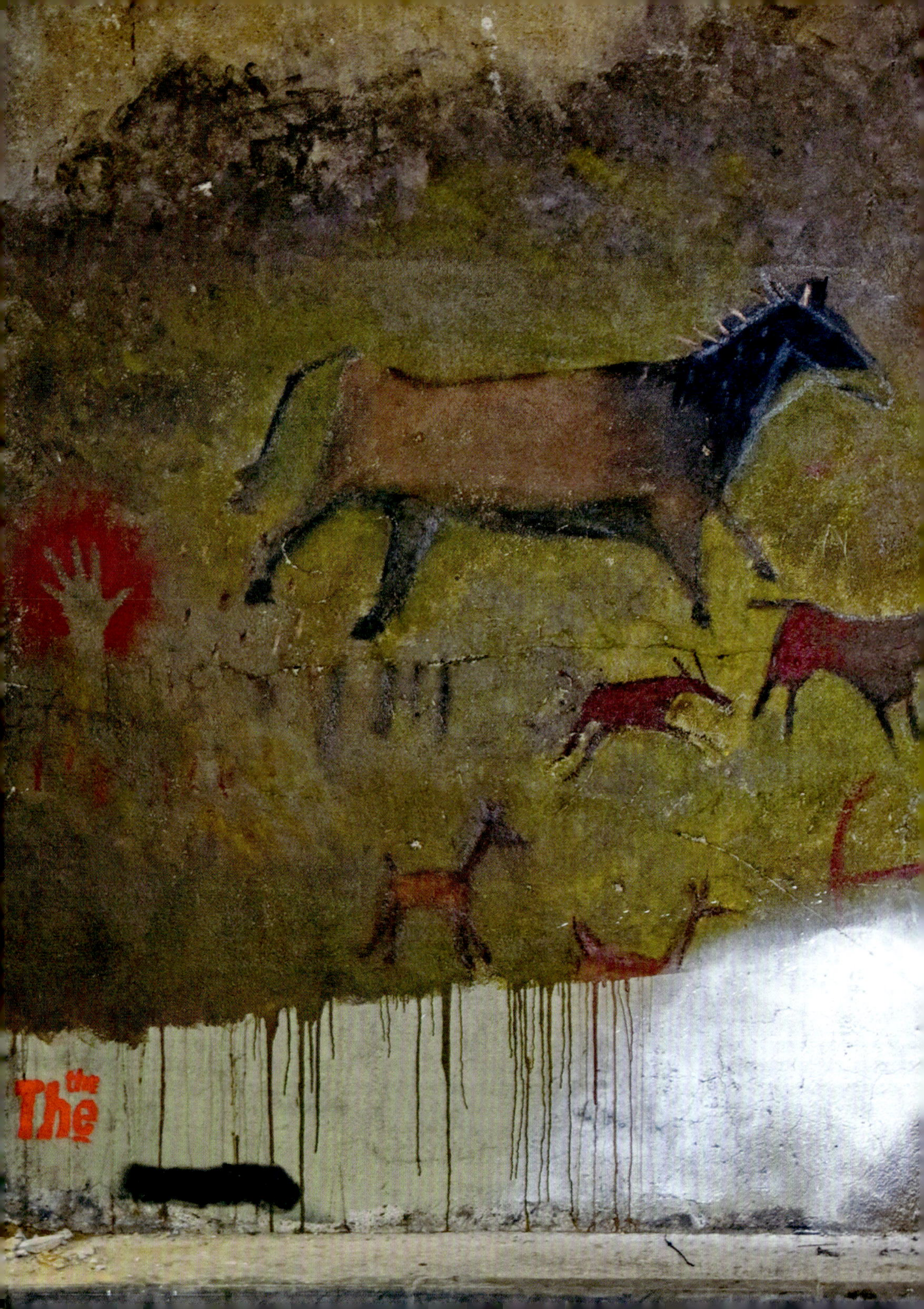

the
The

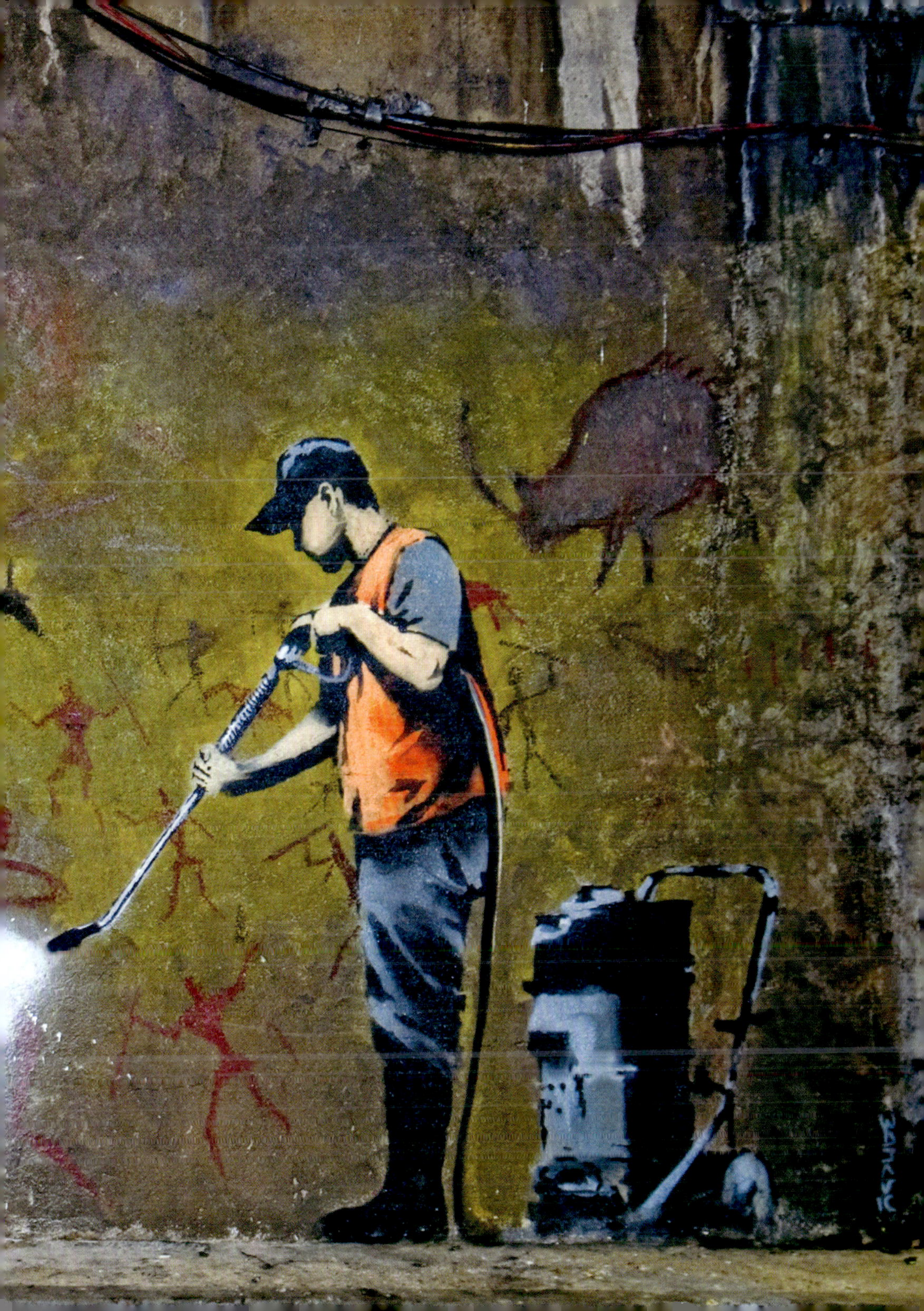

BANKSY'S RUDE POLICE OFFICER SHOWS HIS MIDDLE FINGER AND SENDS A LOUD AND CLEAR MESSAGE TO THE VIEWER. THIS GRAFFITI WORK WAS FIRST PUBLISHED IN PRINT BY "PICTURES ON WALLS" IN 2002.

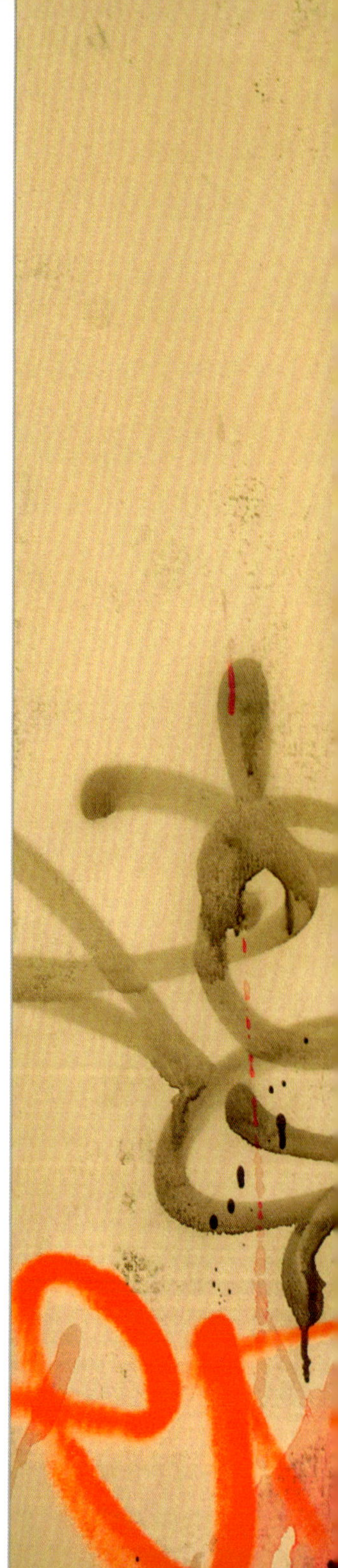

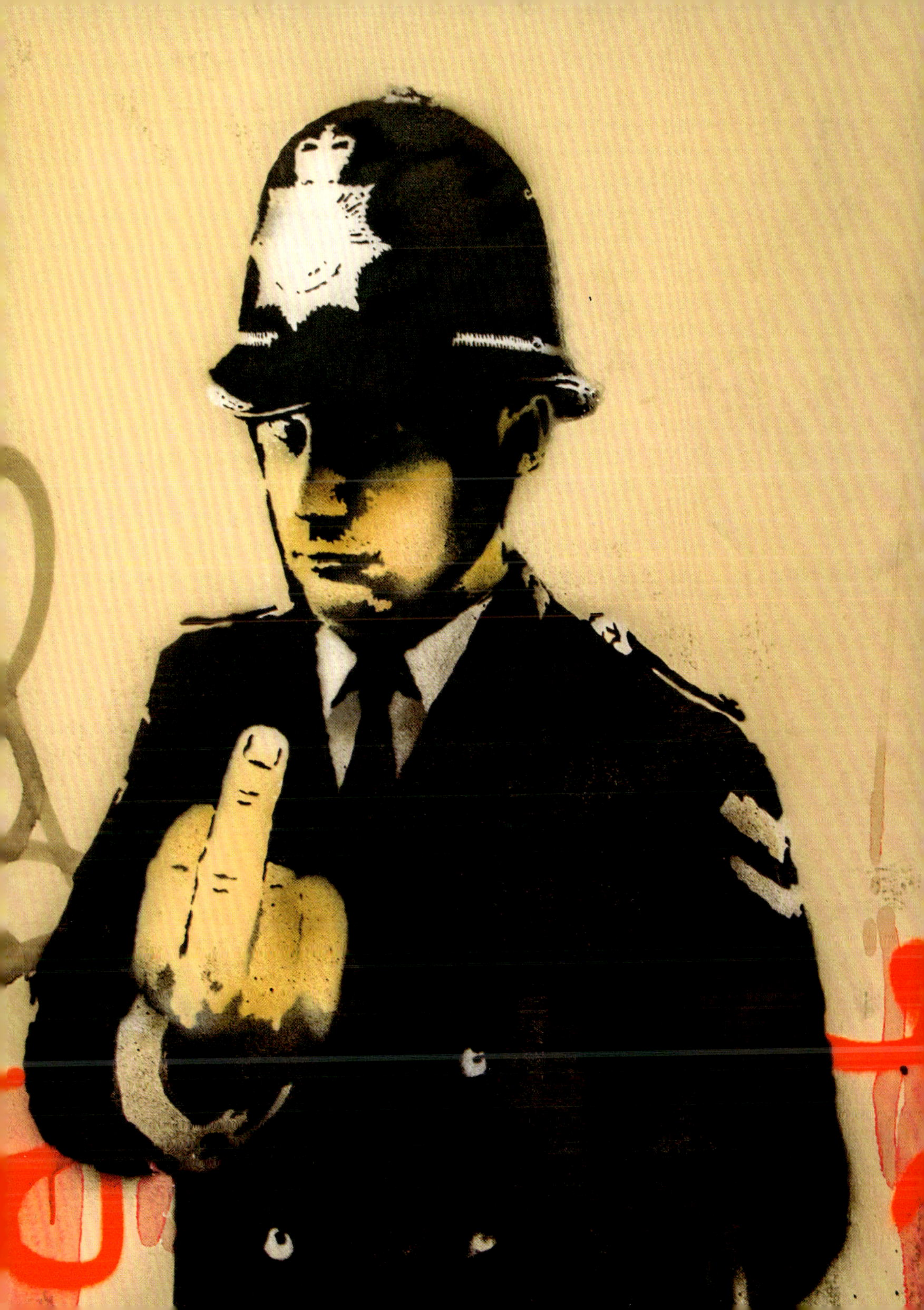

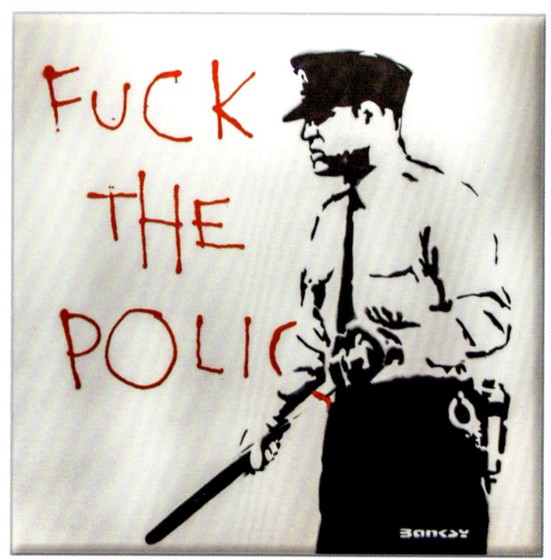

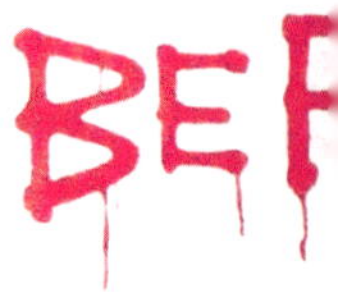

TOP *FUCK THE POLICE – 2000*
RIGHT *STOP ME BEFORE I PAINT AGAIN – 2004*

TWO AMERICAN POLICEMEN ON THE LOOKOUT. WHAT ARE THEY LOOKING FOR? THE SARCASTIC MESSAGES ON THE WALLS LEAVE SOME CLUES. IN BOTH CASES, THE POLICE ARRIVED TOO LATE.

GRAFFITI AREA – LONDON, 2003

40–41 A POLICE OFFICER WITH A POODLE ON A LEASH IS GUARDING AN AREA WHERE PAINTING GRAFFITI IS ALLOWED.

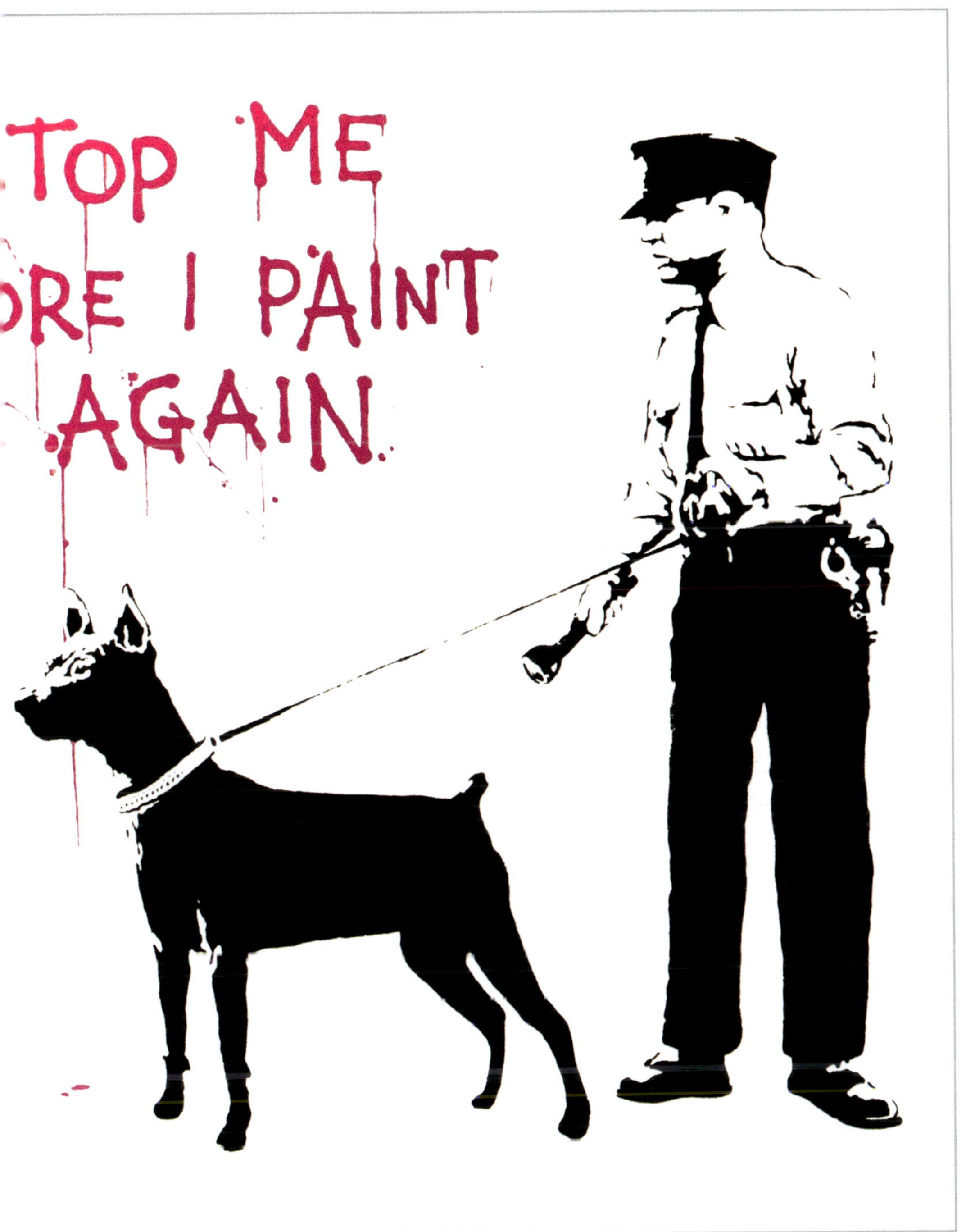
TOP ME
ORE I PAINT
AGAIN.

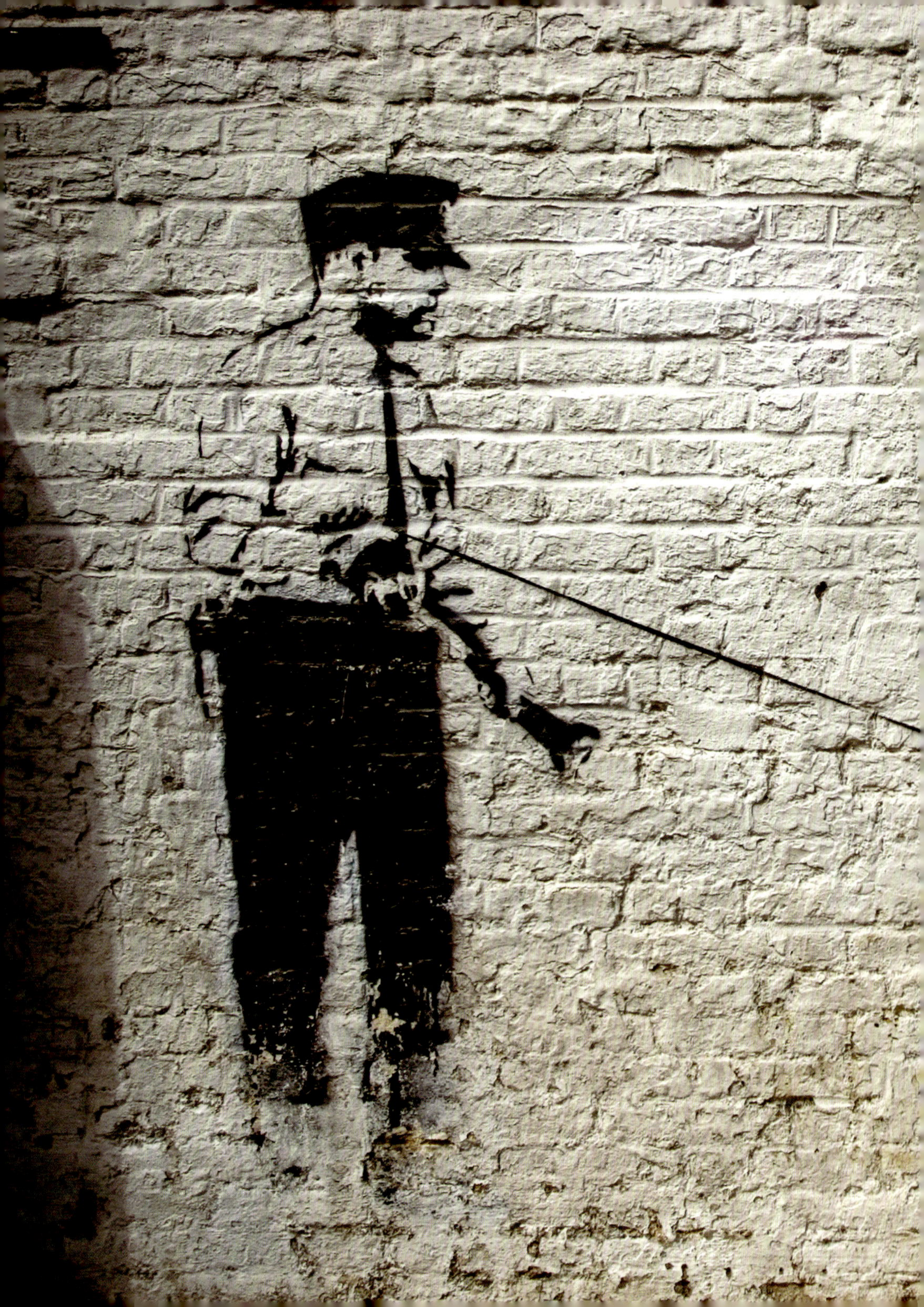

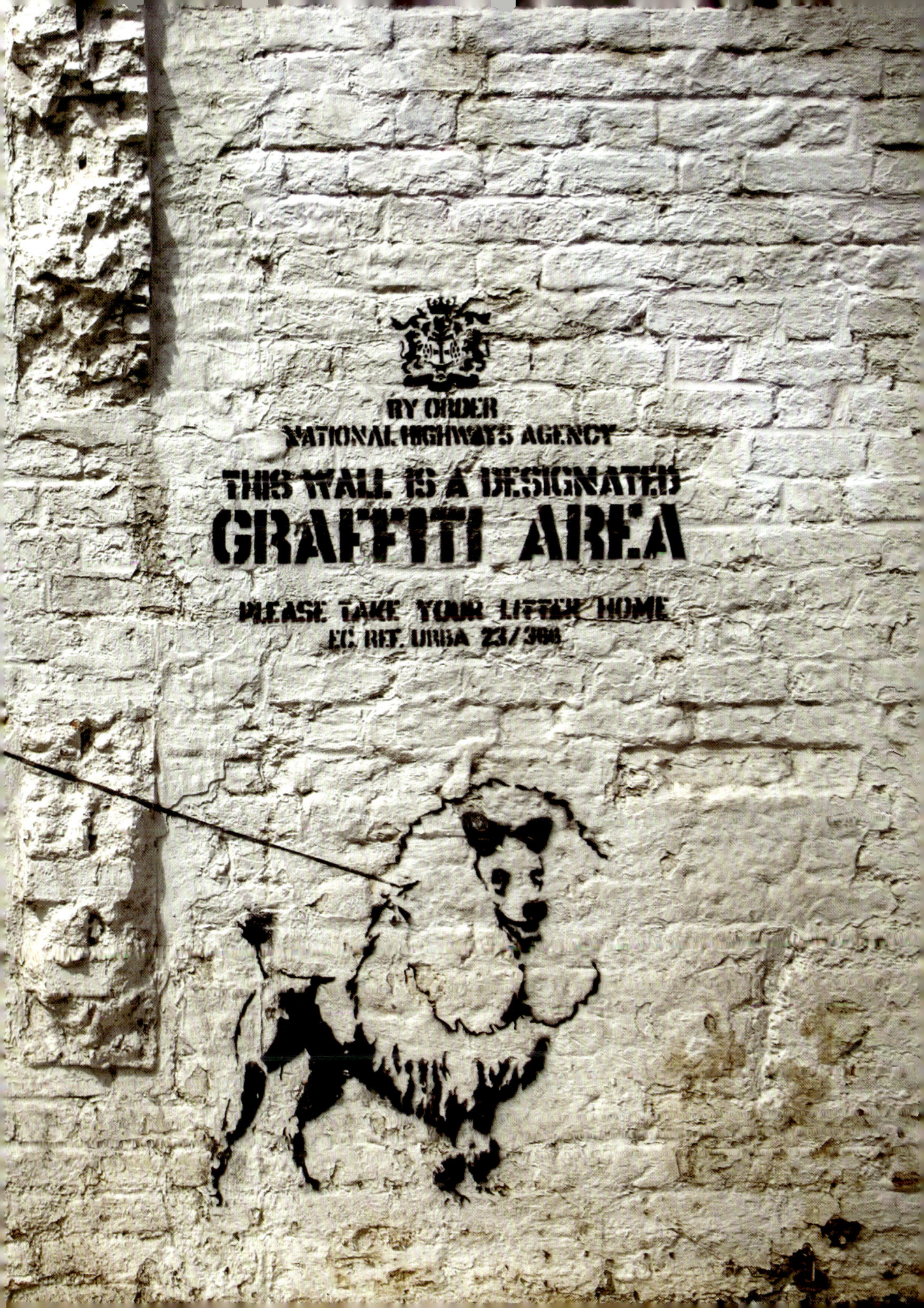
BY ORDER
NATIONAL HIGHWAYS AGENCY
THIS WALL IS A DESIGNATED
GRAFFITI AREA
PLEASE TAKE YOUR LITTER HOME
EC. REF. URBA 23/300

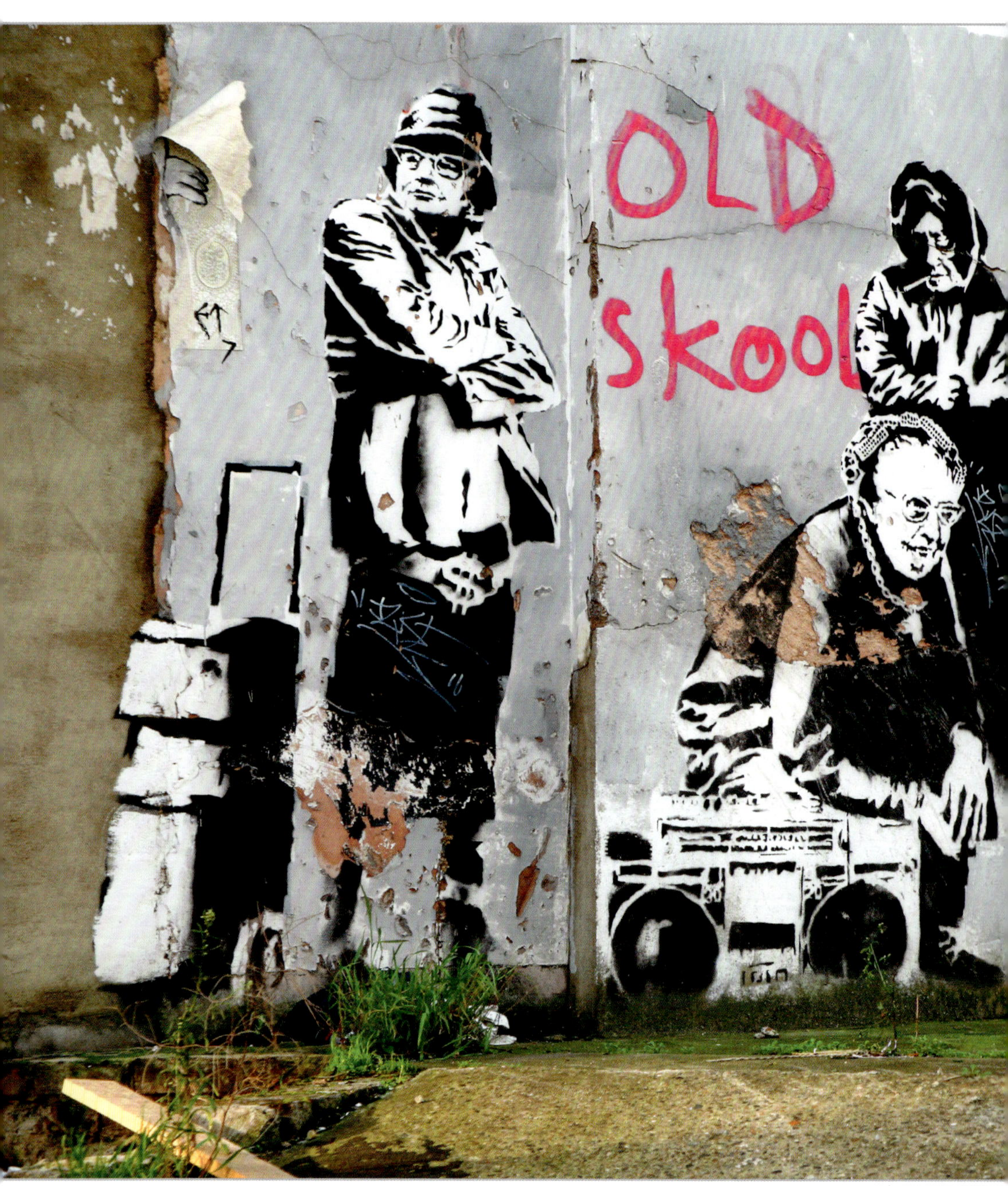
OLD
SKOOL

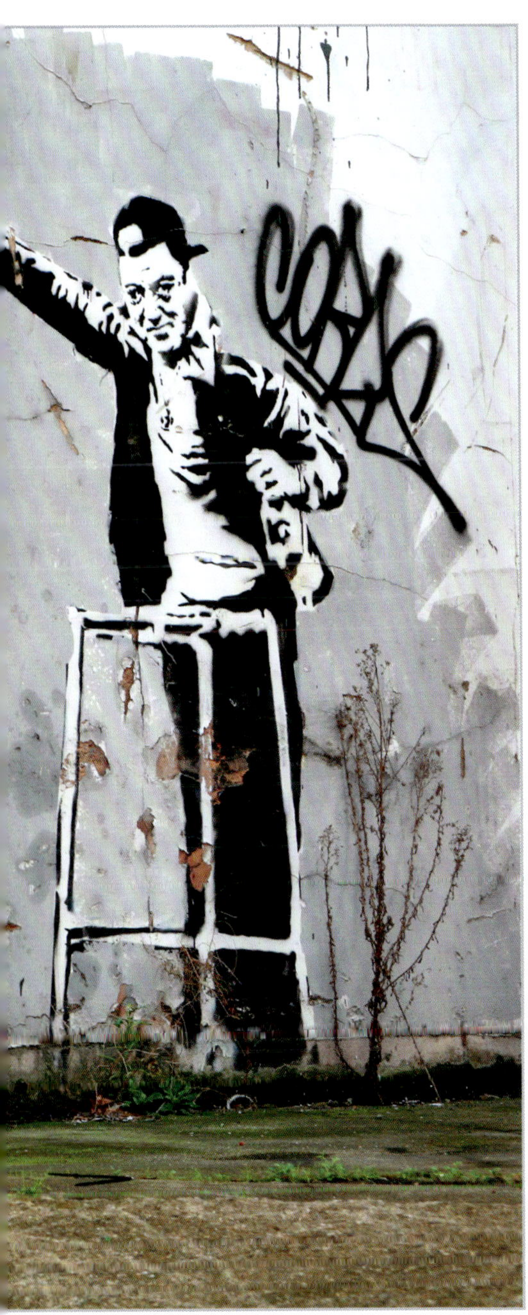

OLD SKOOL – LONDON, 2006

A SHOPPING CART, AN OLD RADIO, AND A WALKING FRAME MAKE UP THE PERFECT SETTING FOR A PUNK BAND OF ELDERLY PEOPLE WHO HAVEN'T GIVEN UP.

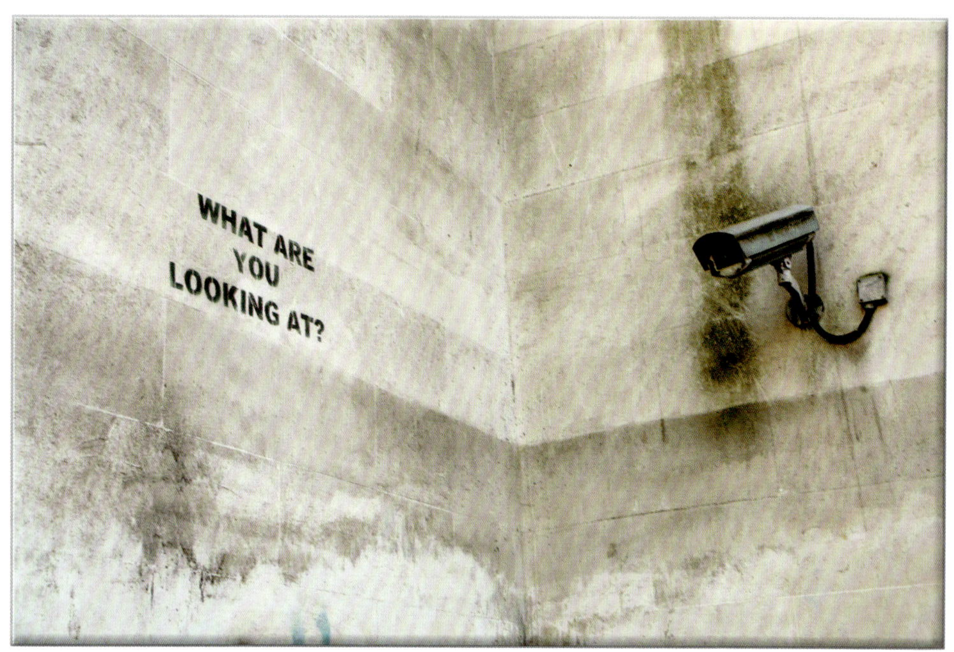

WHAT ARE YOU LOOKING AT? – MARBLE ARCH STREET, LONDON, 2004

BANKSY EXPRESSES HIS DISAPPOINTMENT AT THE "CULTURE OF SURVEILLANCE."

SHOP TILL YOU DROP – LONDON, 2011

THIS WOMAN FREE-FALLING WITH HER SHOPPING CART IN LONDON'S MAYFAIR DISTRICT IS AN EXPLICIT MESSAGE AGAINST UNBRIDLED CONSUMERISM.

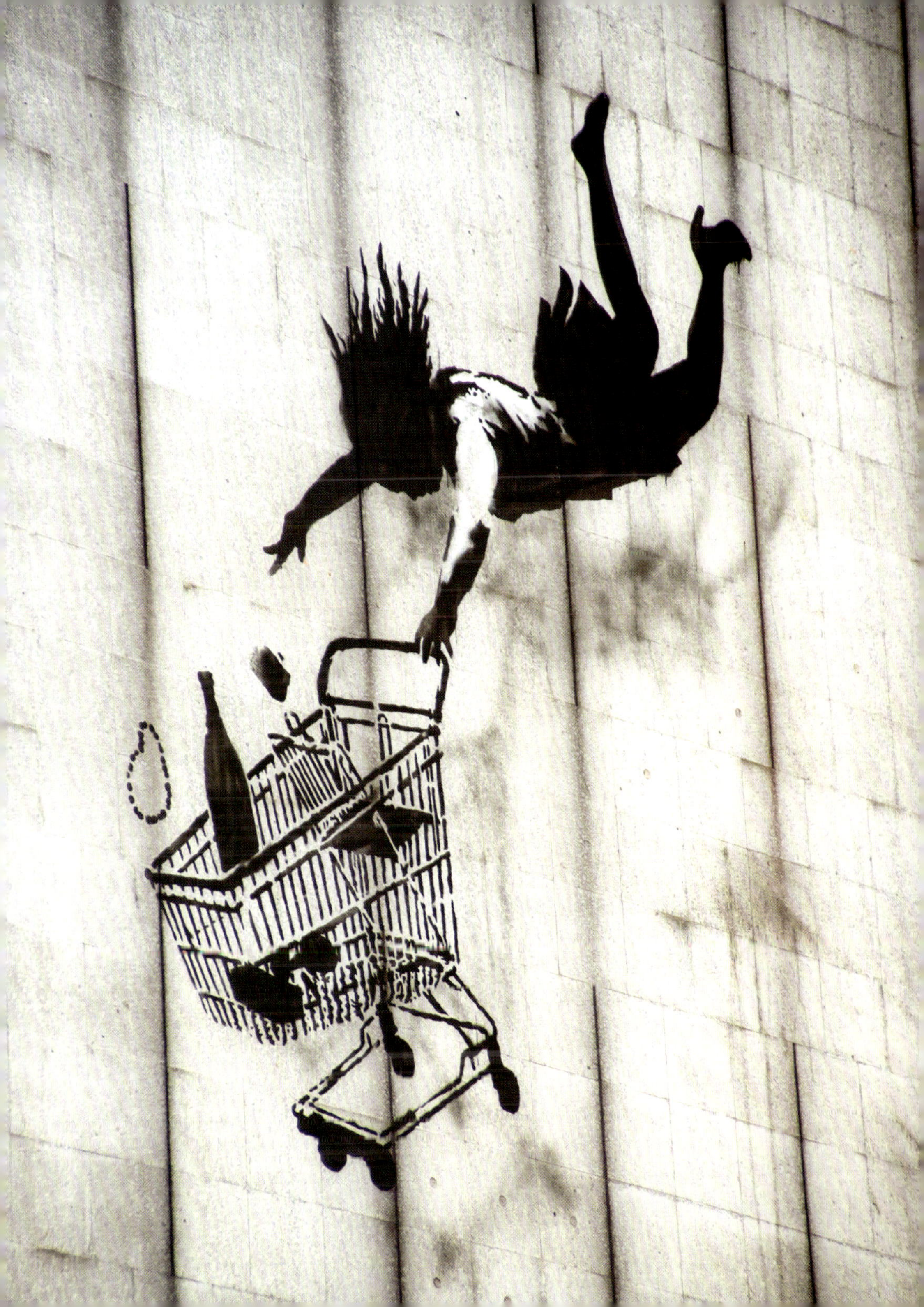

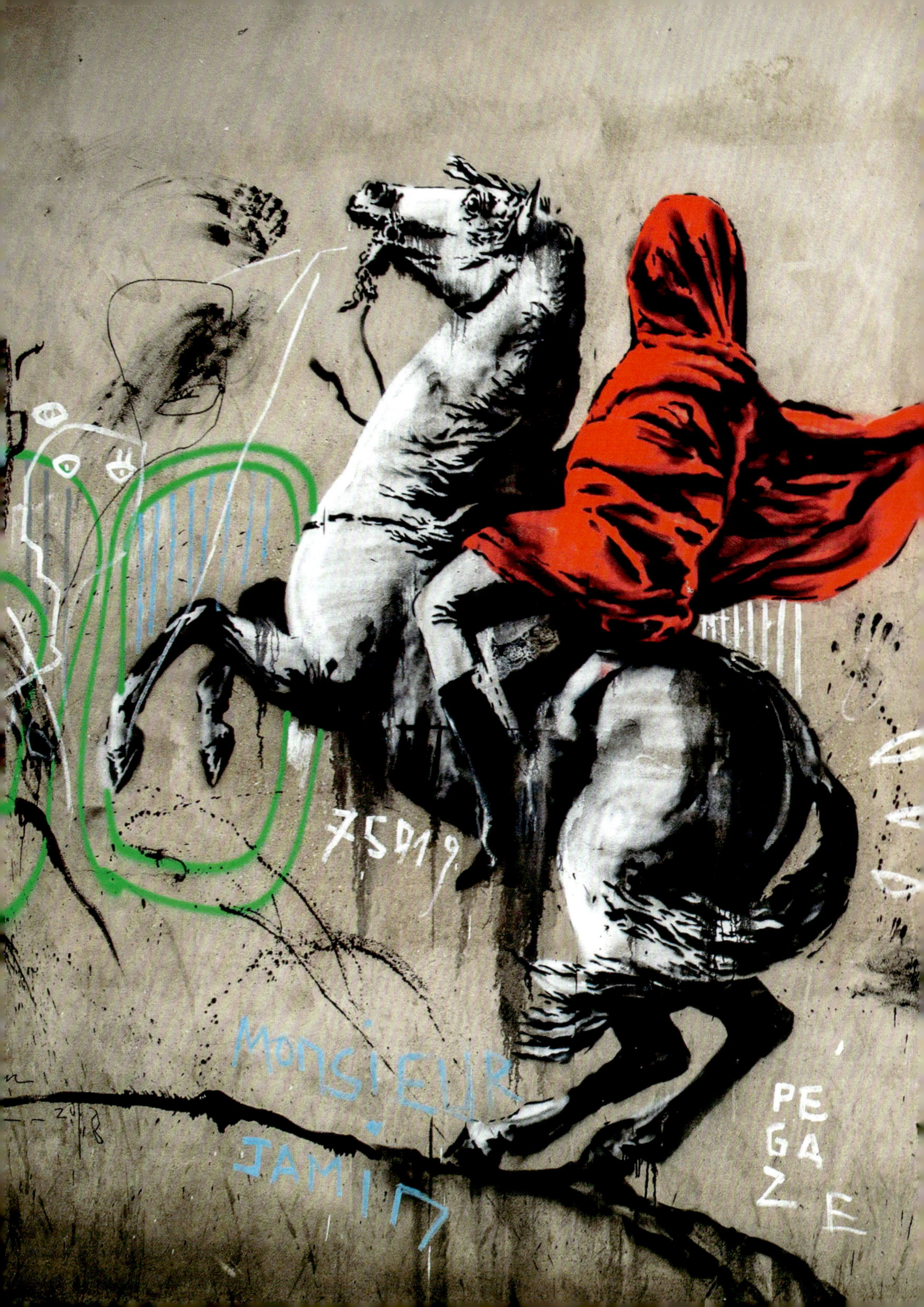

75019
MONSIEUR JAMIN
PE GA ZE

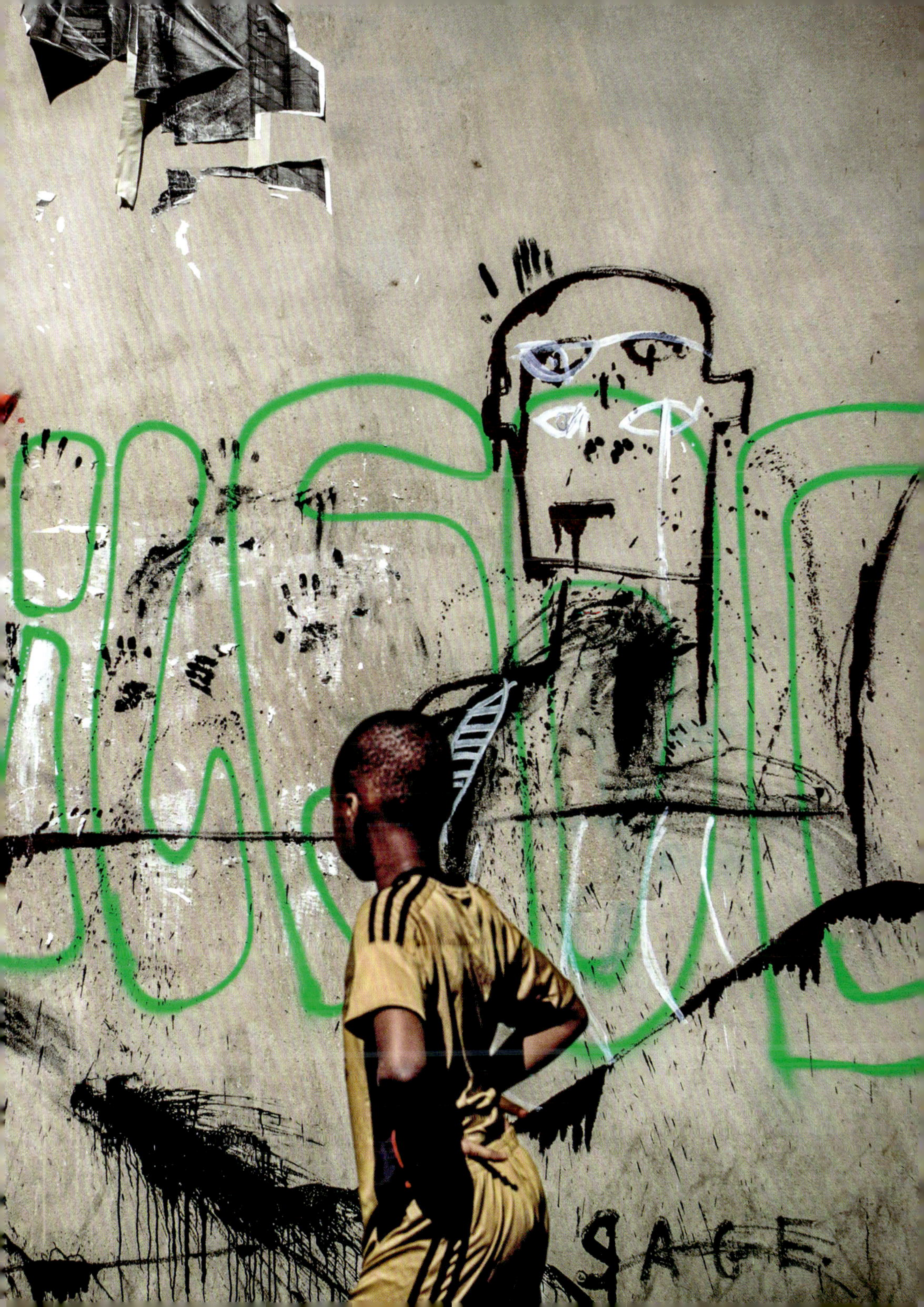

SAGE.

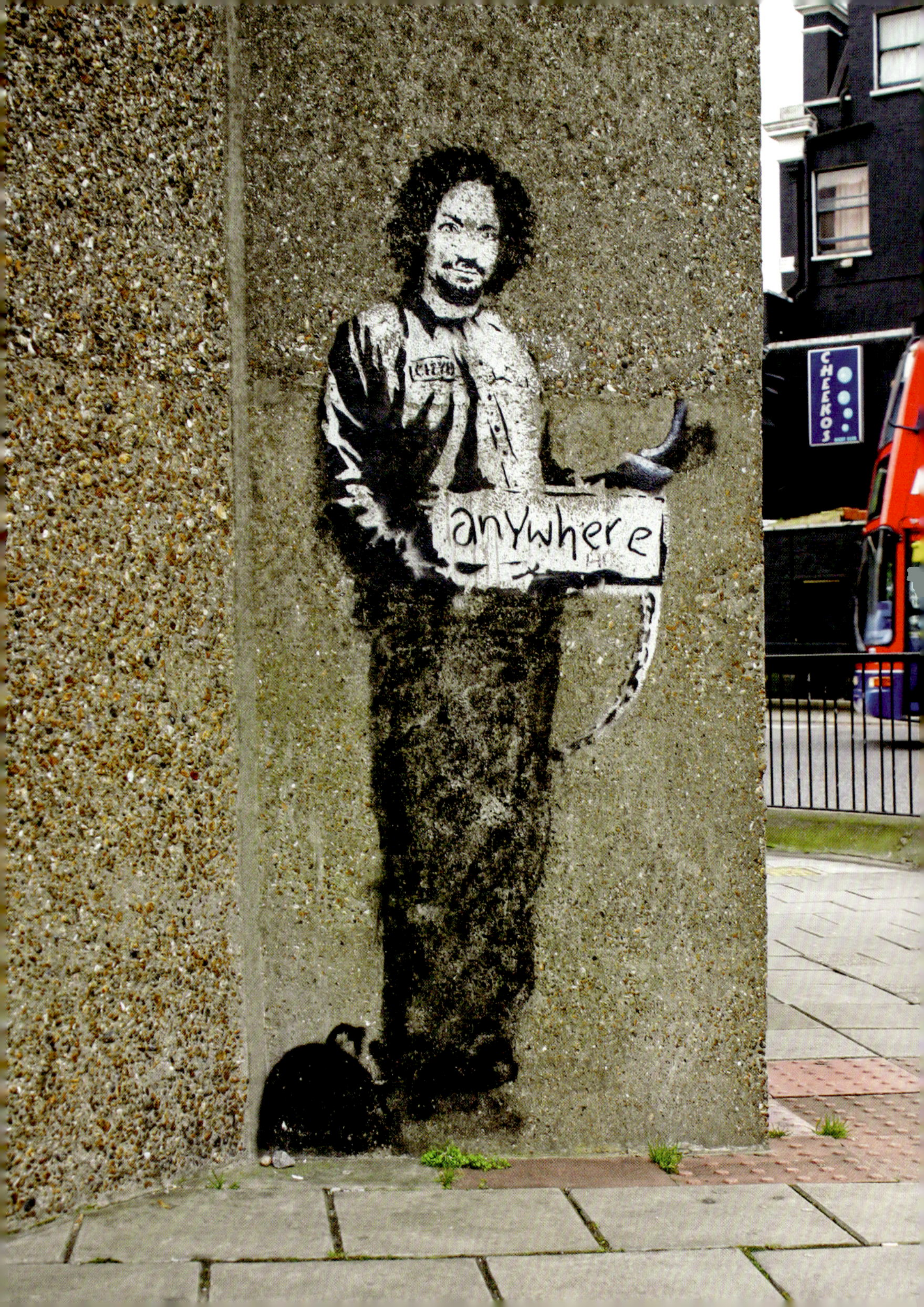

anywhere

46–47 BANKSY REINTERPRETS THE WORK BY JACQUES-LOUIS DAVID TO EXPRESS THE TOTAL LACK OF VISION OF THE FRENCH GOVERNMENT IN DEALING WITH THE ISSUE OF MIGRANTS, WHO AT THAT TIME WERE REJECTED AT THE ALPINE BORDER BY THE FRENCH POLICE.

WHAT IS CHARLES MANSON DOING NEAR THE ARCHWAY SUBWAY STATION IN LONDON? BANKSY URGES US TO PAY MORE ATTENTION TO THE PERSUASIVE INFLUENCE OF OUR SOCIETY'S THREATS SPREADING EVERYWHERE.

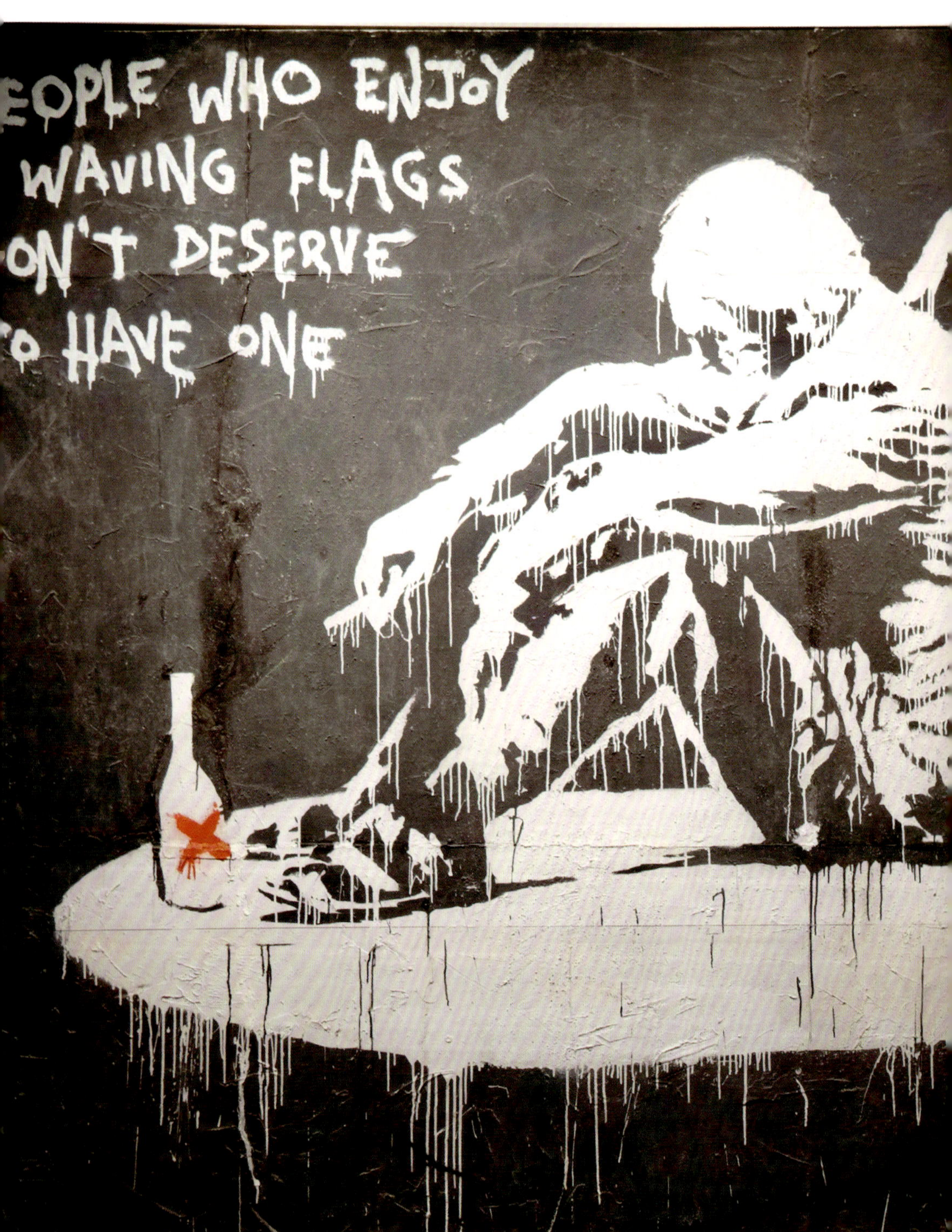
EOPLE WHO ENJOY
WAVING FLAGS
ON'T DESERVE
O HAVE ONE

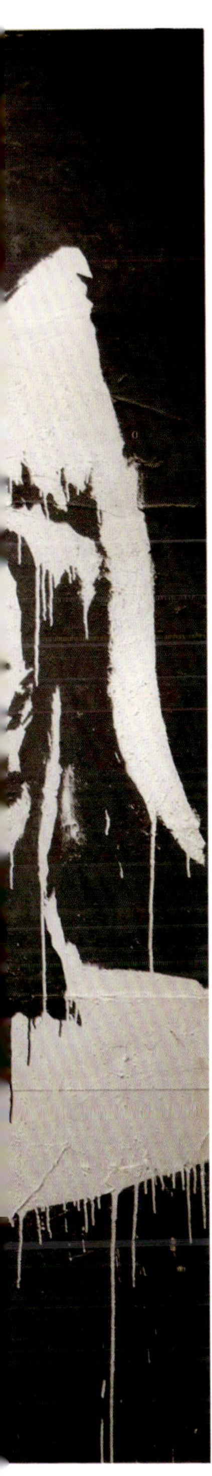

FALLEN ANGEL – LONDON, 2008

"PEOPLE WHO ENJOY WAVING A FLAG DON'T DESERVE TO HAVE ONE." ANYONE CAN FALL, EVEN AN ANGEL. BANKSY INVITES US NOT TO JUDGE LIGHTLY, BUT TO TRY TO UNDERSTAND AND SHARE.

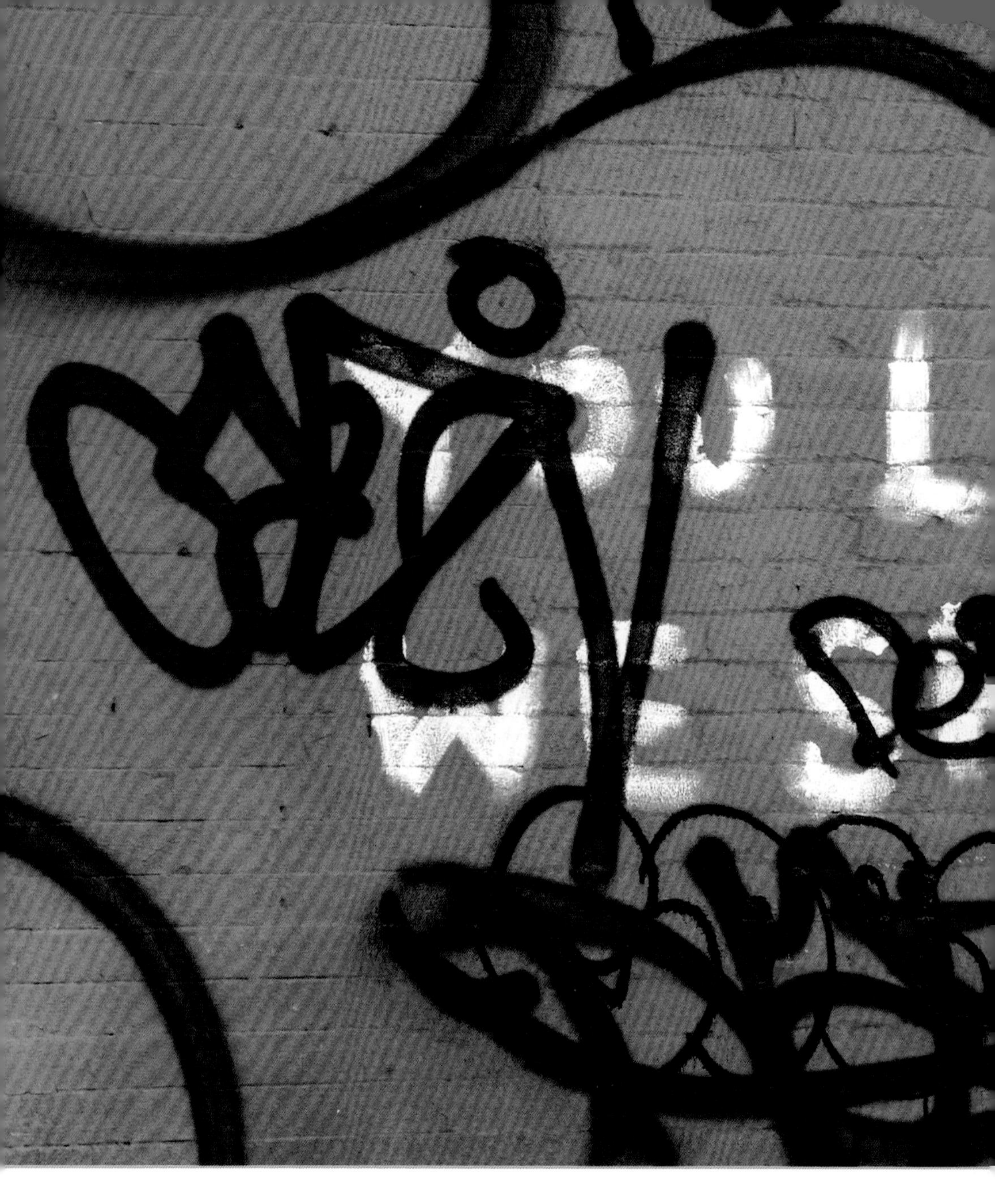

YOU LOOT WE SHOOT - NEW YORK, 2018

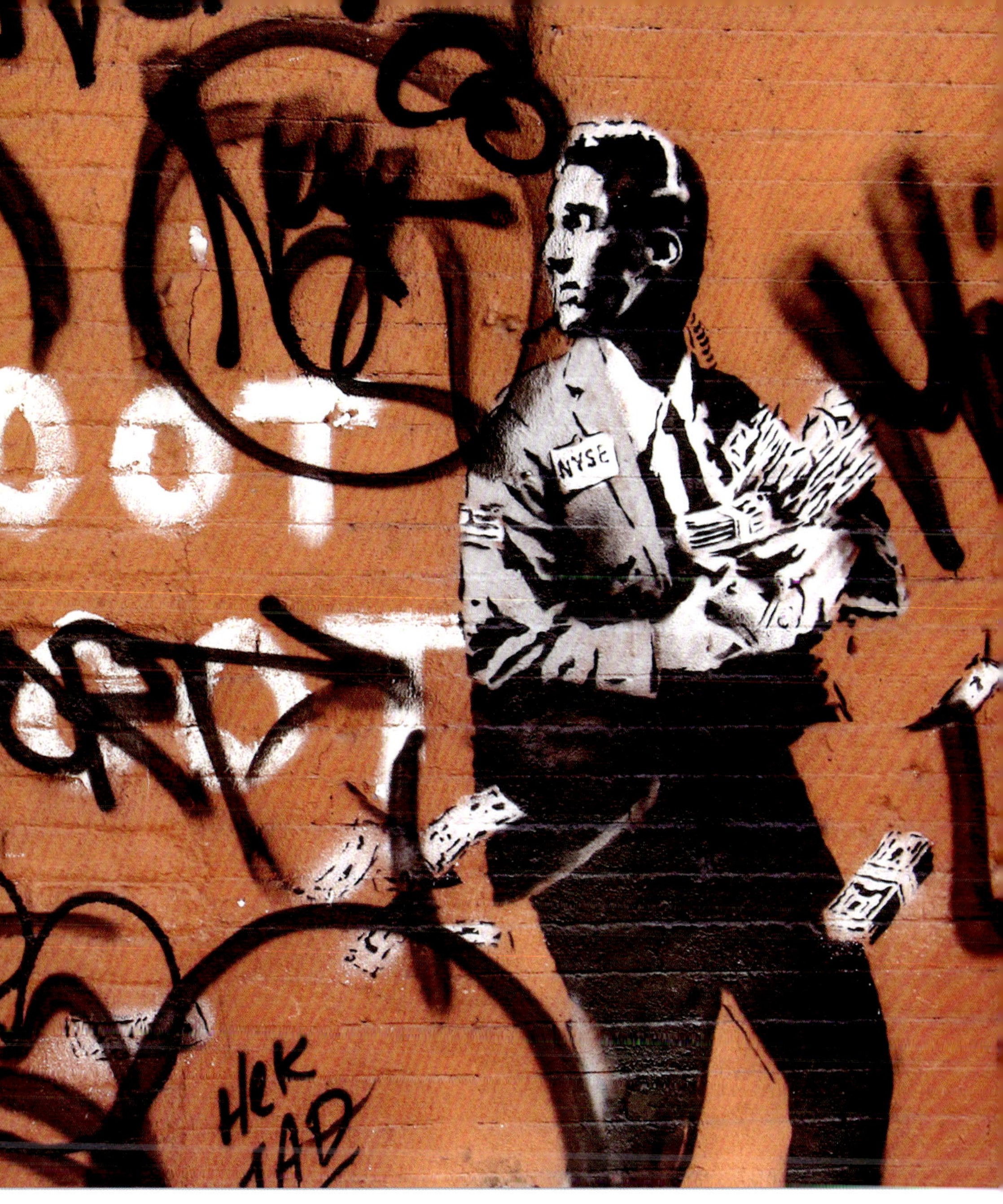

A BROKER ON THE RUN WITH A BUNCH OF MONEY INVITES US TO
REFLECT ON THE CONSEQUENCES OF THE WALL STREET ECONOMY ON
AMERICAN SOCIETY.

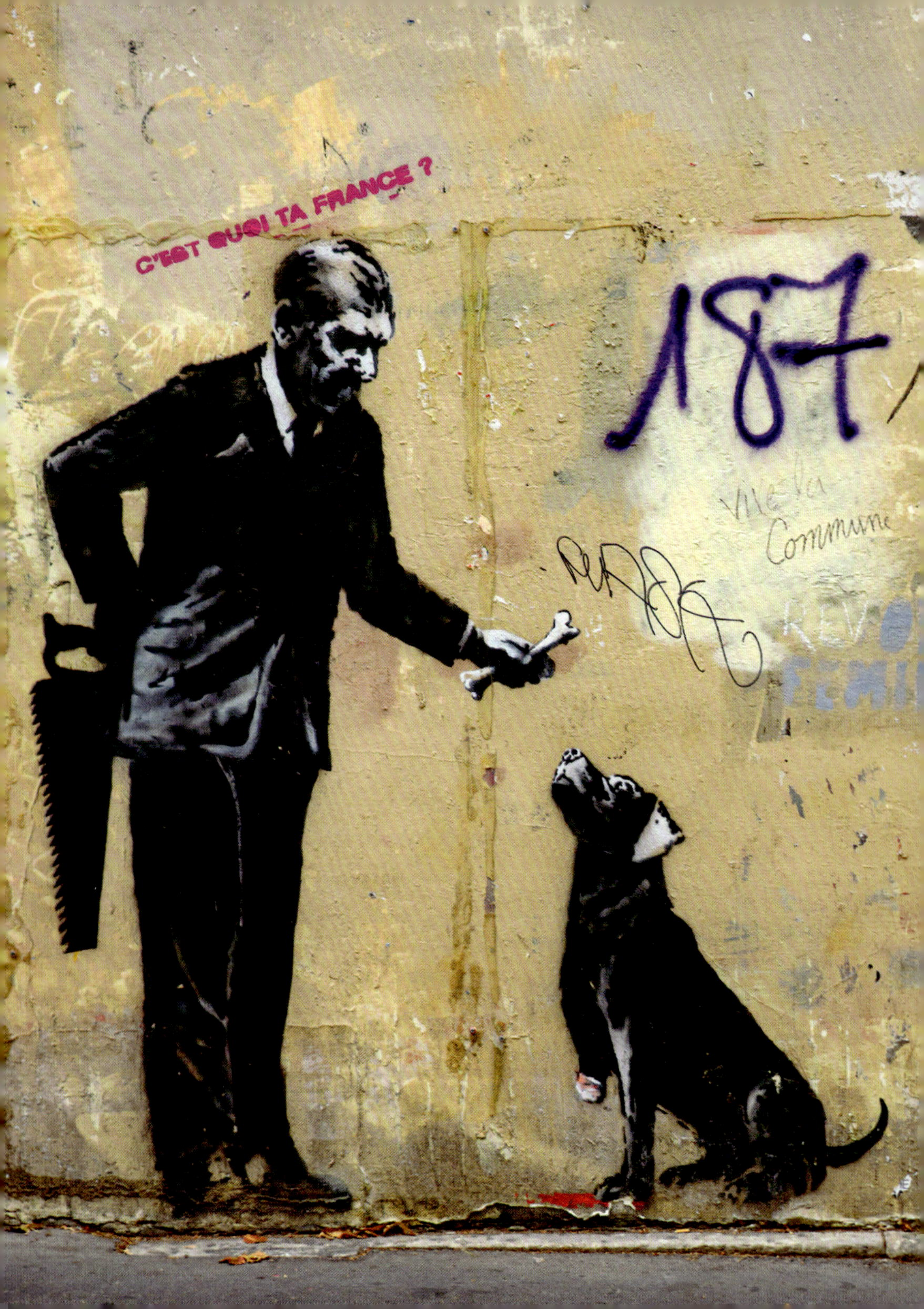
C'EST QUOI TA FRANCE ?
187
vive la
Commune

BANKSY SHOWS THE CONTRADICTIONS OF THE WESTERN CAPITALIST SYSTEM, WHICH FIRST UNFAIRLY APPROPRIATES THE RESOURCES OF THE POOREST PEOPLES IN THE WORLD, THEN PRETENDS TO GIVE THEM HELP.

56–57 "WHAT WE DO IN LIFE ECHOES IN ETERNITY": BANKSY BORROWS A QUOTE FROM THE MOVIE GLADIATOR TO WARN US THAT EVERYTHING WE DO PRODUCES DISTANT ECHOES THAT NO ONE WILL EVER BE ABLE TO COMPLETELY ELIMINATE.

58–59 THIS GRAFFITI WORK EVOKES THE HISTORY OF BRISTOL, AND IN PARTICULAR OF THE REVOLTS AGAINST THE POLICE DURING THE UNAUTHORIZED RAVE PARTIES OF THE '90S.

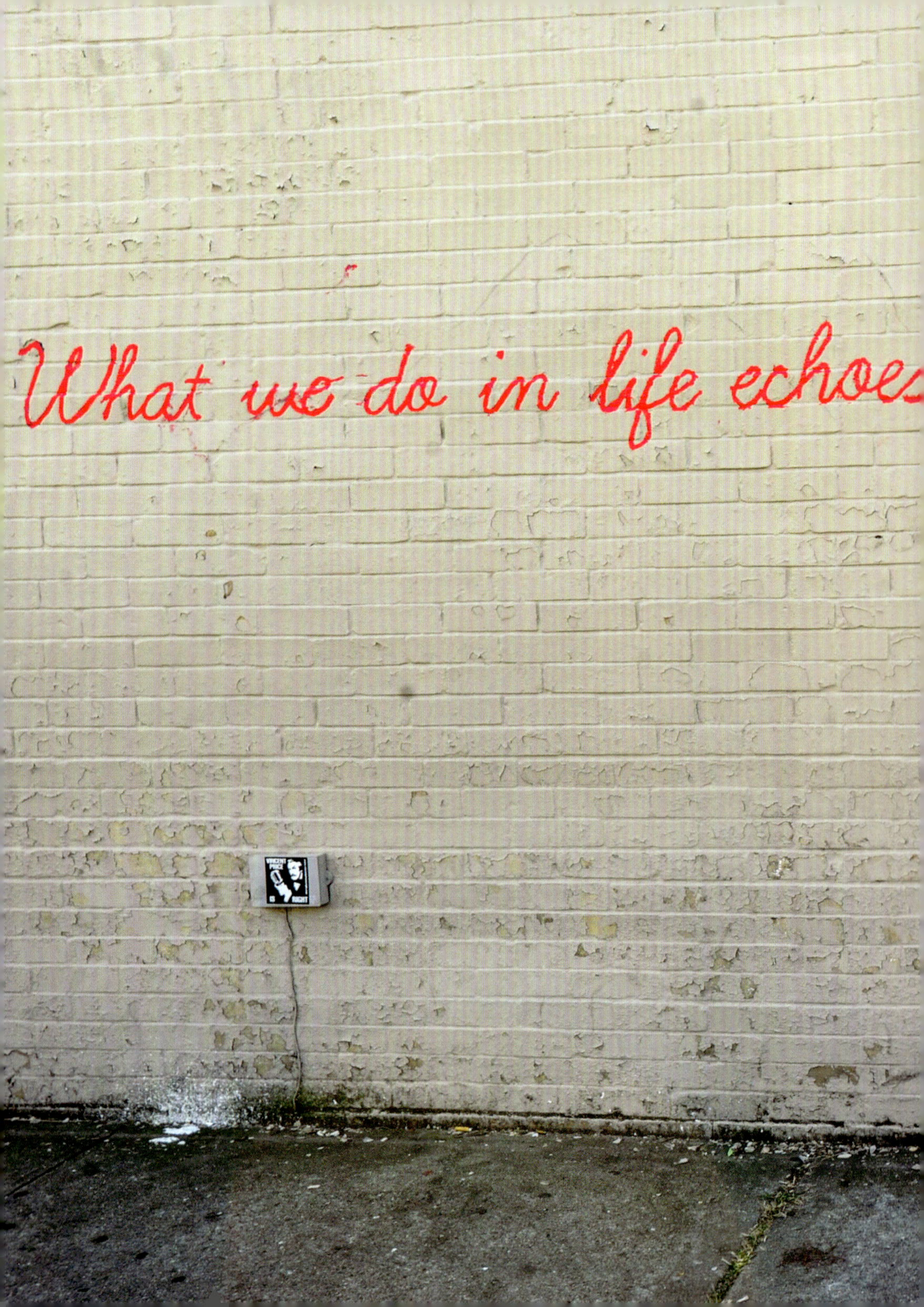

What we do in life echoes
VINCENT PRICE
IS RIGHT

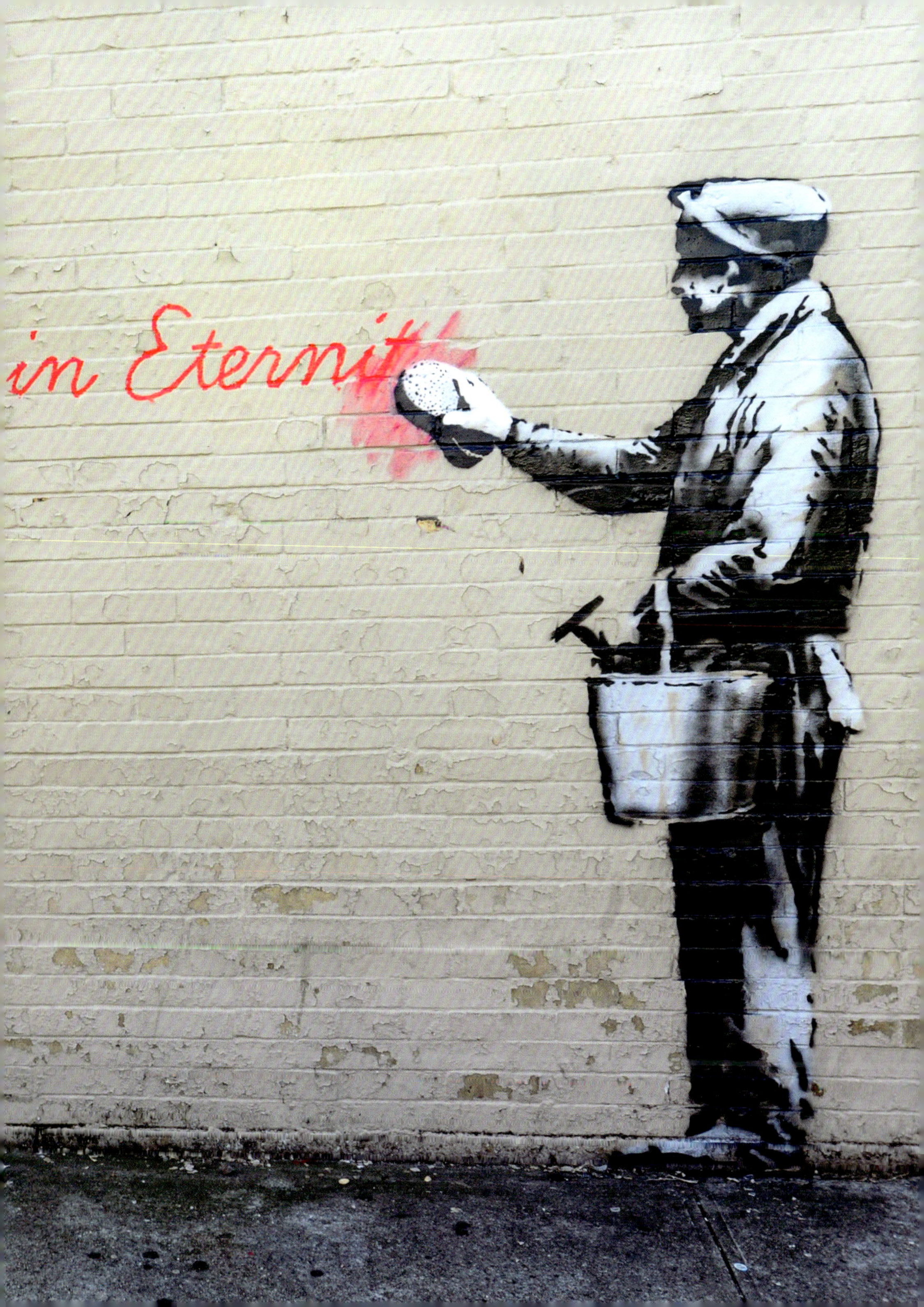
in Eternit

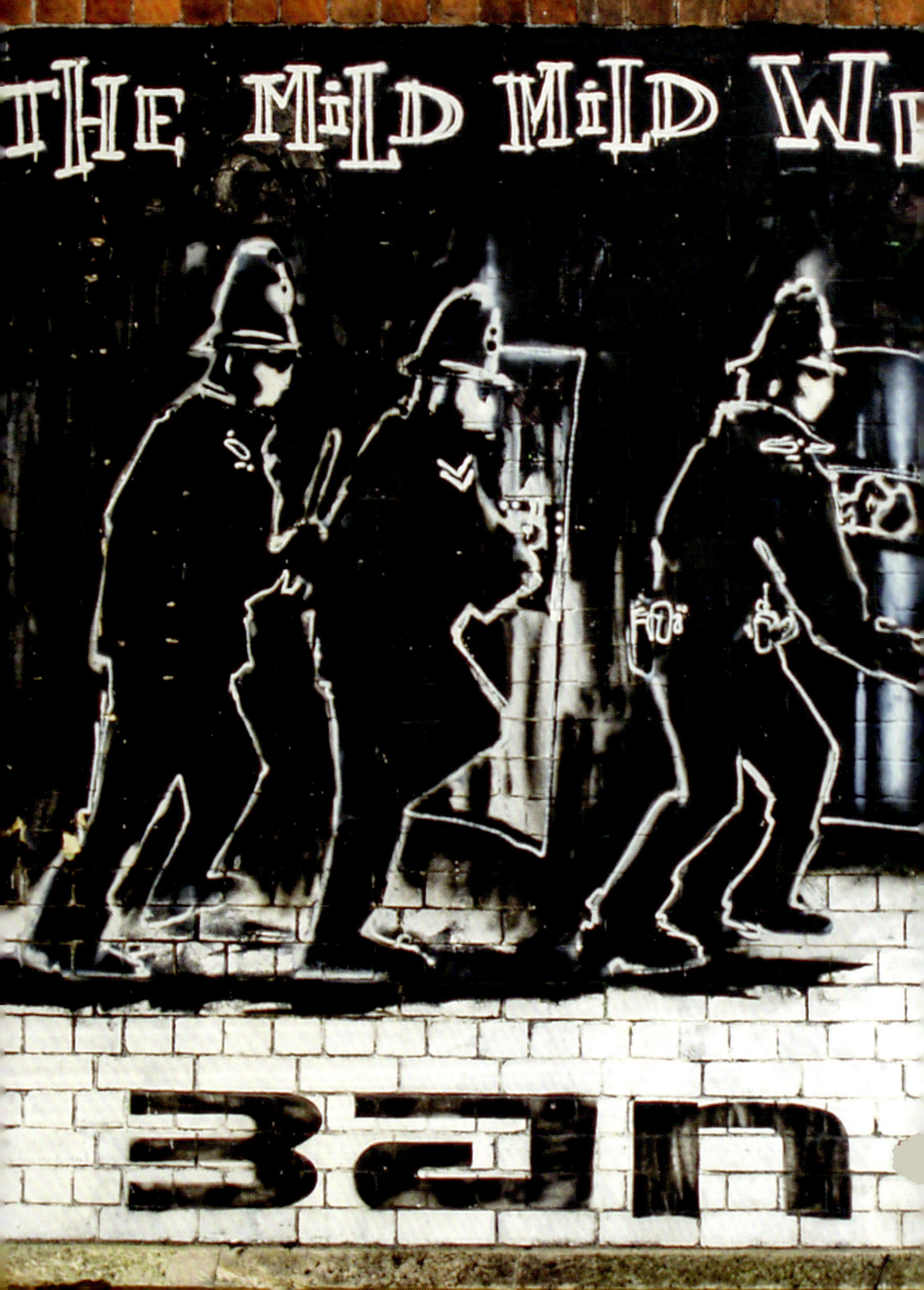
THE MILD MILD W
THE BRIS

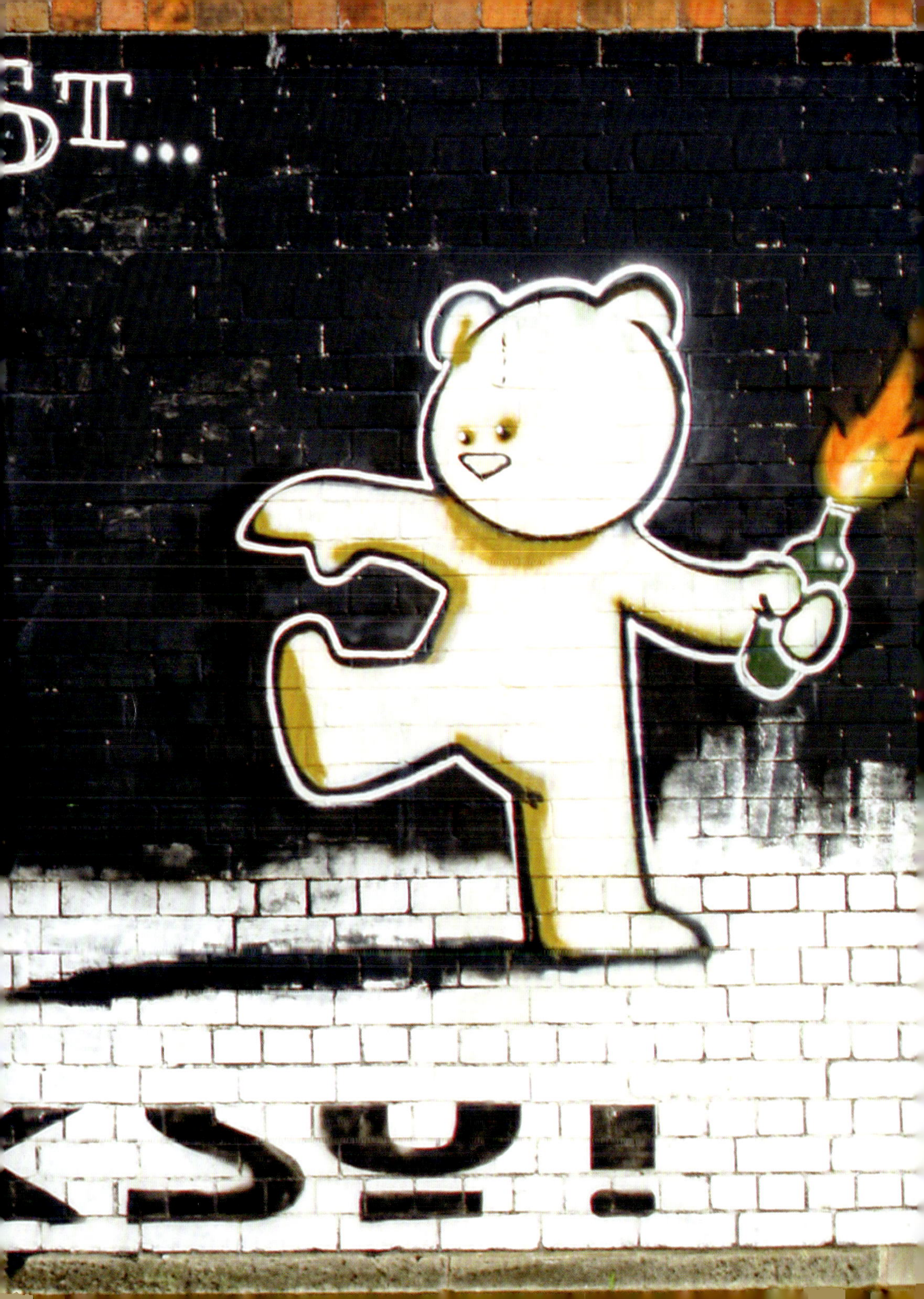
ST...
SU

FIVE POLICEMEN ESCORT A TRUCK WITH AN ENORMOUS STRAWBERRY DONUT ON THE ROOF, AS IF IT WAS A GOVERNMENT AUTHORITY. THE POLEMICAL INTENT TOWARD THE POLICE SUBSERVIENT TO THE POWER OF CAPITALISM IS EVIDENT.

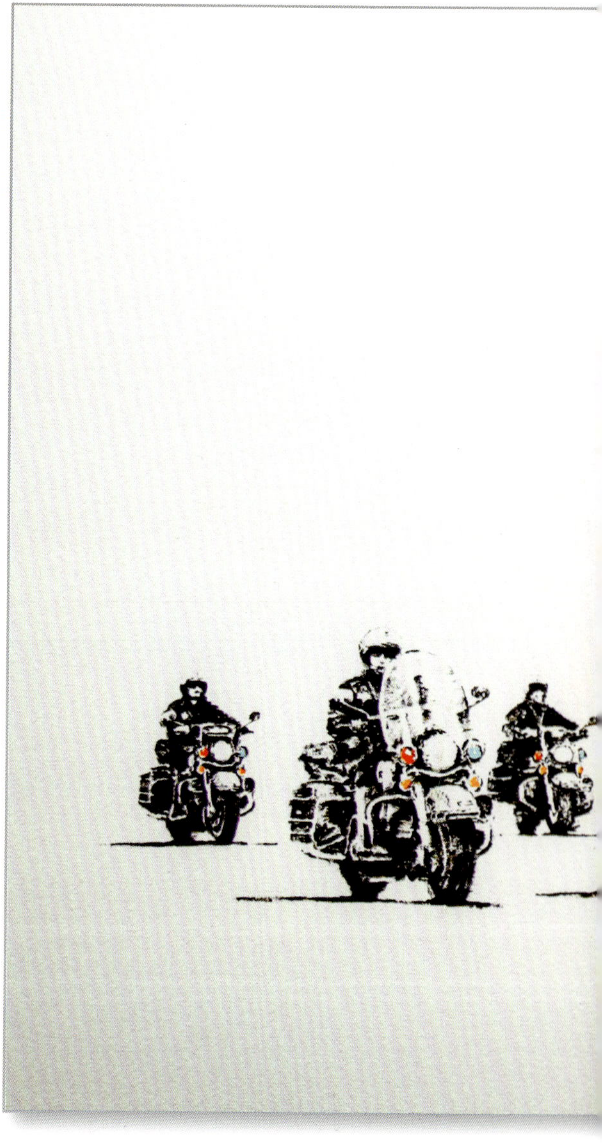

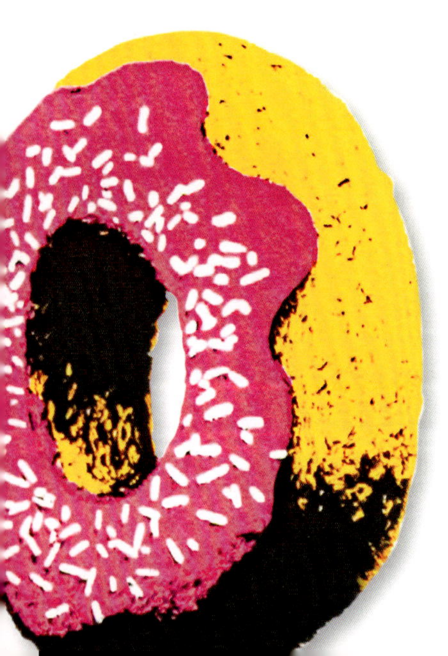

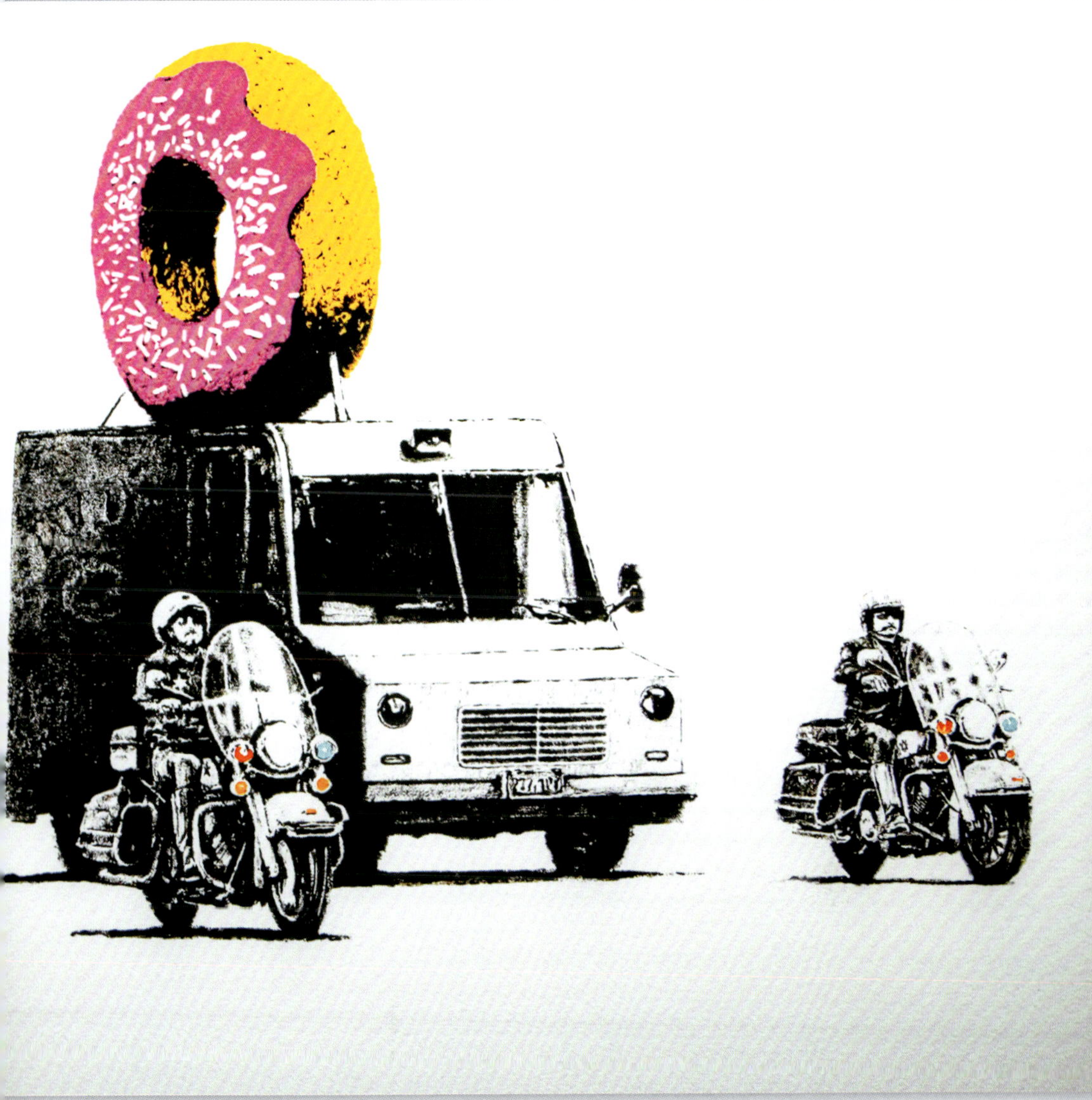

62–63 BANKSY IRONICALLY RECALLS ONE OF THE MOST MEMORABLE MASS ARRESTS IN BRITISH HISTORY, WHICH OCCURRED IN 1985. THE POLICEMEN IN RIOT GEAR ARE CHEERFULLY RUNNING IN THE FLOWERY FIELD ON WHICH THE FESTIVAL THAT TRIGGERED THE REVOLTS SHOULD HAVE TAKEN PLACE.

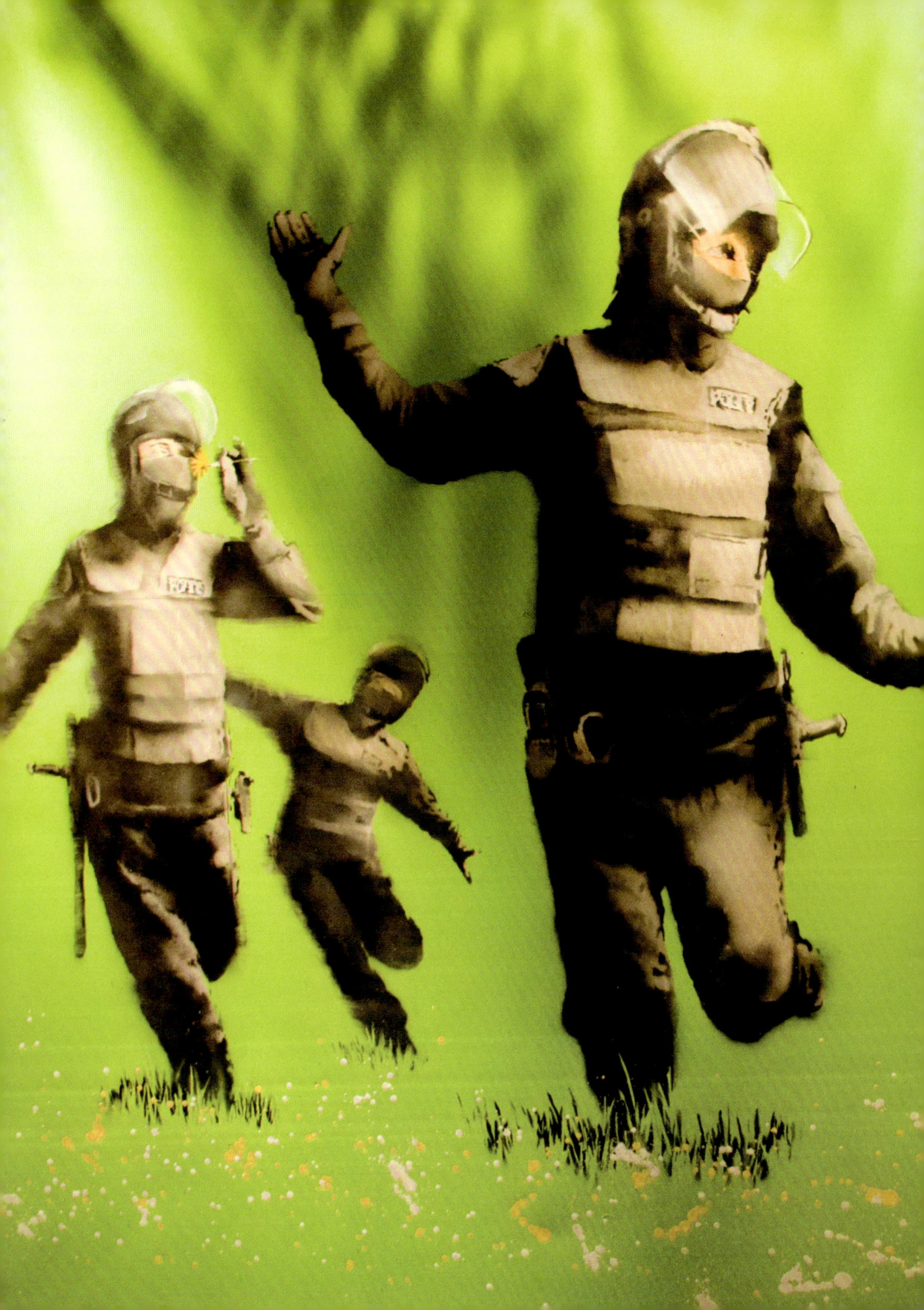

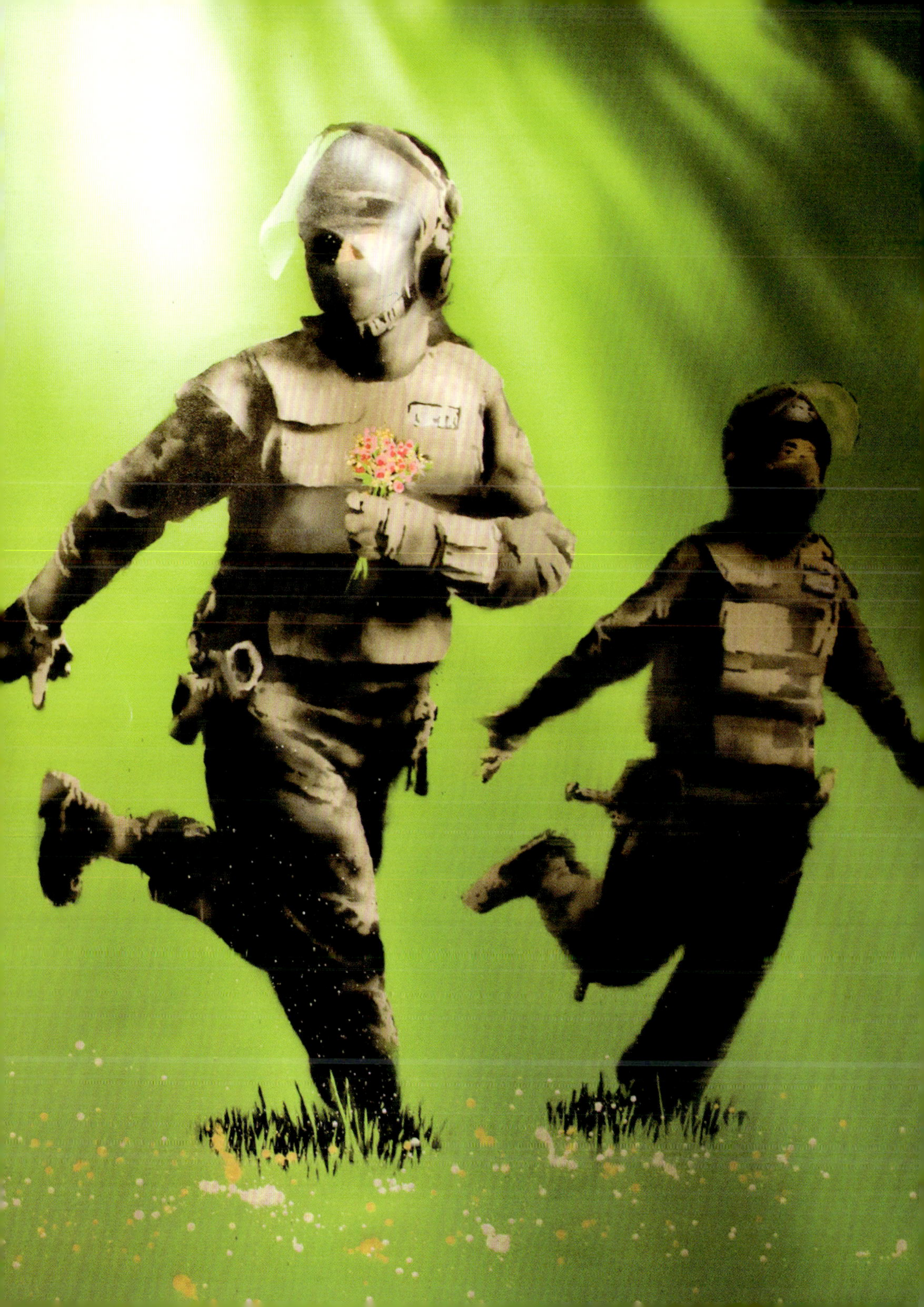

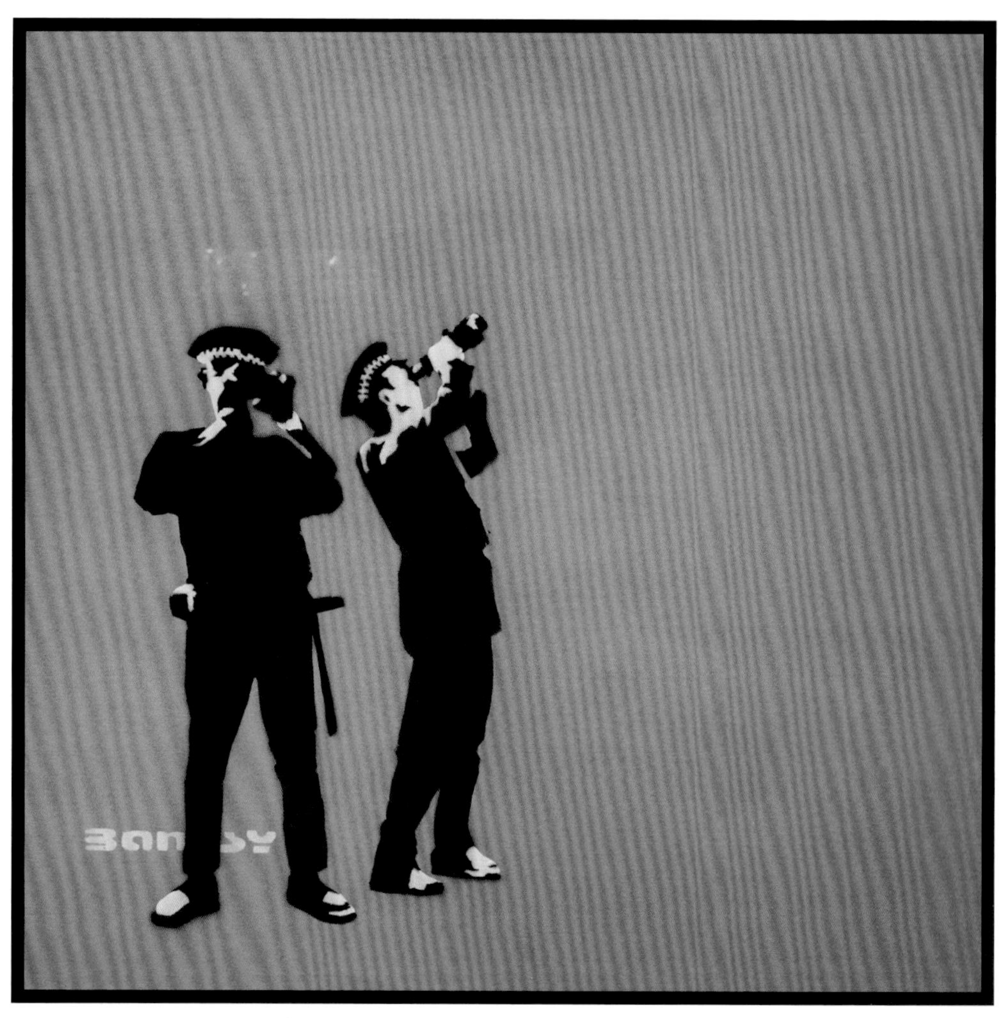

TWO POLICE OFFICERS ON A PINK BACKGROUND ARE LOOKING THROUGH THEIR BINOCULARS IN DIFFERENT DIRECTIONS, WITHOUT KNOWING WHAT THEY ARE LOOKING FOR.

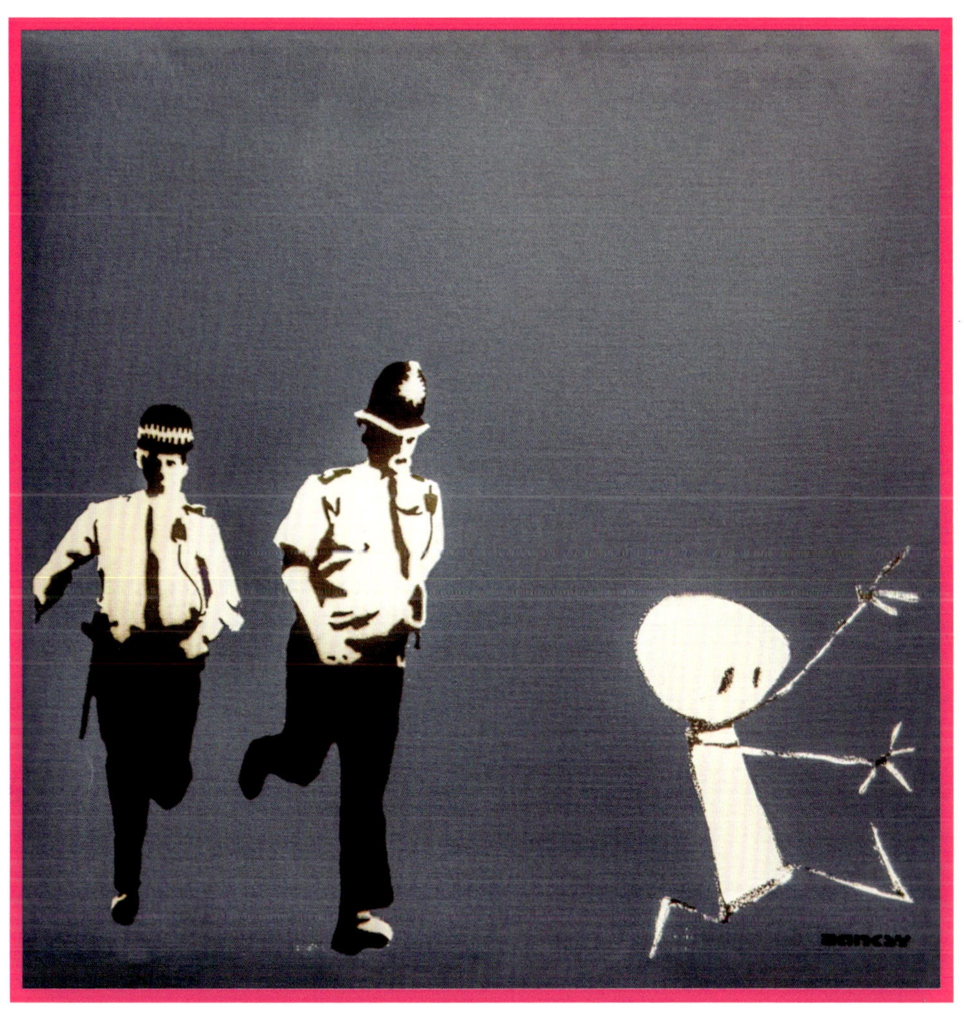

STICK POLICE – 2004

THE POLICE ARE CHASING AN IMAGINARY CHARACTER, WITH NO CLEAR SENSE OF PRIORITIES.

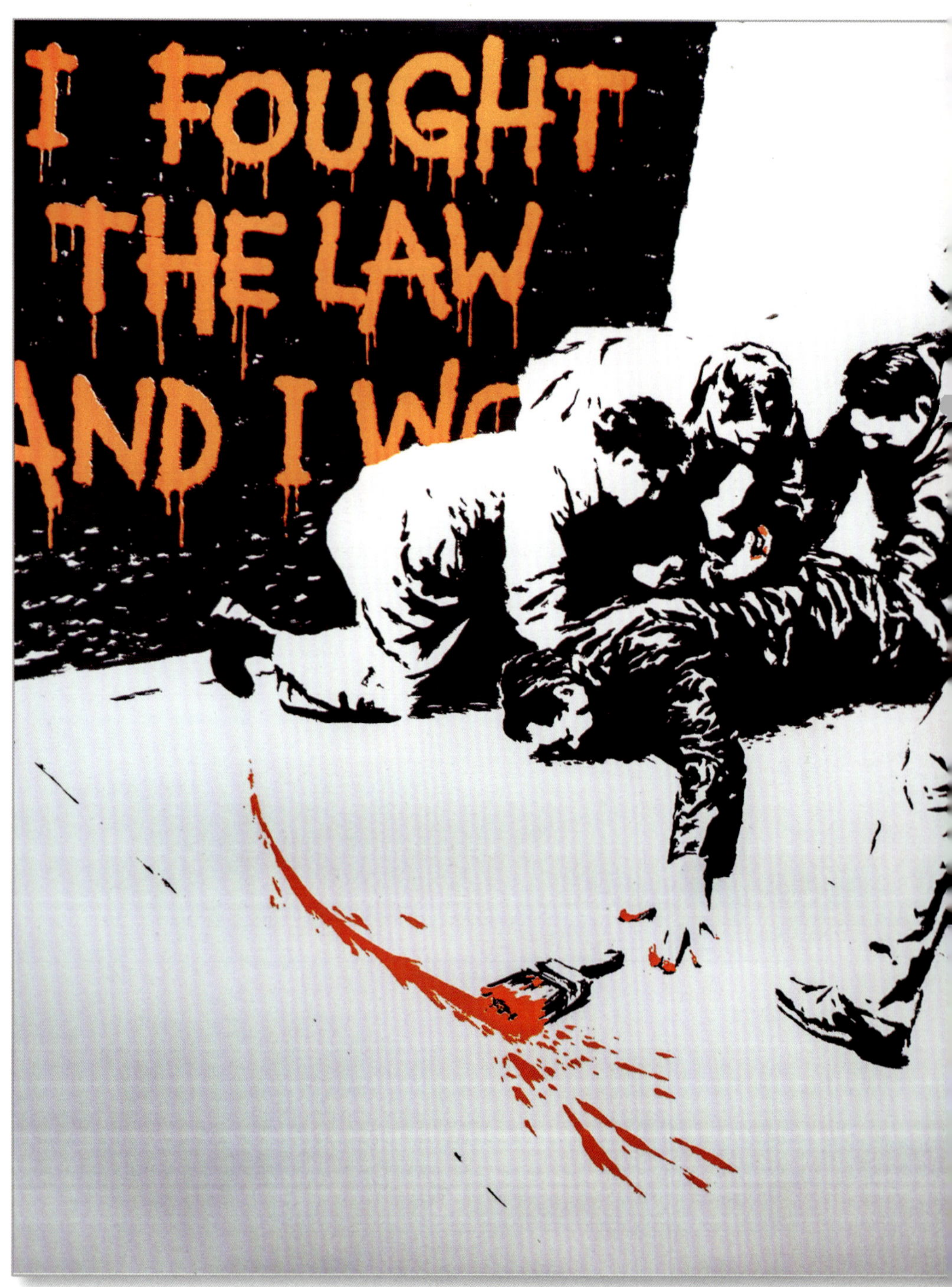

I FOUGHT
THE LAW
AND I WO

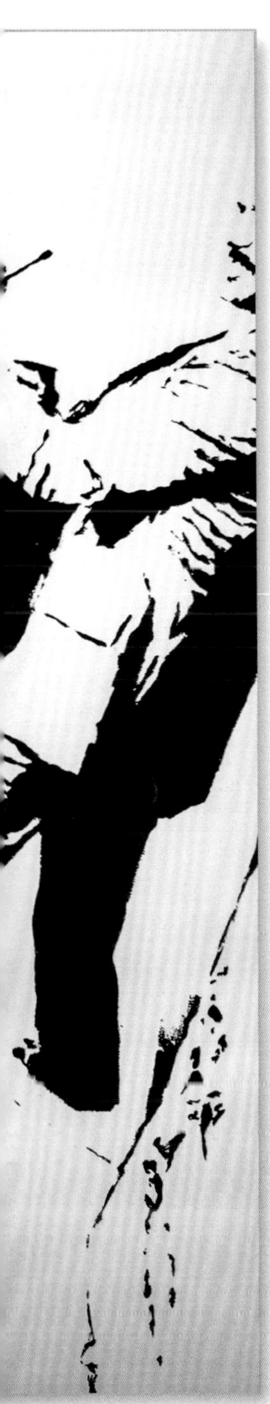

A GRAFFITIST IS PINNED TO THE GROUND AFTER PAINTING ON A WALL THE WORDS "I FOUGHT THE LAW AND I WON." THIS WORK REFERS TO THE FAILED ASSASSINATION ATTEMPT ON PRESIDENT RONALD REAGAN BY JOHN HINCKLEY IN 1981.

THE WORDS "SUPER SOFT" ON THE SIDE OF AN ICE CREAM TRUCK INVITE US TO REFLECT ON POLICE BRUTALITY.

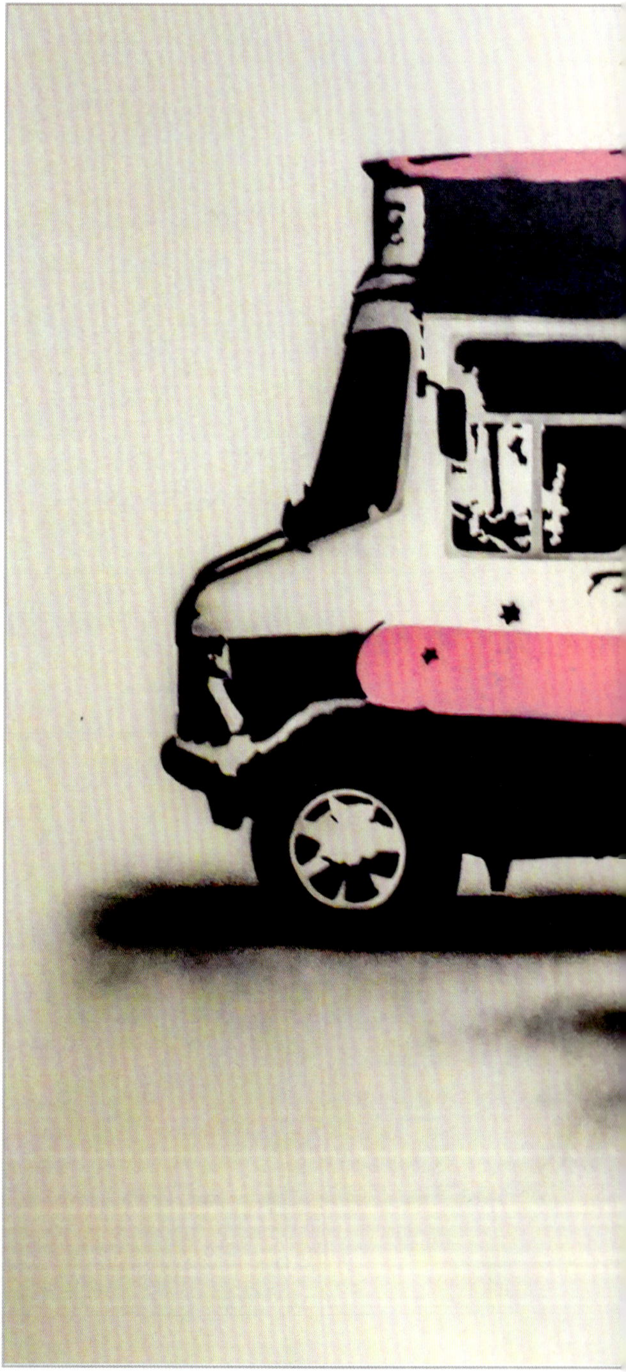

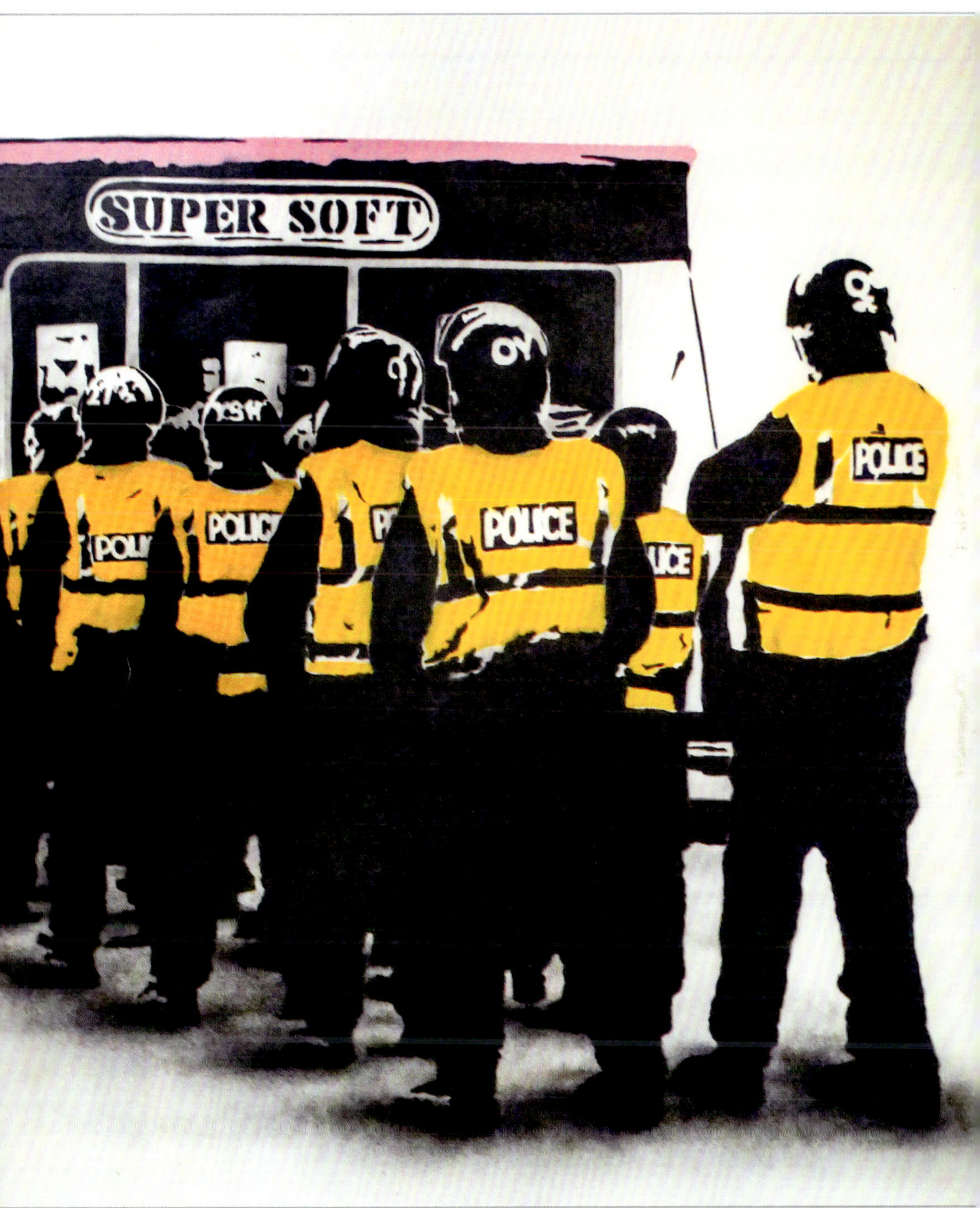
SUPER SOFT
POLICE
POLICE
POLICE
POLICE
POLICE

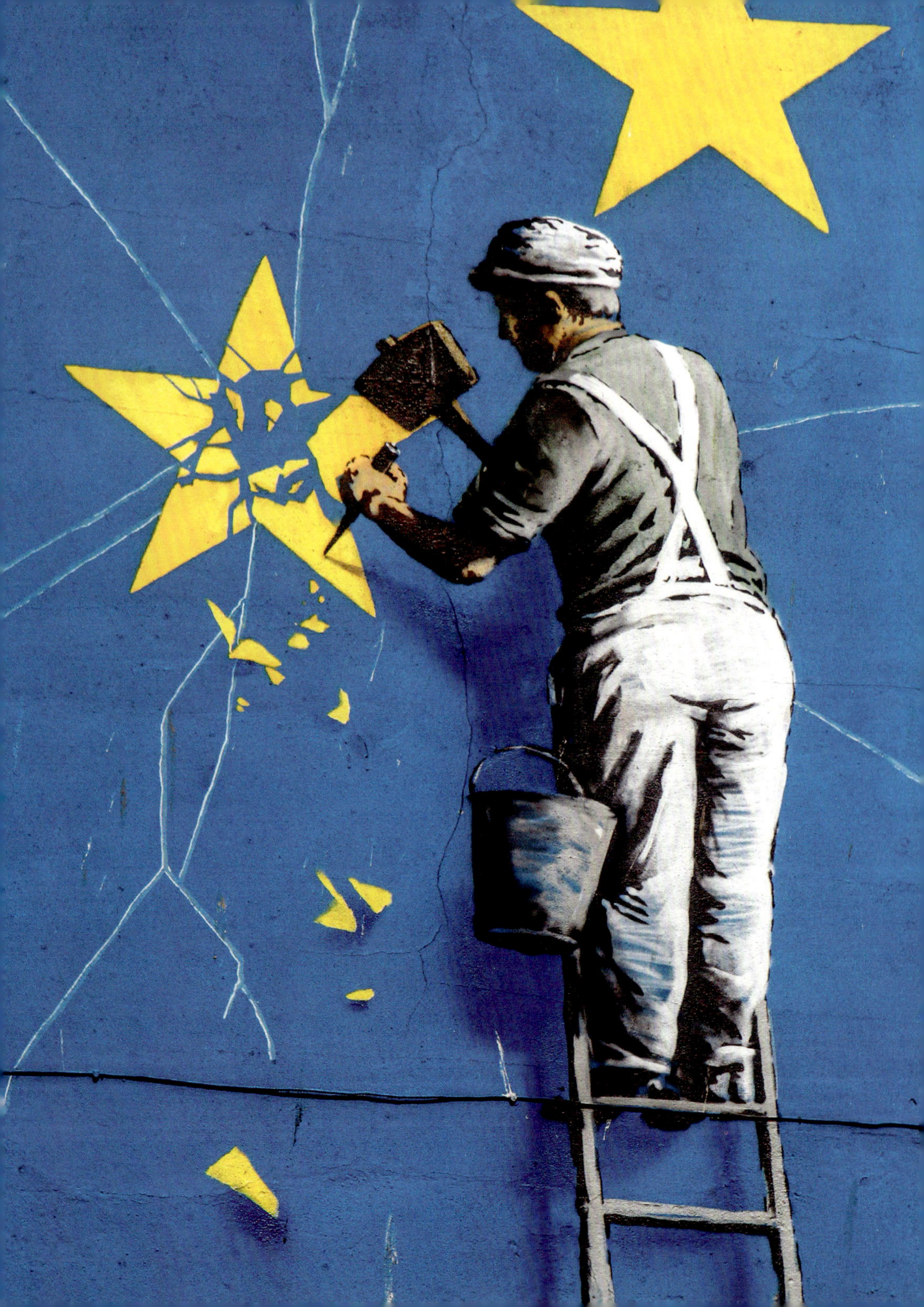

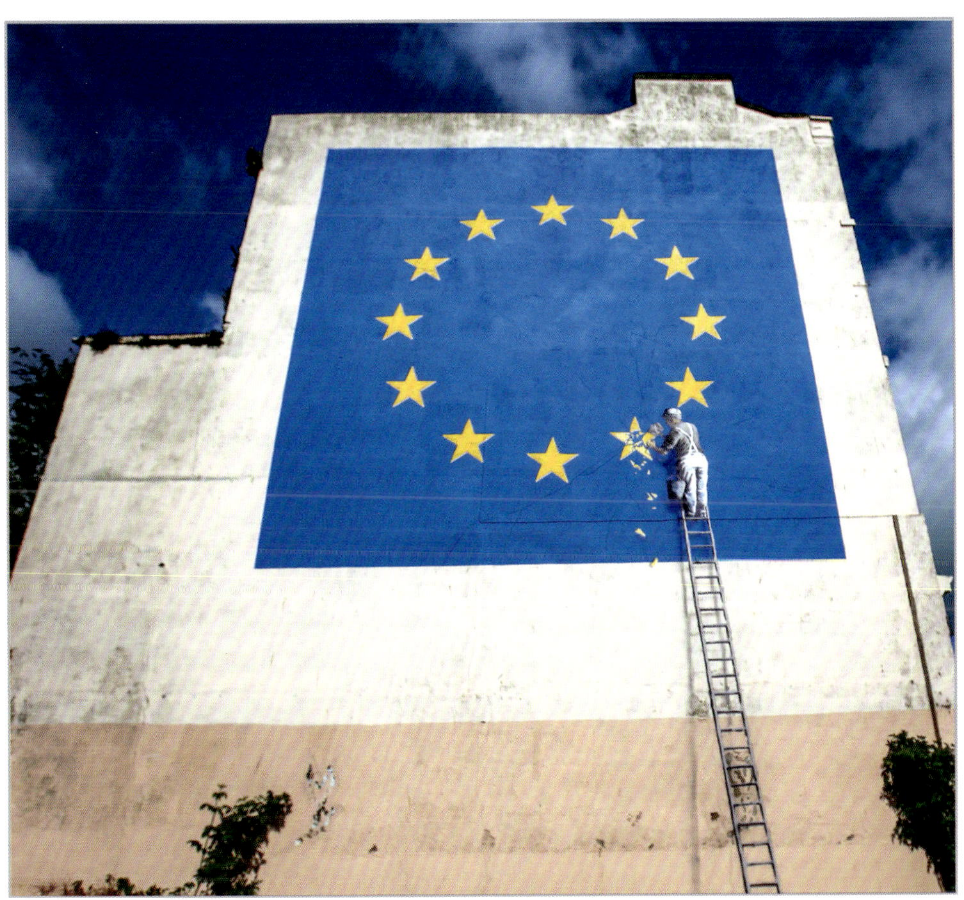

THIS GRAFFITI WORK IS LOCATED IN DOVER, AND IT PORTRAYS A WORKER UP A LADDER ARMED WITH A HAMMER AND CHISEL WHILE REMOVING A STAR FROM A HUGE EUROPEAN UNION FLAG.

WHAT A FOOD OF RUBBISH

72–73 THE PERVASIVENESS OF THE WELL-KNOWN BRITISH SUPERMARKET CHAIN IS ALSO FOUND IN THE TRASH.

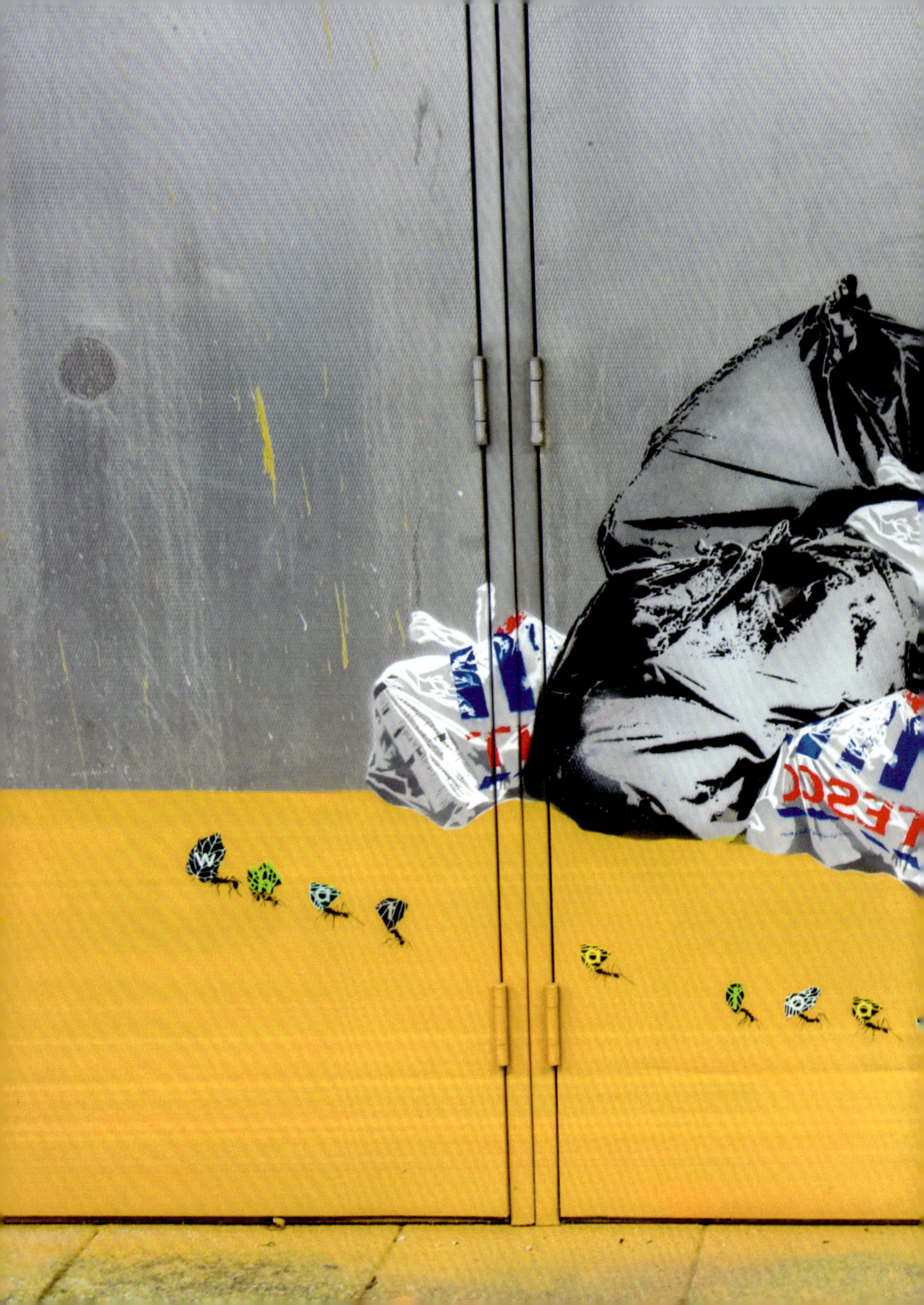
TESCO
TESCO
W

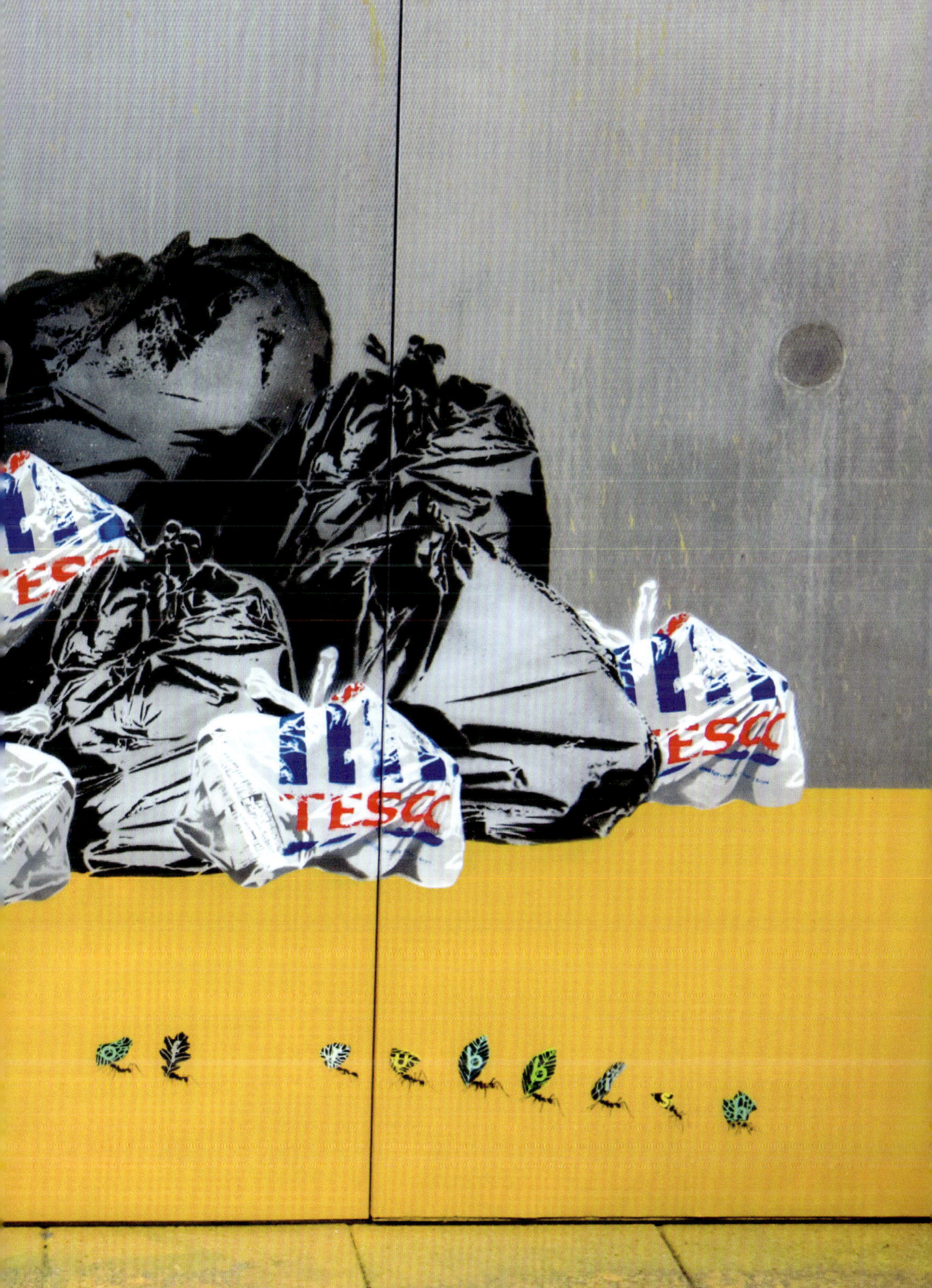

TESCO
TESCO
TESCO

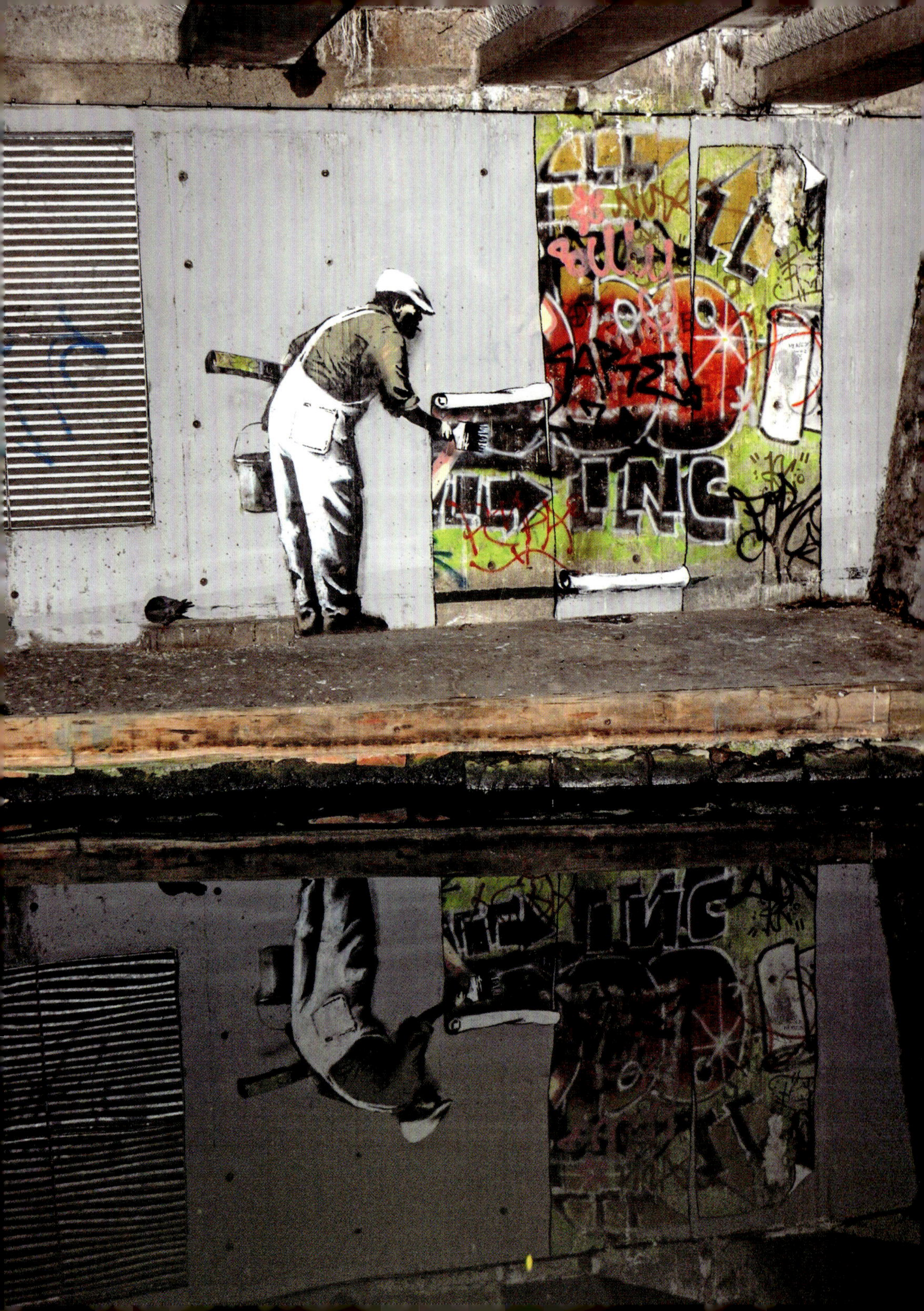

IN 2009, BANKSY STARTED ONE OF THE MOST THRILLING WARS IN LONDON'S STREET ART SCENARIO. HIS CHOICE TO COVER PART OF A GRAFFITI WORK MADE BY KING ROBBO IN 1985 NEAR REGENT'S CANAL STARTED A FEUD THAT LASTED SEVERAL YEARS.

CRAZY HORSES RIDING THROUGH THE LOWER EAST SIDE TO A WIKILEAKS SOUNDTRACK – NEW YORK, 2013

76–77 THIS WORK WAS MADE ON THE SIDE OF A CAR AND A TRUCK, AND IT WAS ACCOMPANIED BY THE TRAGIC AUDIO RECORDING OF A THREE-MINUTE AIR STRIKE ON UNARMED CIVILIANS THAT OCCURRED IN BAGHDAD IN 2007 AND THAT WAS TAKEN FROM THE COLLATERAL MURDER VIDEO LEAKED ON WIKILEAKS BY CHELSEA MANNING IN 2010.

IKEA PUNK – BEDDINGTON FARM ROAD, CROYDON, 2009

78–79 WHILE CAPITALISM IS MAKING THE WORLD COLLAPSE, A PUNK GUY EXPRESSES ALL HIS FRUSTRATION WHEN FACED WITH SOME ASSEMBLY INSTRUCTIONS.

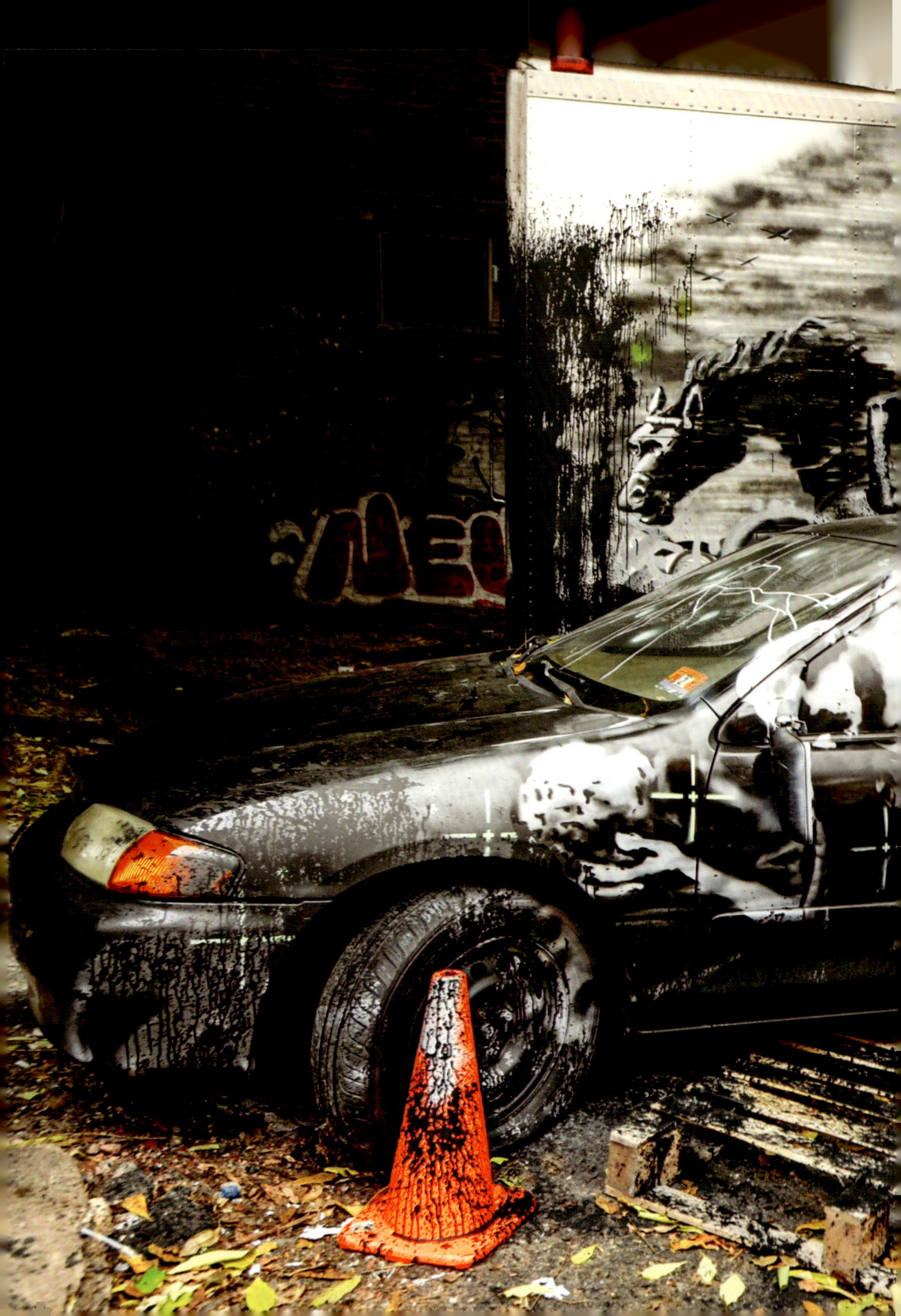

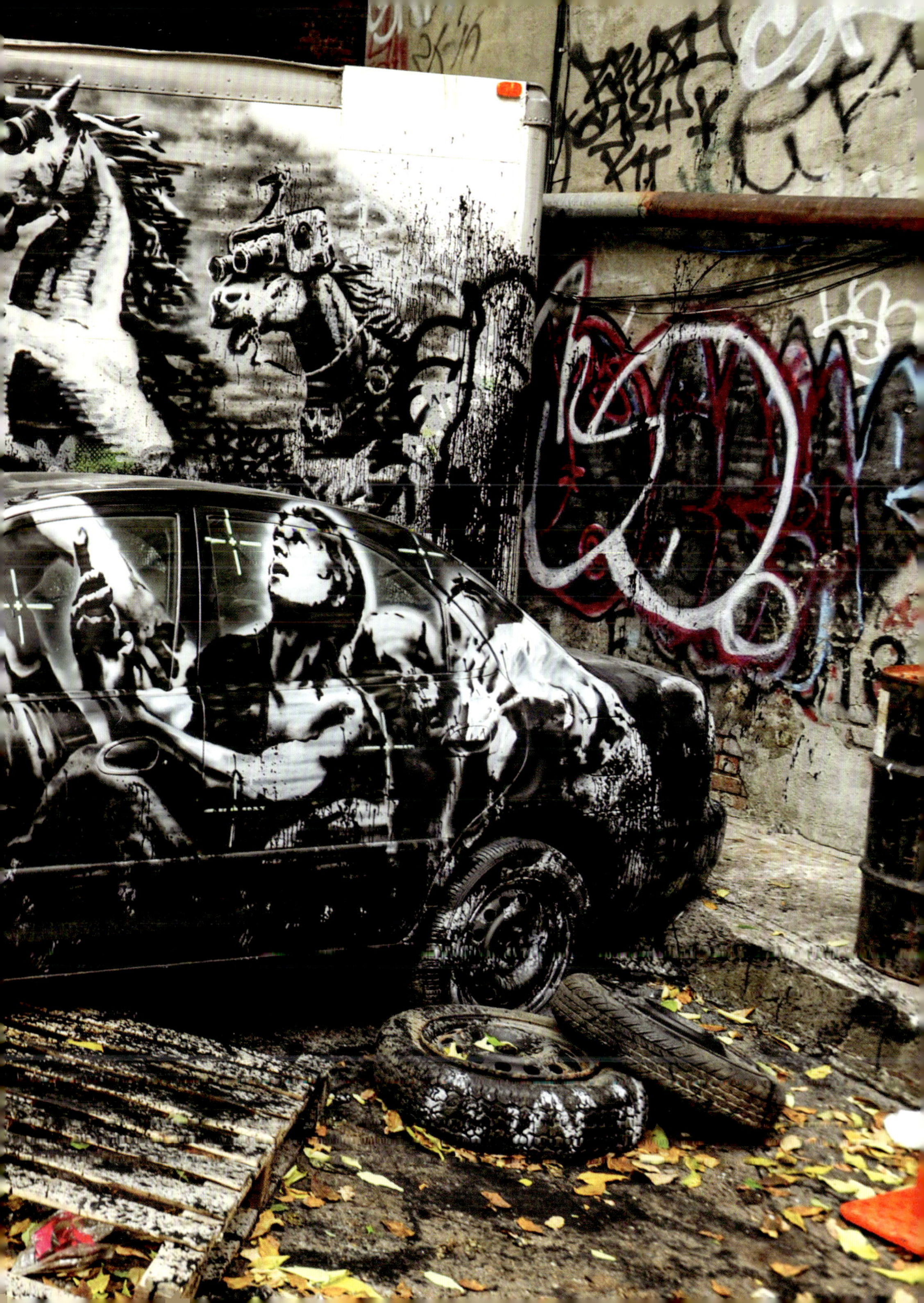

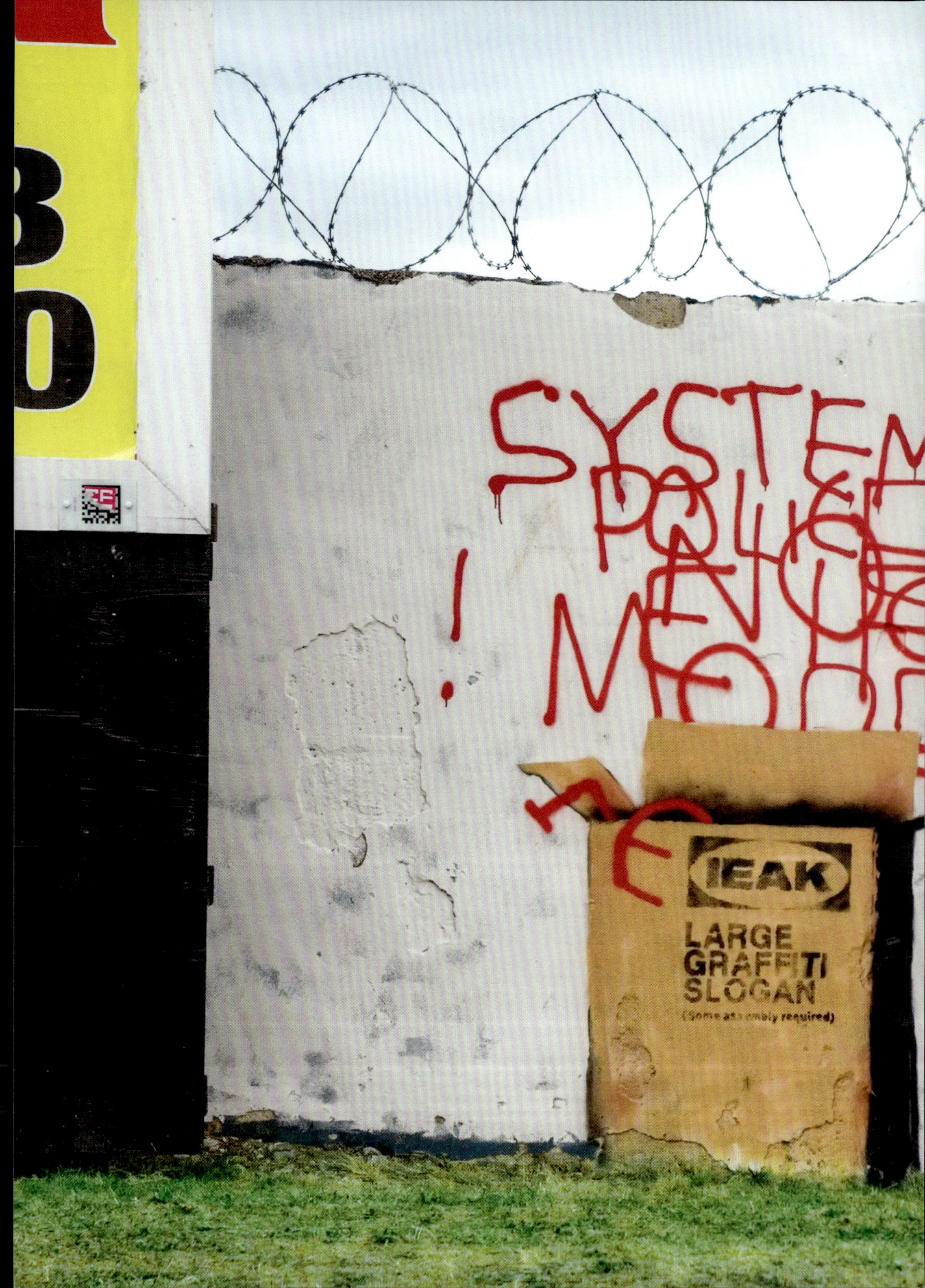

SYSTEM
POLICE
MENACE
MOB

IEAK
LARGE
GRAFFITI
SLOGAN
(some assembly required)

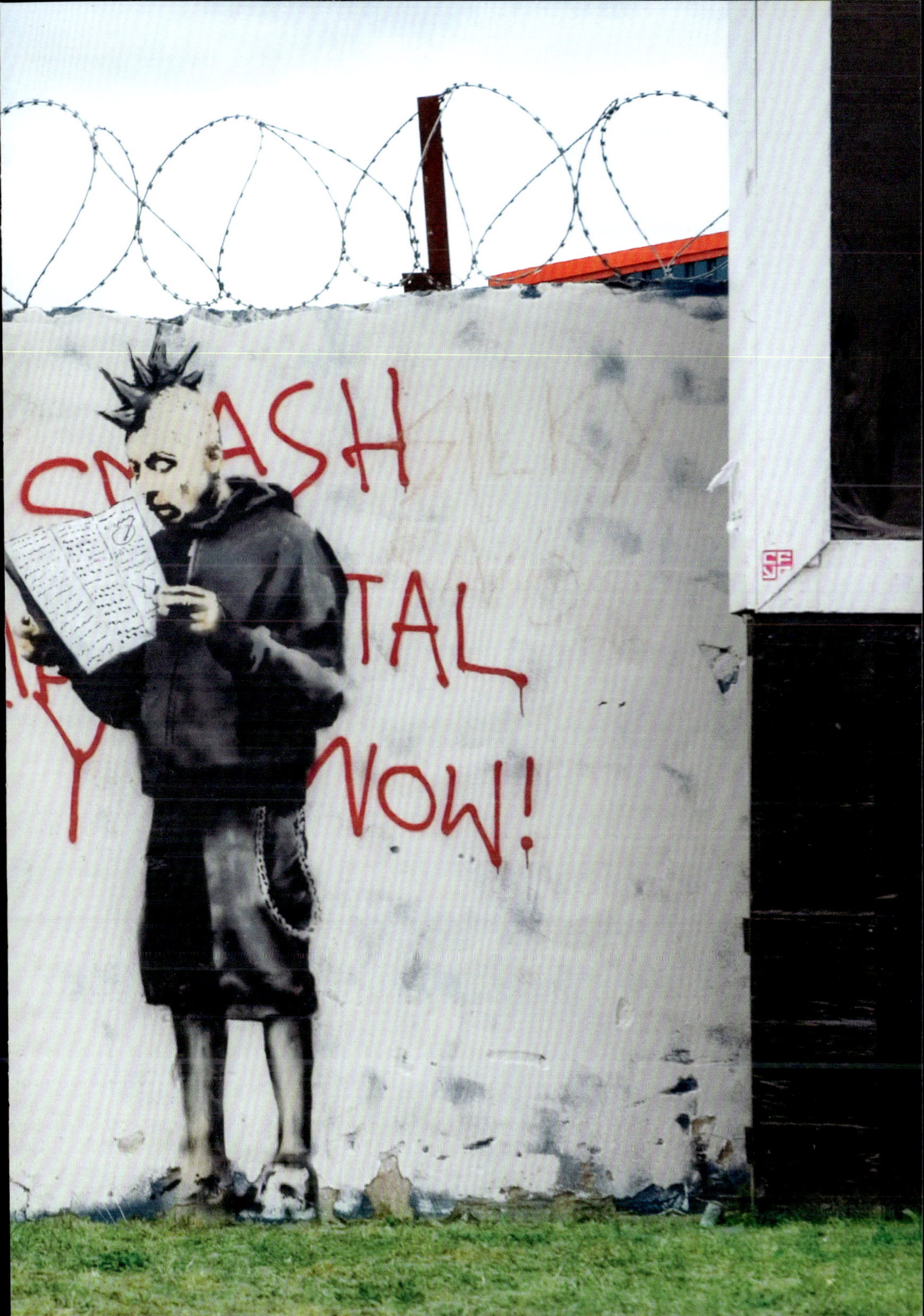

SMASH
TAL
NOW!

BANKSY IRONICALLY REINTERPRETS JEAN-MICHEL BASQUIAT'S WORK TO EMPHASIZE THE DIFFERENT TREATMENT THAT STREET ART RECEIVES OUTSIDE MUSEUMS.

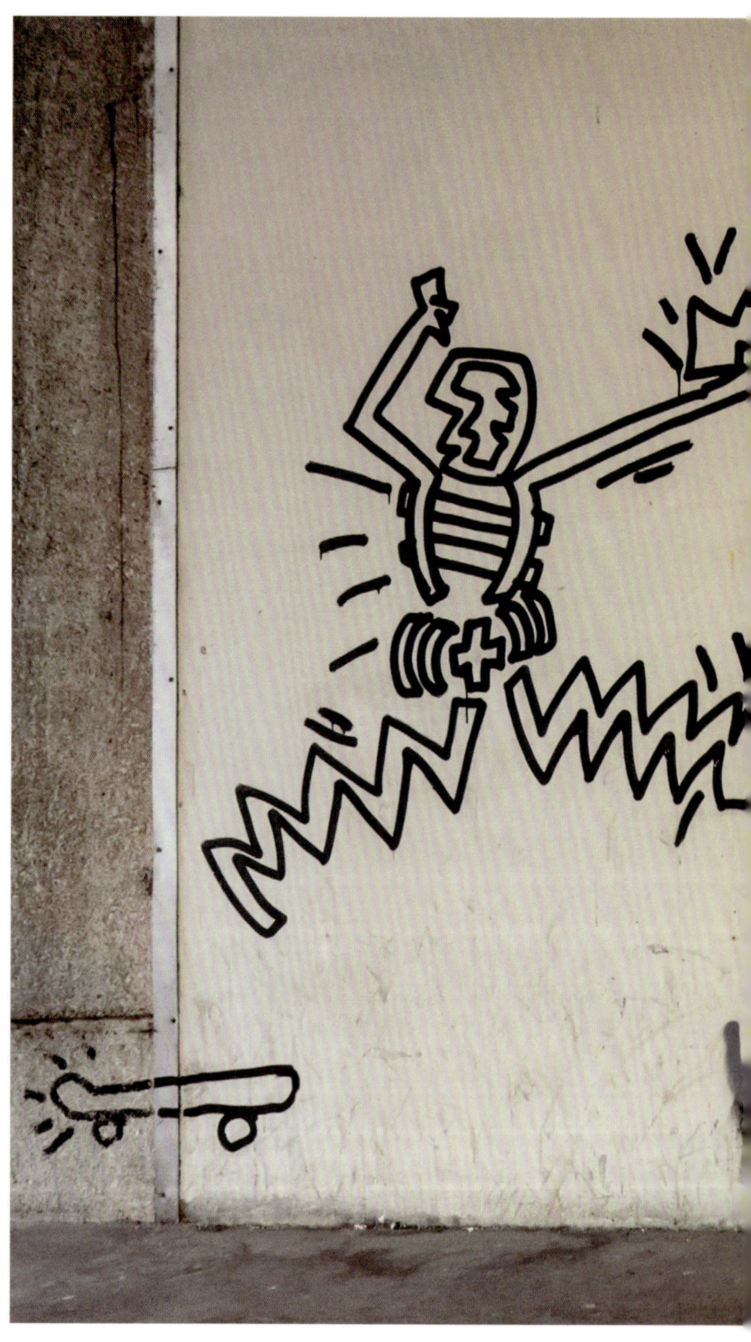

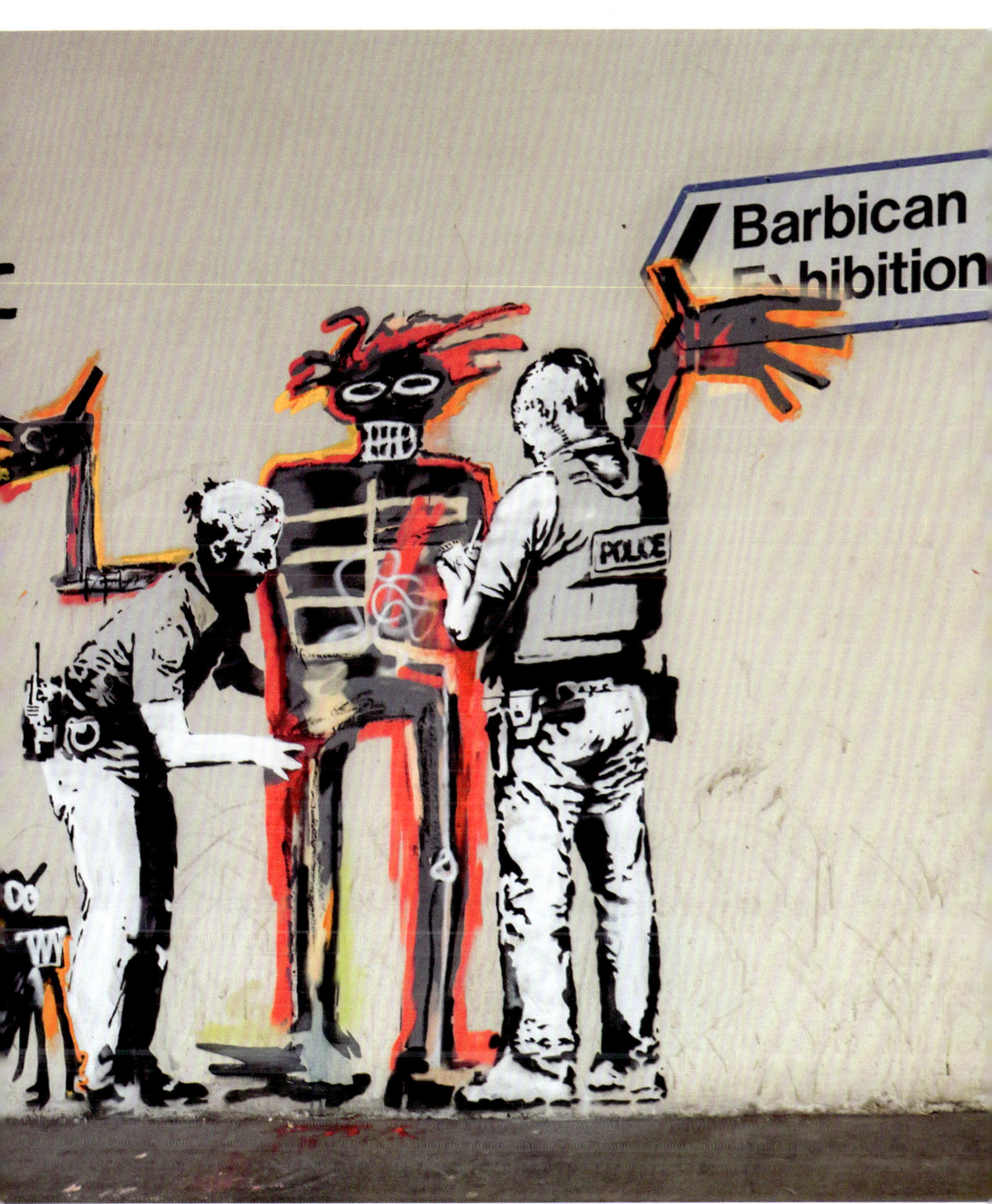
Barbican
Exhibition
POLICE

BANKSY PAINTED THIS GRAFFITI WORK ON THE WALL OF THE BROOK YOUNG PEOPLE'S CLINIC, IN BRISTOL. IT DEPICTS A NAKED MAN HANGING FROM HIS LOVER'S WINDOW TO ESCAPE HER HUSBAND WHO CAME HOME UNEXPECTEDLY.

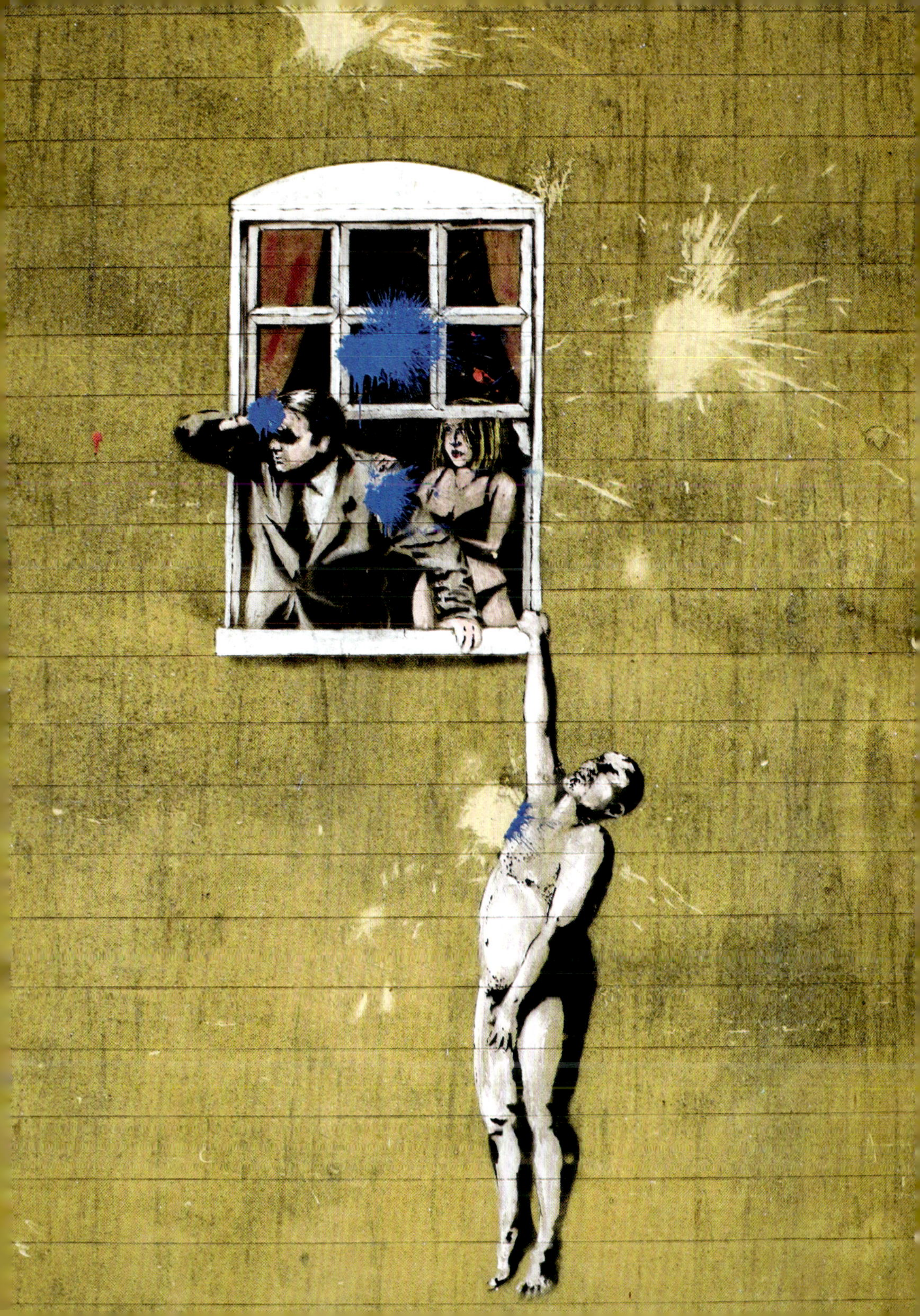

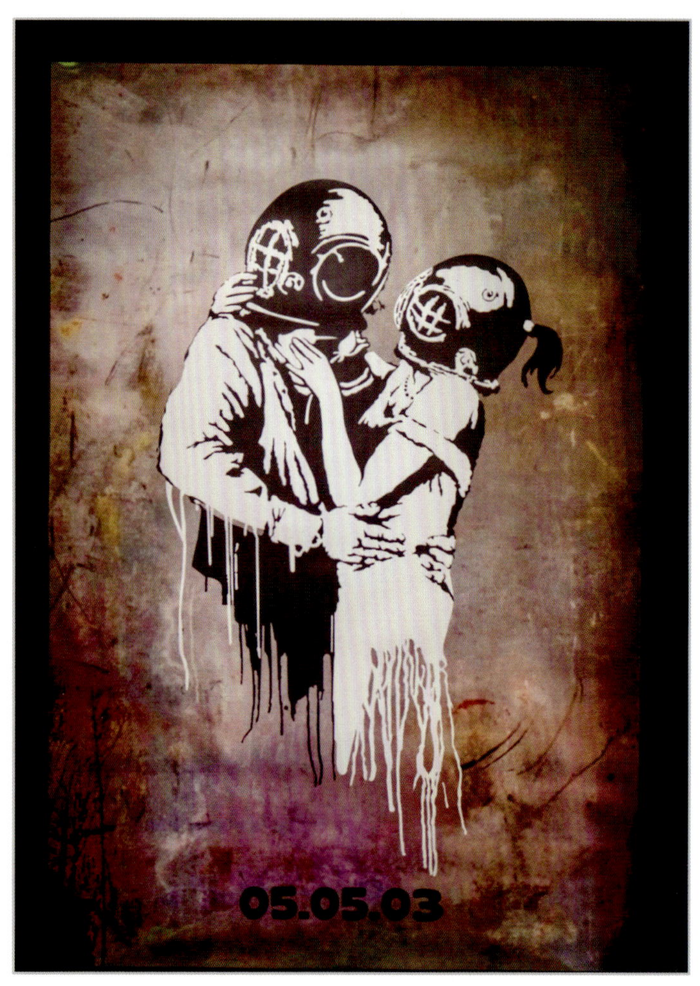

TANK – EMBRACING COUPLE AND DRIP DINNER – 2003

BODY LANGUAGE EXPRESSES THE FEELINGS OF THESE TWO COUPLES, DESPITE THE BIG DIVING HELMETS. BOTH THESE GRAFFITI ARE STUDIES FOR THE THE ENGLISH ROCK BAND BLUR'S THINK TANK ALBUM.

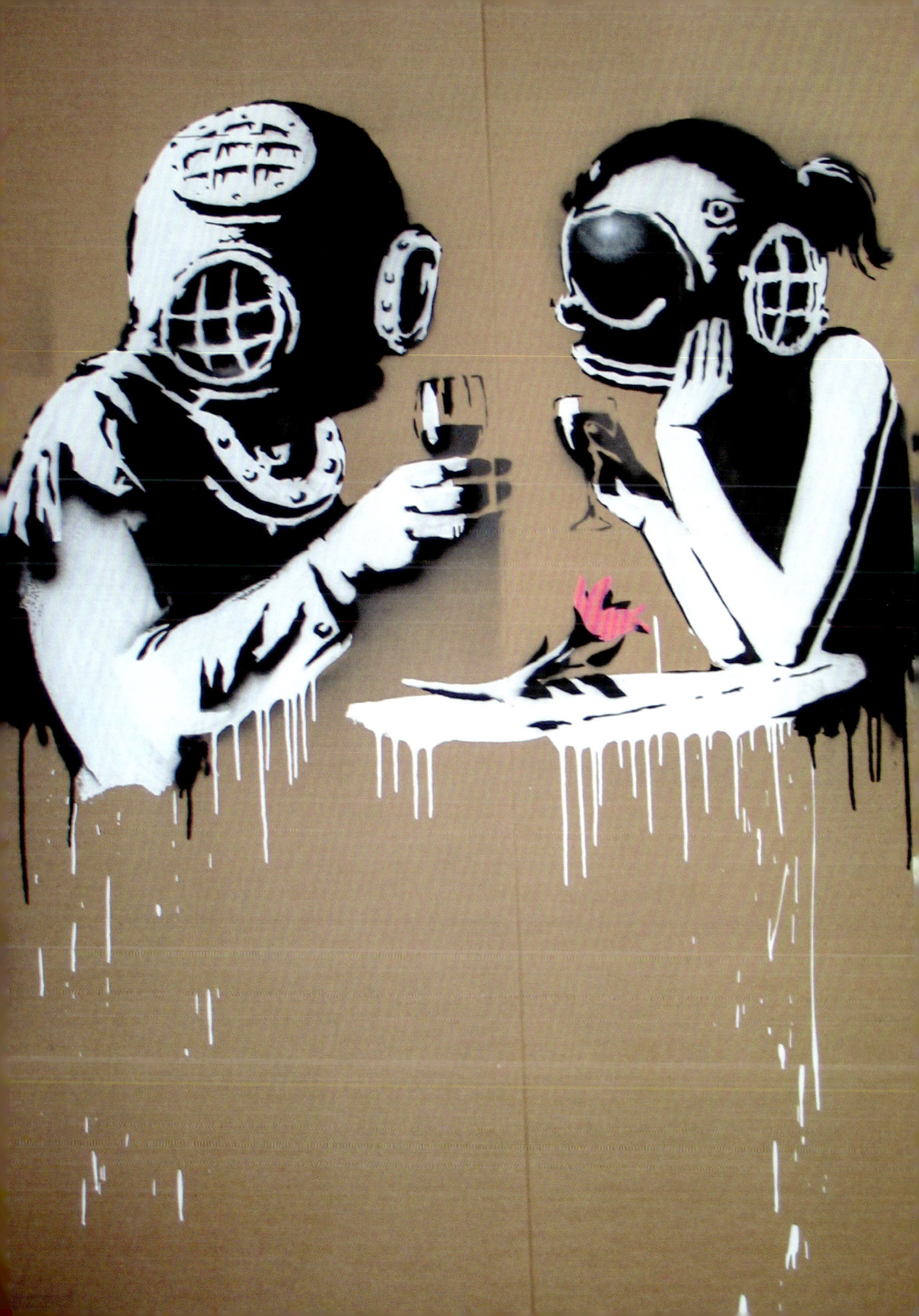

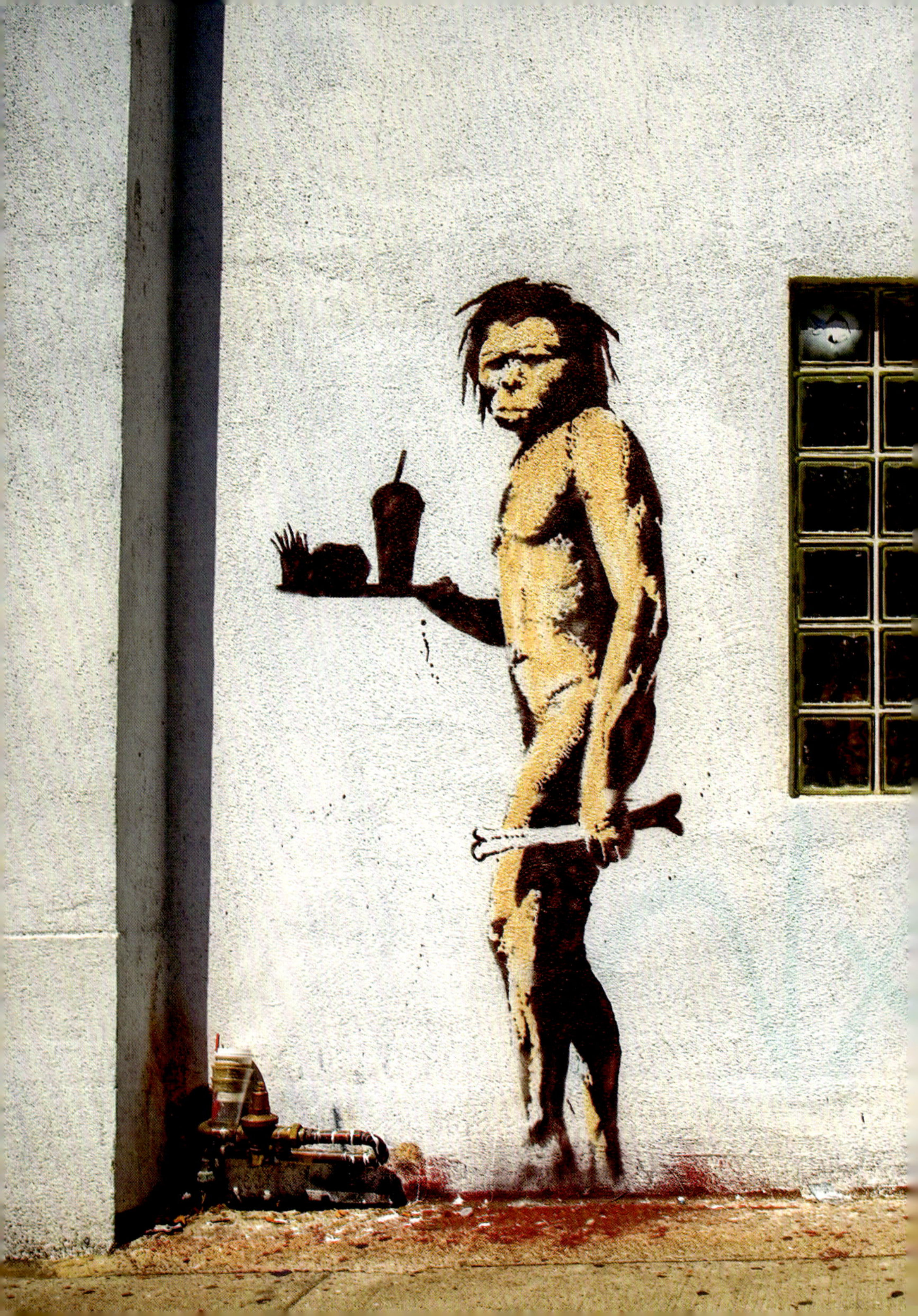

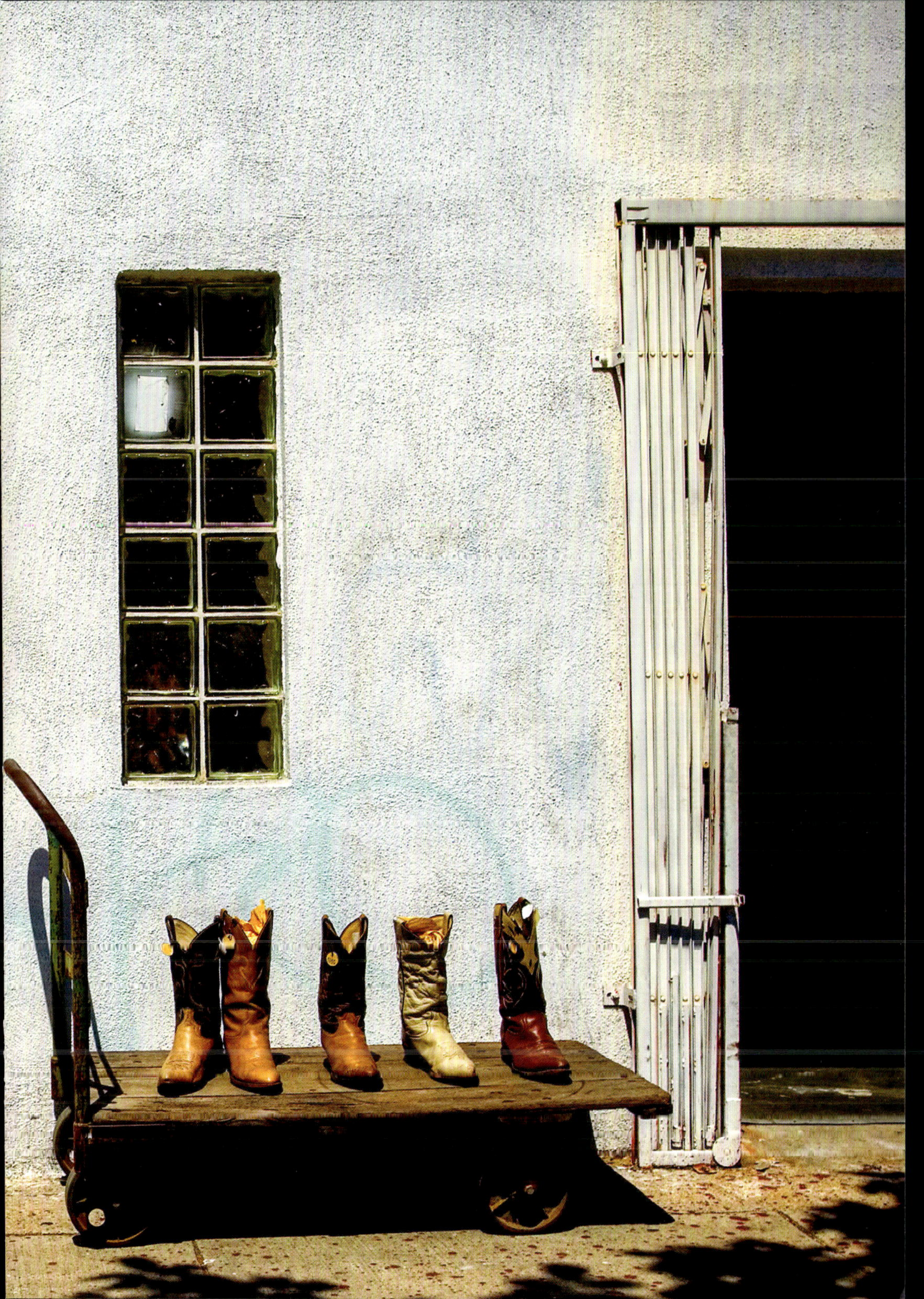

86–87 BANKSY'S CRITICISM OF AMERICAN SOCIETY AND THE FAST-FOOD WORLD COMES STRAIGHT FROM PREHISTORY!

YEARS AFTER HURRICANE KATRINA, BANKSY DENOUNCES THE SLOW RECONSTRUCTION OF NEW ORLEANS BY PORTRAYING PRESIDENT ABRAHAM LINCOLN AS A HOMELESS MAN WANDERING THE STREETS OF THE CITY.

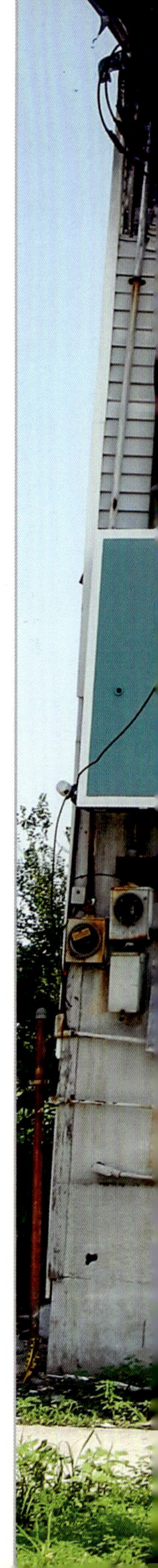

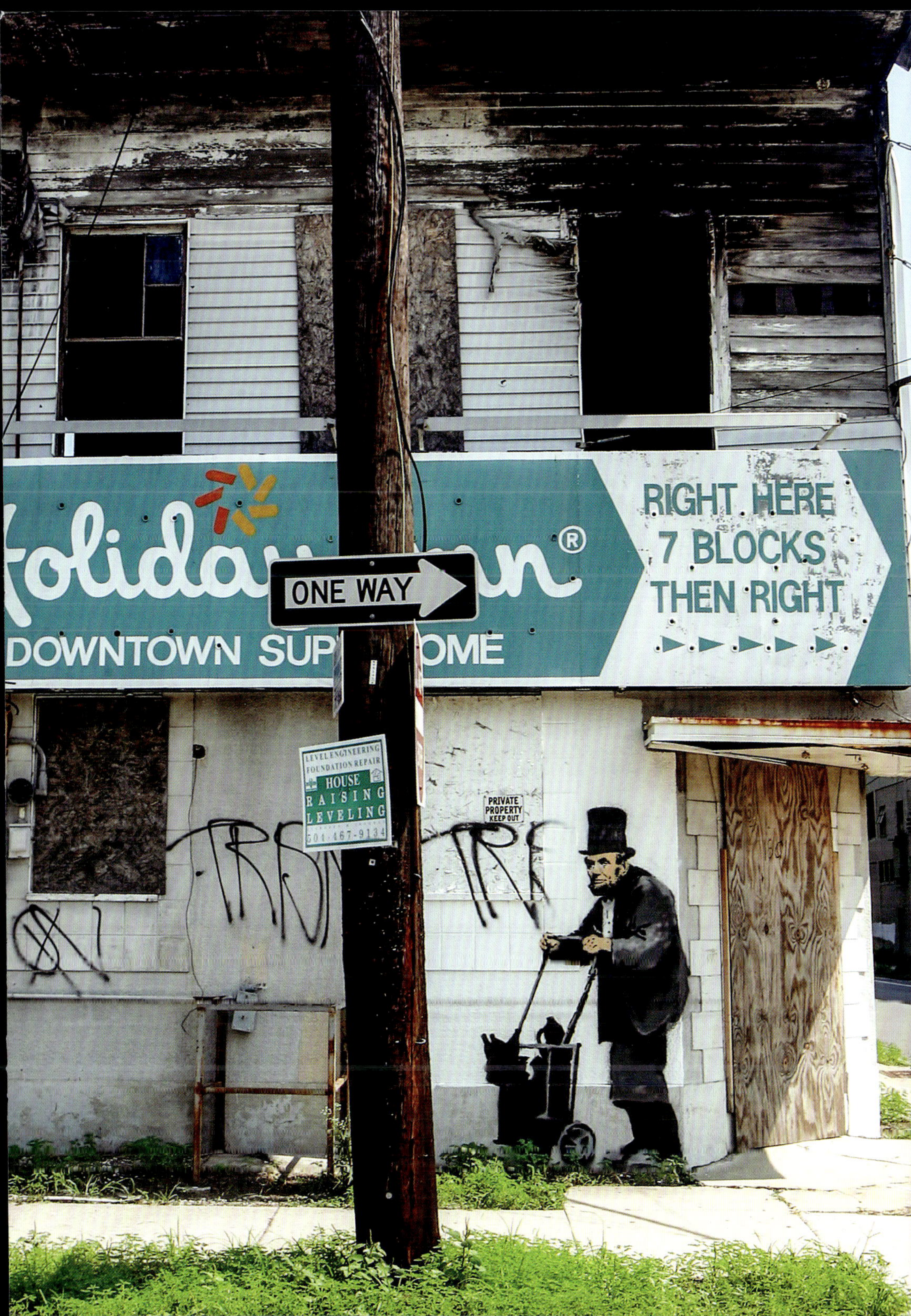
Holiday Inn ®
DOWNTOWN SUPER HOME
RIGHT HERE
7 BLOCKS
THEN RIGHT
ONE WAY
LEVEL ENGINEERING
FOUNDATION REPAIR
HOUSE
RAISING
LEVELING
504-467-9134
PRIVATE
PROPERTY
KEEP OUT

A WOMAN SNEEZES AND LOSES HER DENTURES: BANKSY'S WAR AGAINST COVID-19 GOES VIRAL.

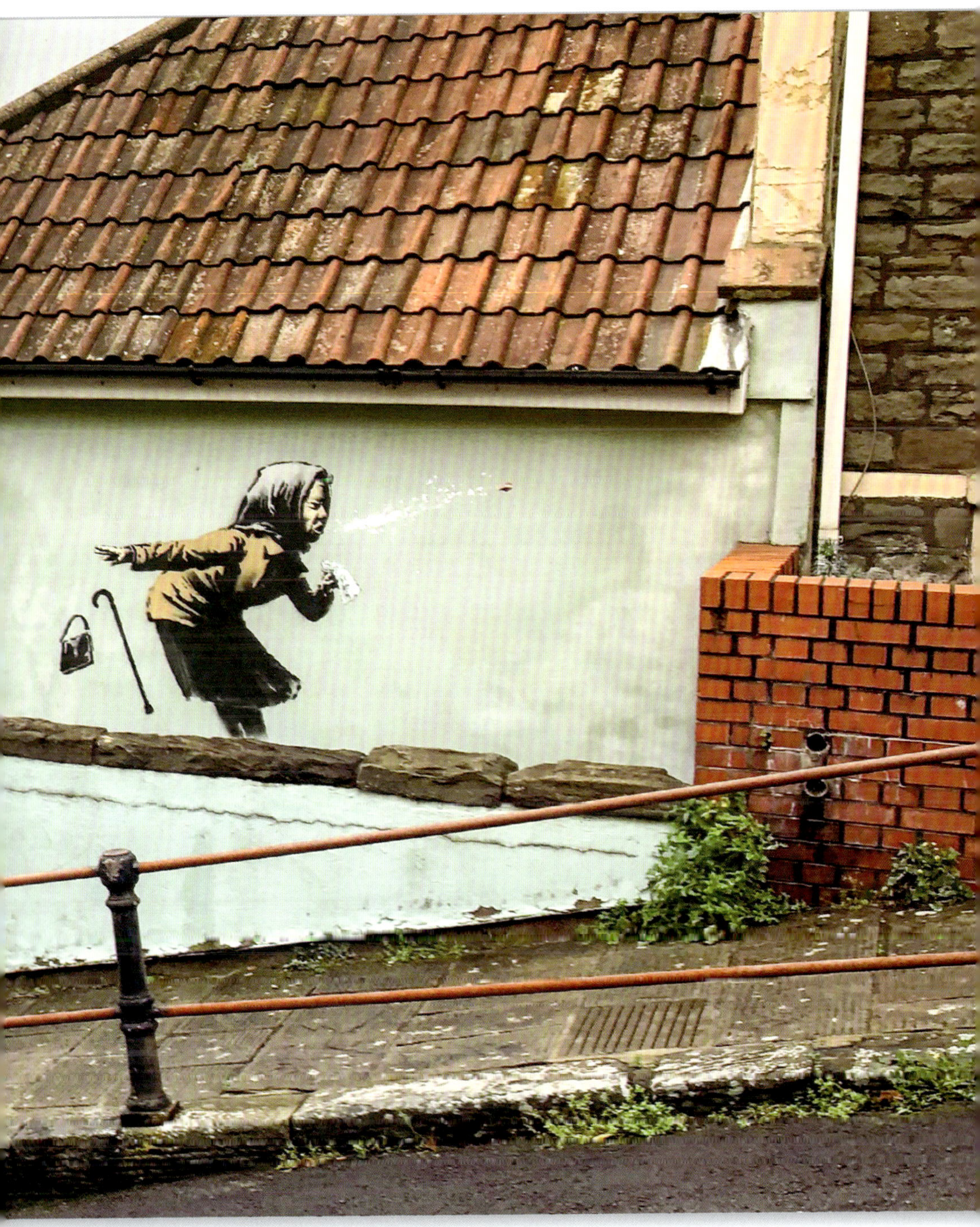

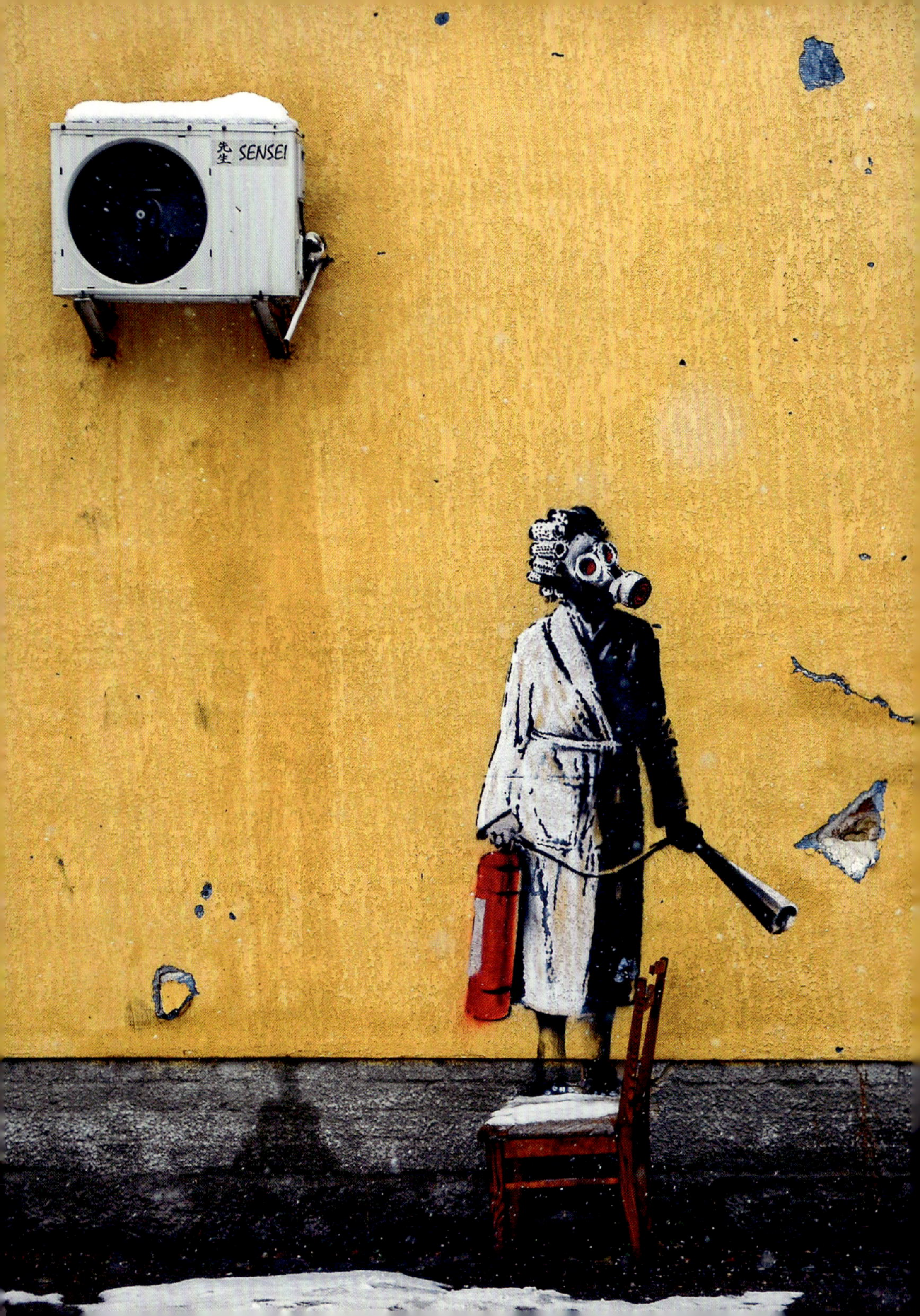
先生 SENSEI

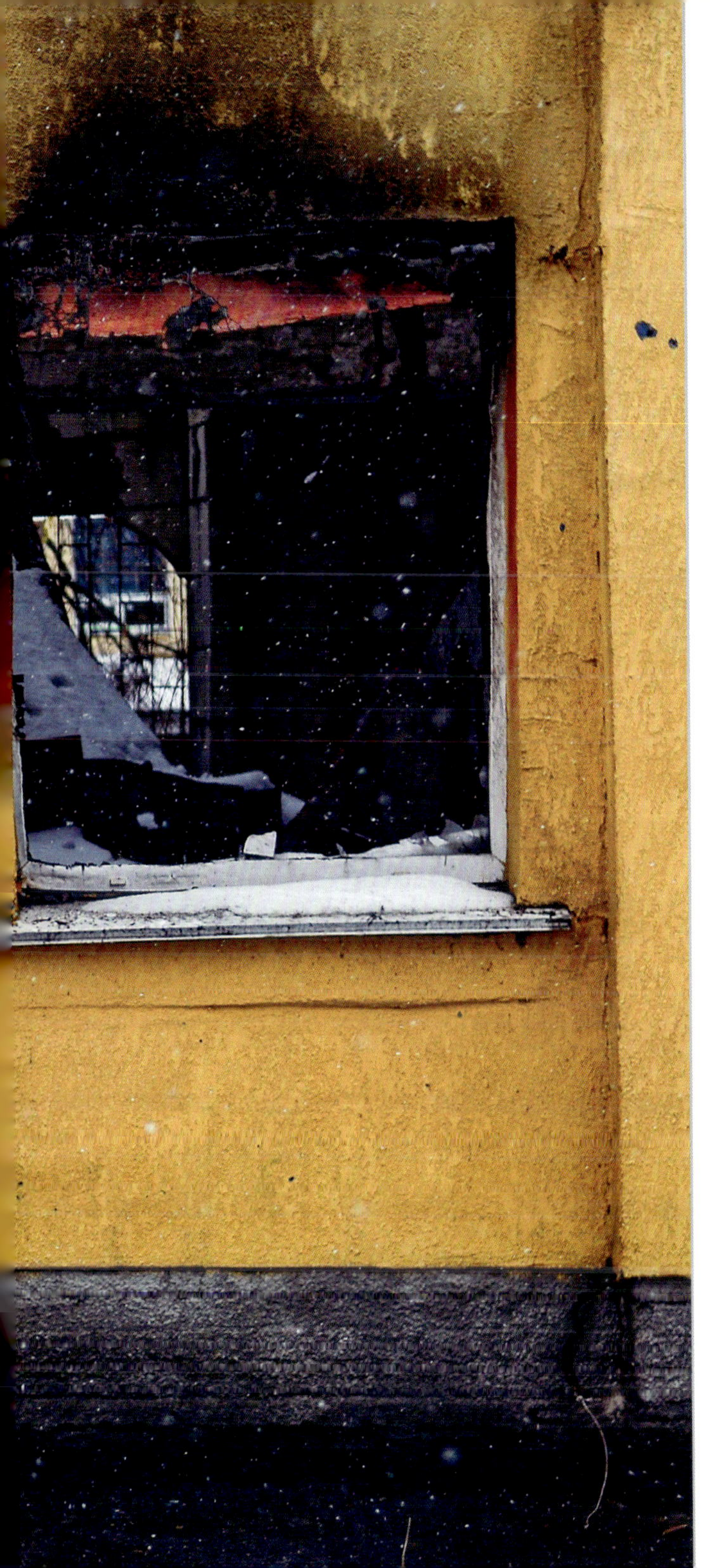

IN UKRAINE, THIS WOMAN WITH A GAS MASK AND A FIRE EXTINGUISHER IN HER HANDS BECOMES THE SYMBOL OF RESISTANCE TO ADVERSITY CAUSED BY AN UNJUST WAR.

ABOUT THE AUTHOR

ALESSANDRA MATTANZA is a multi-award-winning writer and journalist, screenwriter, fine art photographer, and multimedia artist, and she lives between Munich, New York, San Francisco, Los Angeles, and Paris. She has collaborated with several magazines, including *Forbes, Vanity Fair, Elle, Cosmopolitan, How to Spend It, Icon, F,* and *Natural Style,* and she also writes novels and murder mysteries for several publishing houses. She won several awards for best articles and books at the Annual Southern California Journalism Awards and the SoCal Journalism Awards, in Los Angeles. Among the many awards she has received, she also won first prize in the nonfiction category for the books *C215 #christianguemy: Stencil Art* and the first *Banksy* book, and third prize for *Street Art: 20 Famous Artists Talk About Their Vision.* As an artist, she created the projects and media campaigns *www.newyorkblackandwhite.org,* exhibited at the Kunstlabor 2 museum, linked to the MUCA Museum in Munich, and *www.abetterplanetabetterworld.com,* presented in a major exhibition at the United Nations Headquarters of New York in 2023 and at the Italian Mission to the UN in New York until 2025. This last project for the environment was inspired by the book *SOS Planet Earth: Voices for a Better World,* published by National Geographic and White Star.

ABOUT THE CAPTIONS AUTHOR

LUCA GRECO is a copywriter, social media manager, and art blogger. After graduating in philosophy and completing a master's degree in marketing and communication from the IED in Turin, he collaborated with important communication agencies in Turin. An attentive observer of reality, Luca loves sharing his way of interpreting it by constantly experimenting with new forms of digital communication on his news and cultural study blog called "Fatti e Fabulae" (www.fattiefabulae.com). He is currently copywriter and social media manager for an important Italian digital experience company. Since 2022, he has been social media management professor of the Social Innovation, Communication, and New Technologies course at the University of Turin.

PHOTO CREDITS

Project Handling: Weiß-Freiburg GmbH – Grafik & Buchgestaltung
Translation: Carlotta Cappato
Editing: Abby Young
Editing and proofreading: John Stilwell
Editorial Direction at Prestel: Curt Holtz
Production at Prestel: Martina Effaga

Printed in China

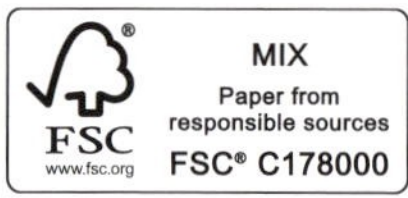

ISBN 978-3-7913-9309-4
www.prestel.com

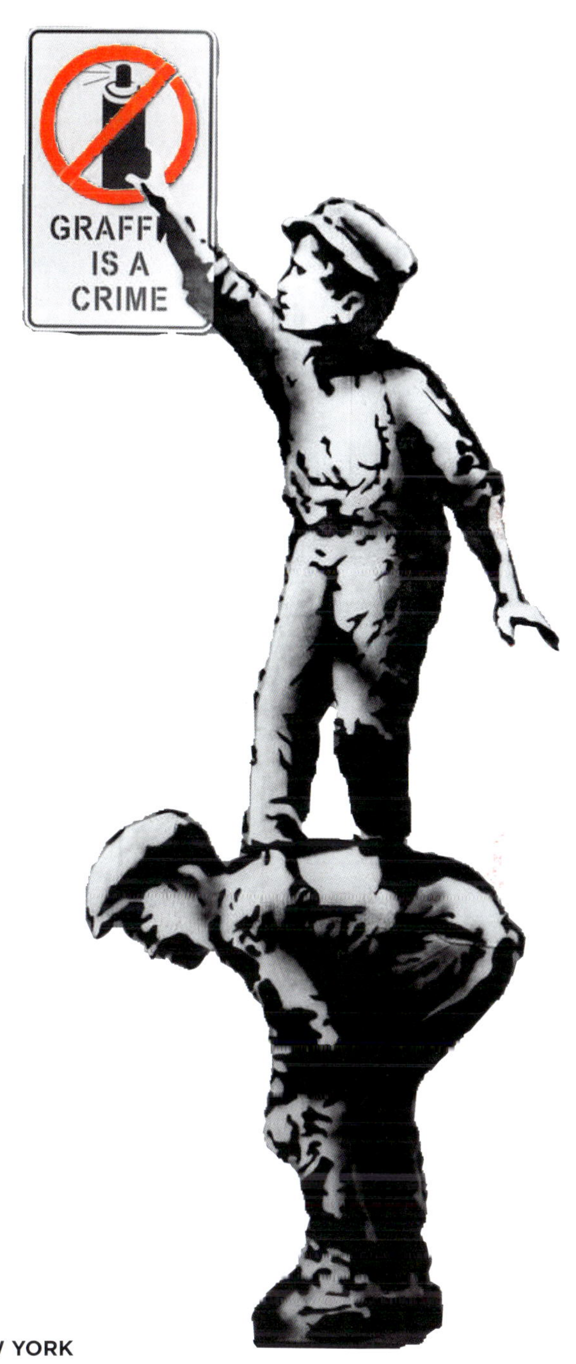

PRESTEL

MUNICH · LONDON · NEW YORK

CHILDREN

ALESSANDRA MATTANZA

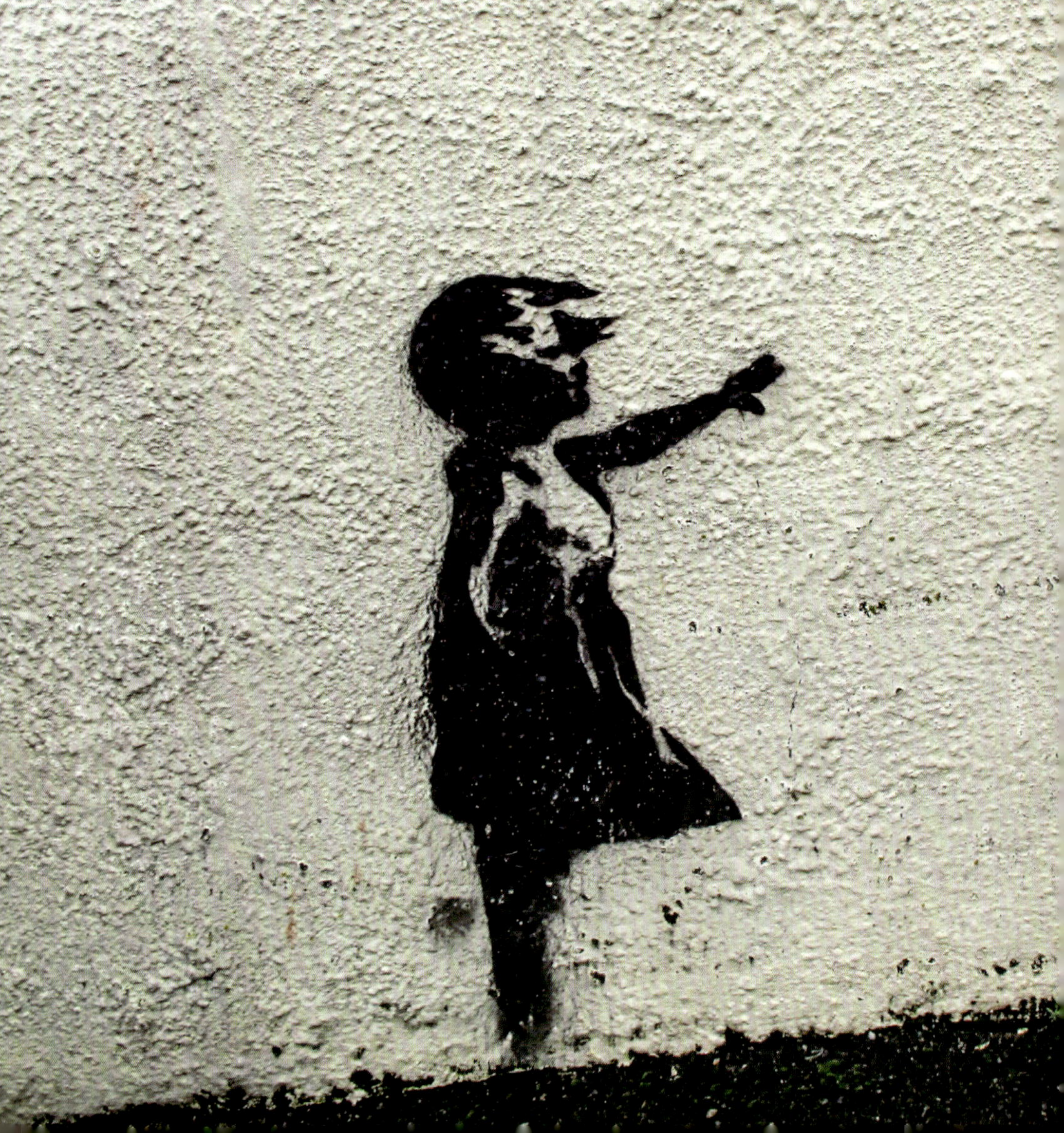

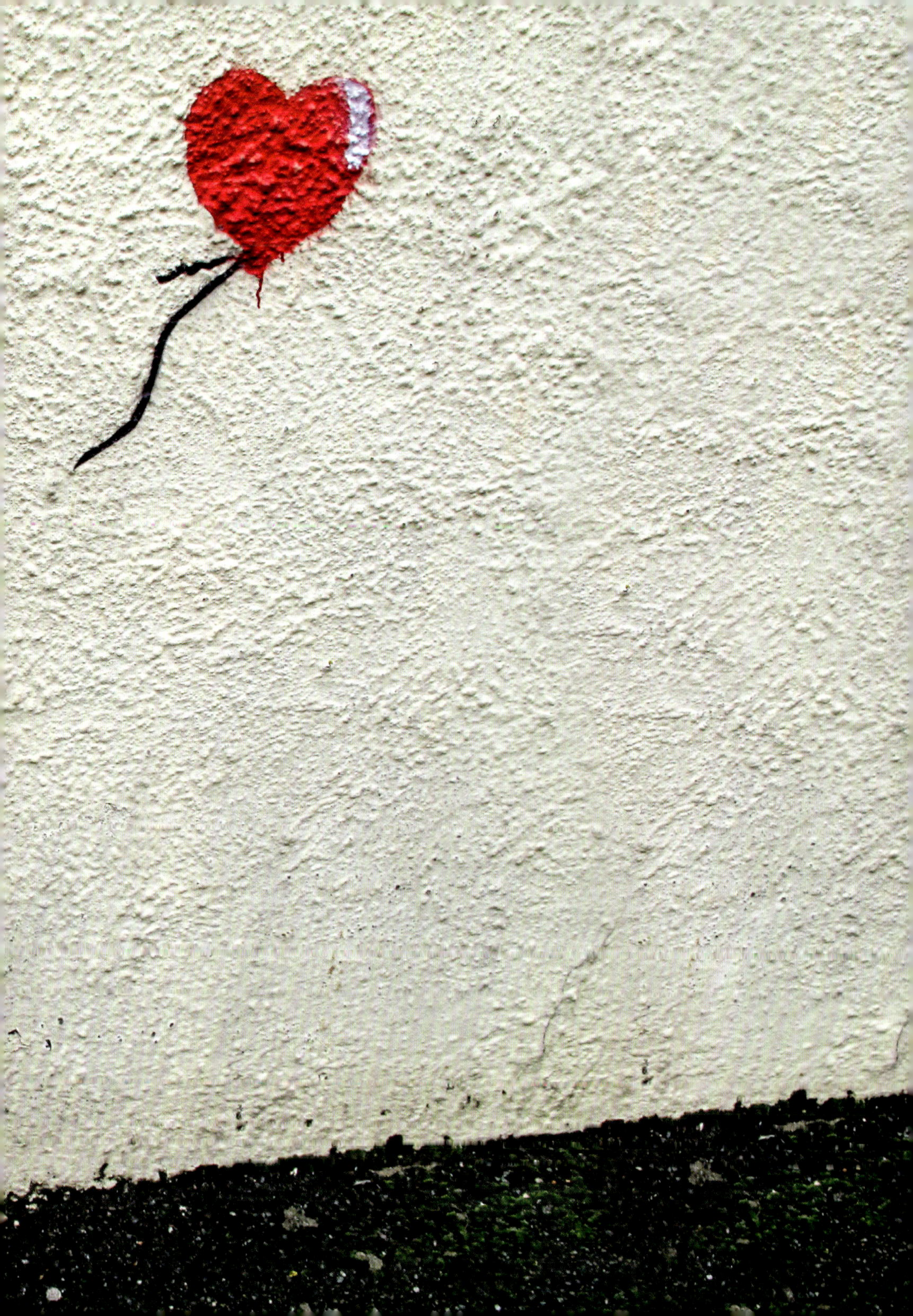

CHILDREN AT PLAY

**"CHILDREN BEGIN BY LOVING THEIR PARENTS; AS THEY GROW OLDER THEY JUDGE THEM; SOMETIMES THEY FORGIVE THEM."
OSCAR WILDE**

CHILDREN ARE SYMBOLS OF INNOCENCE, PURITY, AUTHENTICITY, AND TRUTH. THEY ARE THE LIGHT OF OUR UNIVERSE. HOPE, DREAMS, AND HAPPINESS LIE IN THEM. CHILDREN ARE A KEY ELEMENT IN BANKSY'S OEUVRE, AND HIS STENCILS WOULD NOT BE THE SAME WITHOUT THEM.

Banksy's children are actually a tool to reveal the ills of humanity. They look like innocent children playing, but their smiles belie a deeper meaning and an ominous feeling of darkness and danger.

Girl with Balloon first appeared in 2002. She is Banksy's most famous child, a stencil that has become iconic. She lets her red balloon go, with wind blowing through her hair, and she pulls on your heartstrings every time you look at her. It is difficult to get your mind off this picture because it represents various aspects of life, evoking a

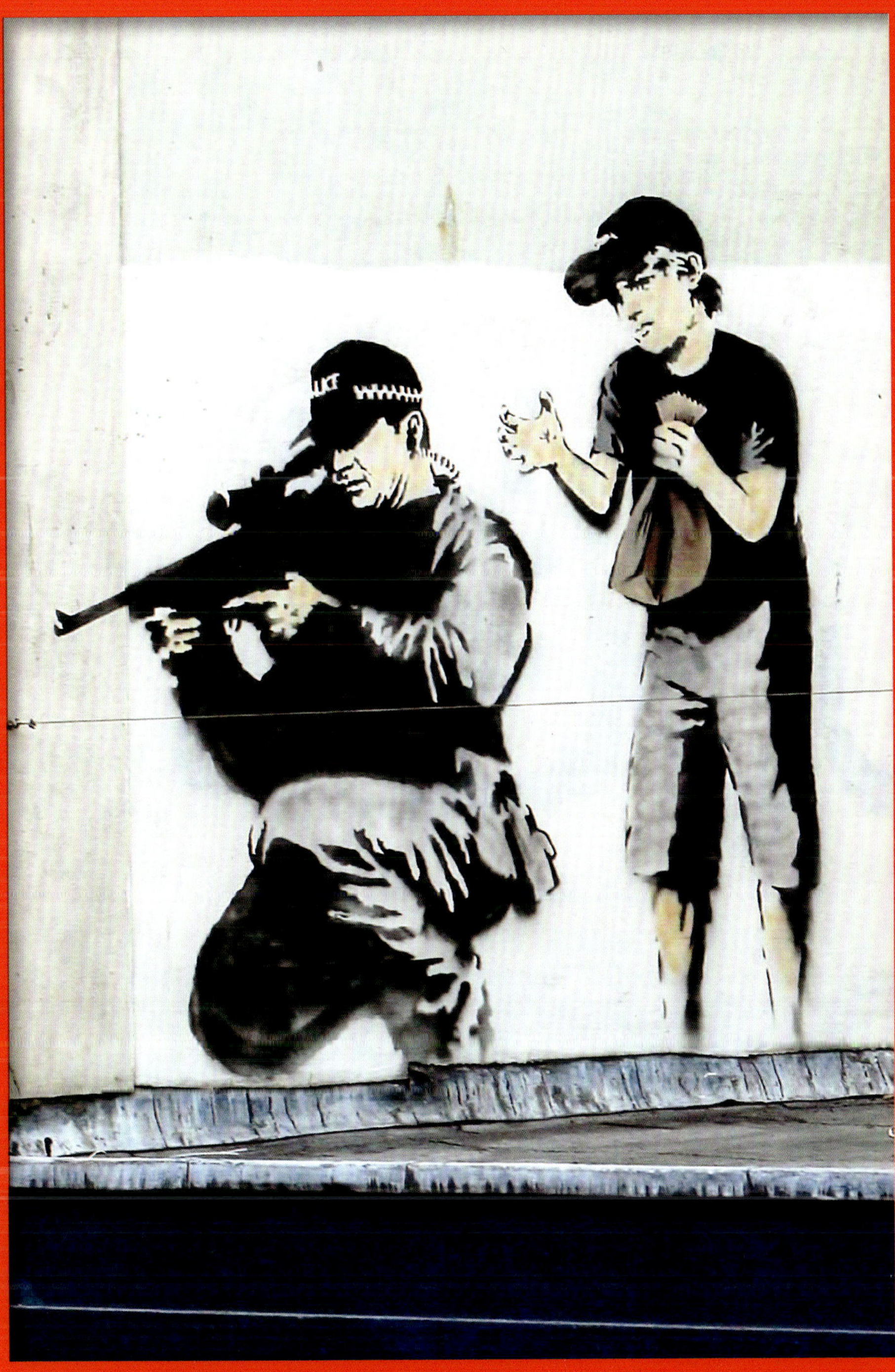

range of emotions and feelings that always vary according to the observor and how they are feeling at that particular moment. "And isn't that what street art and graffiti are all about?" Banksy would ask point-blank, because he loves when people take risks and face challenges, exchanging their views and getting out of their comfort zone. Some people interpret this beautiful and moving work as the loss of innocence, some as the pursuit of a dream, while others as the letting go of something toward another world, toward hope. Many people just love it regardless of its meaning. What's certain is that in that child's hand there is great hope.

When it first appeared along the stairs of Waterloo Bridge in London's Southbank, *Girl with Balloon* was accompanied by the message "There Is Always Hope" written on the wall. Since then, this little girl stretching her hand toward her balloon has almost become Banksy's second signature, appearing in several variants throughout the world. Whenever he wants to make an impression, his *Girl with Balloon* appears.

Banksy's aggressiveness and subversive spirit toward the system seem to melt like an iceberg in the sun in front of a child's smile. At the same time, he lets children communicate the values he most believes in: peace, love, fighting against all sorts of injustices, satire, and harsh criticism of the capitalist world and the globalized society constantly controlling us.

Banksy shows an incredible sense of protection toward children because he feels they are endangered by the violence of wars and the manipulative influence of TV and video games. Banksy believes children must be safeguarded and that we should all commit to ensuring that they won't lose their innocence too soon.

His 2007 *Girl Frisking Soldier,* depicting a little girl frisking a soldier by the Western Wall of Bethlehem, encourages us to reflect in this regard. The message is that in Palestine, as in many other parts of the world where war looms and values are distorted, anything can happen, everything is uncertain, and children end up being tragically turned into little adults.

In *Kids on Guns,* a boy and a girl are portrayed standing on a hill made of weapons. They're looking at each other, she is holding a red balloon, and he has a teddy bear in his hand. It is a clear image of innocence violated by war, of children forced to deal with weapons instead of their toys. Hope is still in the air, though. One might think that with these works Banksy aims at encouraging adults to let children inspire them to forget hatred, violence, and oppression, to seek peace and imagine a reassuring future for the generations to come. Banksy believes that one of the most important goals of graffiti and street art is becoming more attuned with young people's minds and communicating with them using appropriate language. This purpose was probably inspired by literature of the past, where children characters often conveyed messages revealing the hidden evils of humanity.

This is evident in the Brothers Grimm's or Hans Christian Andersen's fairy tales, in Lewis Carroll's *Alice in Wonderland*, and in William Blake's

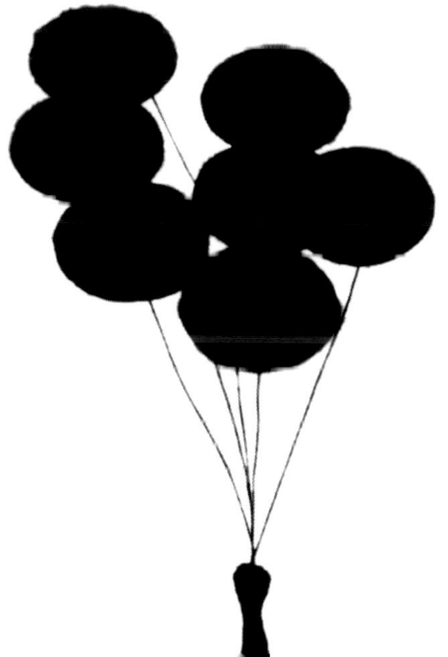

Songs of Innocence and Experience, focusing on corruption and inequality in the adults' world, and on the peril of trusting those we don't know very well. The purpose of fables is often to warn children against hidden risks, to teach them to grow up safely, and to steer them clear of dangers. Likewise, Banksy evidently seeks to encourage reflection in children towards building a better society. Writers and poets use words to tell their stories; Banksy uses stencils just as effectively. He aims to give voice to minorities, to the vast number of invisible people, and to children, whose voices are too often sadly ignored. "A lot of mothers will do anything for their children, except let them be themselves," warns Banksy with concern.

Banksy's children often seem sad, helpless, almost lost, like fallen angels looking for their way or their identity. Sometimes they are playful and fun and evoke empathy in the souls of people observing them. With their seemingly innocuous appearance, they are Banksy's "faithful squires," skilled at making fun of power and conformism. After all, a child, almost akin to a secret agent, can go everywhere without being noticed.

Jack and Jill seem to exemplify all of this. They are a boy and a girl who seem to be running lightheartedly, but they are wearing bulletproof vests emblazoned with the word "POLICE."

In the 2009 *No Ball Games*, two children are playing with a sign reading "No Ball Games" as if it was a ball. Both these works clearly highlight the premature loss of childhood innocence.

With the 2008 *Very Little Helps*, Banksy illustrates a theme that is especially dear to him: his personal fight against consumerism dominating our society. Three children are portrayed solemnly raising the Tesco British supermarket chain flag, while two other children swear allegiance to it with a hand on their chest. The image hits the viewer like a dagger to the heart.

Children are often prevented from looking at graffiti, but they are allowed to witness the horrors caused by humankind and governments, and so, from a very young age, they find themselves exploited by a decadent society on the verge of collapse, a society driving them to unbridled consumerism and to the prevailing superficiality of social media, a society where anyone can become a star for five minutes; it only takes a selfie.

"The people who run our cities don't understand graffiti because they think nothing has the right to exist unless it makes a profit... The people who truly deface our neighborhoods are the companies that scrawl giant slogans across buildings and buses trying to make us feel inadequate unless we buy their stuff... Any advertisement in public space that gives you no choice whether you see it or not is yours, it belongs to you, it's yours to take, rearrange and reuse. Asking for permission is like asking to keep a rock someone just threw at your head," thinks Banksy, worried about the future.

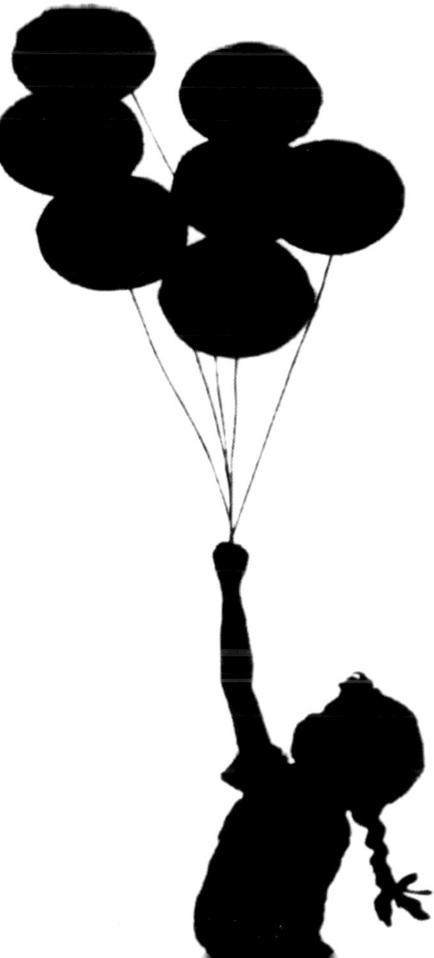

Banksy also seems very knowledgeable about the significance of childhood trauma. Many specialized psychologists constantly point out how the wrongs suffered by a child will have an impact on their whole life. This is especially amplified when the "playground" is a war zone. During the 2022 Russian aggression, Banksy created many works in Ukraine in the worst affected areas. Again, children are often the real heroes. A stencil portrays a man, who could be Russian president Vladimir Putin, knocked out by a child with a judo move. Another one depicts a young gymnast doing a handstand on the broken wall of a bombed-out building, perhaps to boldly declare her will to never give up and to return to normal life as soon as possible.

Banksy's children are also an equally powerful symbol of global injustice. His *Nola*, also known as *Umbrella Girl* or *Rain Girl*, was created in 2008, three years after Hurricane Katrina, in a New Orleans street in the Marigny neighborhood. The little girl is portrayed while sheltering from the rain under a broken umbrella and represents the failure of the American government to protect its people.

Banksy's 2004 *Napalm* has become very popular, and it vociferously denounces the horrors of war. It depicts Phan Thi Kim Phúc, the 9-year-old girl, now an activist, who, in the 1972 *The Terror of War* photo, shot by photographer Nick Út during the Vietnam War, is running alone, horribly burned by napalm, down a road. Banksy portrays her between Mickey Mouse and Ronald McDonald, symbolizing two of the largest corporations in the world. It is a powerful critical image invoking global social justice.

The horror of the original scene thus becomes even stronger and more powerful, leaving an indelible imprint on the heart. The imagery, hard to forget, is able to evoke thirst for justice and change.

Banksy has a very clear vision of this: "The greatest crimes in the world are not committed by people breaking the rules but by people following the rules. It's people who follow orders that drop bombs and massacre villages." He insists: "Fight the fighters, not their wars."

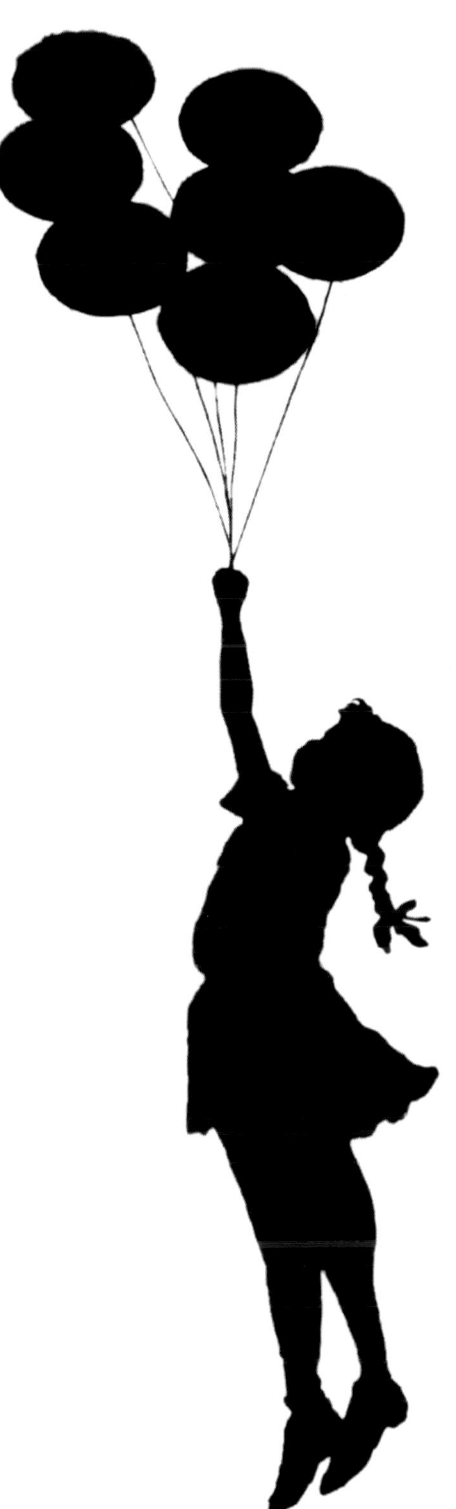

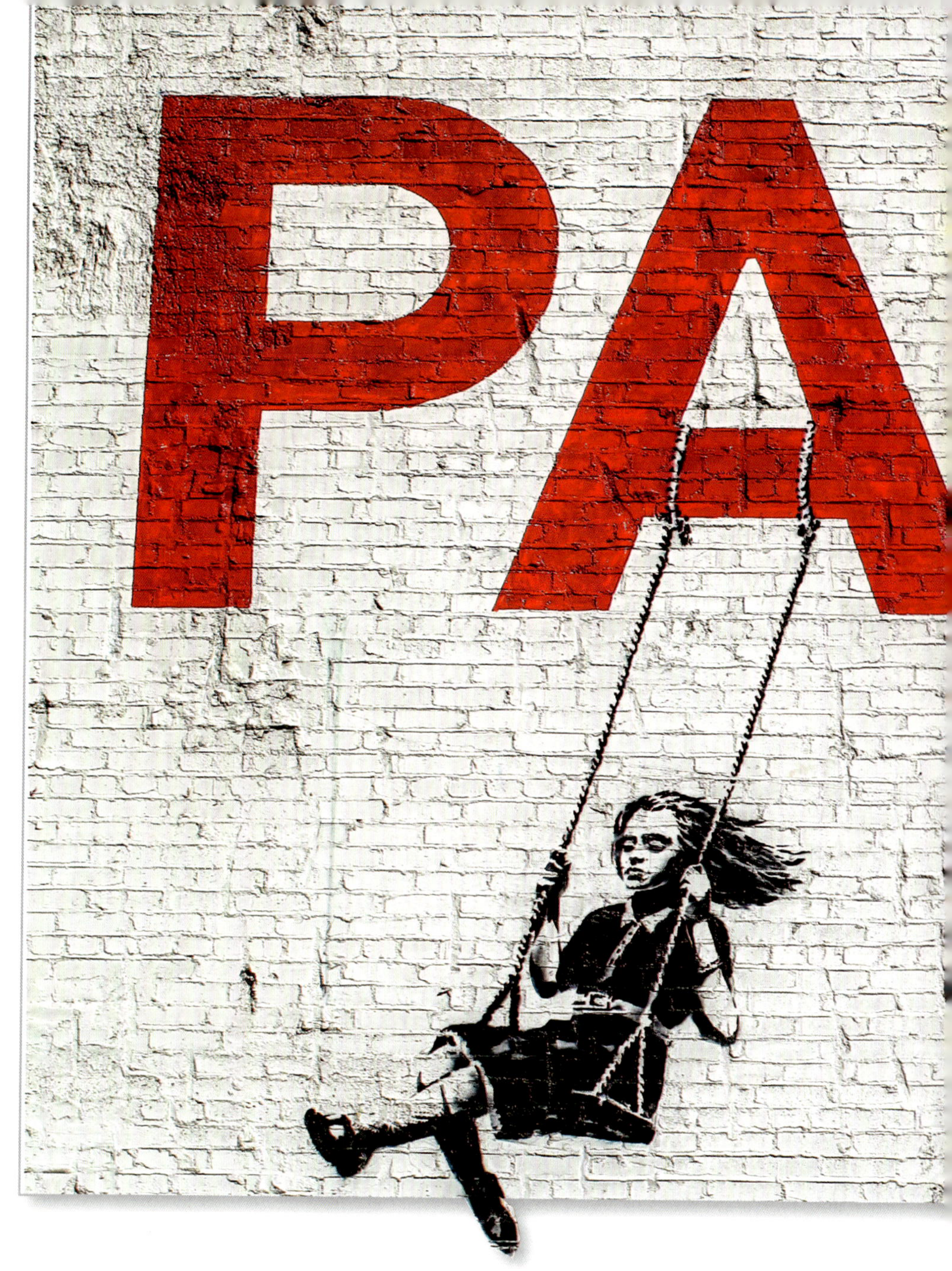

PA

SWING GIRL – LOS ANGELES, 2010

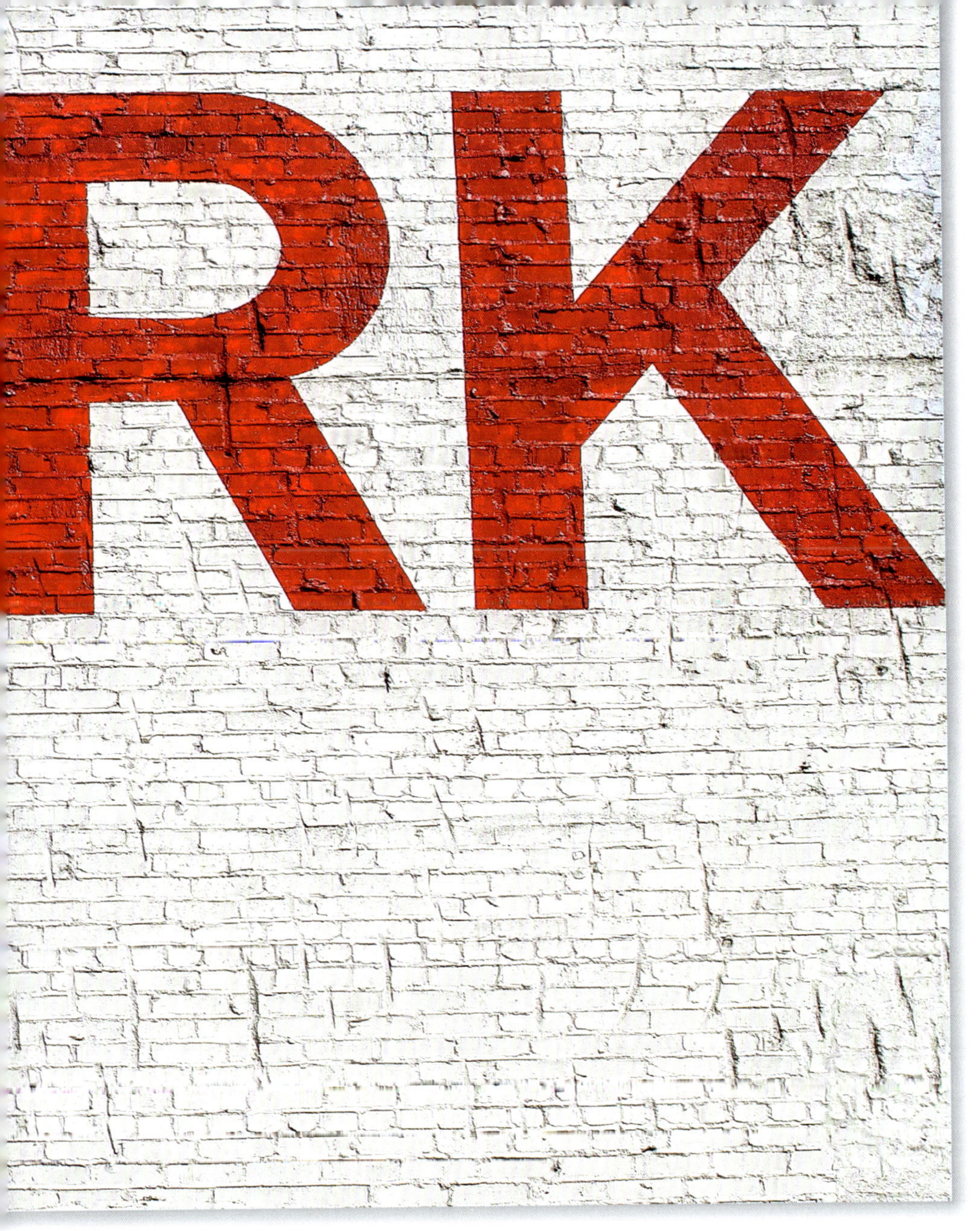

IT SEEMS BANKSY WANTS TO WARN US ABOUT THE NEED TO CREATE MORE PLAYGROUNDS FOR CHILDREN, ALSO IN MAJOR CITIES.

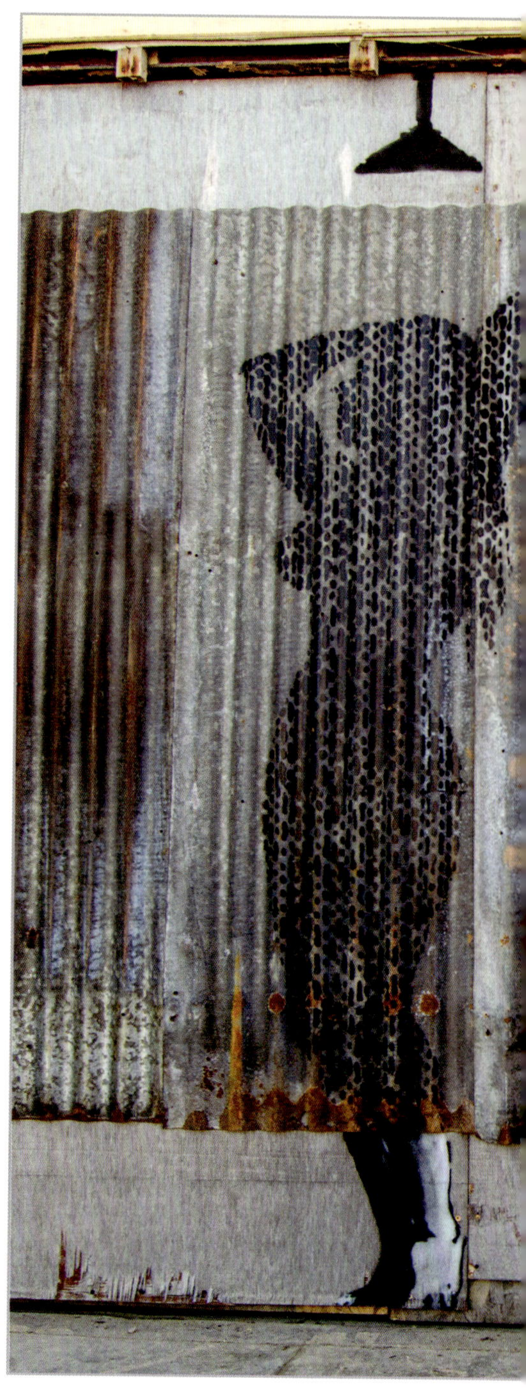

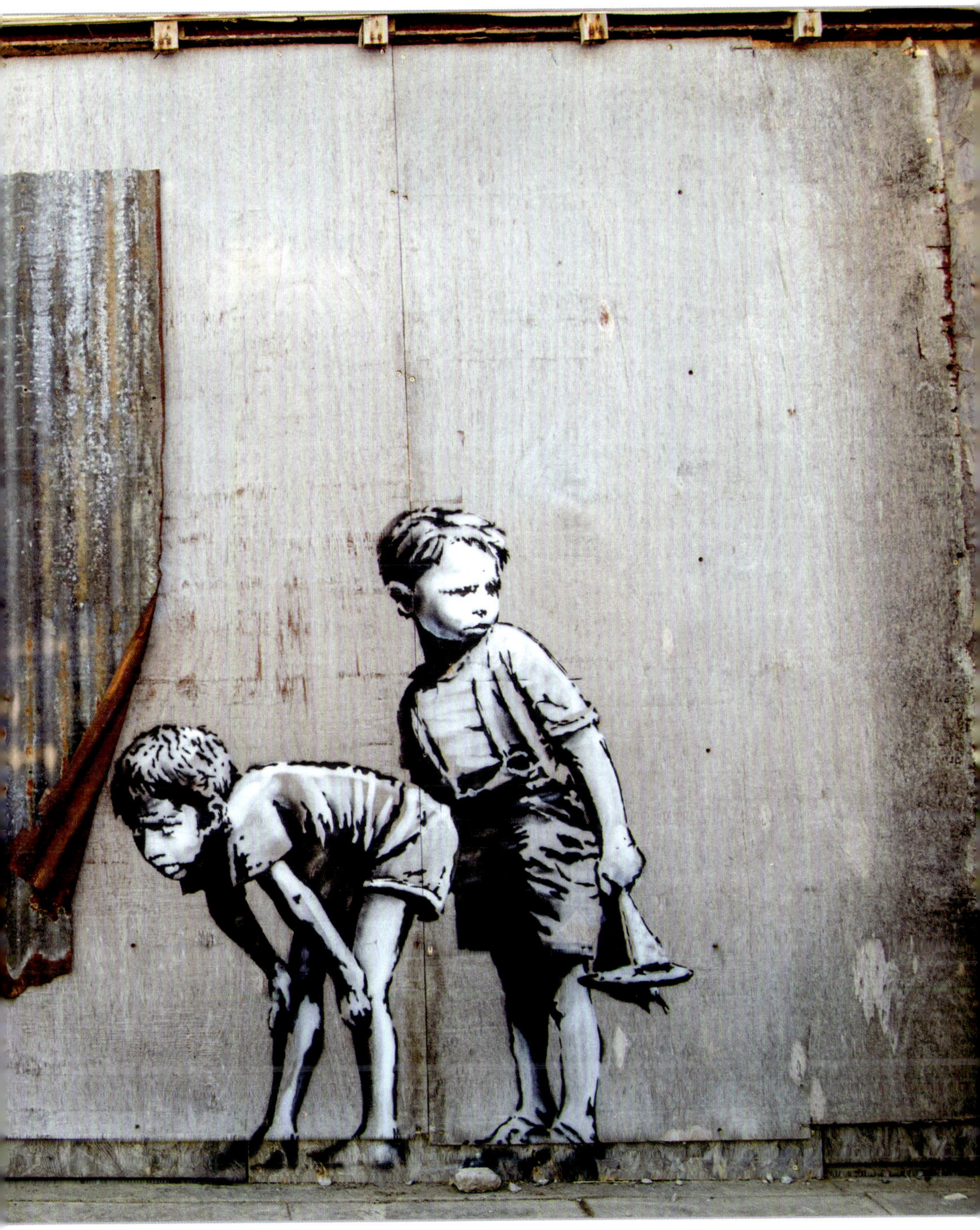

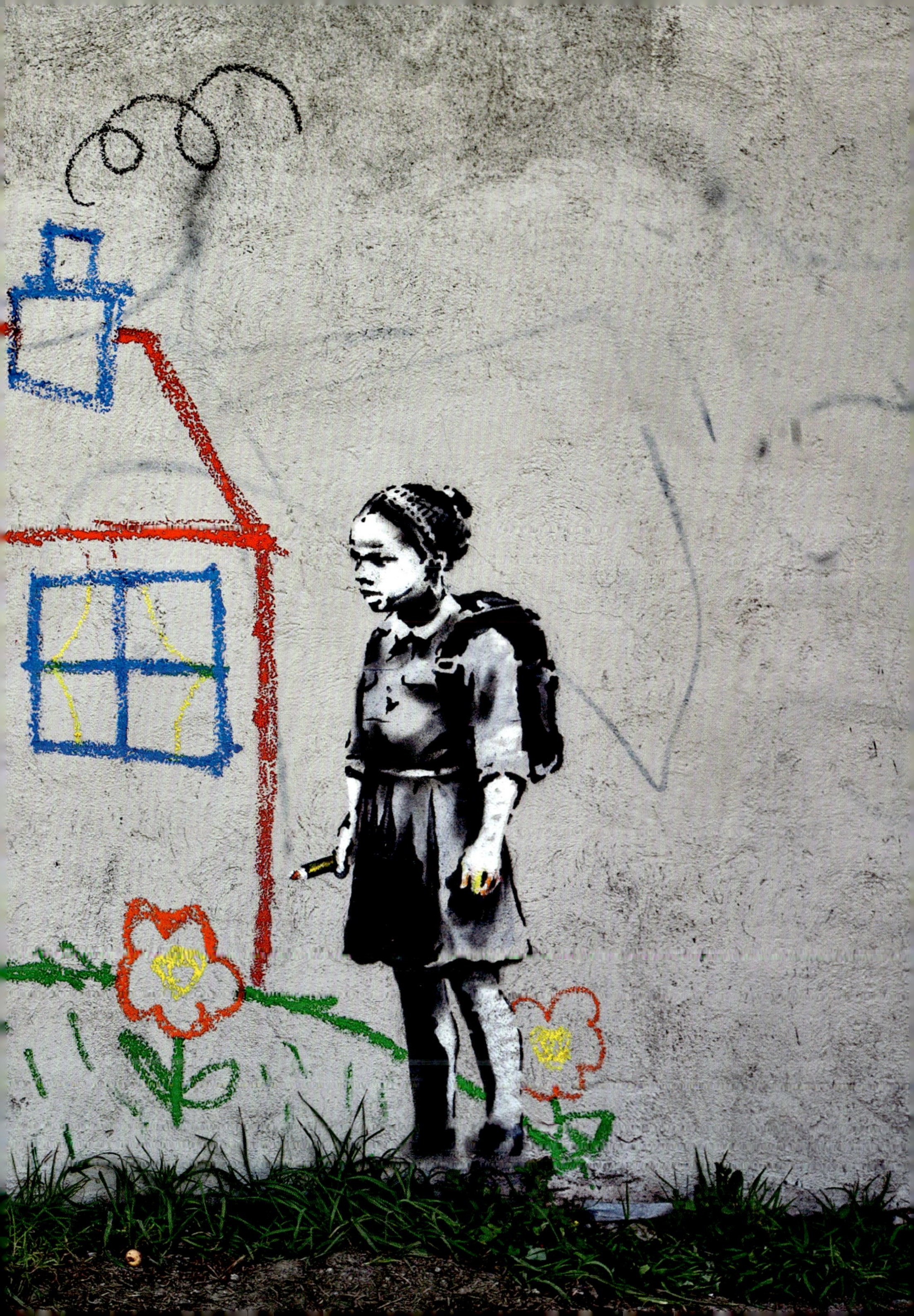

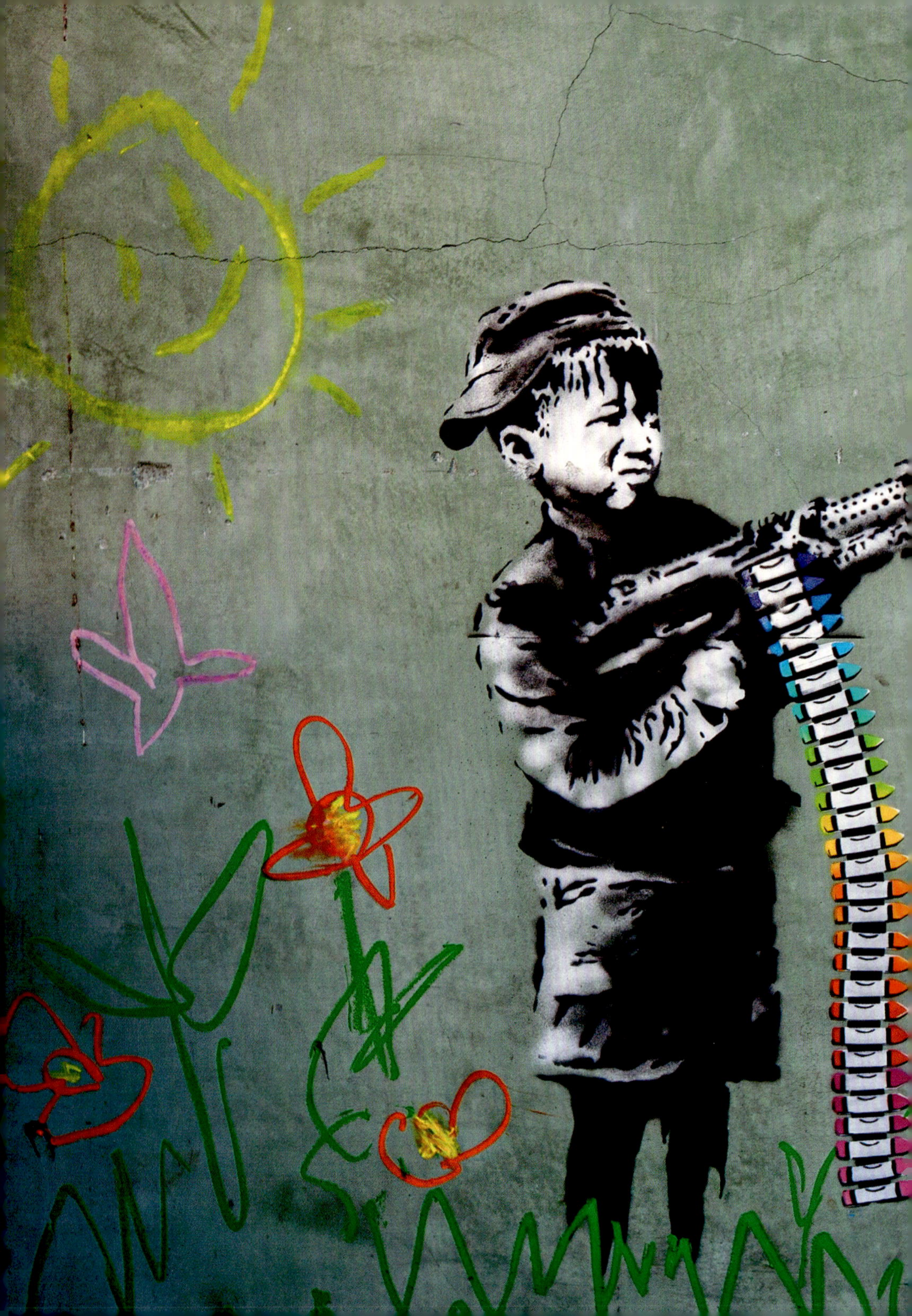

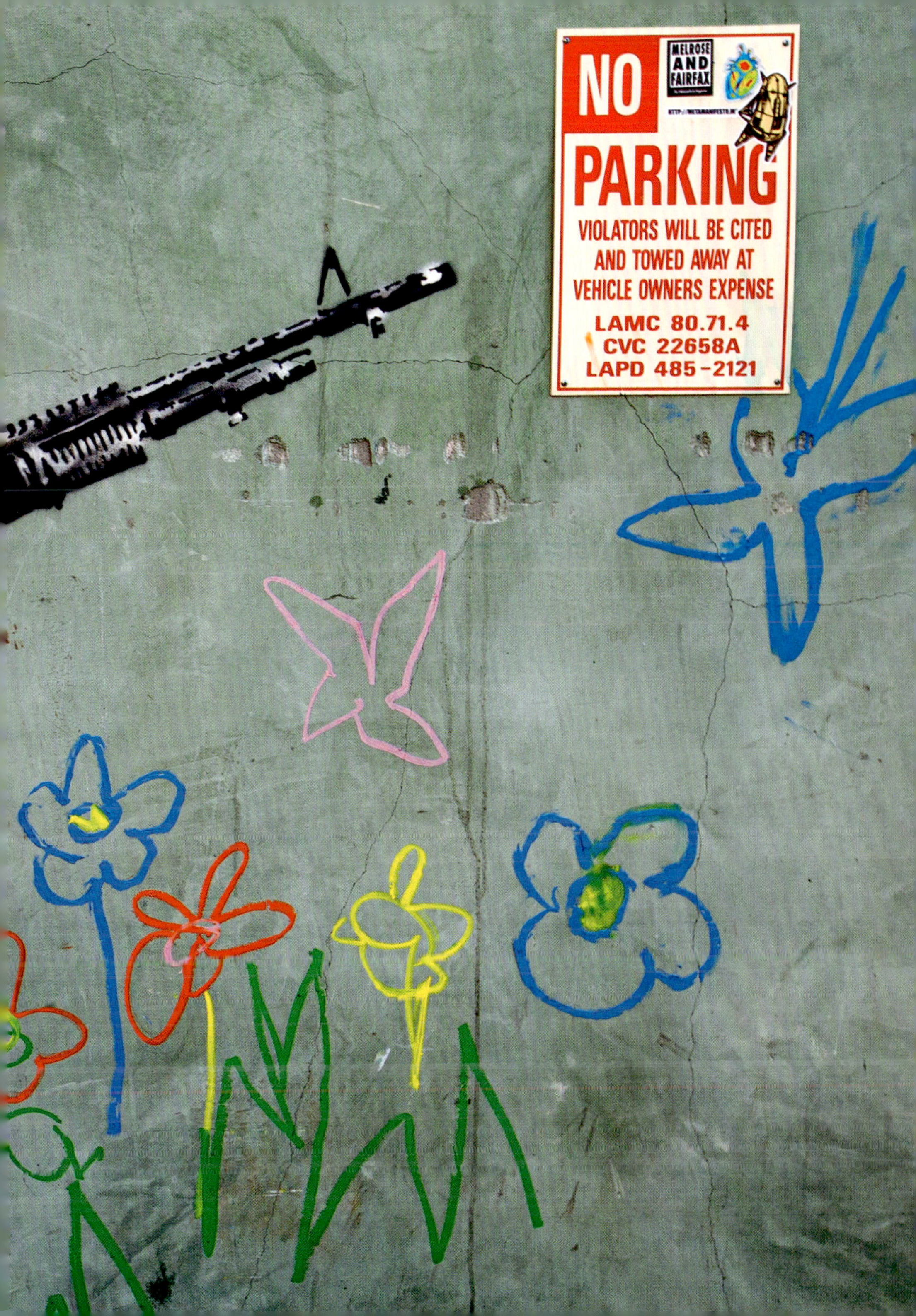
NO
MELROSE
AND
FAIRFAX
PARKING
VIOLATORS WILL BE CITED
AND TOWED AWAY AT
VEHICLE OWNERS EXPENSE
LAMC 80.71.4
CVC 22658A
LAPD 485-2121

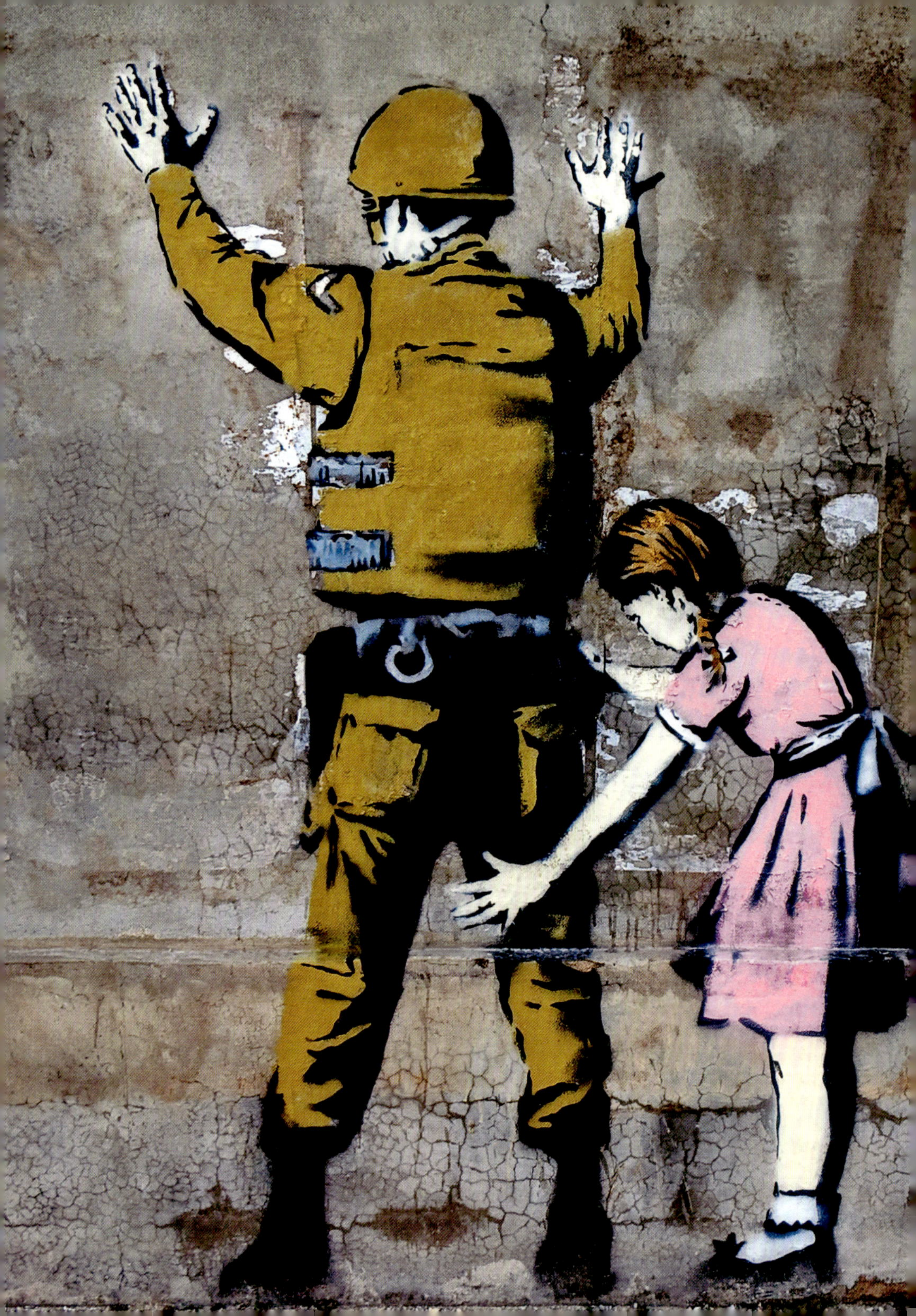

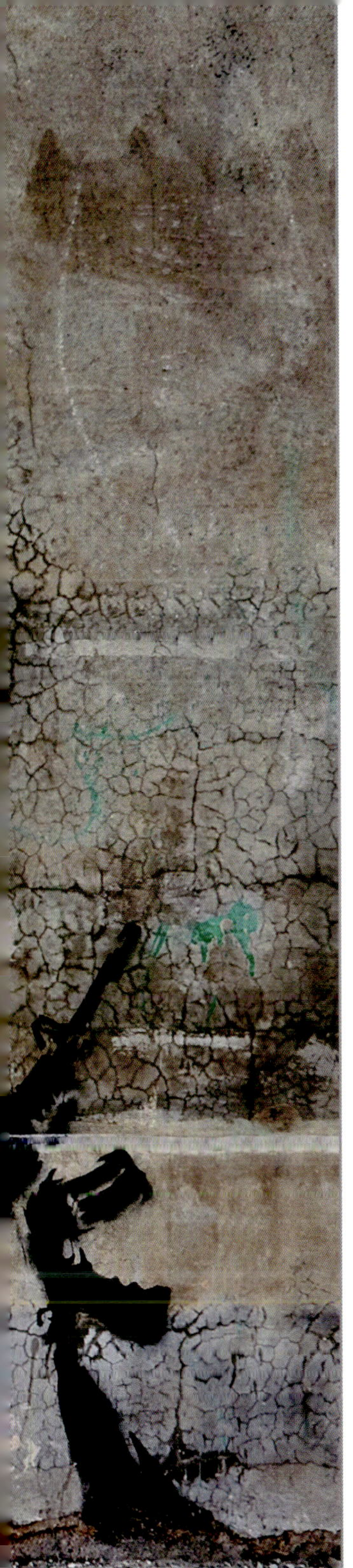

STREET ART HAS THE POWER TO CHANGE THE WORLD AND, IN THIS CASE, TO REVERSE THE ROLES: HERE, IT IS THE ISRAELI SOLDIER WHO IS BEING FRISKED BY A YOUNG GIRL.

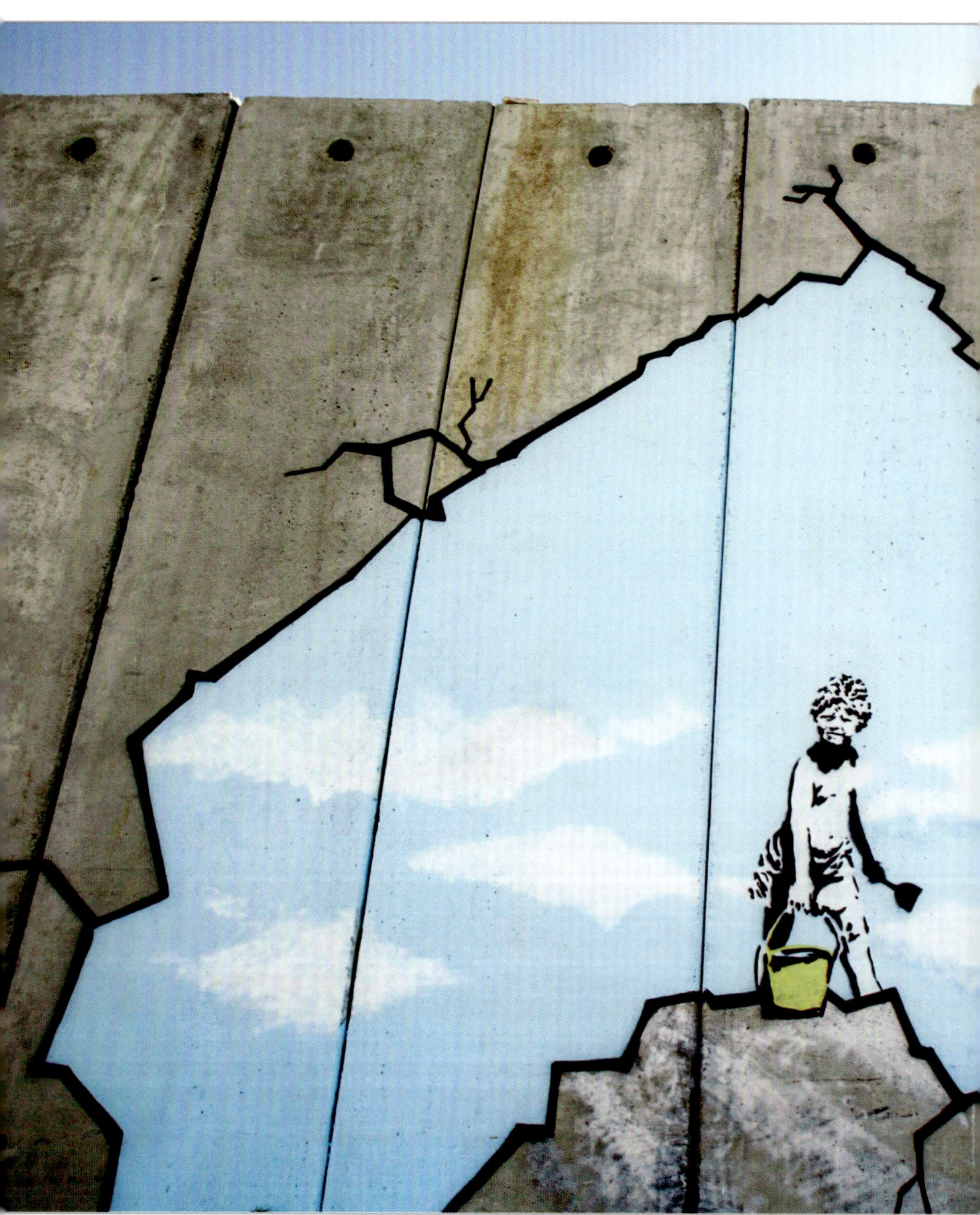

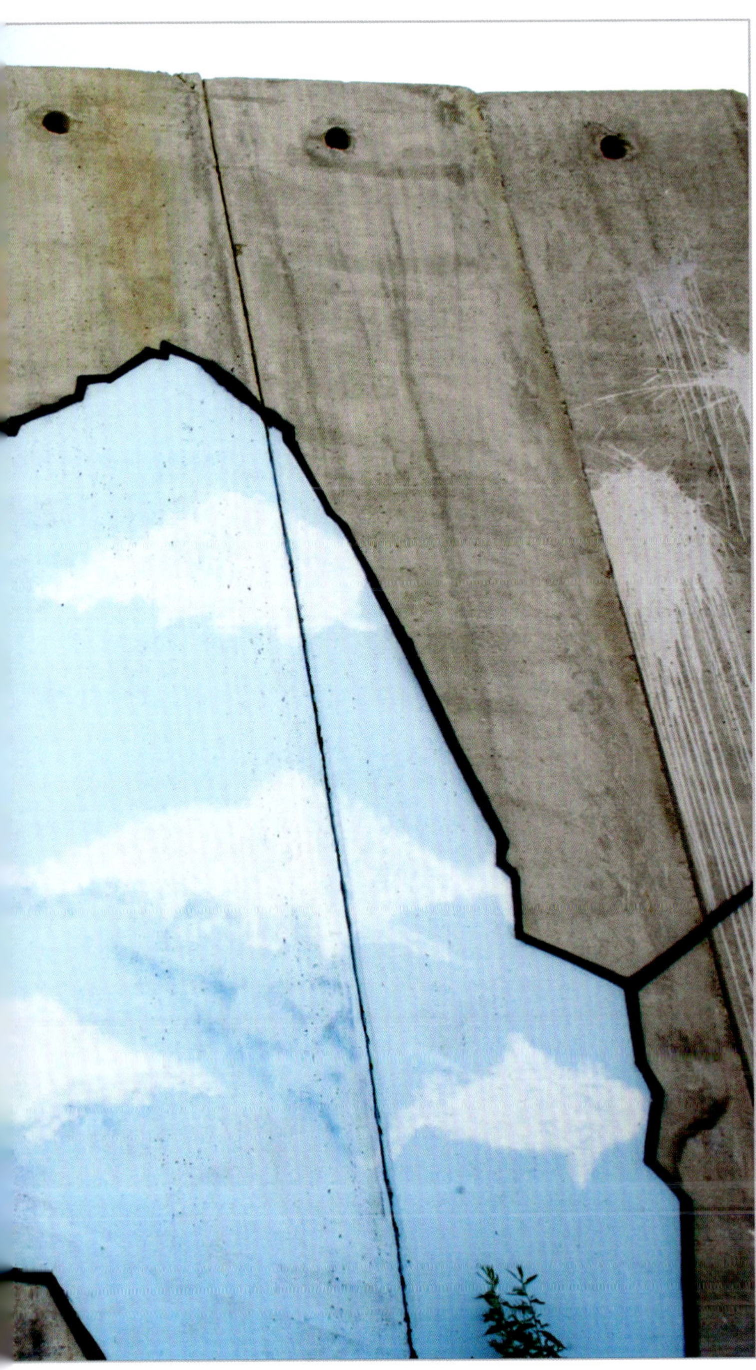

BEYOND THE CRACK IN THE WALL NEAR THE RAMALLAH CHECKPOINT, A BETTER SCENARIO IS POSSIBLE.

A LITTLE GIRL IS HOLDING ON TO A BUNCH OF SEVEN BALLOONS. HER DESTINATION IS BEYOND THE BORDER WALL AND AWAY FROM THE HARDSHIPS OF LIFE.

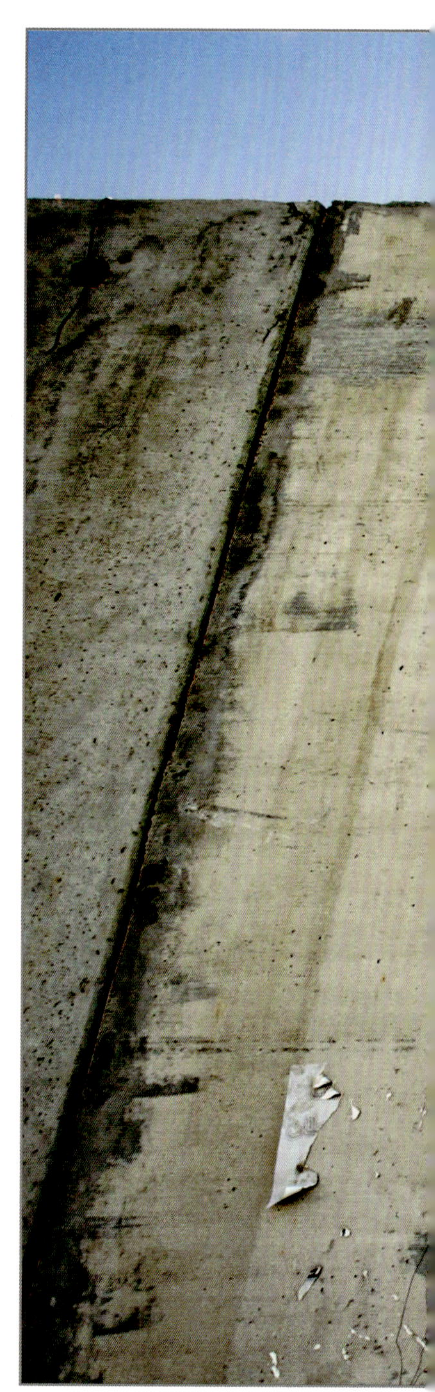

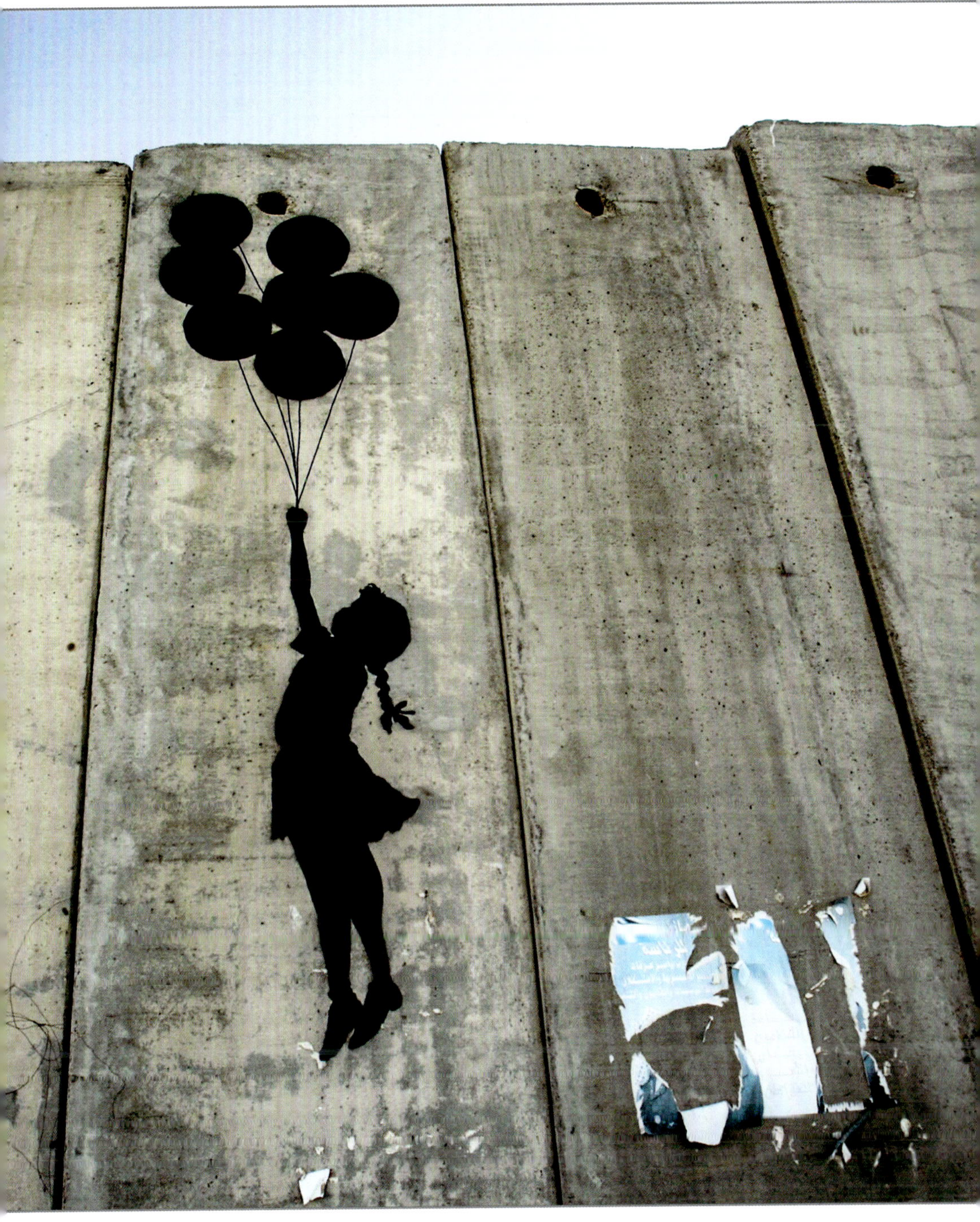

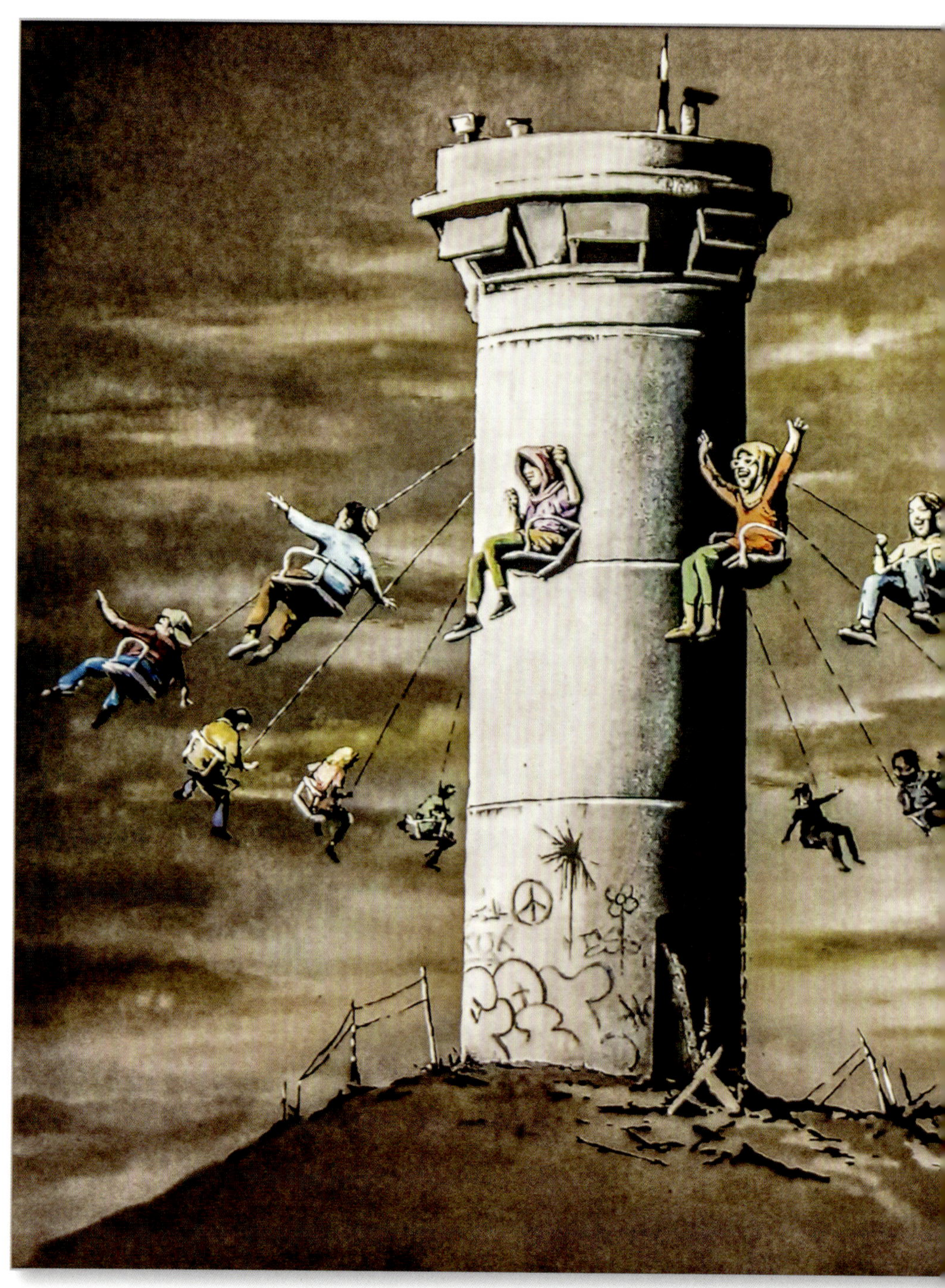

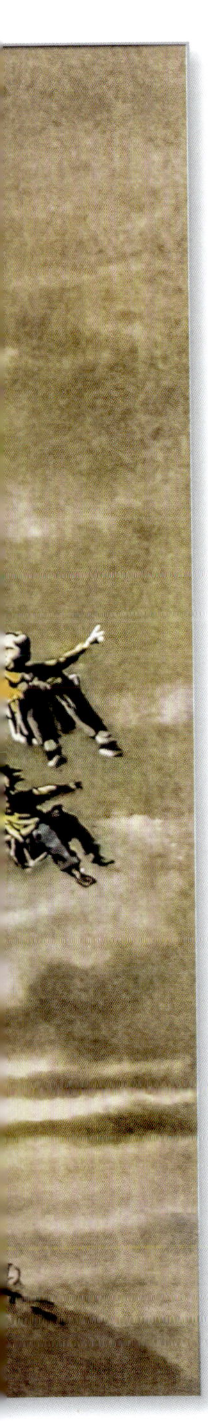

NO WAR COULD LIMIT THE IMAGINATION OF THE CHILDREN OF GAZA. A WATCHTOWER OF THE ISRAELI ARMY IS MAGICALLY TRANSFORMED INTO THE SWING RIDE OF AN AMUSEMENT PARK.

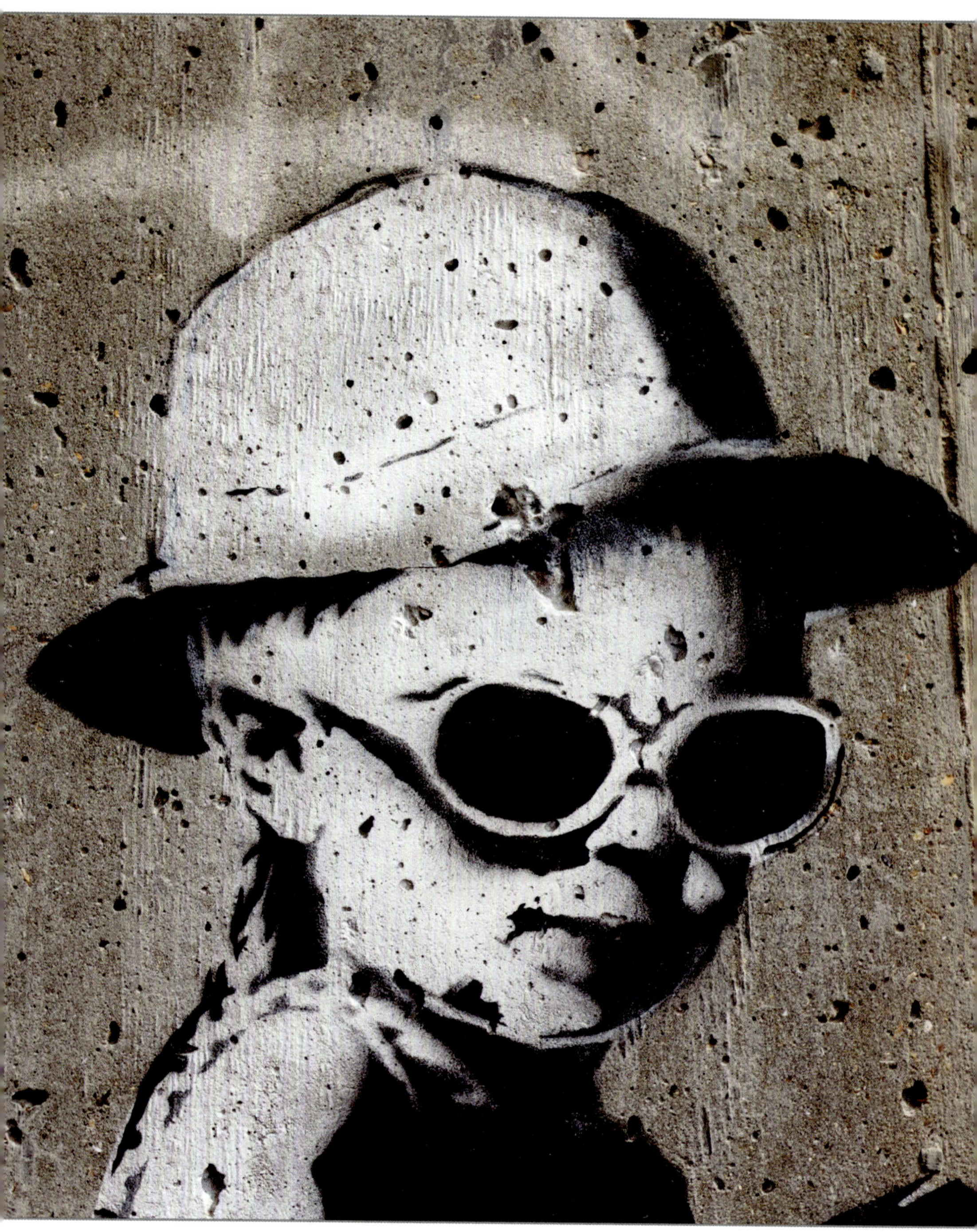

BANKSY'S CRITICISM AGAINST CAPITALISM IS ESPECIALLY EVIDENT HERE. THIS IS NOT THE FIRST TIME HE TARGETED THIS BRITISH MULTINATIONAL, RAILING AGAINST THE RAMPANT CONSUMERISM CONTRASTING WITH SITUATIONS OF EXTREME POVERTY.

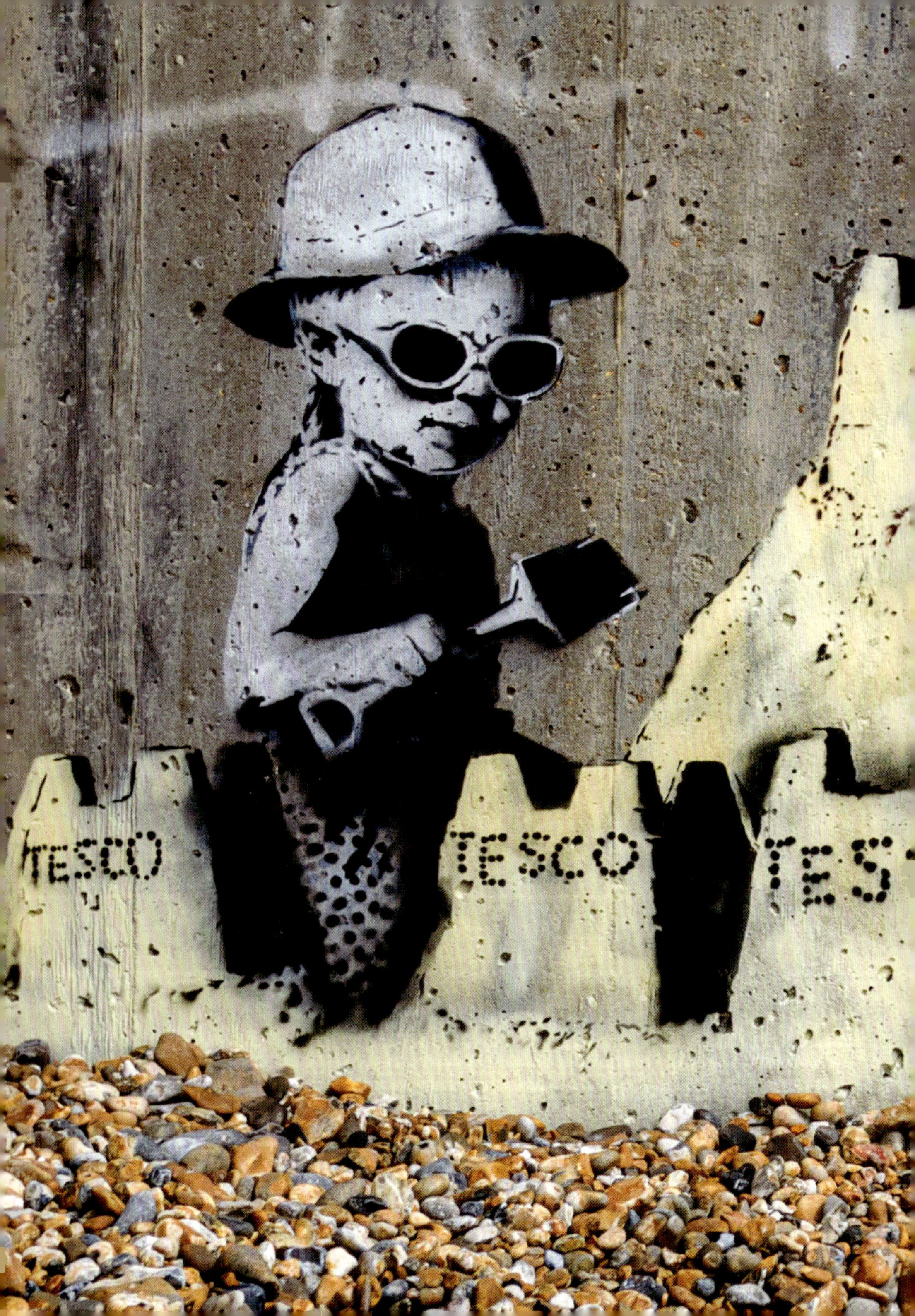

TESCO
TESCO
TES

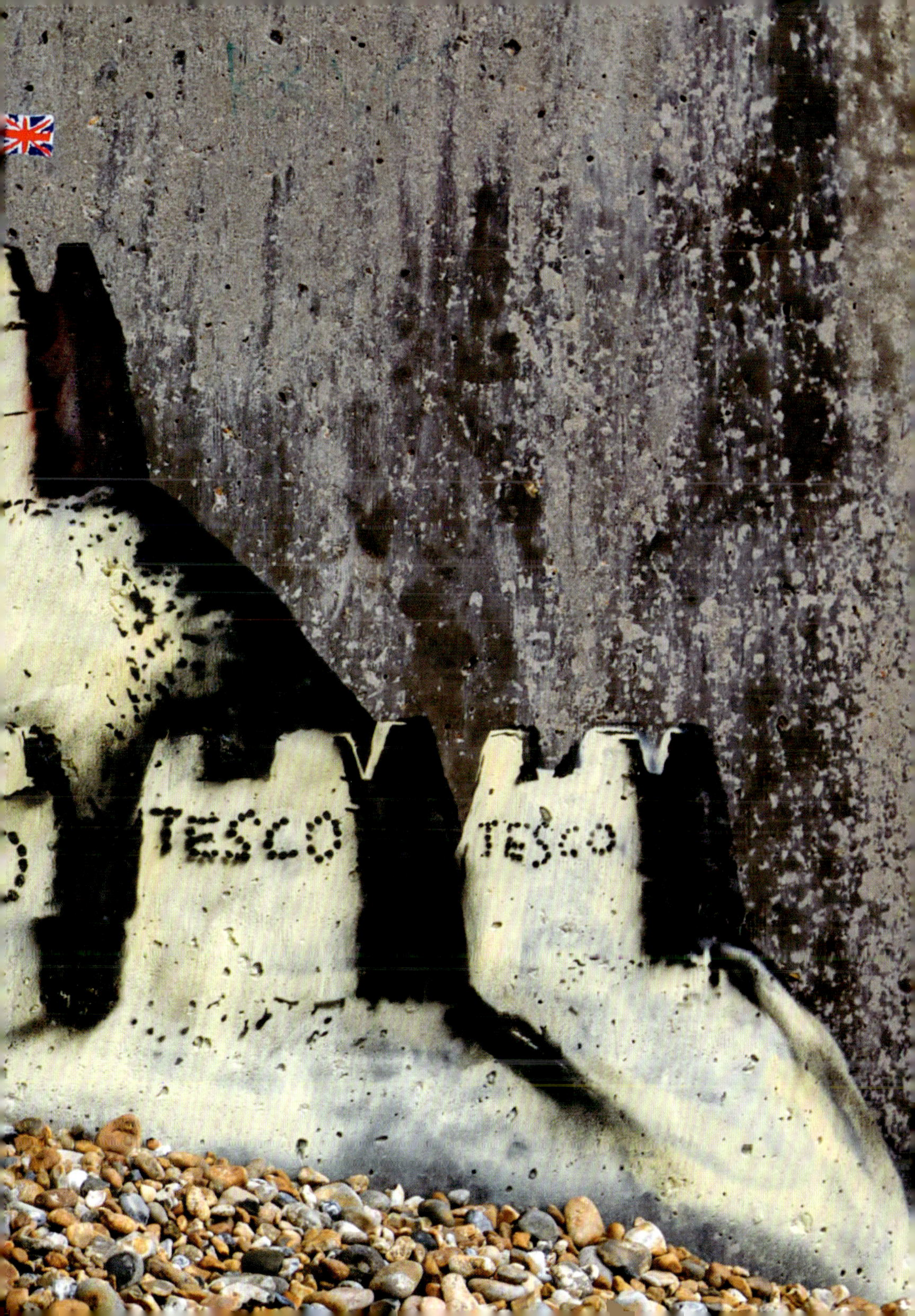

TESCO
TESCO

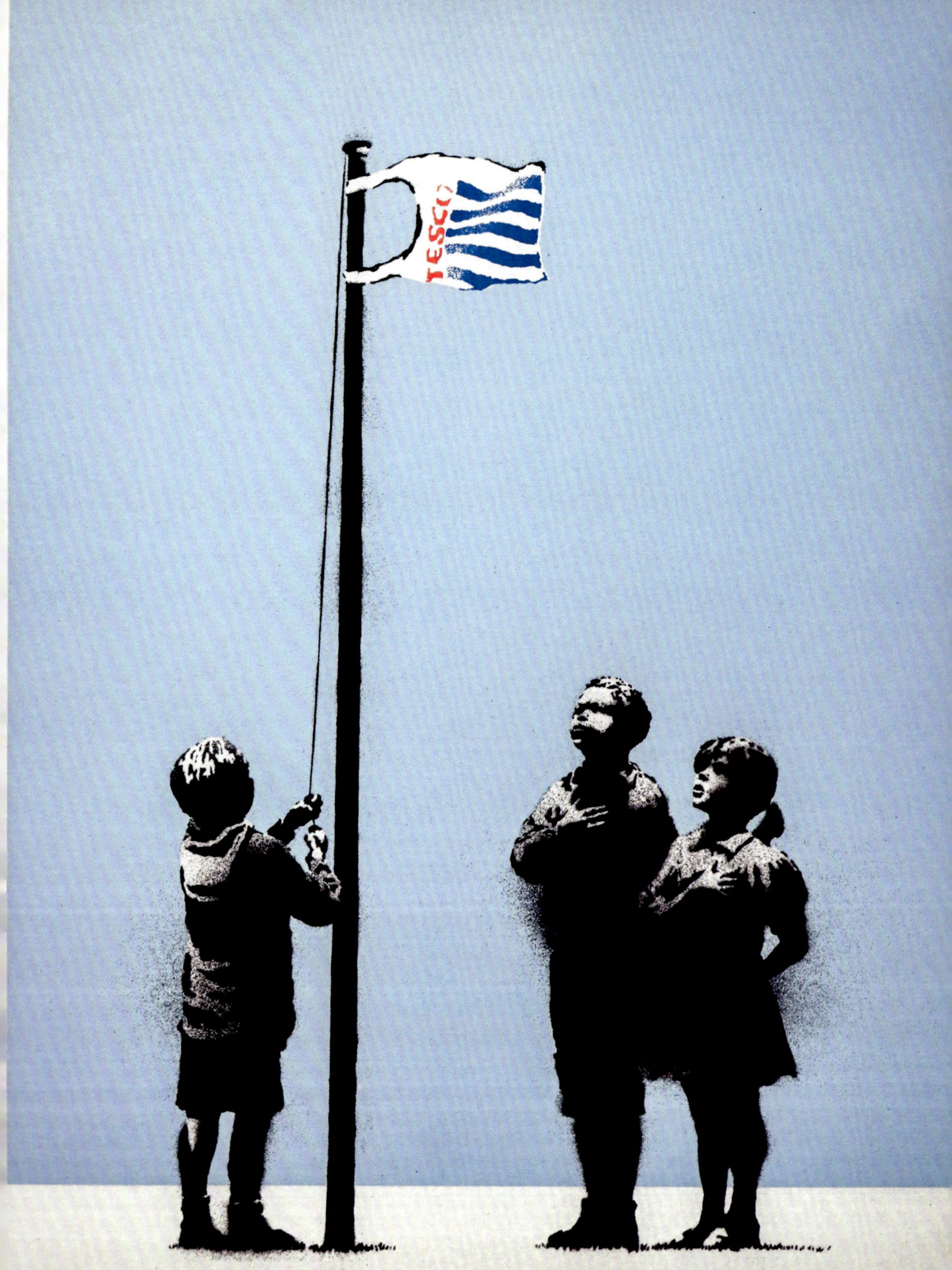
TESCO
220/299
Banksy

THREE CHILDREN ARE SWEARING ALLEGIANCE TO THE FLAG OF TESCO, THE MULTINATIONAL THAT, ACCORDING TO BANKSY, INFLUENCES FUTURE GENERATIONS TOWARD UNBRIDLED CONSUMERISM. THE GRAFFITI WORK FIRST APPEARED IN 2008 ON THE FAÇADE OF A PHARMACY ALONG ESSEX ROAD, LONDON.

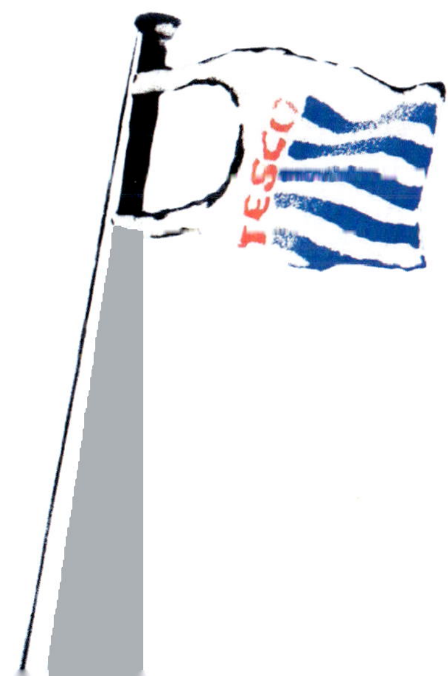

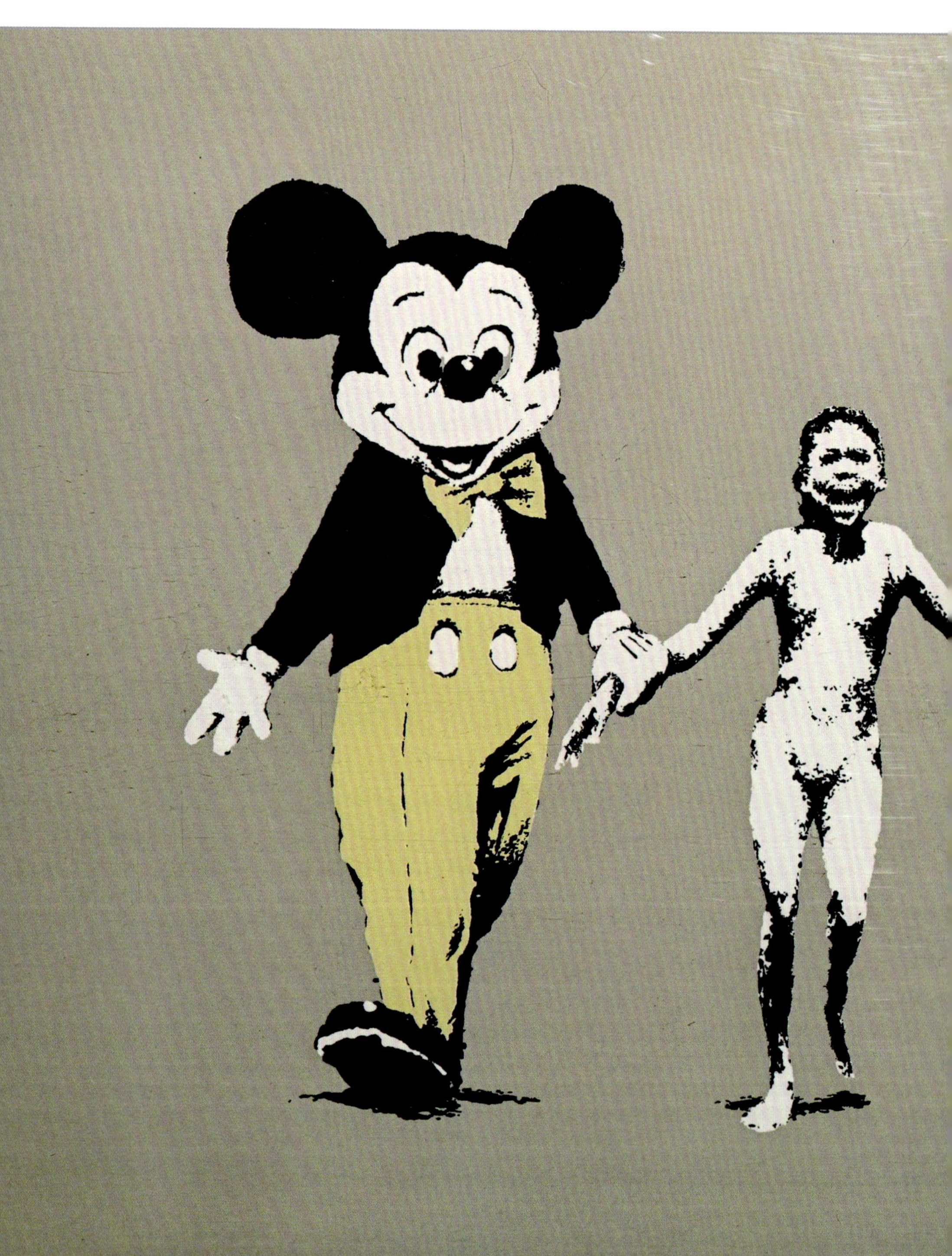

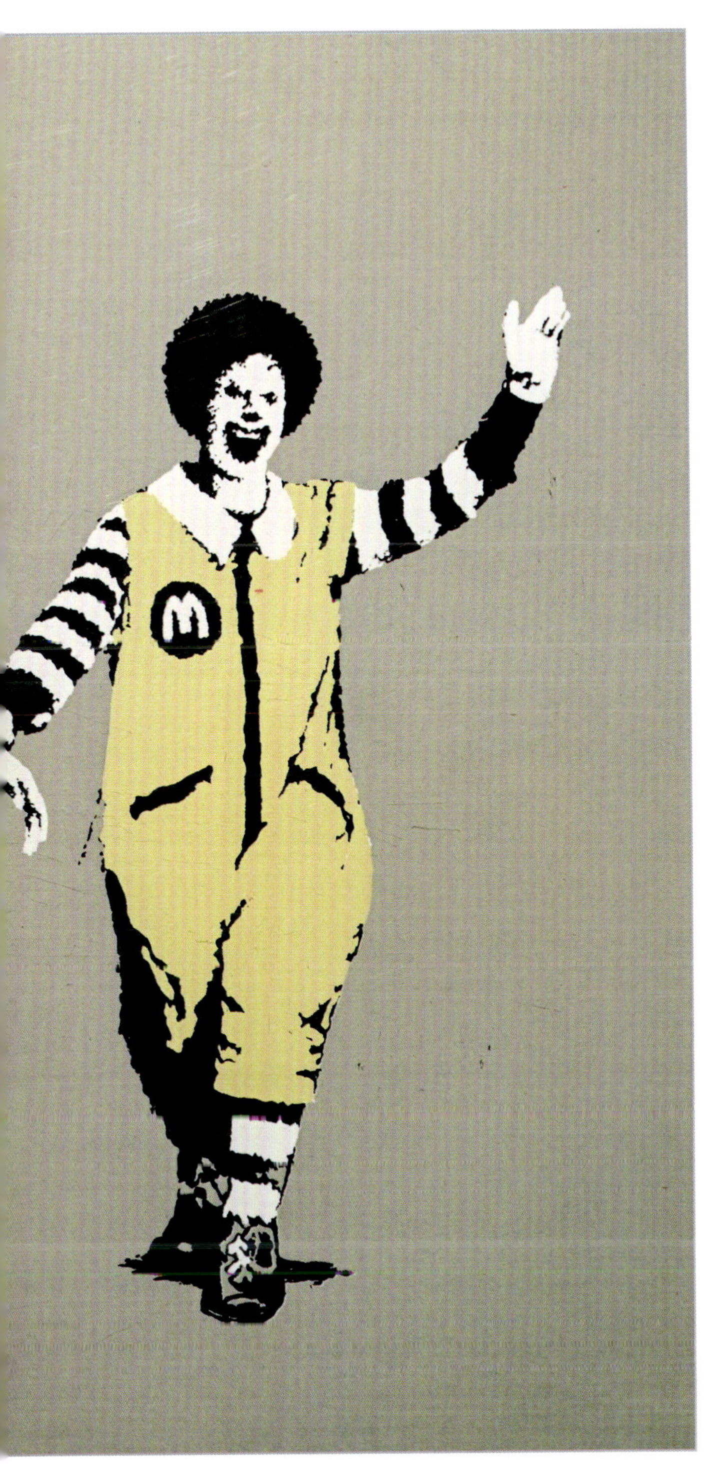

THE LITTLE VIETNAMESE GIRL PHAN THI KIM PHÚC IS PORTRAYED WITH MICKEY MOUSE AND RONALD MCDONALD: TWO ICONS OF CAPITALIST CONSUMERISM.

THE IMAGE OF THIS AFRICAN CHILD CURLED UP,
SURROUNDED BY FLIES AND WITH THE CROWN FROM
A WELL-KNOWN FAST-FOOD CHAIN ON HIS HEAD, IS
EXTREMELY MOVING.

38–39 THIS WORK OF GRAFFITI IS AN ACT OF
SOLIDARITY TO SUPPORT DANIEL HALPIN, KNOWN
AS "TOX," CONDEMNED FOR HIS GRAFFITI,
JUDGED AS QUALITATIVELY UNACCEPTABLE AND
THUS RESPONSIBLE FOR SPOILING THE CITY'S
APPEARANCE.

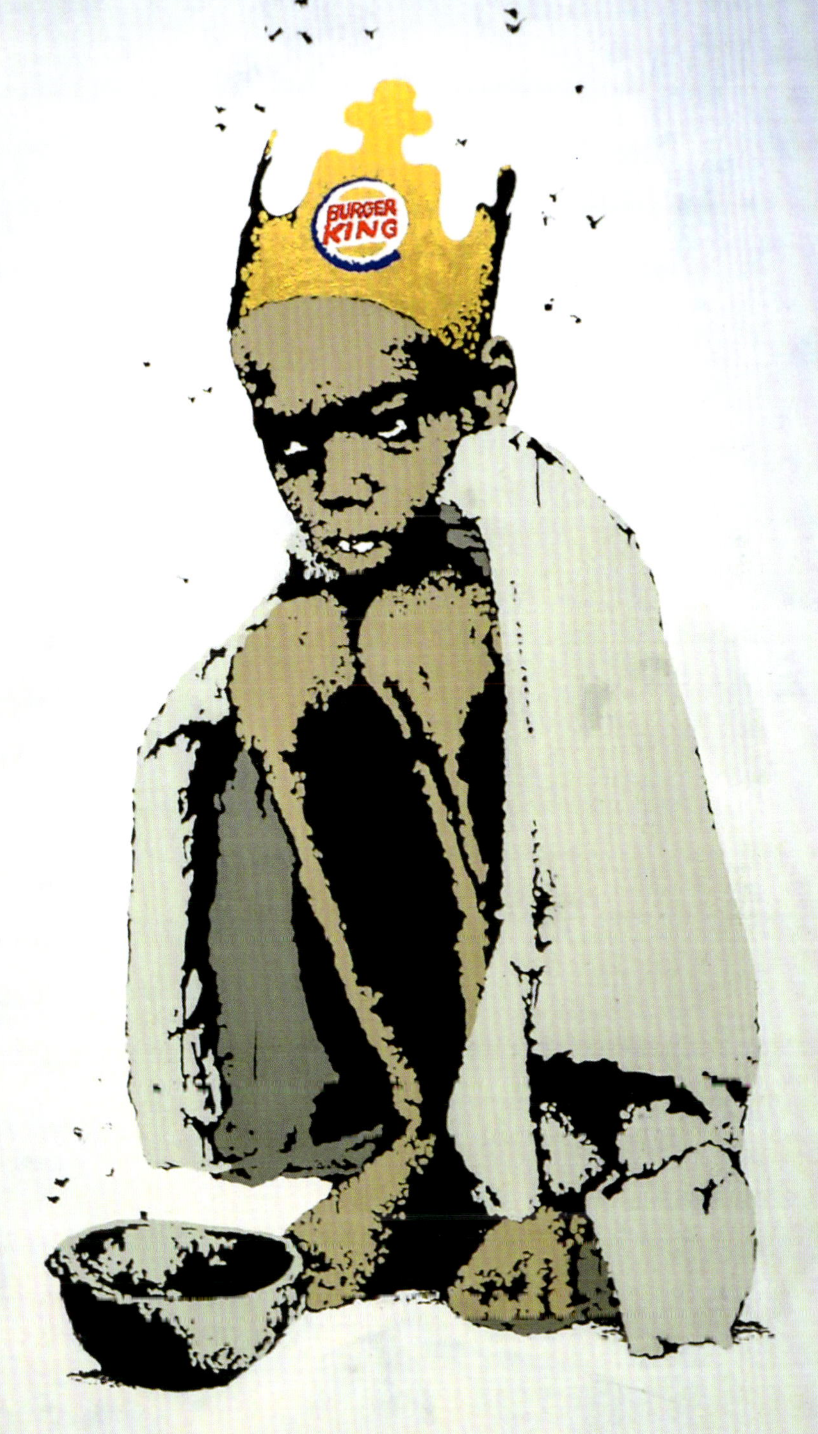

BURGER KING

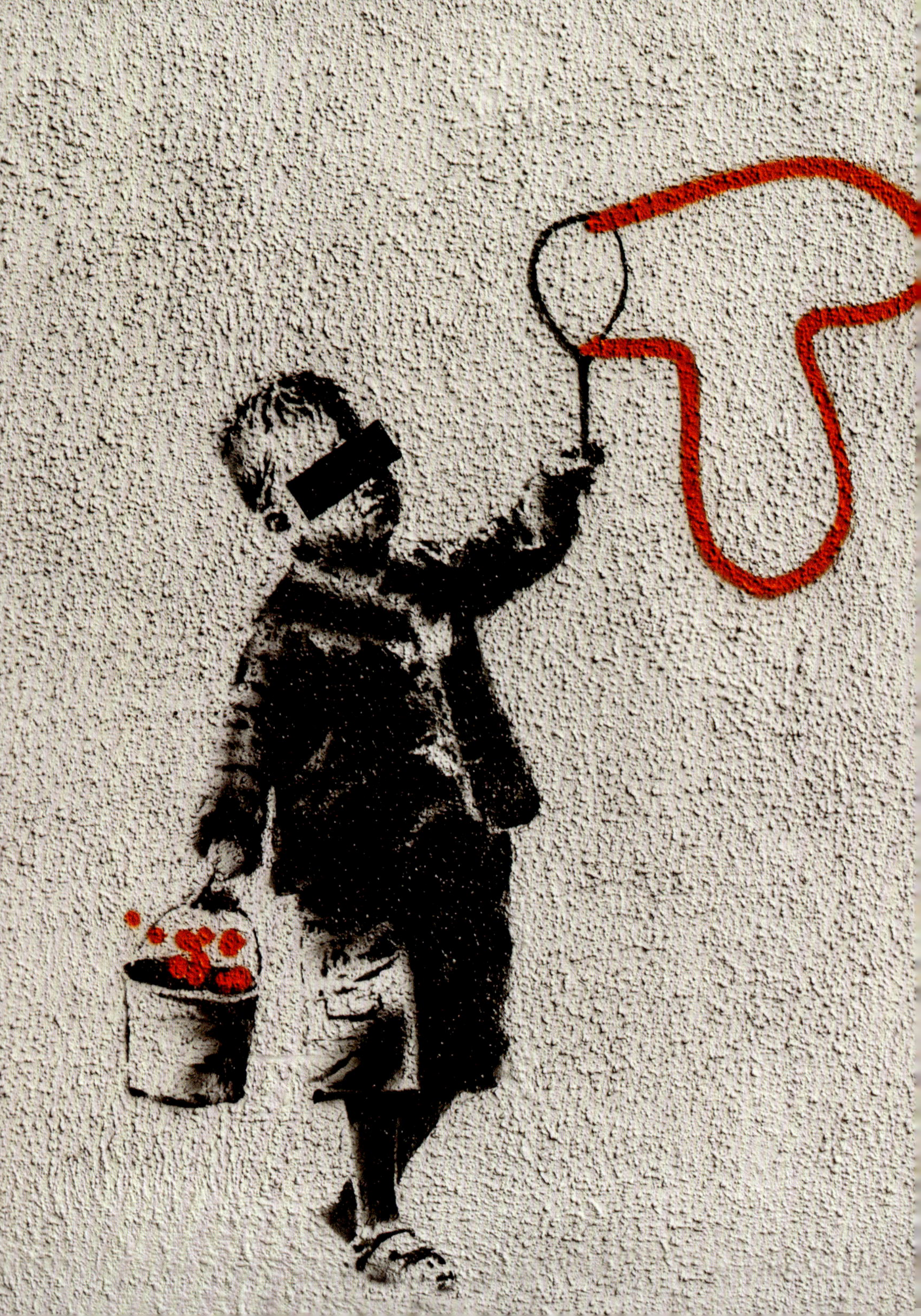

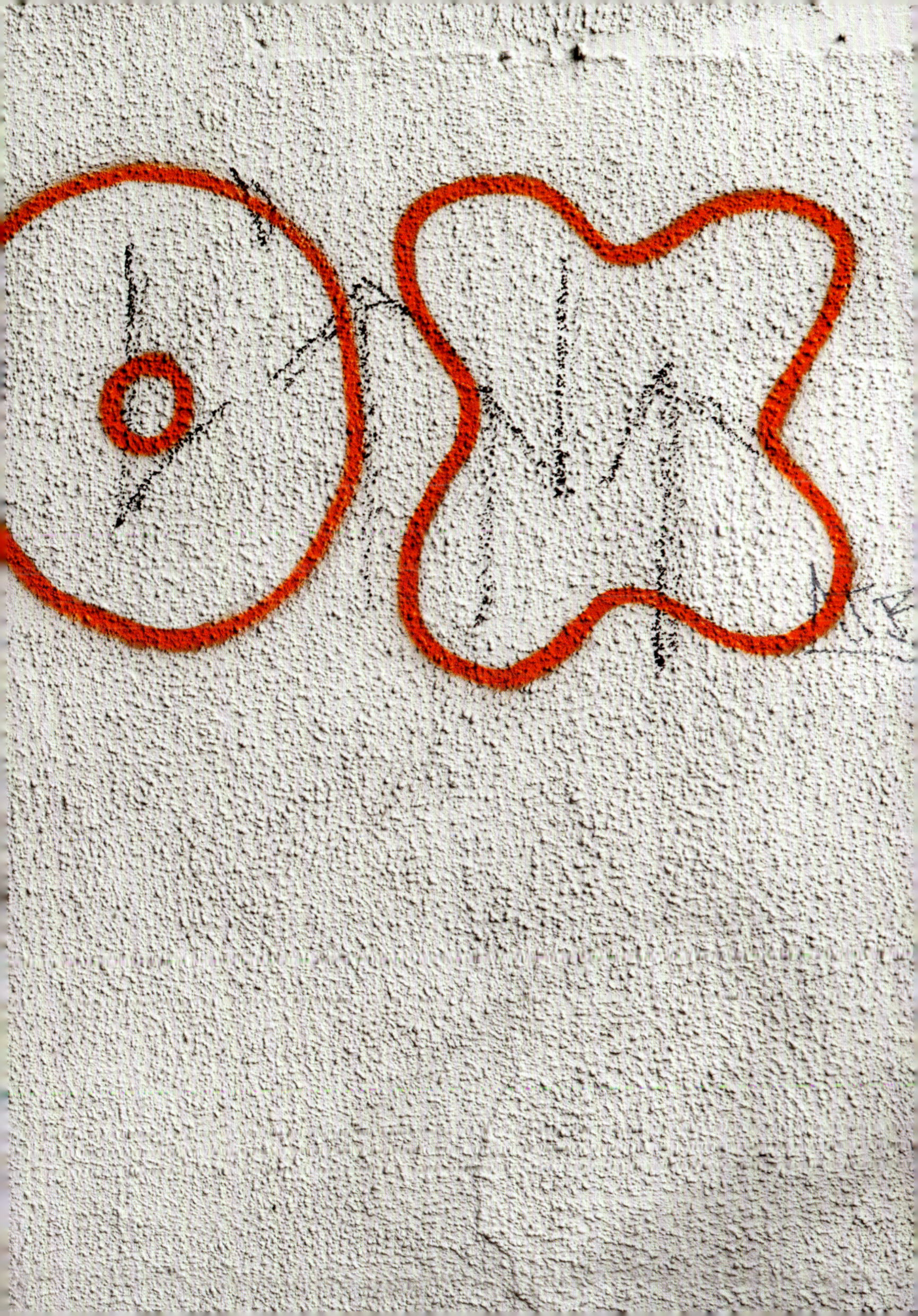

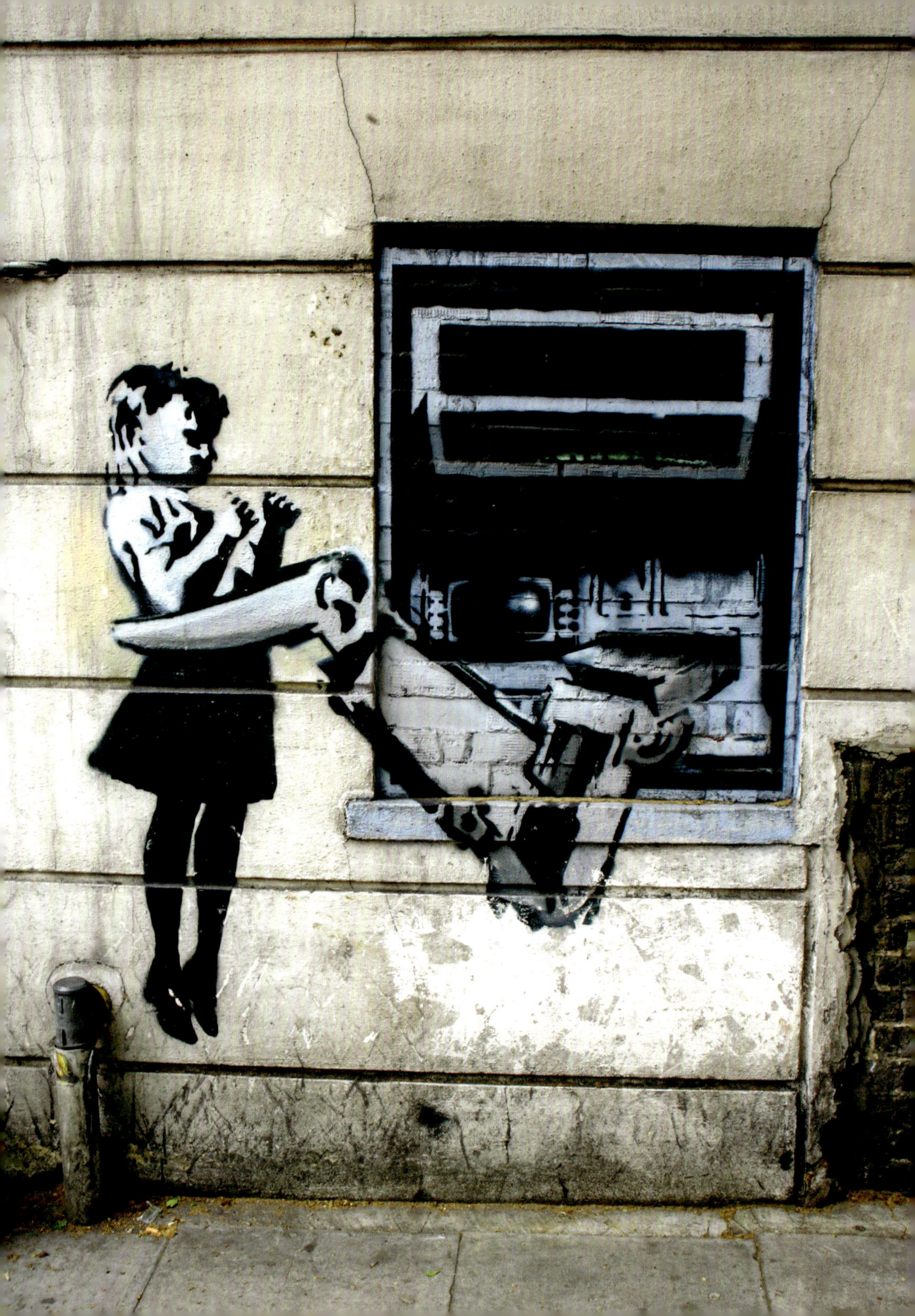

THE CORRUPTIVE POWER OF CAPITALISM IS HERE REPRESENTED AS A ROBOTIC ARM STICKING OUT FROM A CASH MACHINE AND LIFTING A LITTLE GIRL OFF THE GROUND.

THE EXTREMELY RIGID RULES OF GOVERNMENTS WILL NEVER BE ABLE TO LIMIT THE IMAGINATION OF TWO CHILDREN PLAYING WITH A SIGN AS IF IT WAS A BALL.

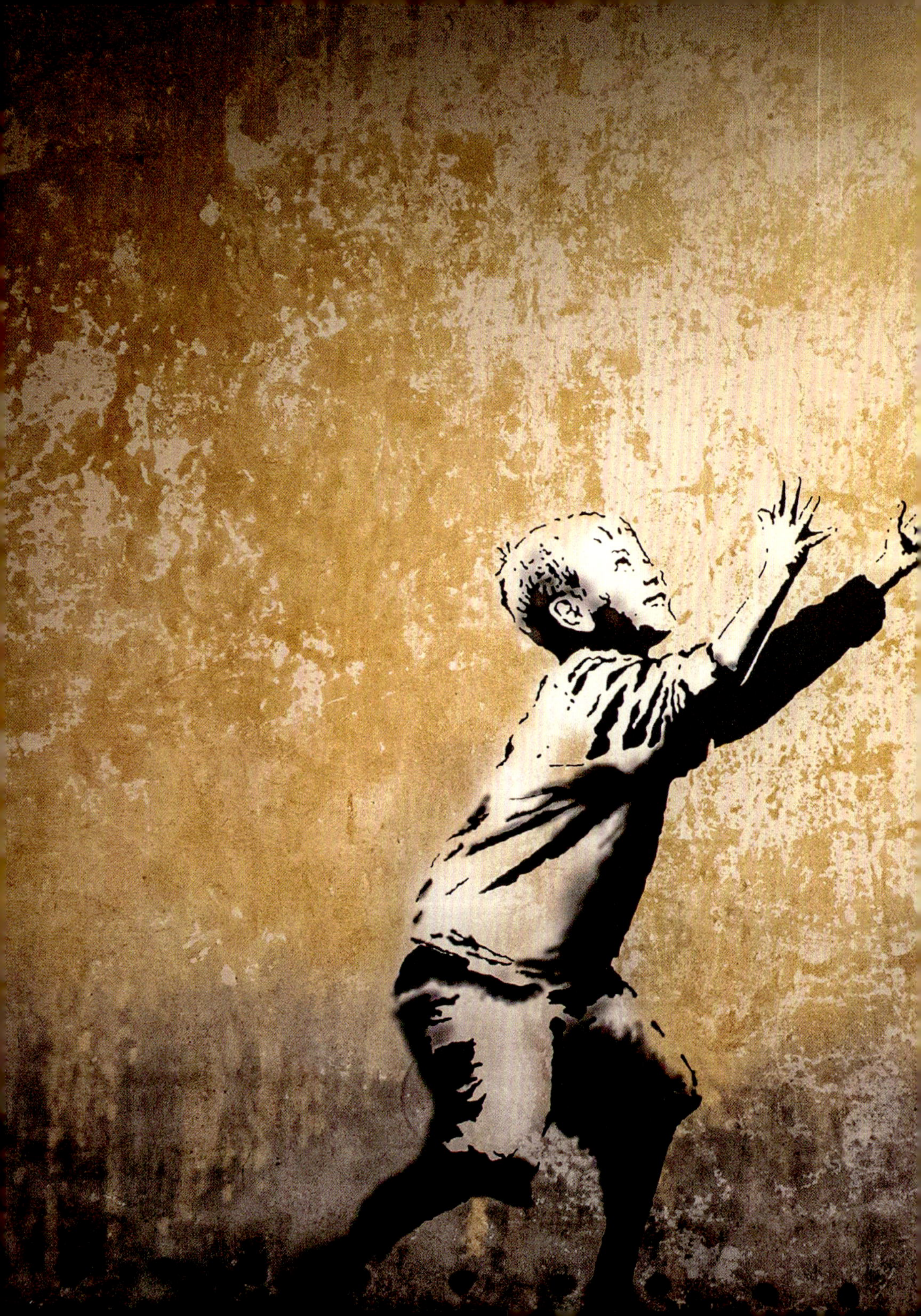

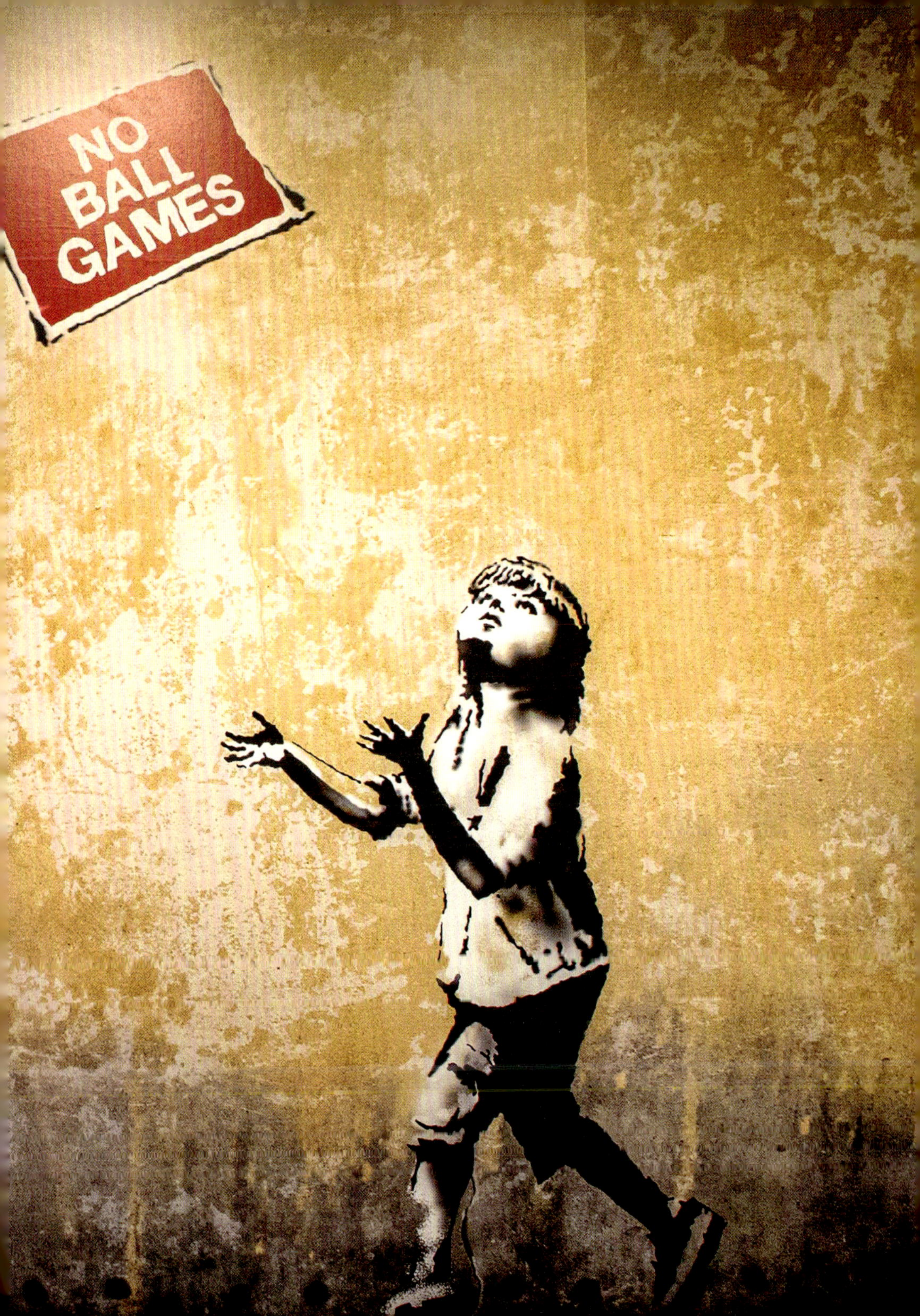

NO
BALL
GAMES

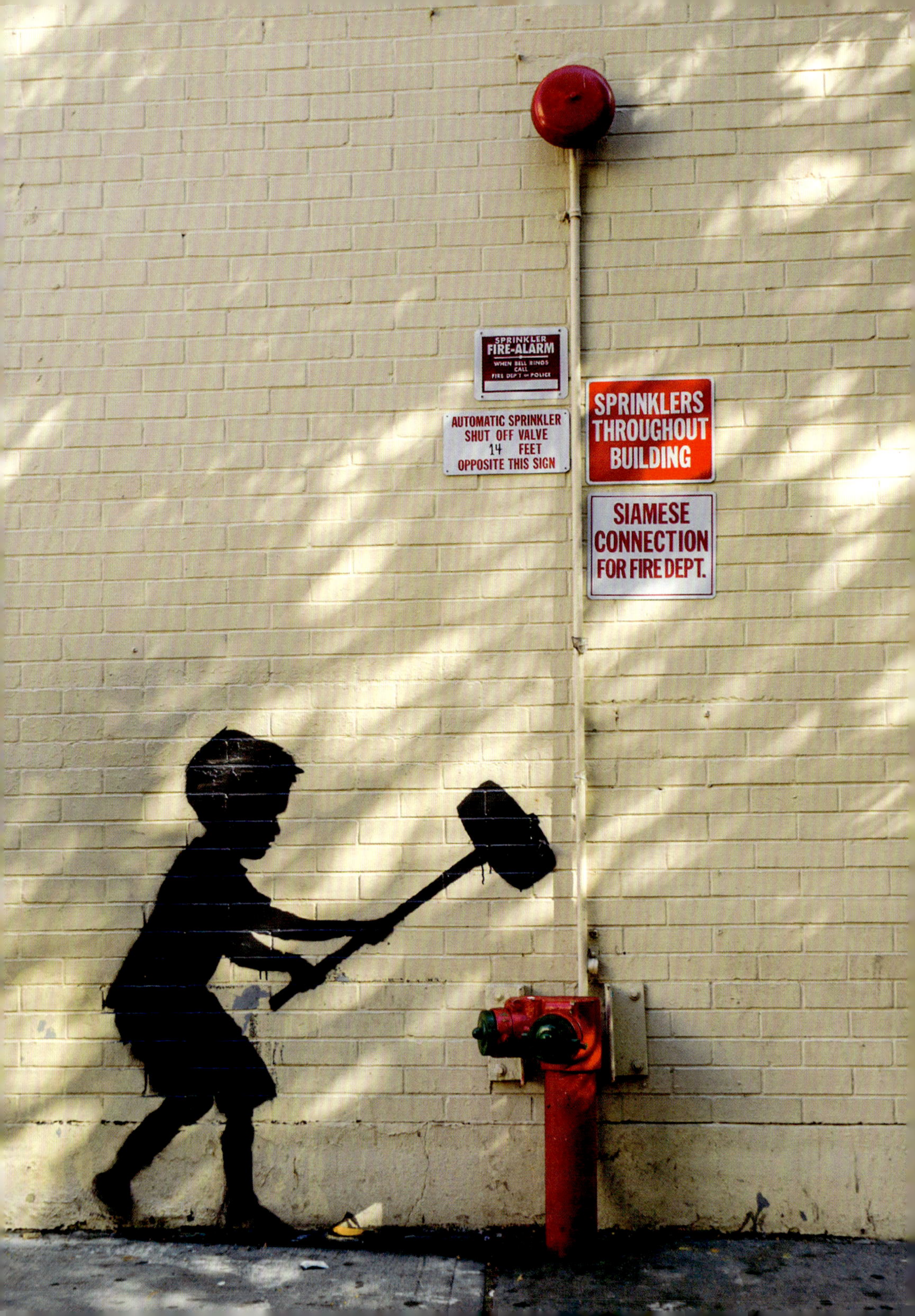

SPRINKLER
FIRE-ALARM
WHEN BELL RINGS
CALL
FIRE DEP'T or POLICE
AUTOMATIC SPRINKLER
SHUT OFF VALVE
14 FEET
OPPOSITE THIS SIGN
SPRINKLERS
THROUGHOUT
BUILDING
SIAMESE
CONNECTION
FOR FIRE DEPT.

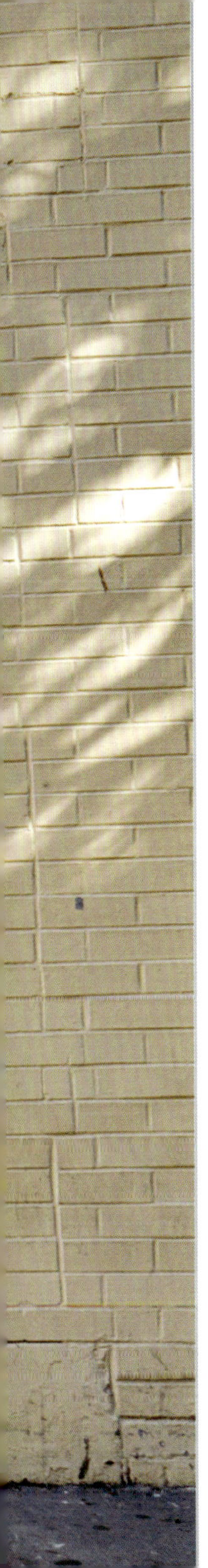

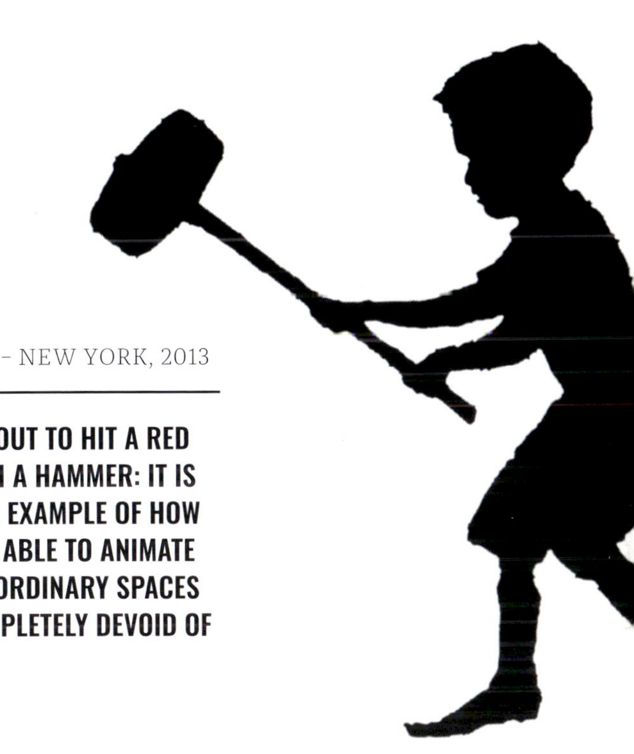

HAMMER BOY – NEW YORK, 2013

A CHILD IS ABOUT TO HIT A RED HYDRANT WITH A HAMMER: IT IS A SUCCESSFUL EXAMPLE OF HOW STREET ART IS ABLE TO ANIMATE OBJECTS AND ORDINARY SPACES THAT ARE COMPLETELY DEVOID OF ART.

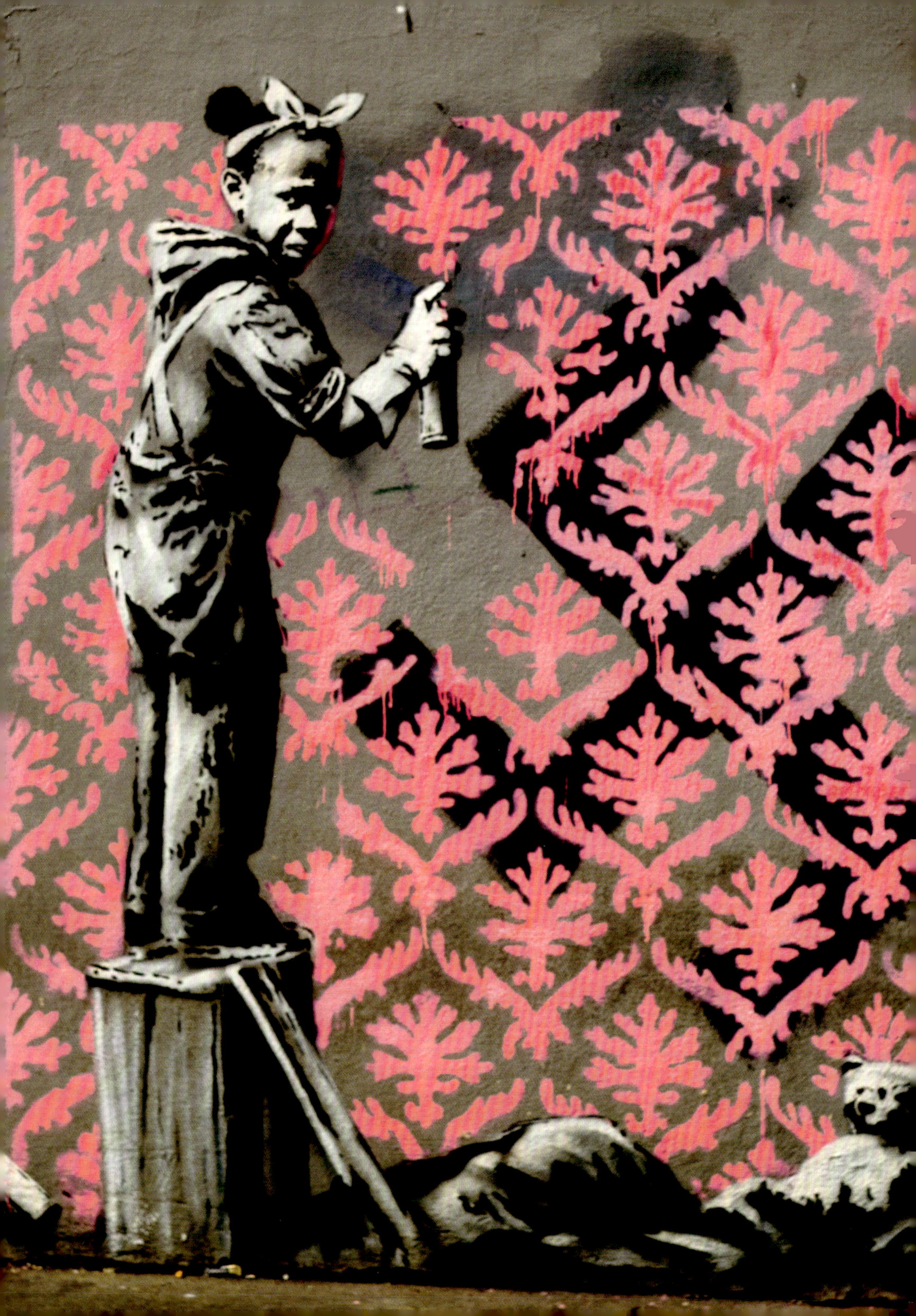

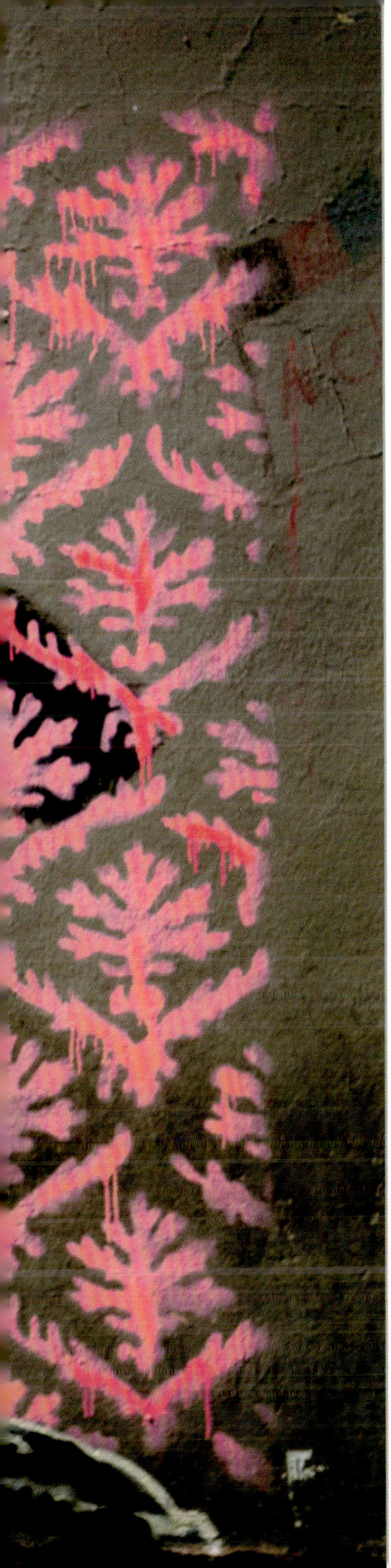

*LITTLE GIRL COVERING
A SWASTIKA* – PARIS, 2018

**A BETTER WORLD IS POSSIBLE,
AS THIS LITTLE REFUGEE GIRL
TEACHES US BY COVERING
A SWASTIKA WITH PINK
DECORATIONS REMINISCENT
OF VICTORIAN WALLPAPER.**

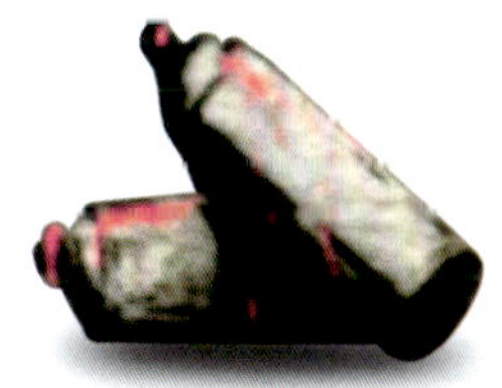

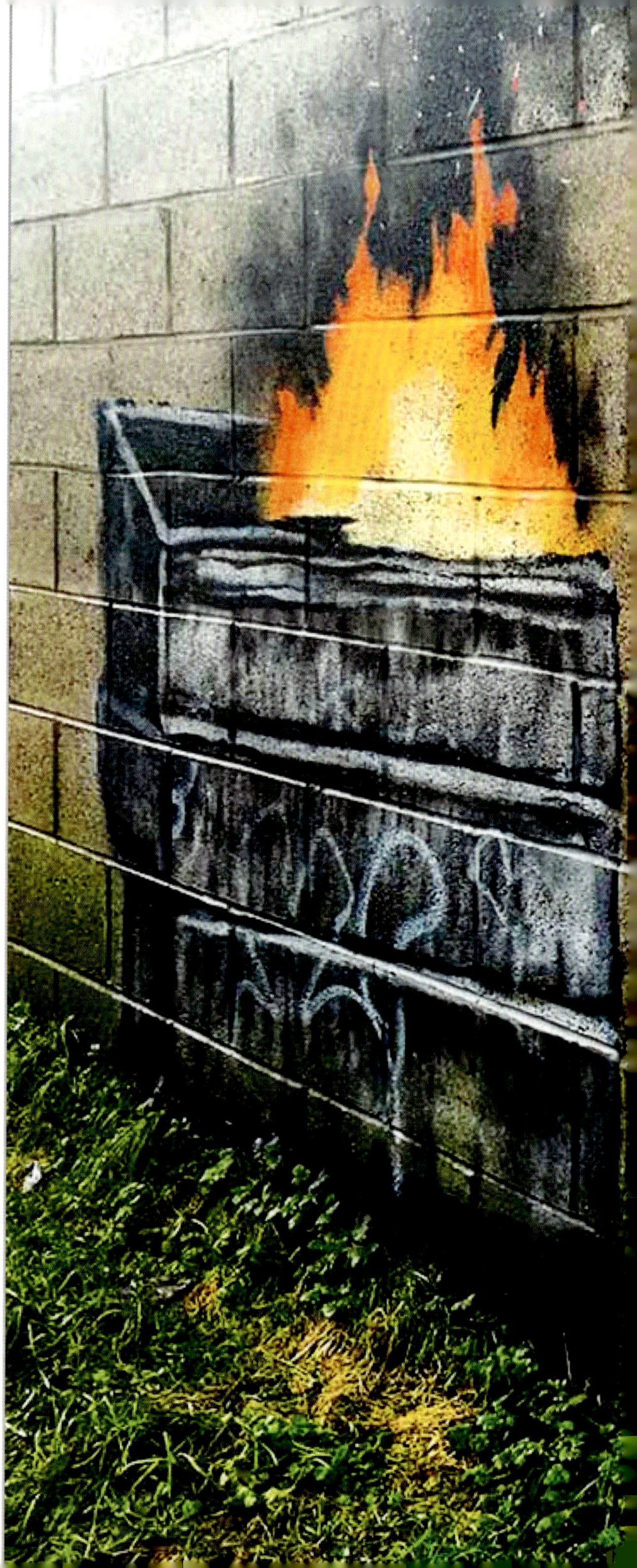

SEASON'S GREETINGS – PORT TALBOT, WALES, 2018

A CHILD WITH A WINTER HAT AND SCARF IS PLAYING WITH THE ASH COMING FROM A BURNING DUMPSTER AS IF IT WAS SNOW.

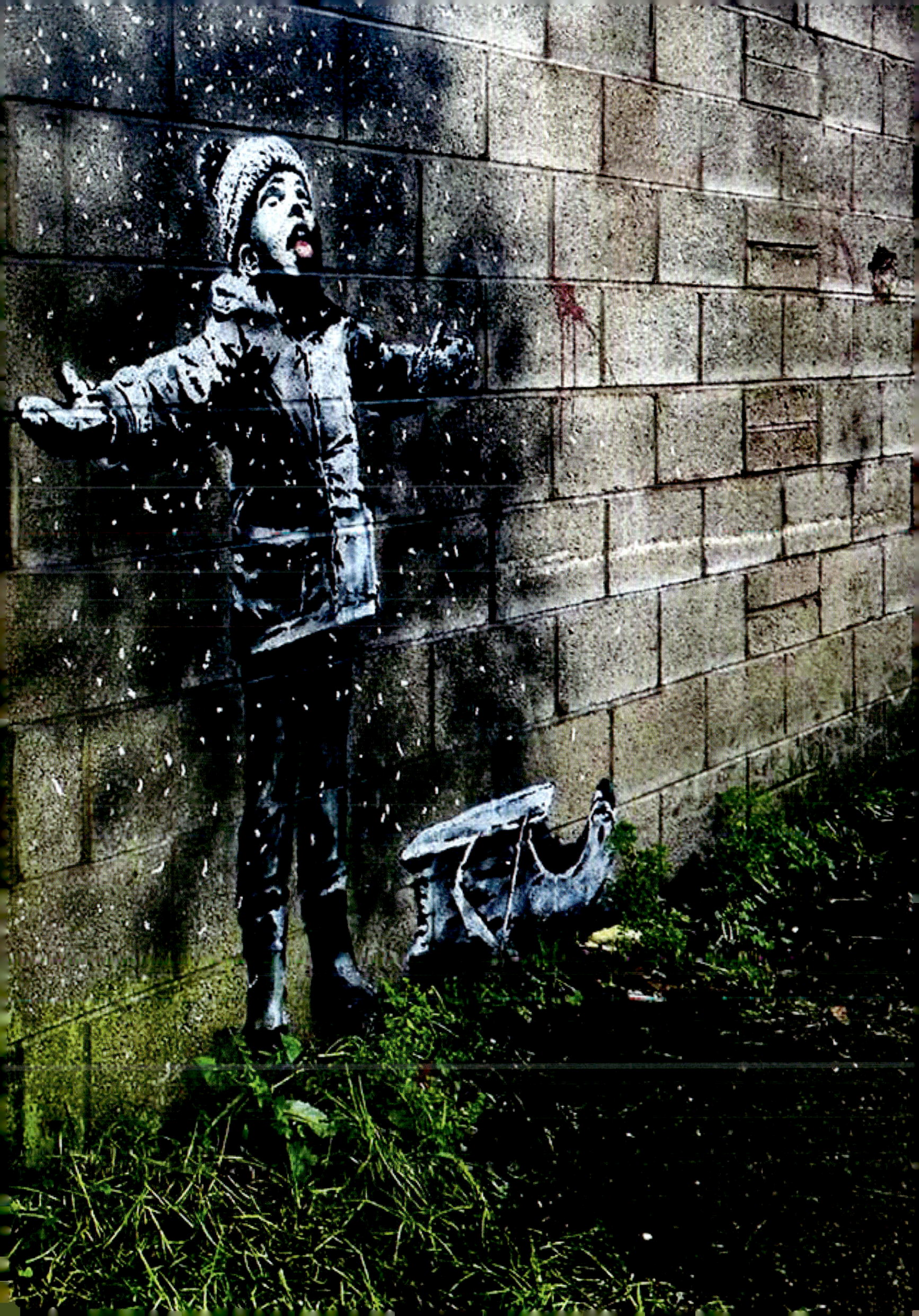

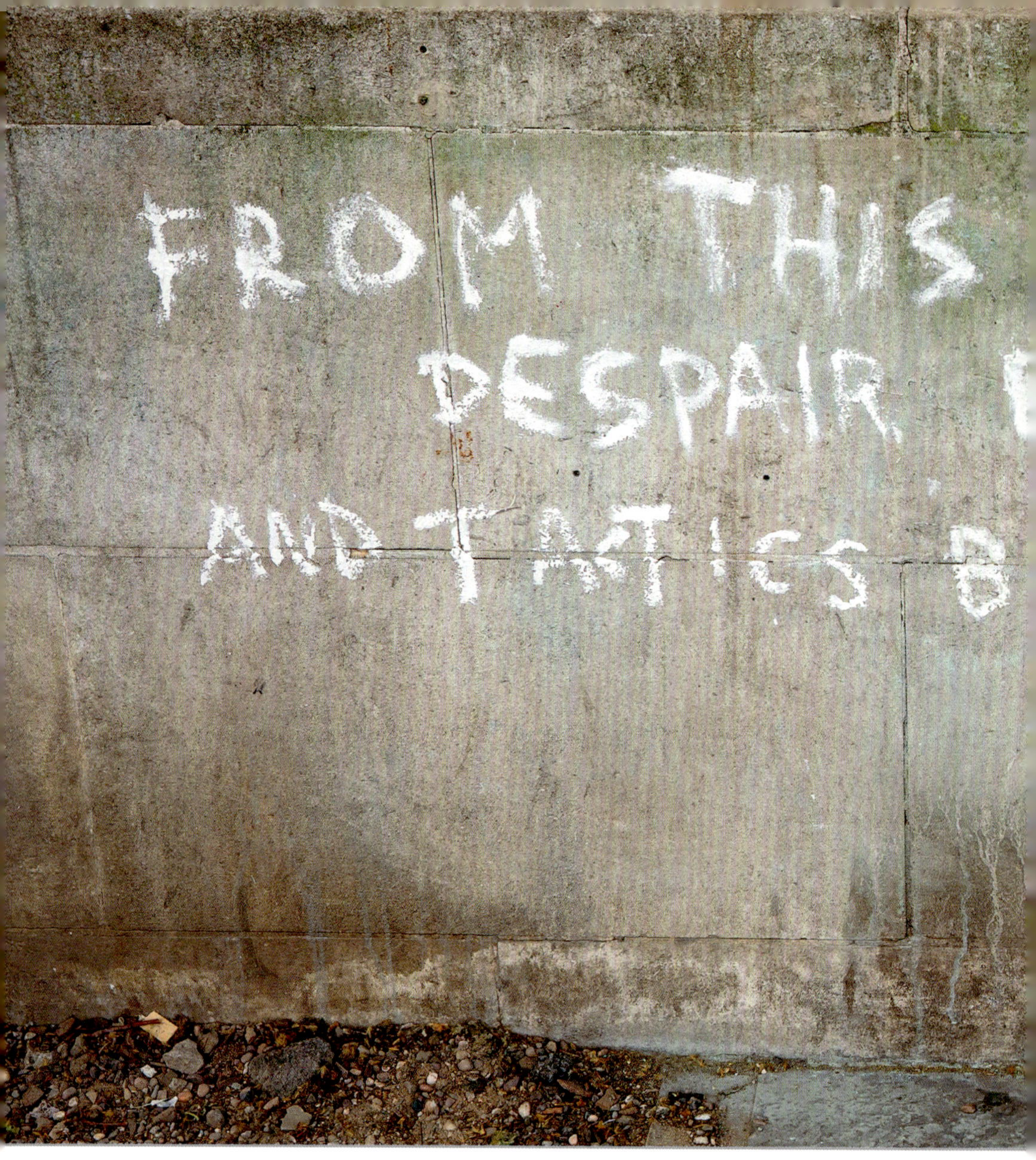

CHILD AT MARBLE ARCH – LONDON, 2019

**CLIMATE CHANGE: "FROM THIS MOMENT DESPAIR ENDS,
AND TACTICS BEGIN" (RAOUL VANEIGEM).**

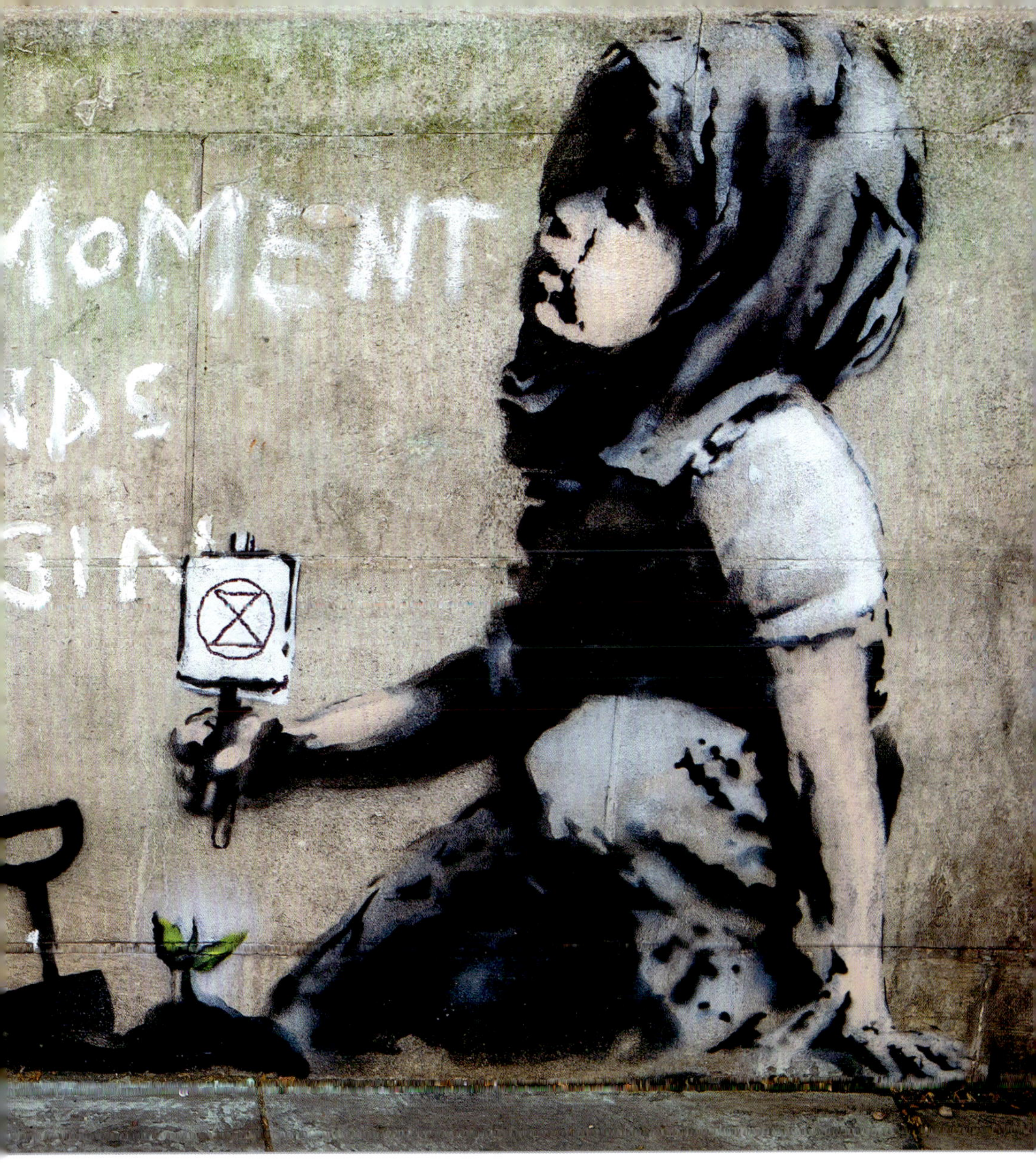

JACK AND JILL – 2005

52–53 NOTHING IS AS IT SEEMS: TWO CHILDREN ARE CHEERFULLY RUNNING, BUT THEY ARE WEARING POLICE BULLETPROOF VESTS.

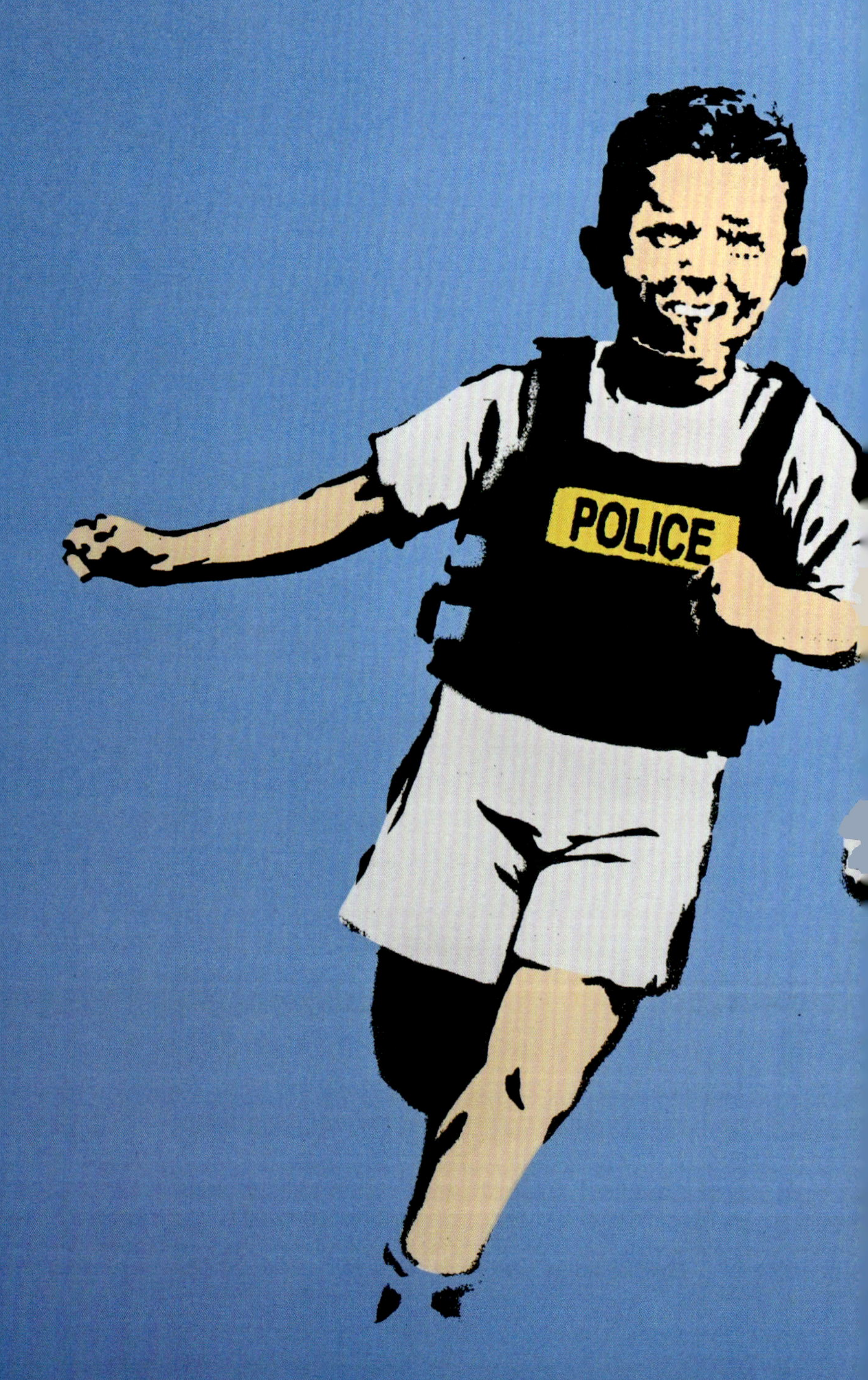
POLICE

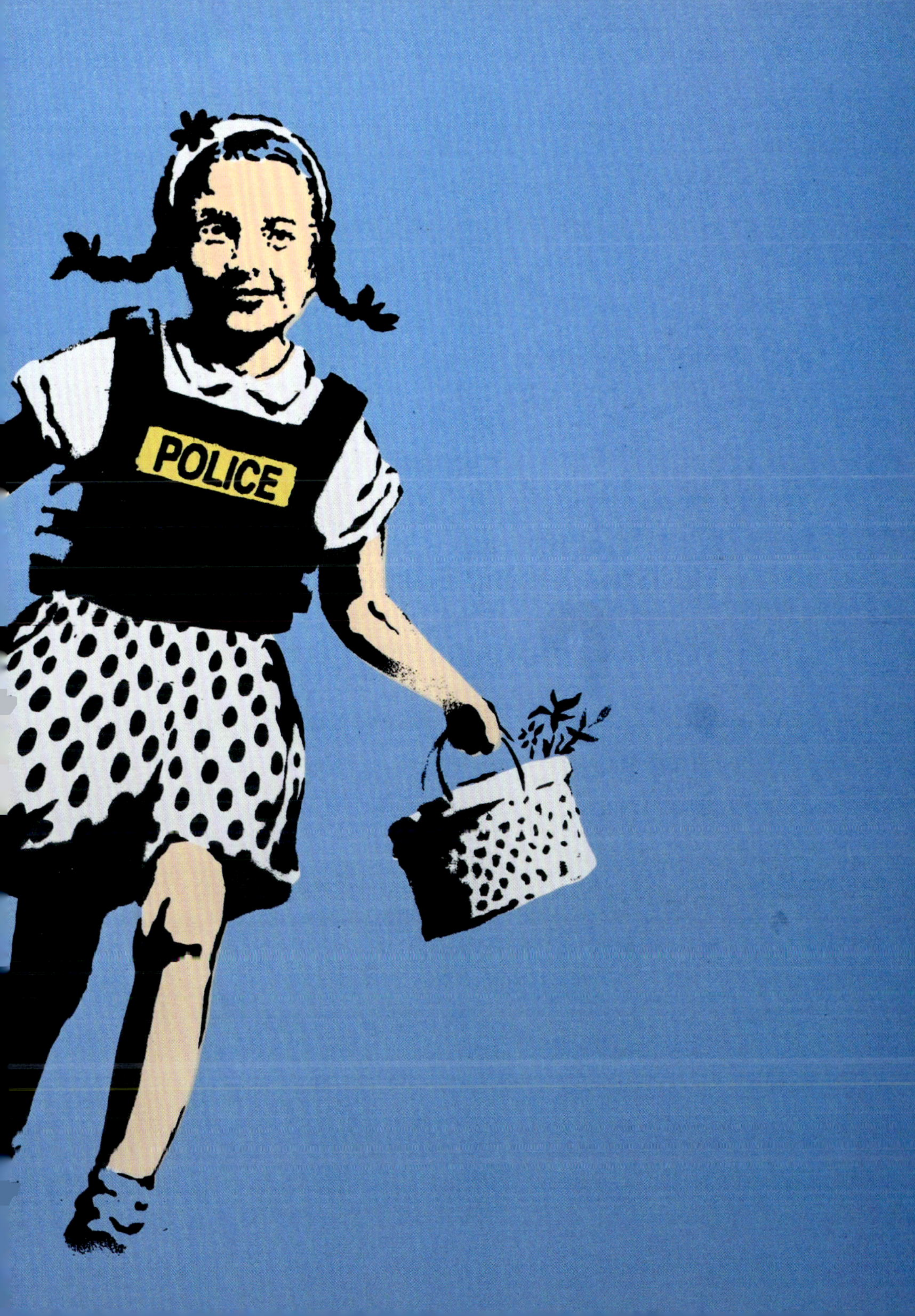
POLICE

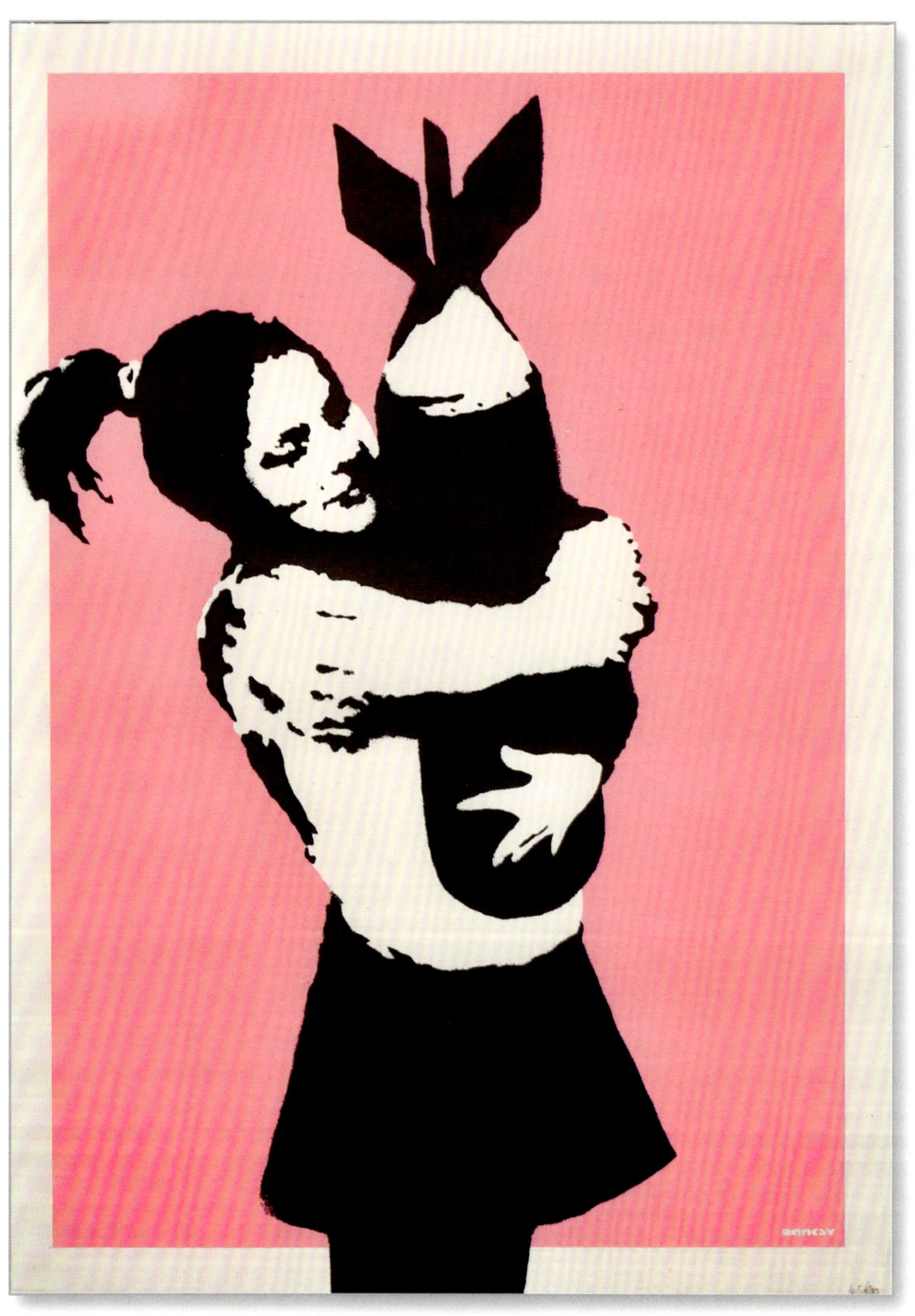

BOMB HUGGER – 2003

A LITTLE GIRL IS HUGGING A BOMB AS IF IT WERE A SOFT TOY: ONLY REAL LOVE HAS THE POWER TO DEFUSE THE THREAT OF A BOMB.

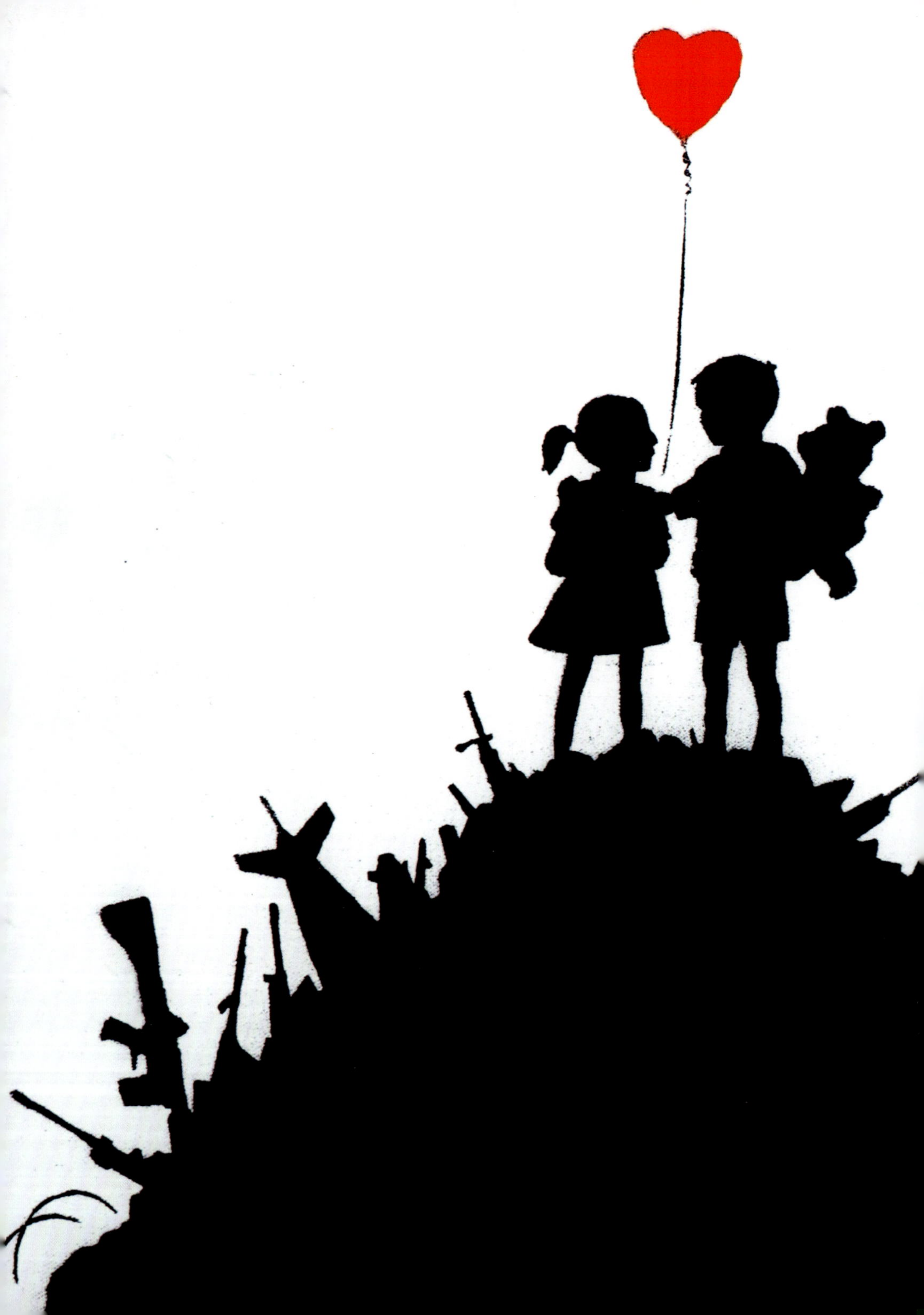

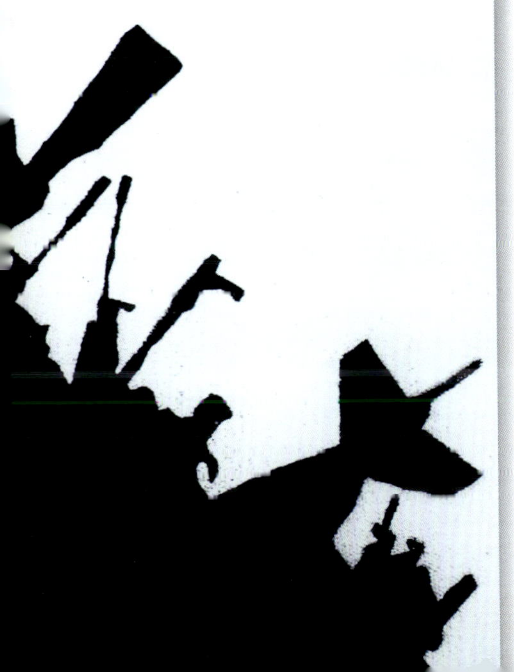

A BOY AND A GIRL ON A MOUND OF WEAPONRY HOLD A RED HEART-SHAPED BALLOON IN THEIR HANDS: WILL INNOCENCE AND LOVE BE ABLE TO SAVE THE WORLD FROM WAR AND OPPRESSION?

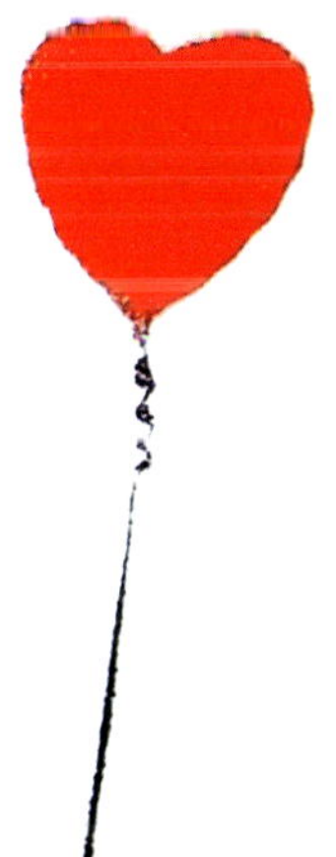

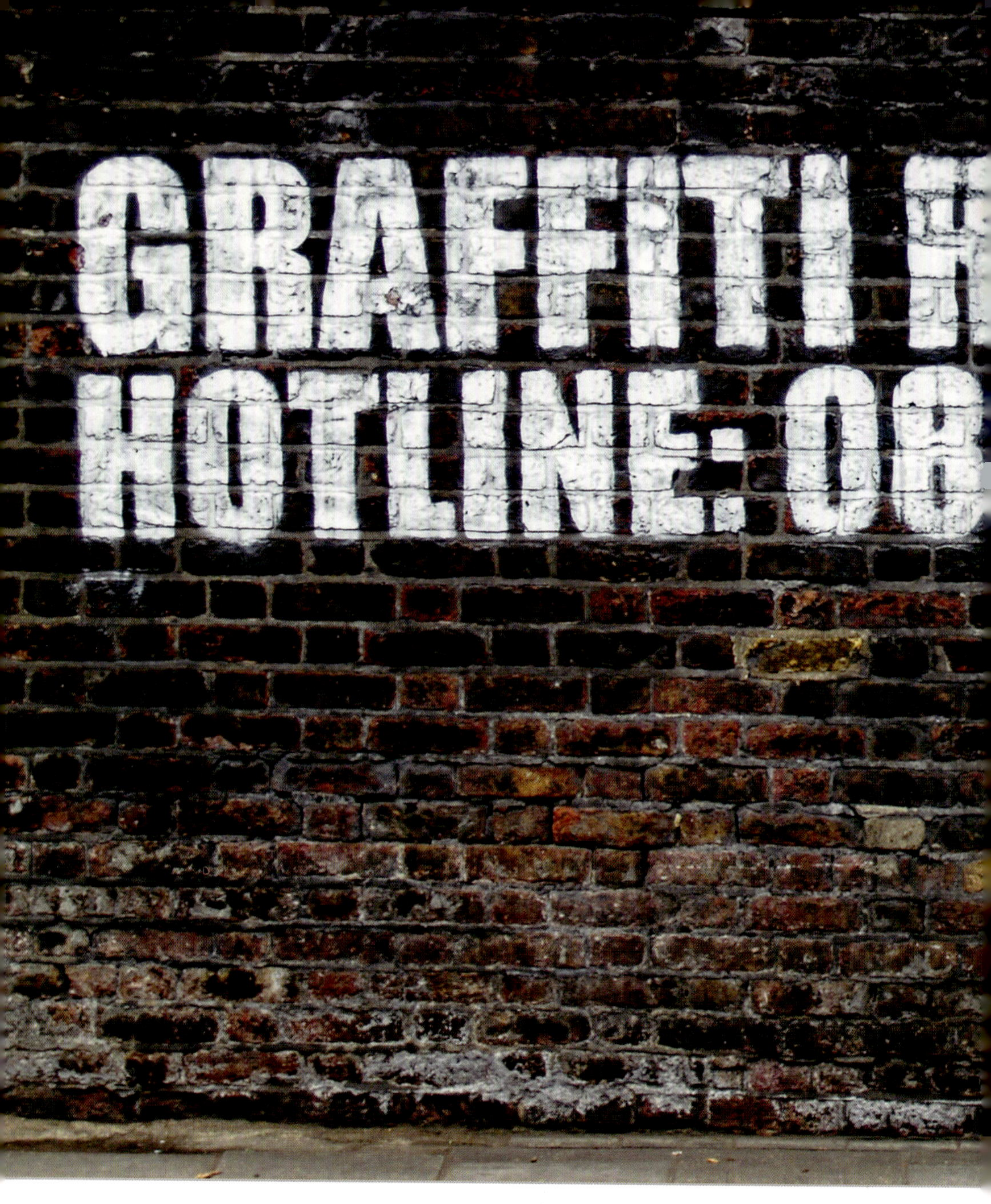

PENTONVILLE ROAD – LONDON, 2006

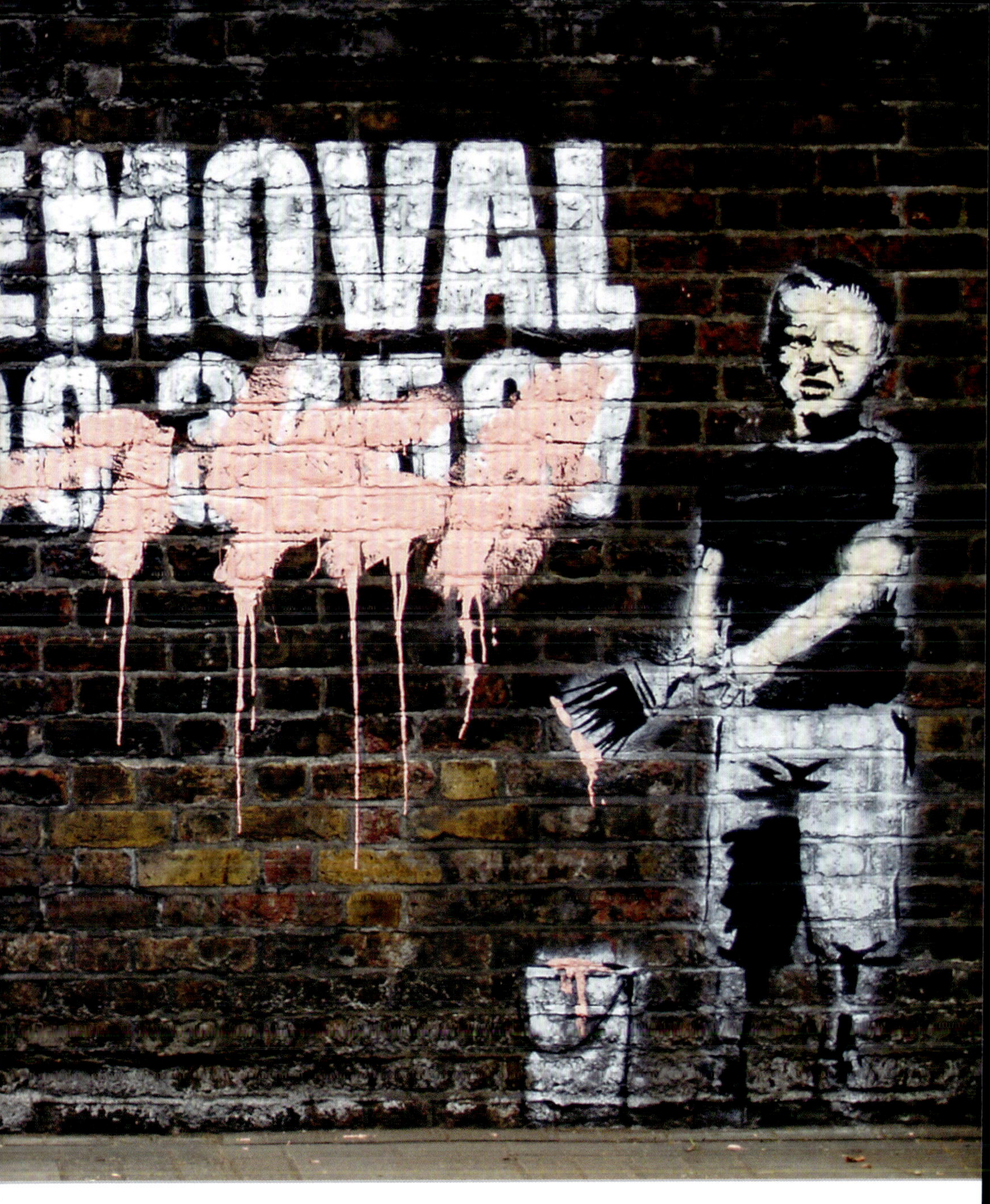

BANKSY'S IRONIC TRIBUTE TO A GRAFFITI
REMOVAL HOTLINE.

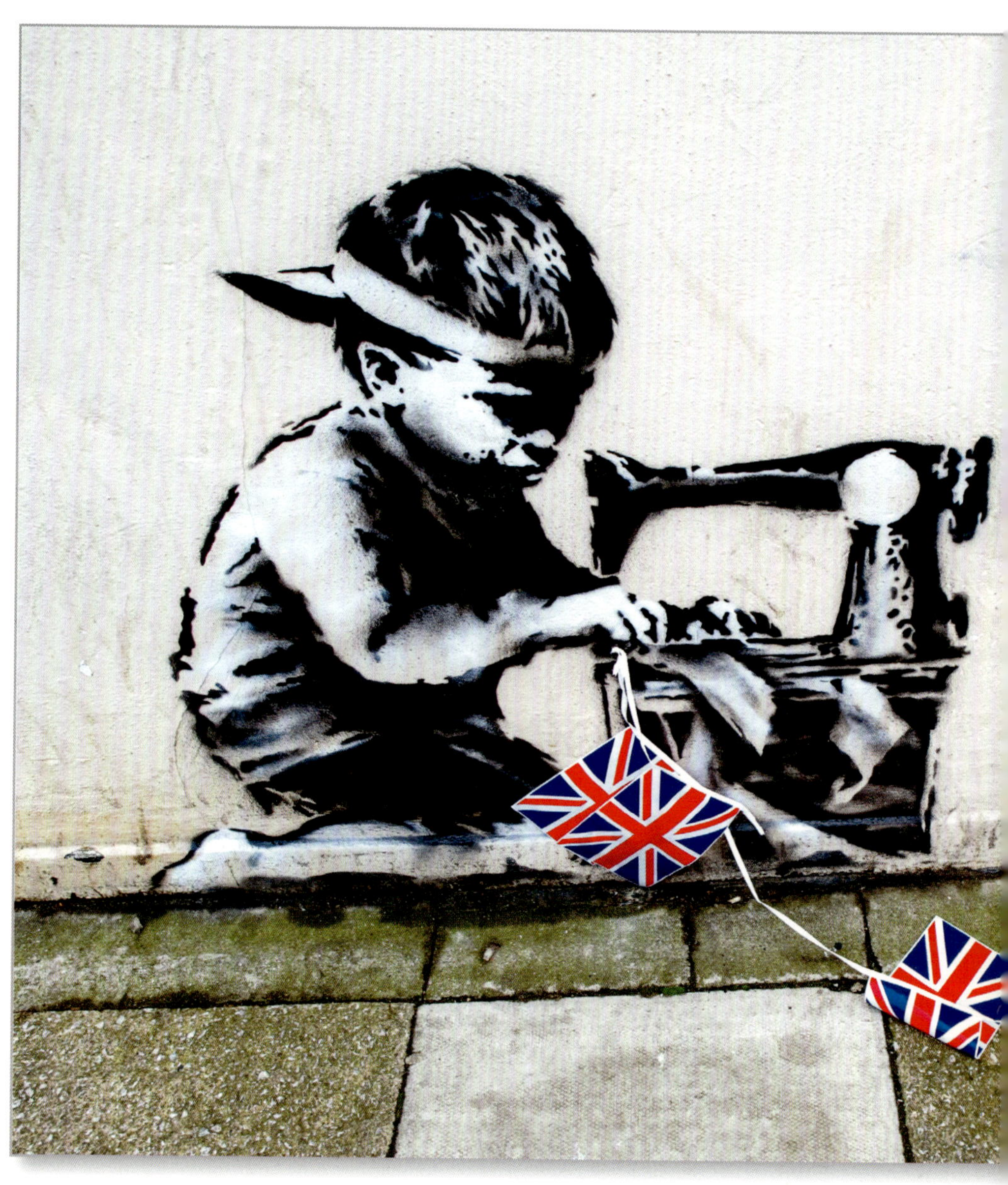

BANKSY DENOUNCES THE EXPLOITATION OF CHILD LABOR ON THE OCCASION OF QUEEN ELIZABETH II'S DIAMOND JUBILEE AND THE 2012 LONDON OLYMPICS.

WE ARE ALL IN THE SAME BOAT – NICHOLAS EVERITT PARK, LOWESTOFT, ENGLAND, 2021

62–63 THREE CHILDREN PRETEND TO BE SAILING IN THE OPEN SEA ON A SINKING SHIP. THE YOUNGEST ONE AT THE STERN IS TRYING TO DO EVERYTHING HE CAN TO SAVE THE CREW, WHILE THE ONE AT THE BOW IS BRAVELY LOOKING AHEAD THROUGH HIS TELESCOPE.

WE'R
IN THE
BO

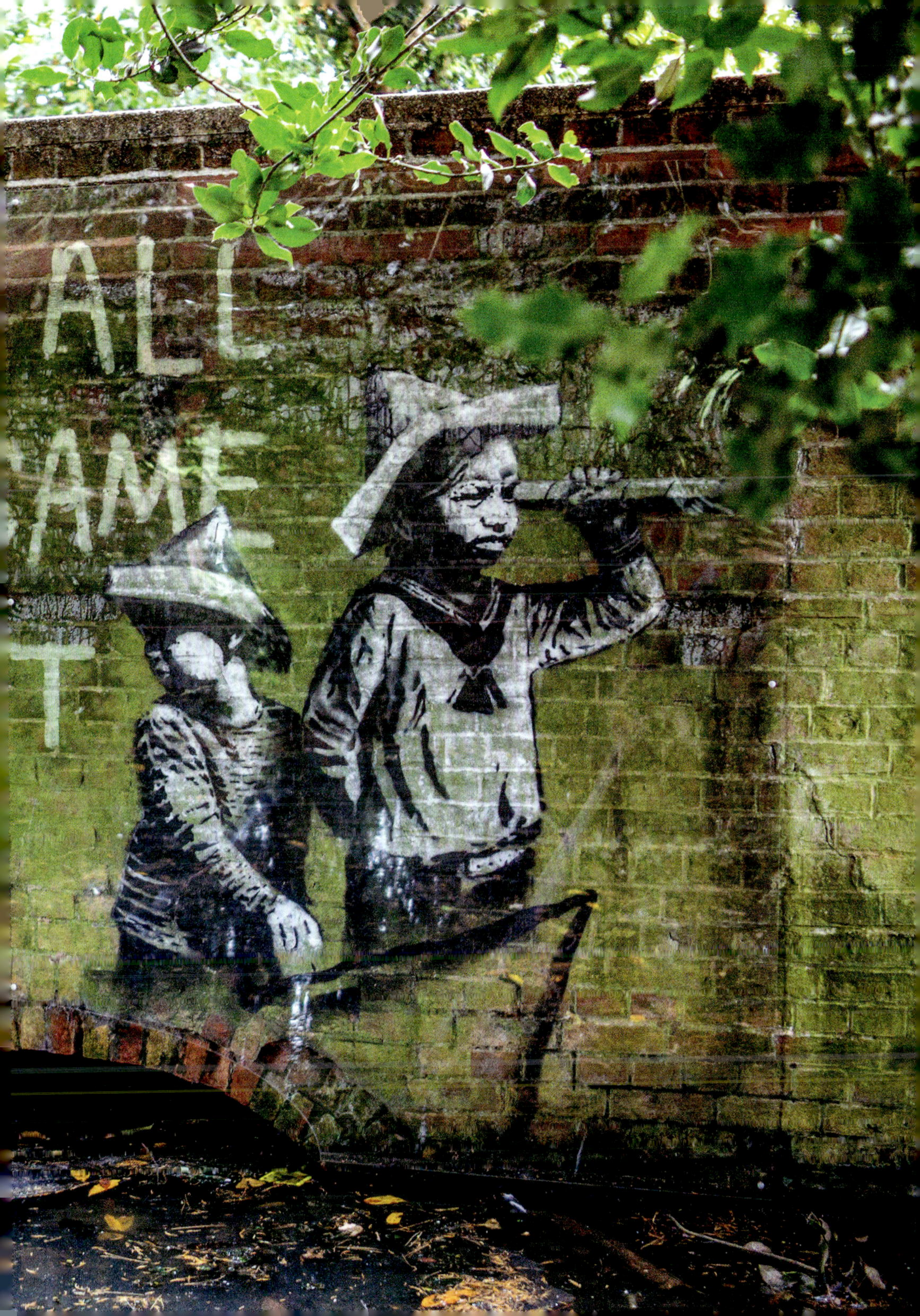

ALL
AME
T

AFTER ALL, HAPPINESS AND FUN LIE IN THE SIMPLEST THINGS: A LITTLE GIRL IS HAVING FUN USING AN OLD TIRE AS A HULA-HOOP.

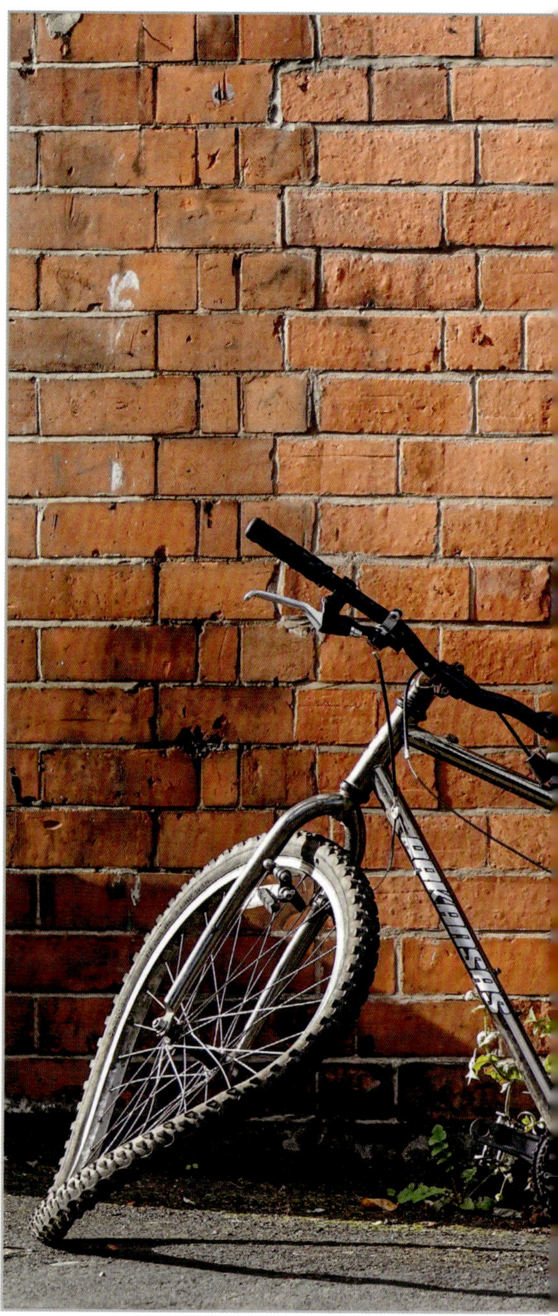

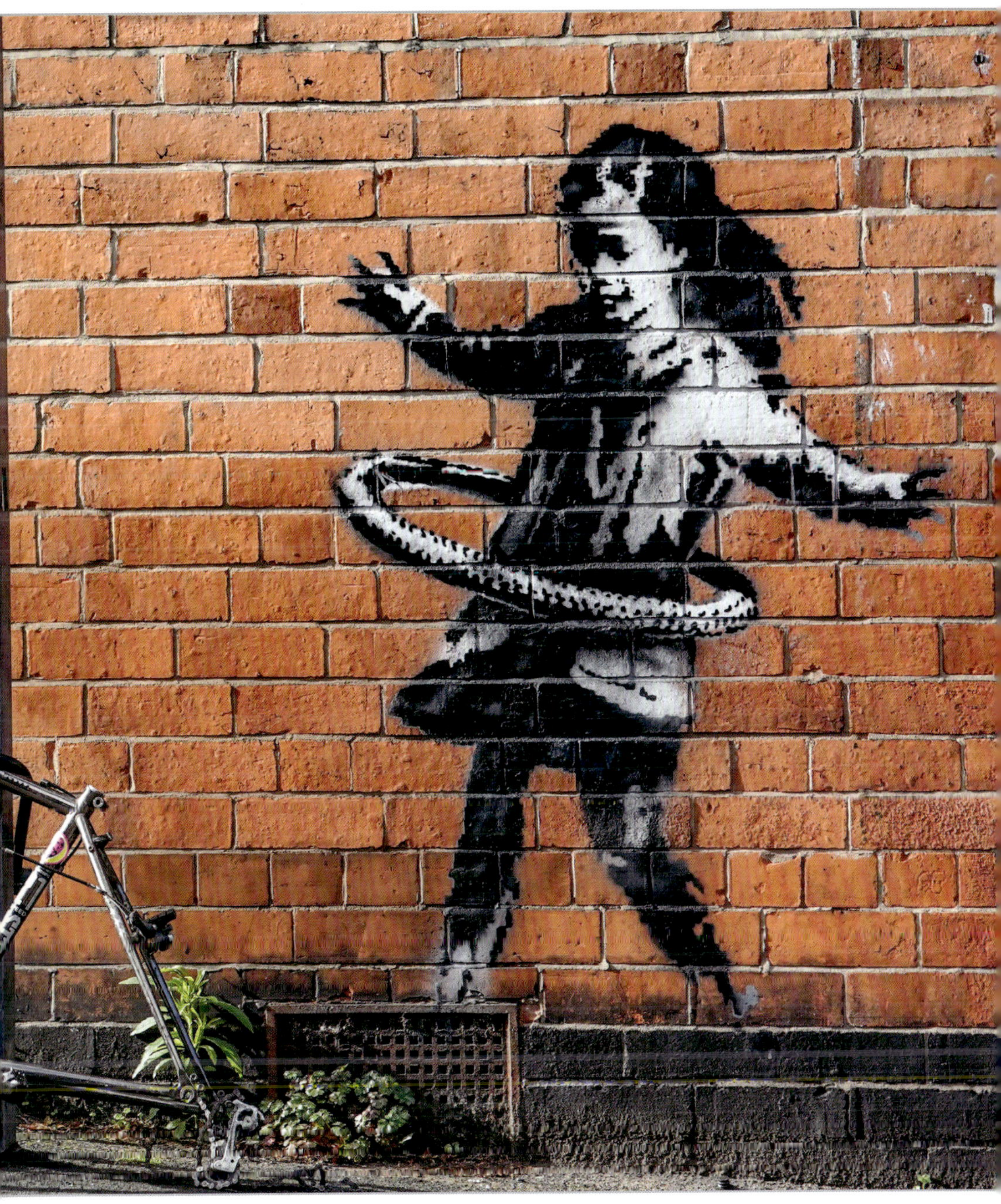

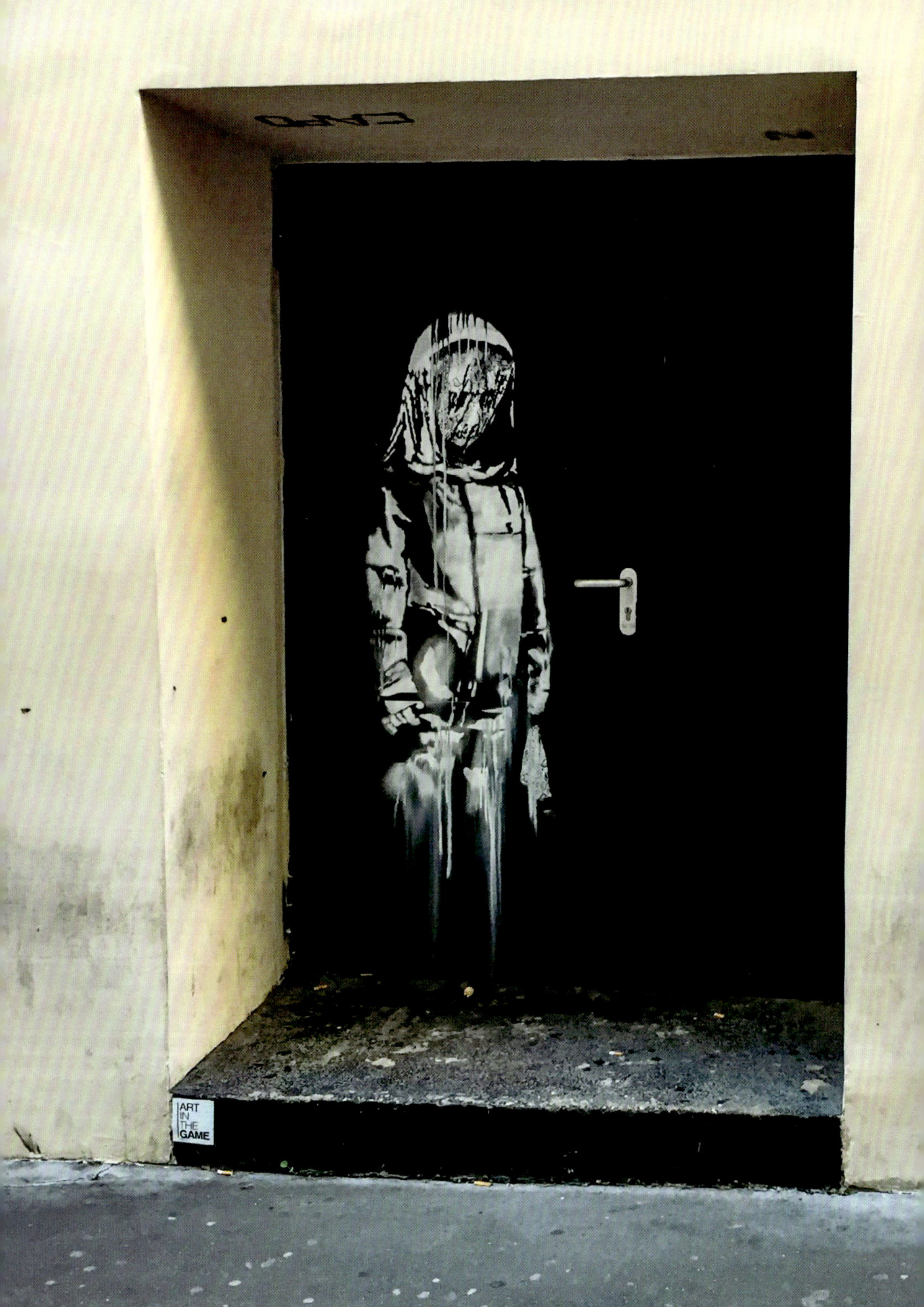
ART
IN
THE
GAME

A GRIEVING LITTLE GIRL CRIES AT THE EMERGENCY
EXIT DOOR OF THE BATACLAN THEATER, IN PARIS.
IT IS BANKSY'S TRIBUTE TO THE 90 VICTIMS OF THE
ATTACK OF NOVEMBER 13, 2015.

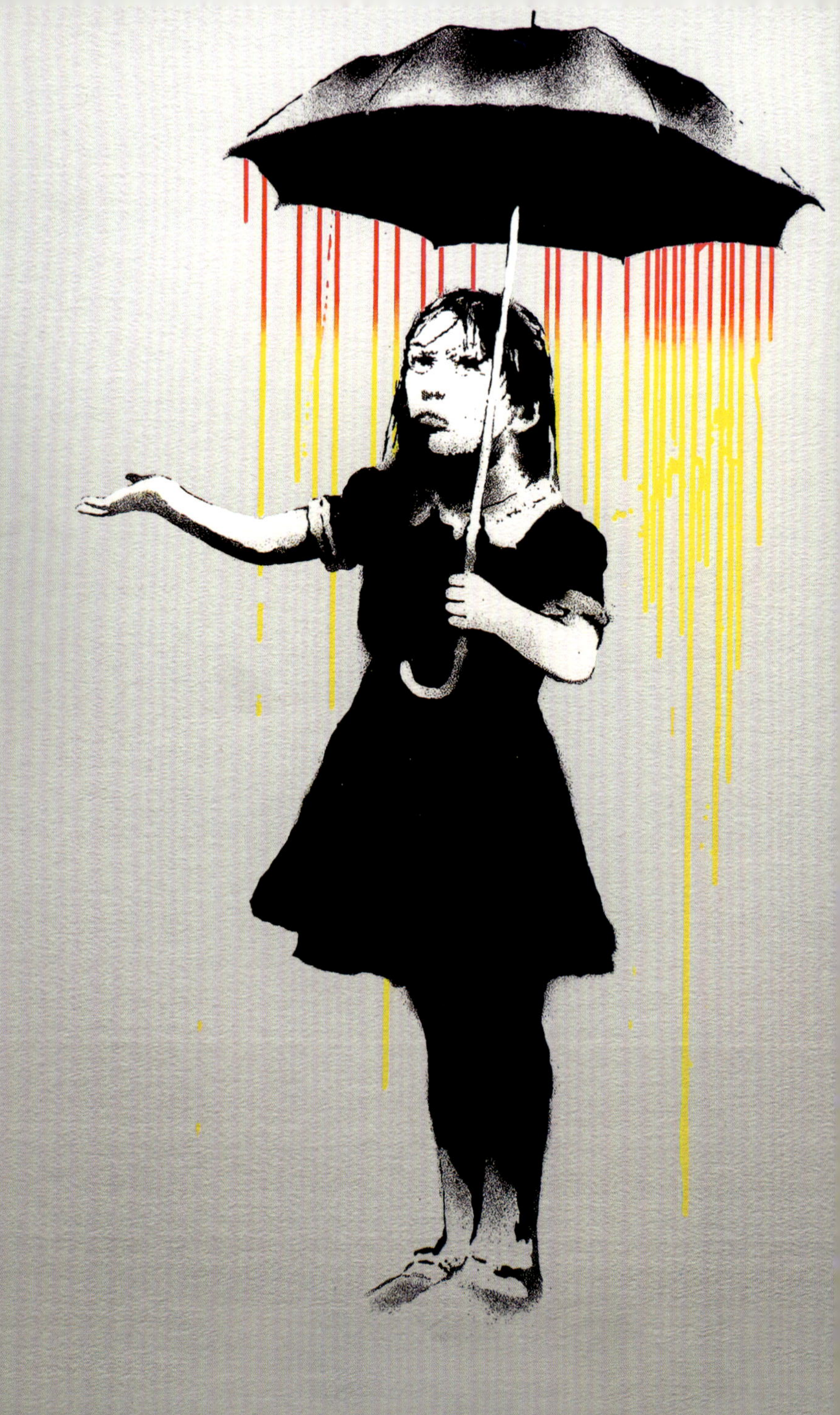

WHAT IS MEANT TO PROTECT US CAN SOMETIMES PROVE HARMFUL. THE RAIN FALLING THROUGH THIS GIRL'S UMBRELLA DENOUNCES THE FAILURE OF THE ANTI-FLOODING MEASURES DURING THE 2005 HURRICANE KATRINA IN NEW ORLEANS.

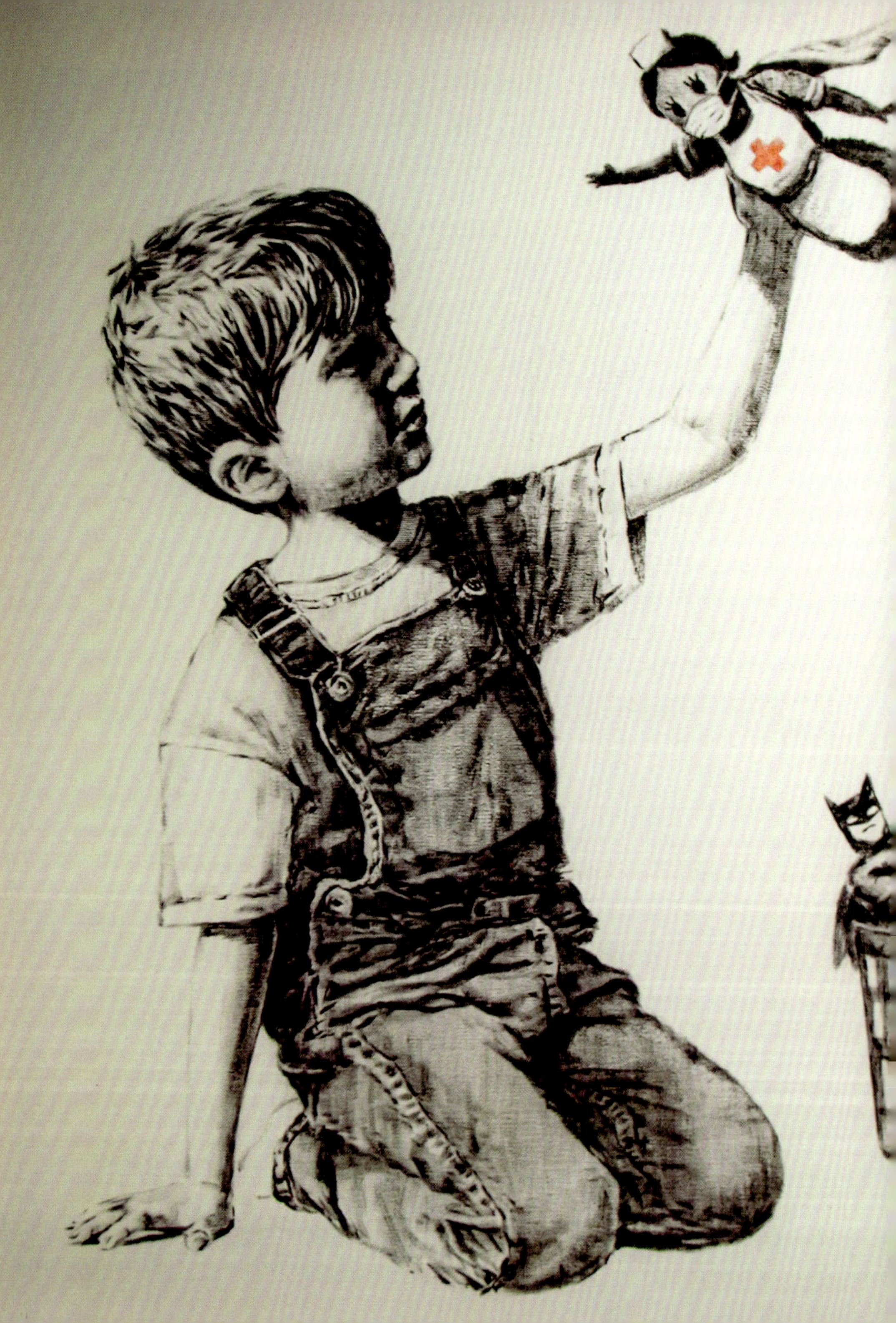

A CHILD PLAYING WITH
SUPERHEROES GRABS A NURSE
DOLL. BANKSY CELEBRATES THE
SACRIFICE OF THE NATIONAL
HEALTH SERVICE STAFF DURING
THE PANDEMIC. THIS WORK WAS
DONATED TO SOUTHAMPTON
GENERAL HOSPITAL, ENGLAND.

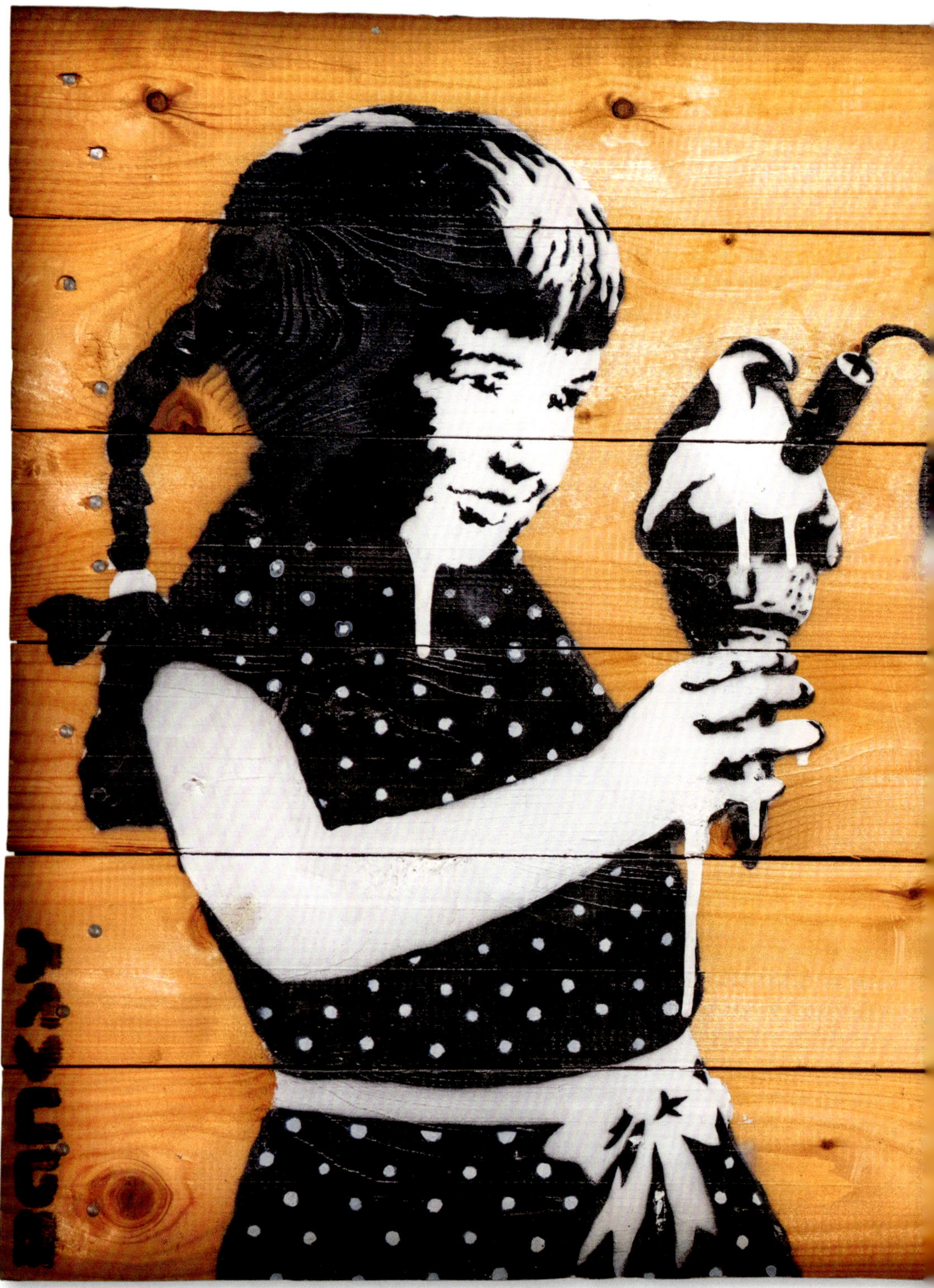

THE FRAGILITY OF CHILDHOOD SHINING THROUGH THIS GIRL'S INNOCENT EYES IS THREATENED BY THE STICK OF DYNAMITE OMINOUSLY STICKING OUT FROM HER ICE CREAM: BANKSY'S BITTER REFLECTION ON LIFE.

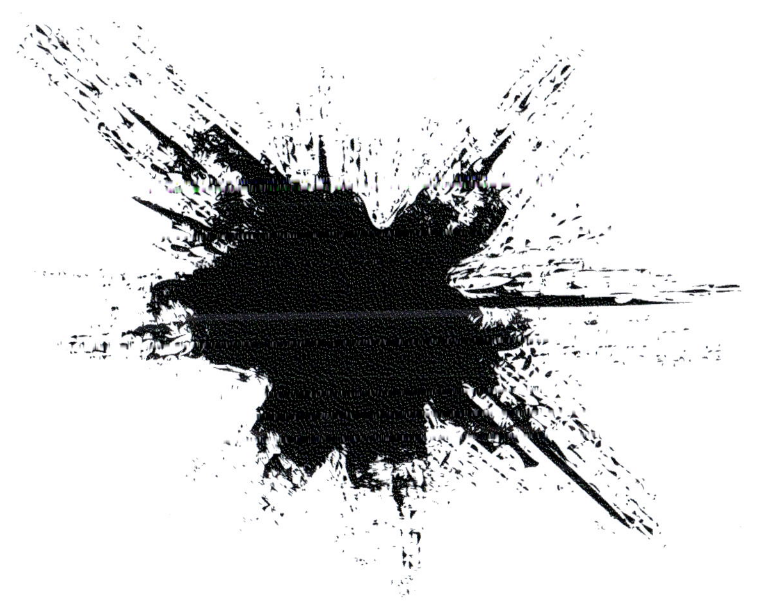

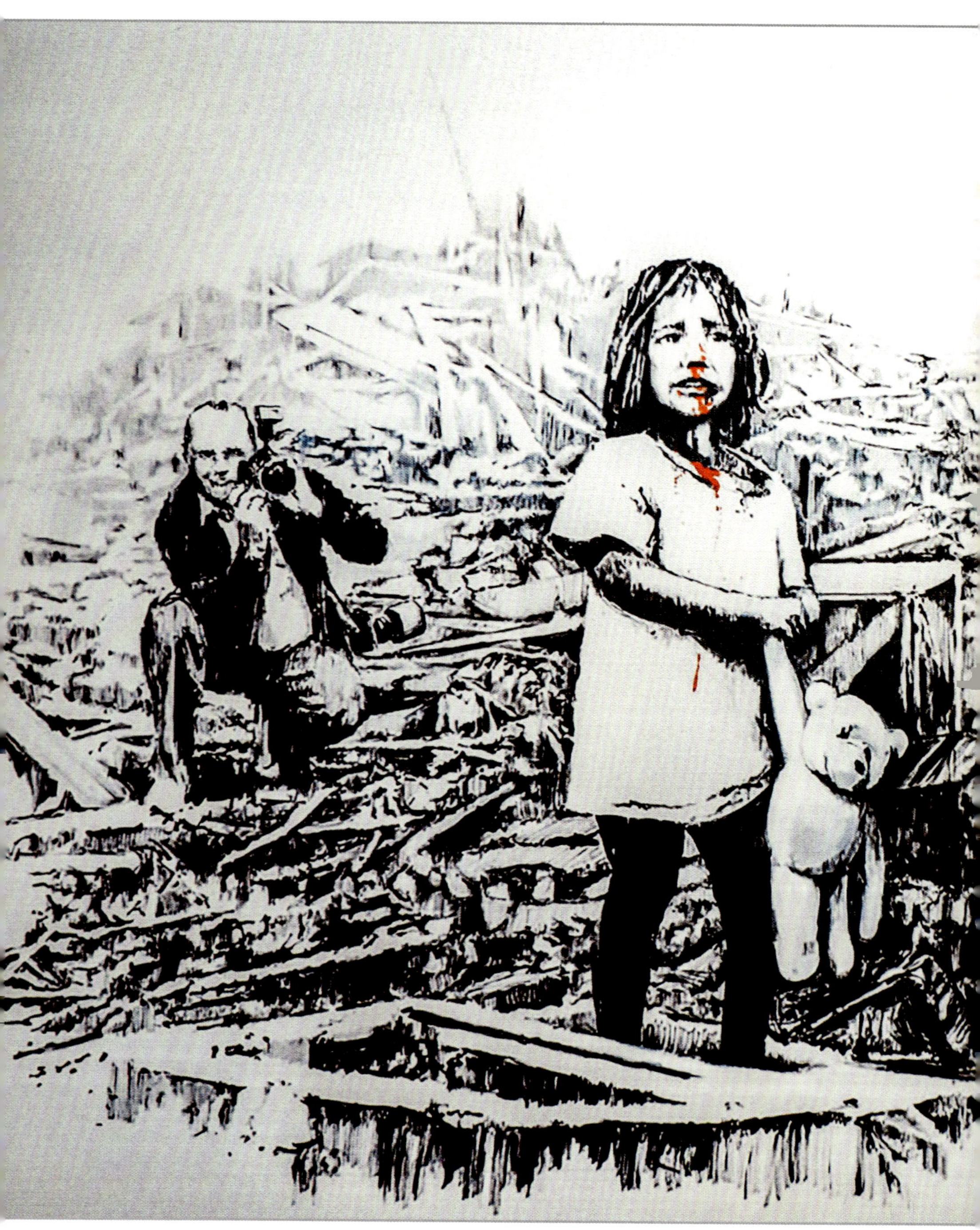

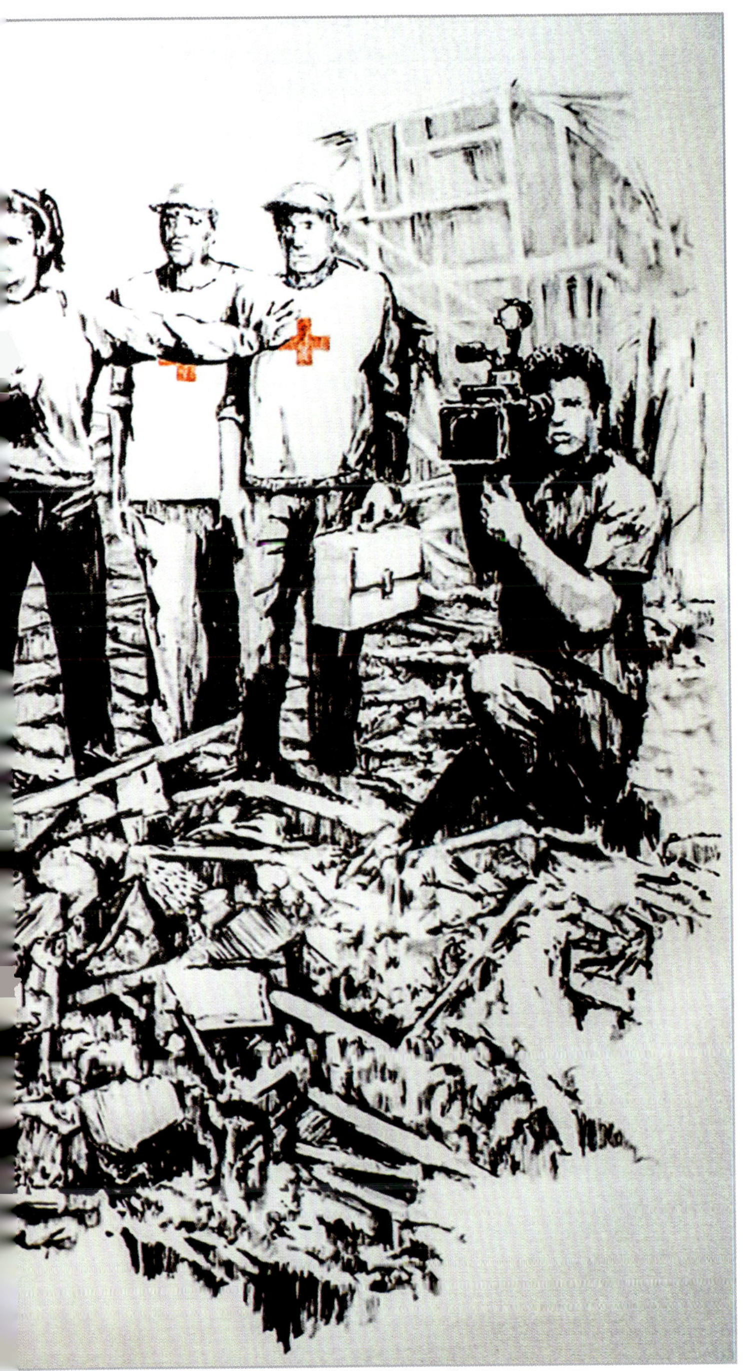

GIRL WITH FILM CREW – 2006

AS IN A MOVIE, A WOUNDED LITTLE GIRL IS WALKING OVER THE RUBBLE. BEHIND HER BACK, A MOVIE CREW CONTINUES ITS WORK WITH TRAGIC INDIFFERENCE AND INCREDIBLE CYNICISM.

IN BORODIANKA, A YOUNG JUDOKA KNOCKS A GIANT PUTIN OUT, THUS BECOMING THE SYMBOL OF UKRAINIAN RESISTANCE AGAINST THE RUSSIAN INVASION OF FEBRUARY 24, 2022.

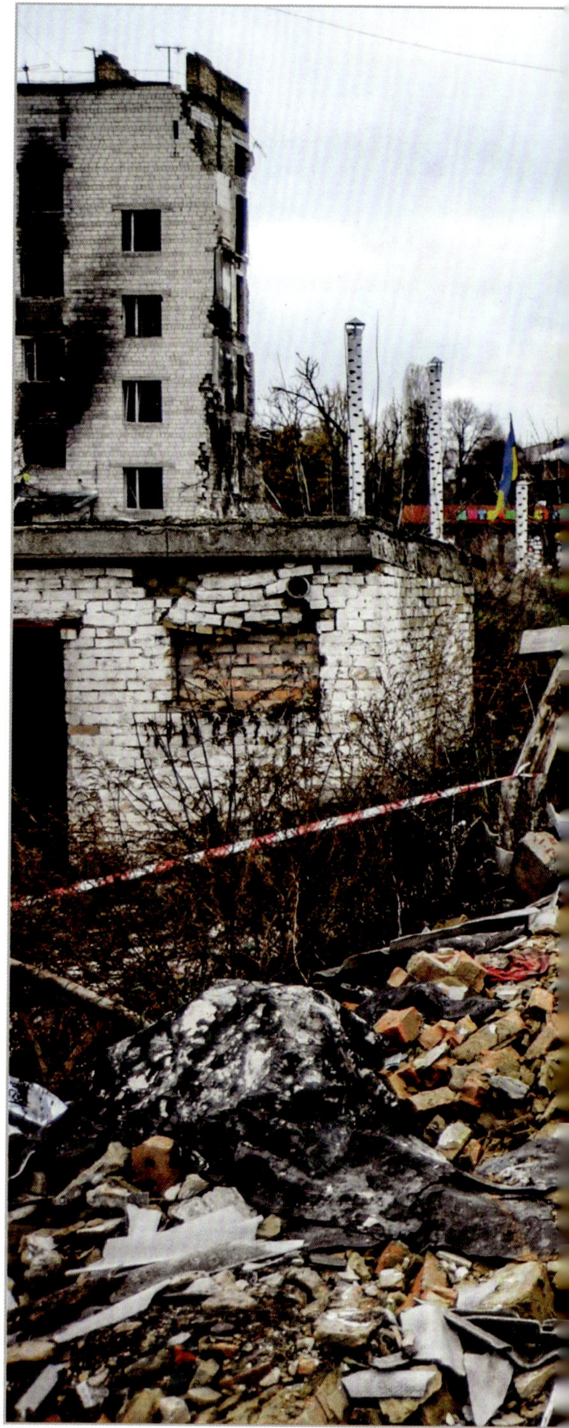

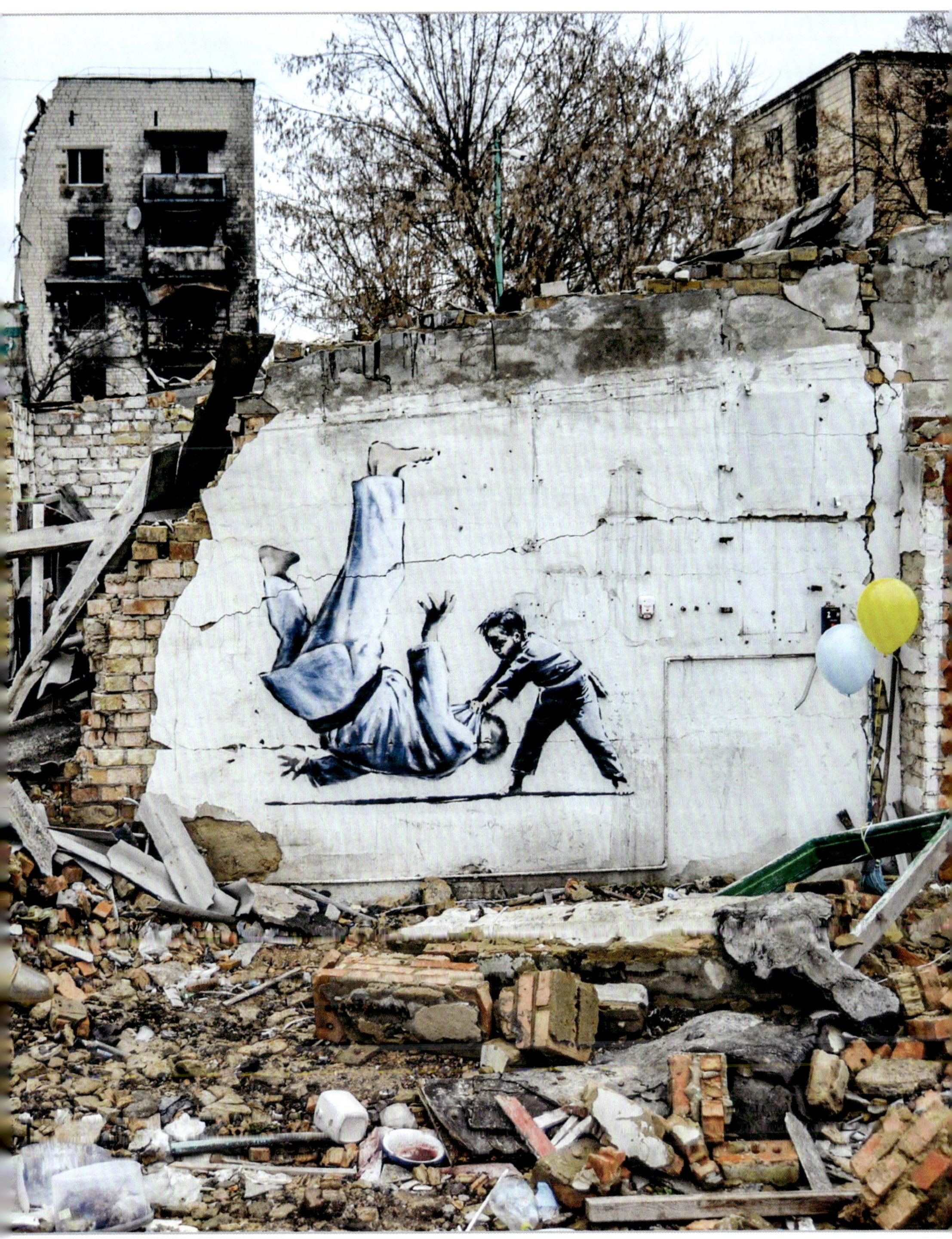

IT'S 2016 AND THE YOUNG COSETTE FROM VICTOR HUGO'S LES MISÉRABLES IS CRYING BECAUSE OF A TEAR GAS CLOUD. THE FRENCH FLAG RIPPED TO SHREDS STANDS OUT IN THE BACKGROUND. A QR CODE SHOWS A VIDEO SHOT IN CALAIS DURING A POLICE RAID AGAINST MIGRANTS.

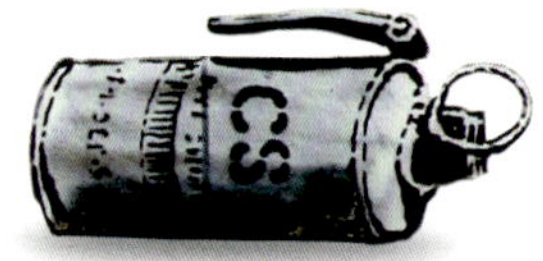

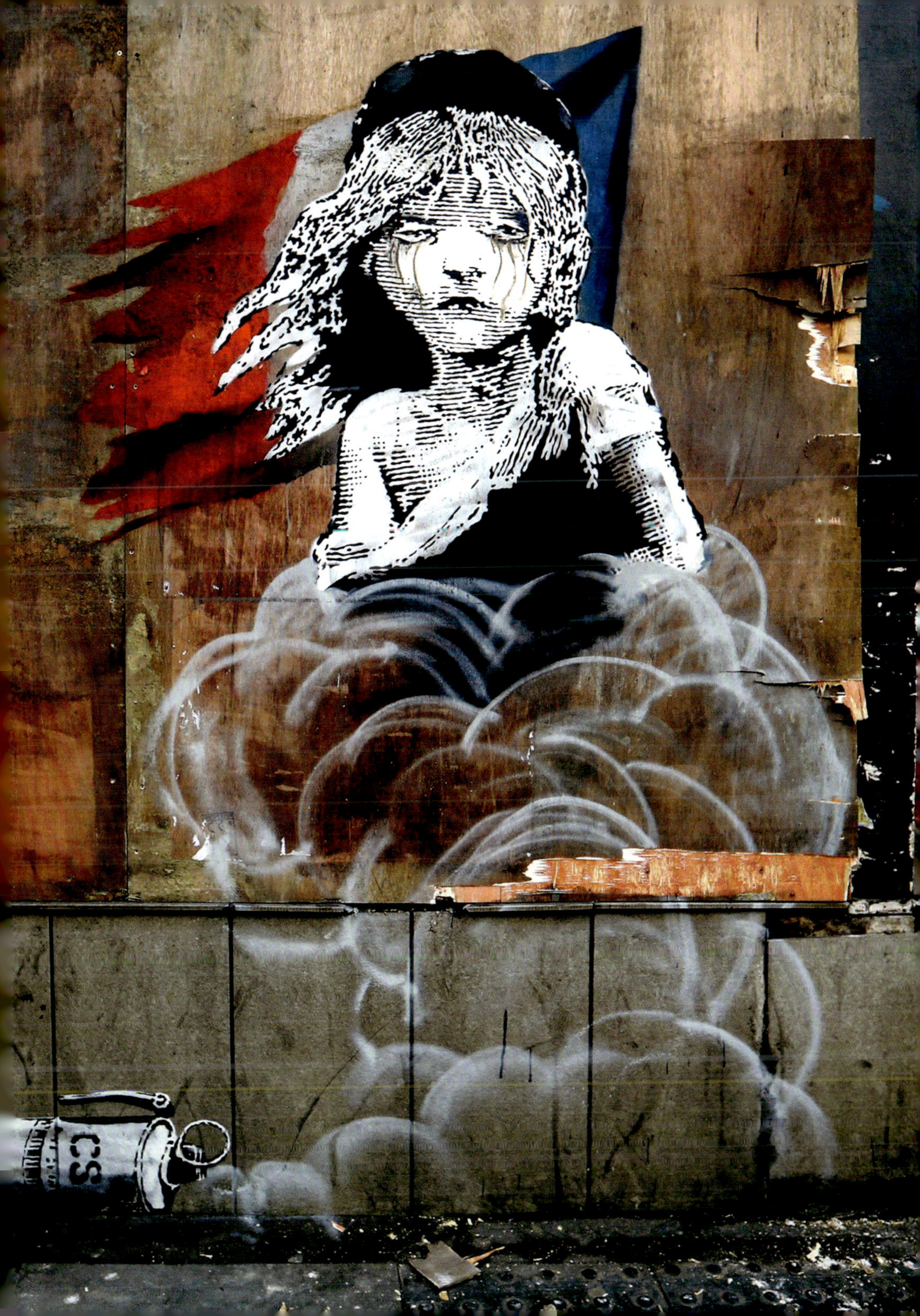
CS

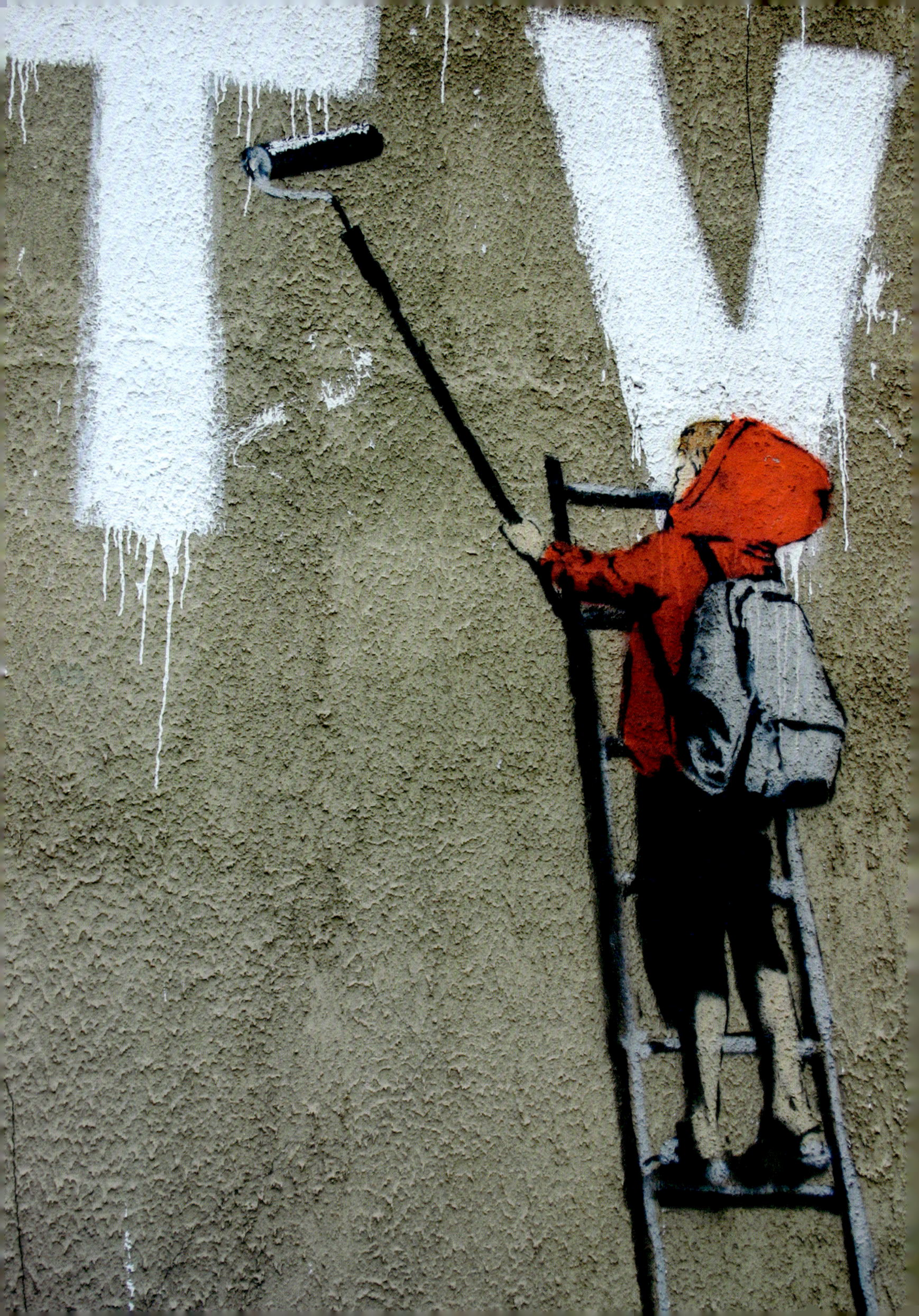

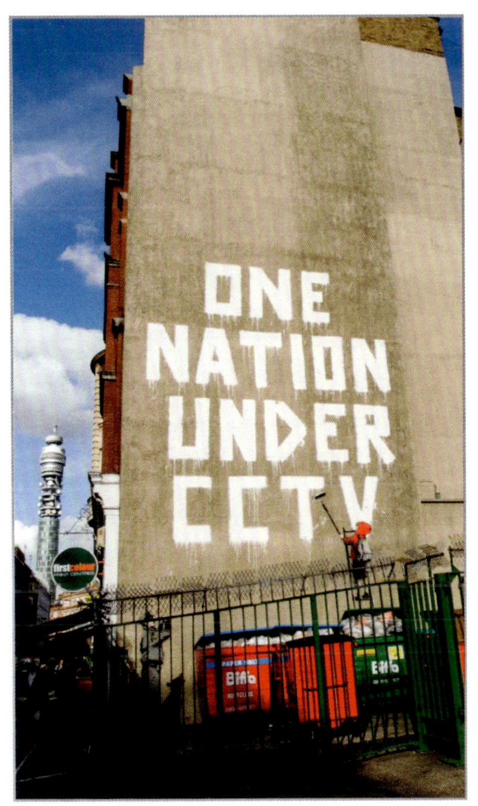

*WE ARE NEVER ALONE: ONE NATION UNDER CCTV –
NEWMAN STREET, LONDON, 2007*

A LITTLE BOY IS PAINTING "ONE NATION UNDER CCTV" ON A
ROYAL MAIL BUILDING WHILE BEING WATCHED BY A POLICE
OFFICER, A CLEAR CRITIQUE OF EXCESSIVE GOVERNMENT
CONTROL. IT IS NO COINCIDENCE THIS GRAFFITI WORK WAS
PAINTED NEXT TO A SECURITY CAMERA.

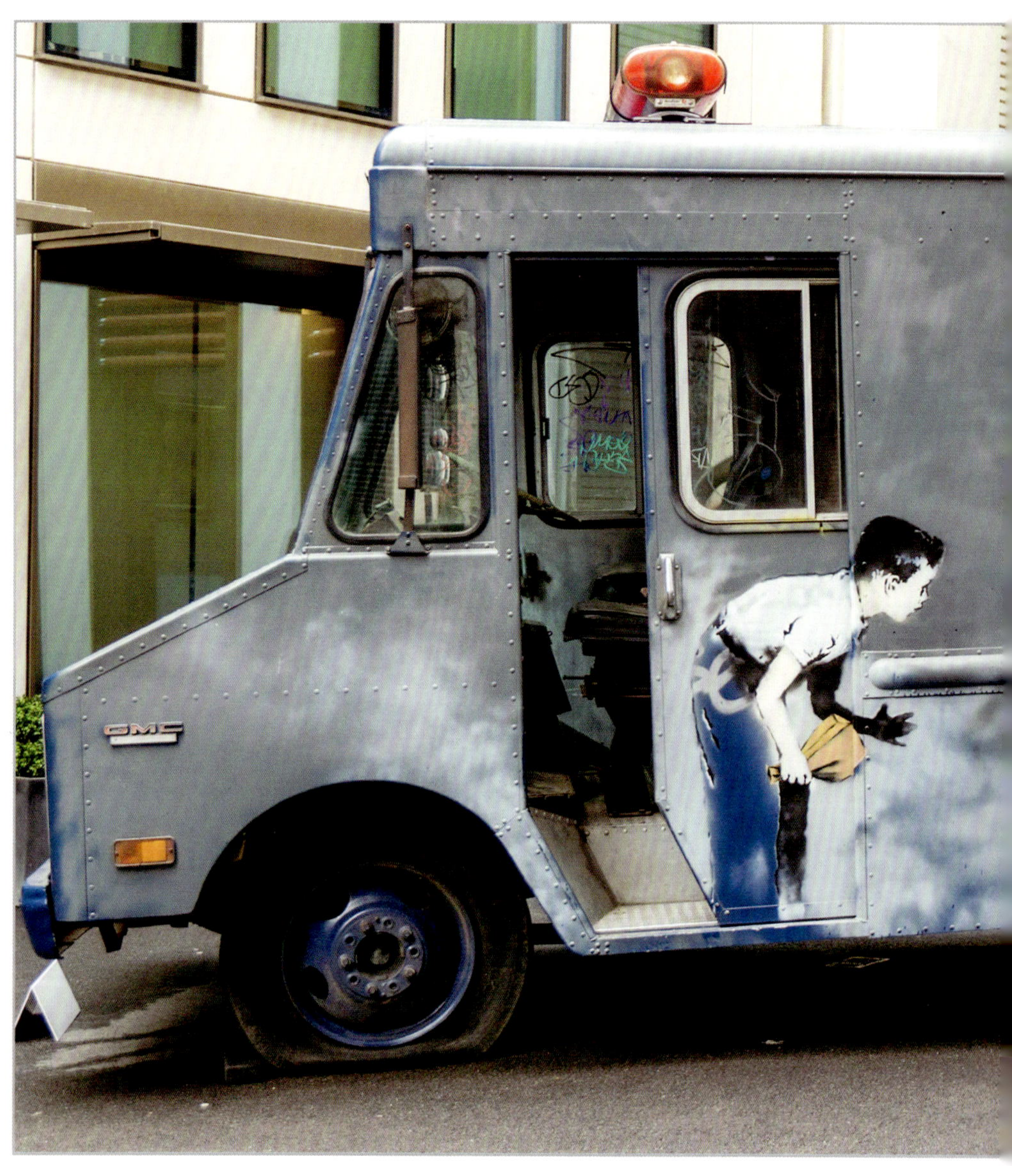

SWAT VAN - LOS ANGELES, 2006

A SWAT TEAM, STANDING READY, IS BEING HOODWINKED BY A LITTLE BOY.

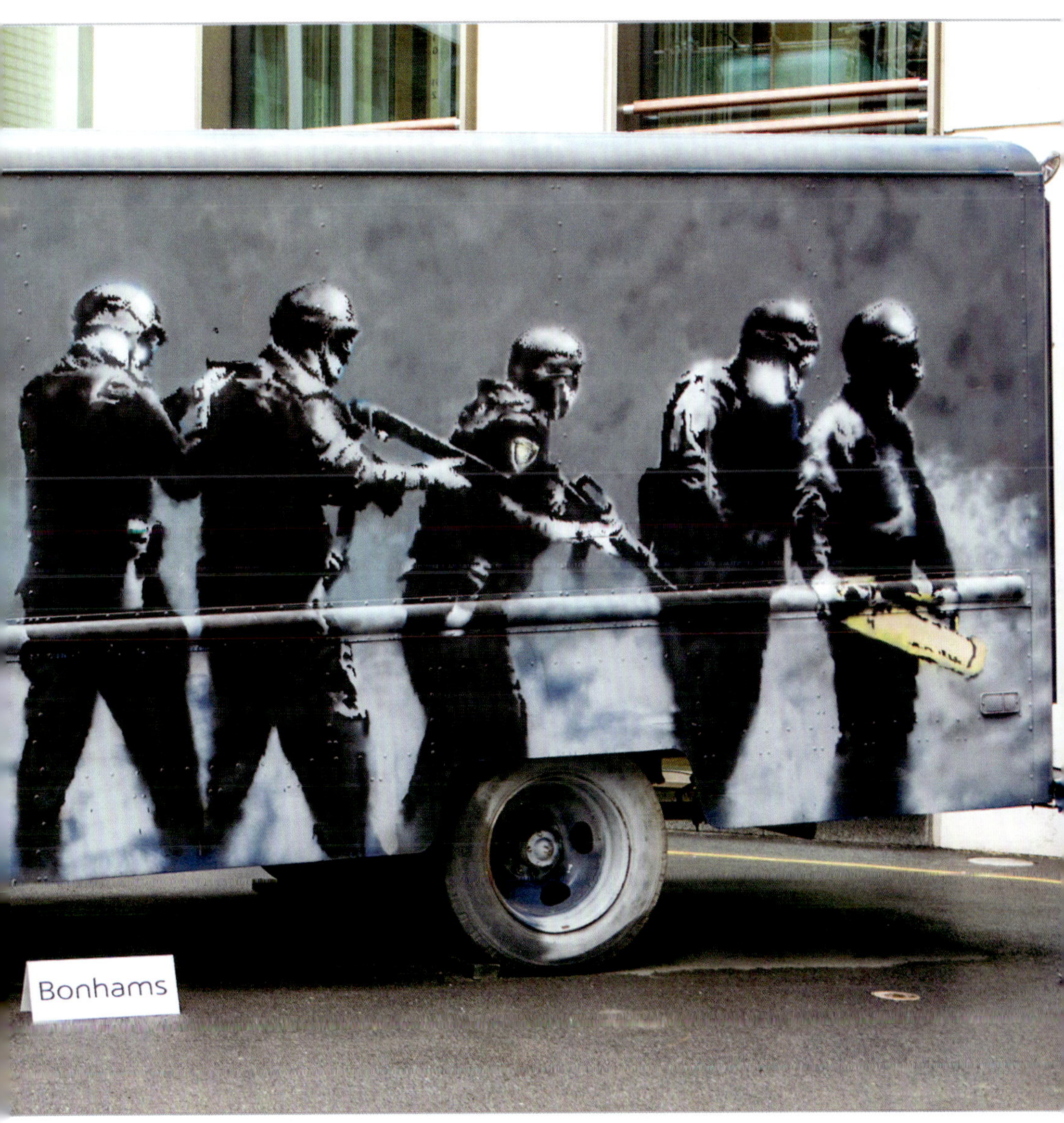

GHETTO 4 LIFE – BRONX, NEW YORK, 2013

84–85 A WORK OF GRAFFITI "SERVED ON A PLATE OF PROVOCATIONS"!

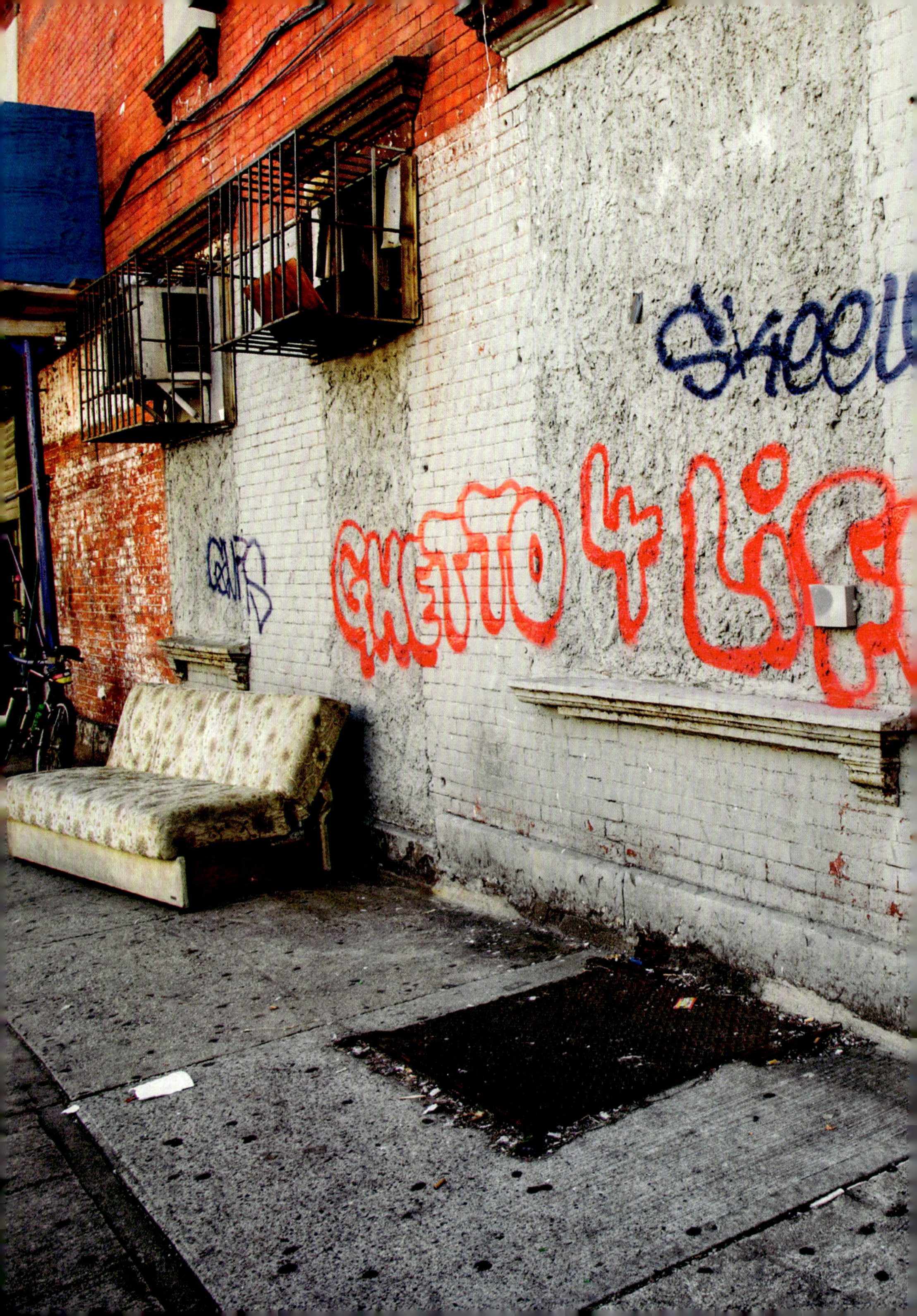

GHETTO 4 LIFE

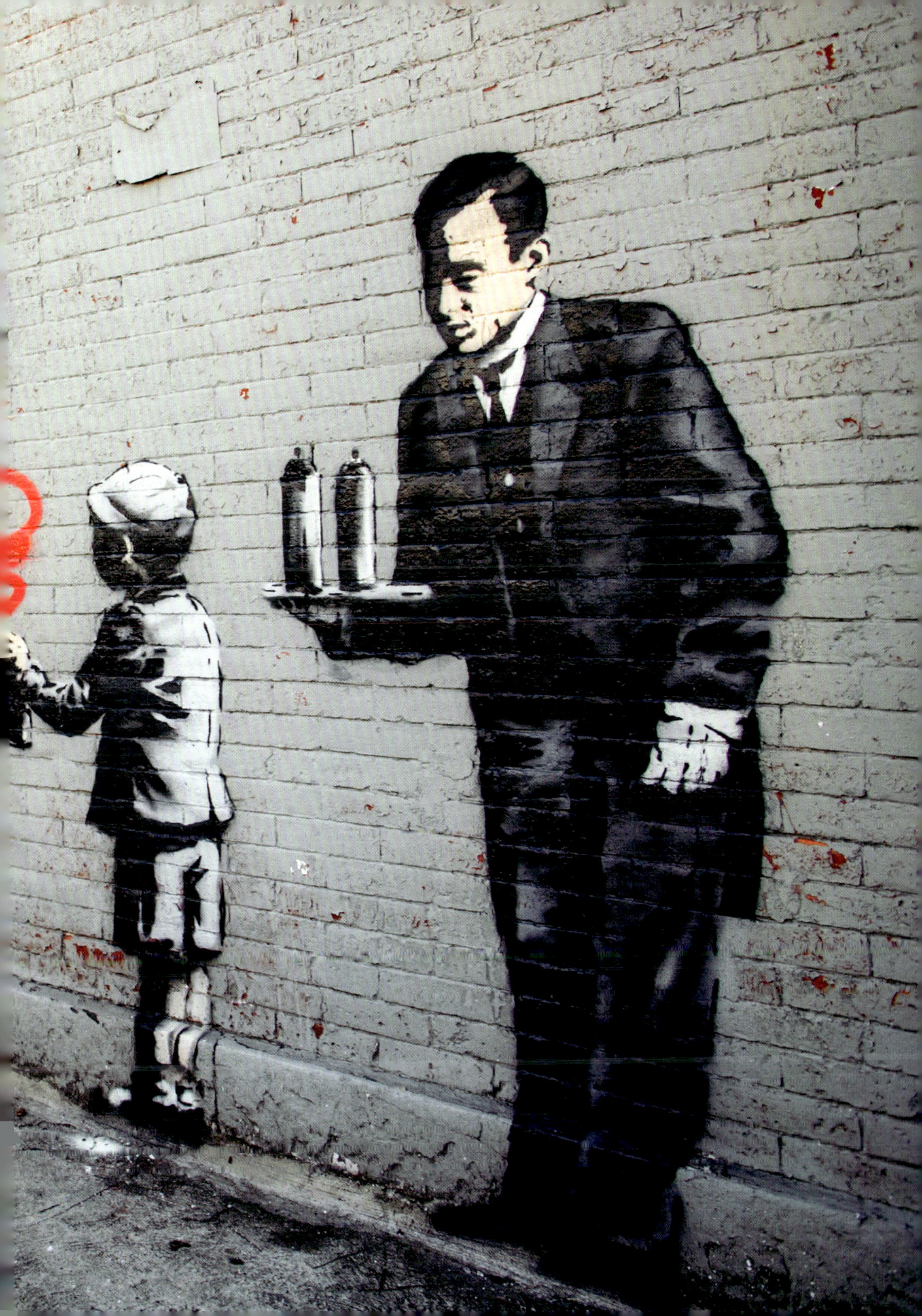

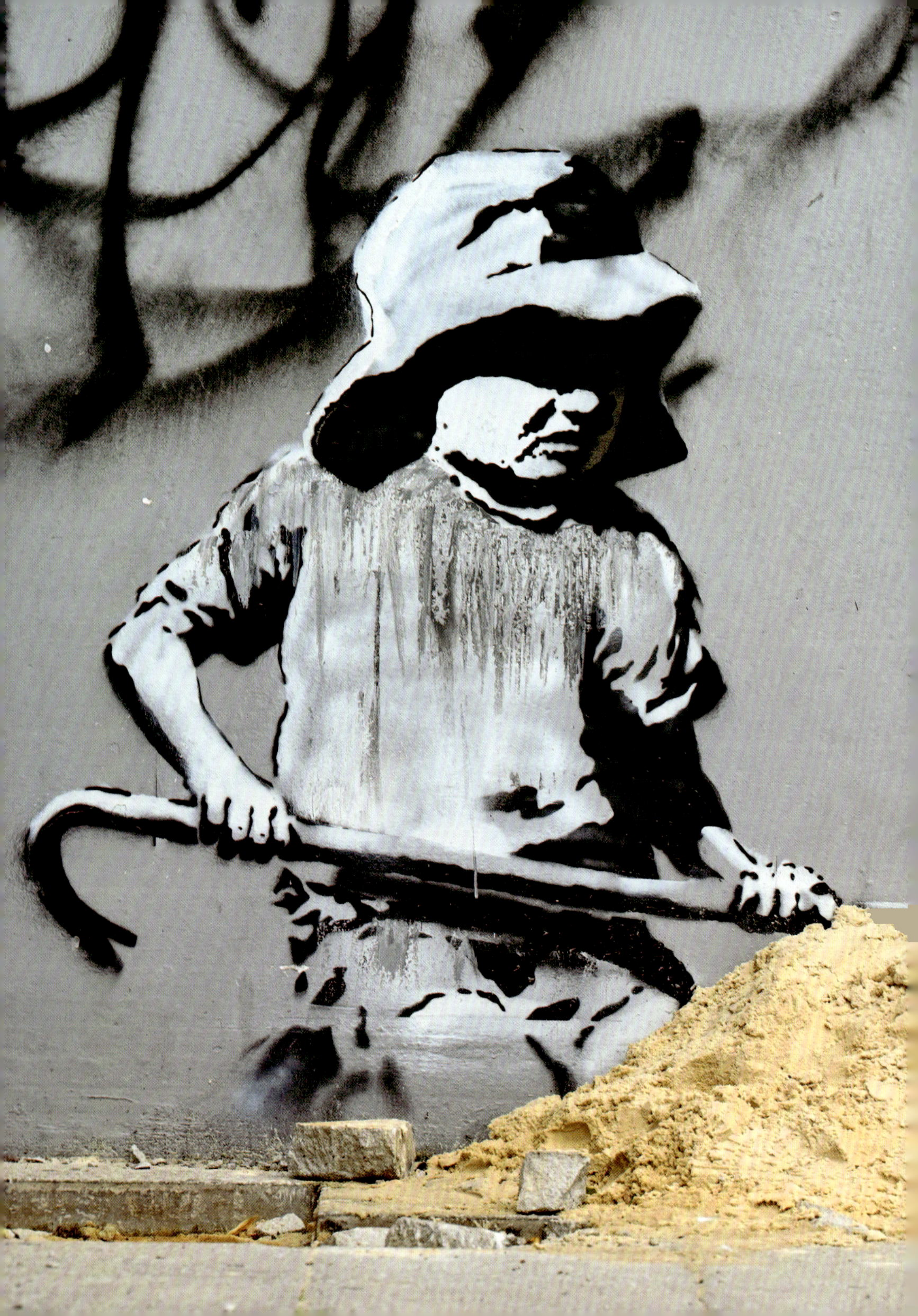

THIS WORK ORIGINALLY PORTRAYED A CHILD HOLDING A CROWBAR IN HIS HANDS WITH A SANDCASTLE IN FRONT OF HIM.

88–89 A CLEAR AND SAD WARNING MESSAGE IS SENT OUT BY THIS DISHEARTENED LITTLE GIRL HOLDING A RED BALLOON THAT IS ALSO THE LETTER O IN THE WORD "NO."

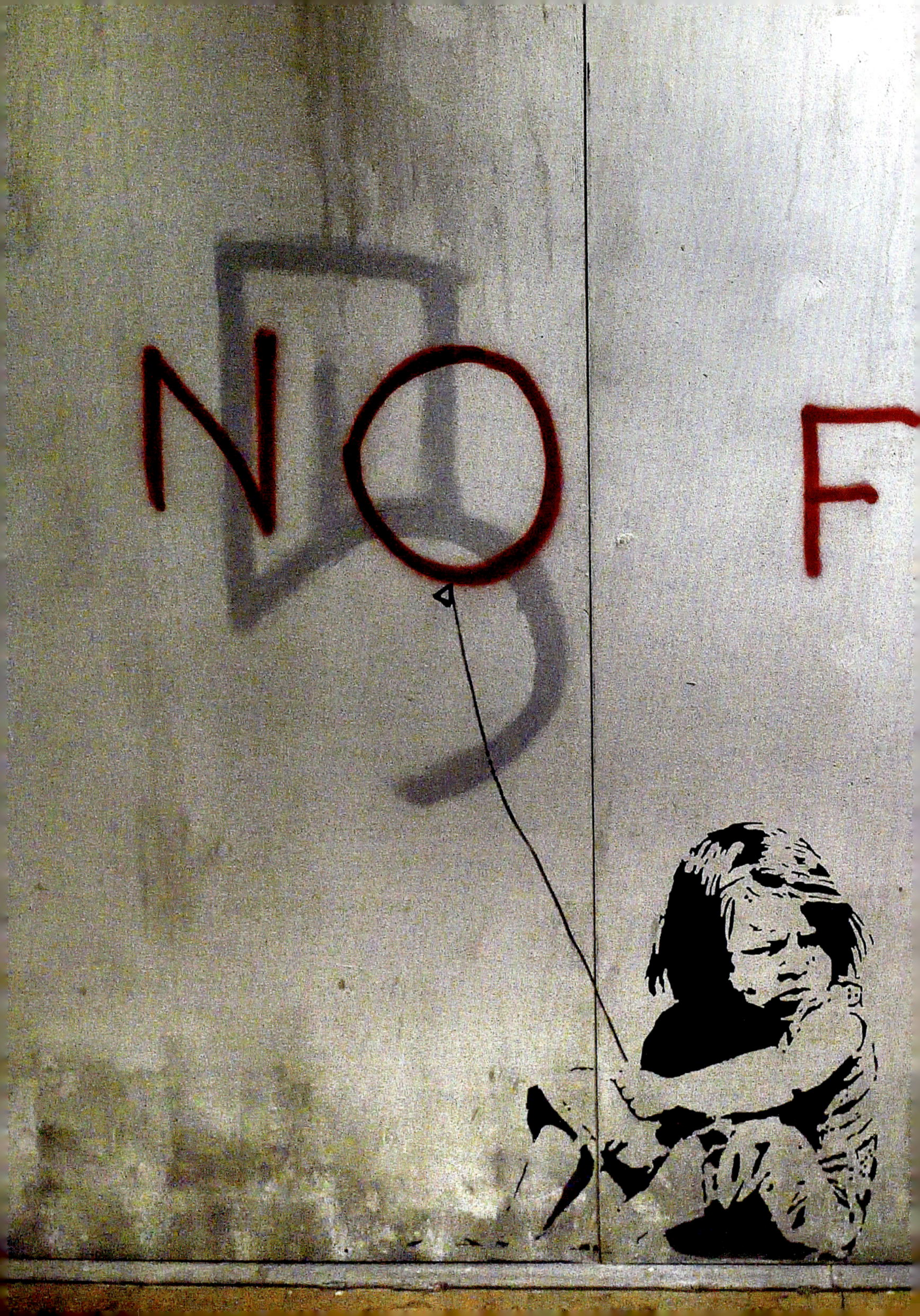

NO
F

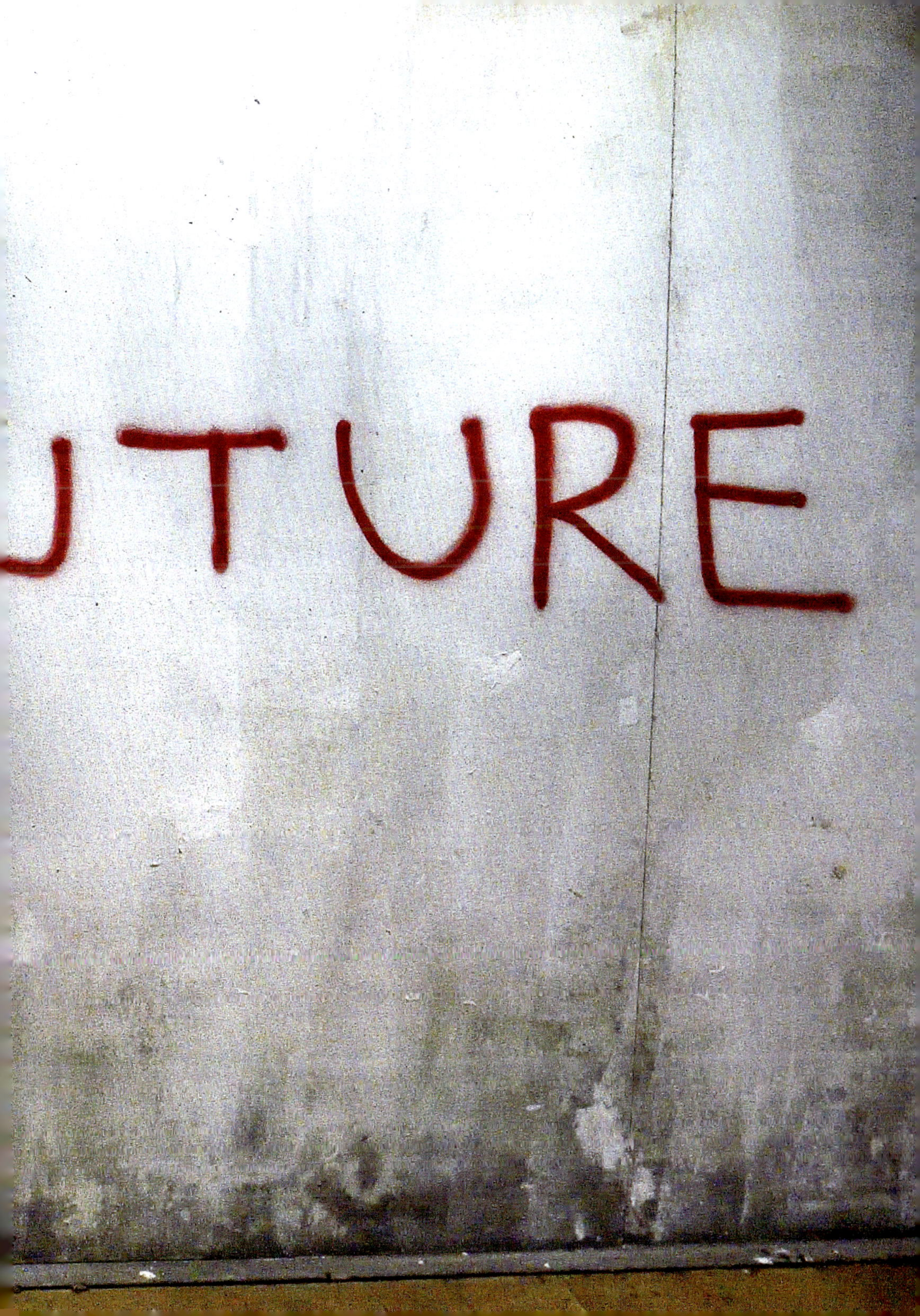

UTURE

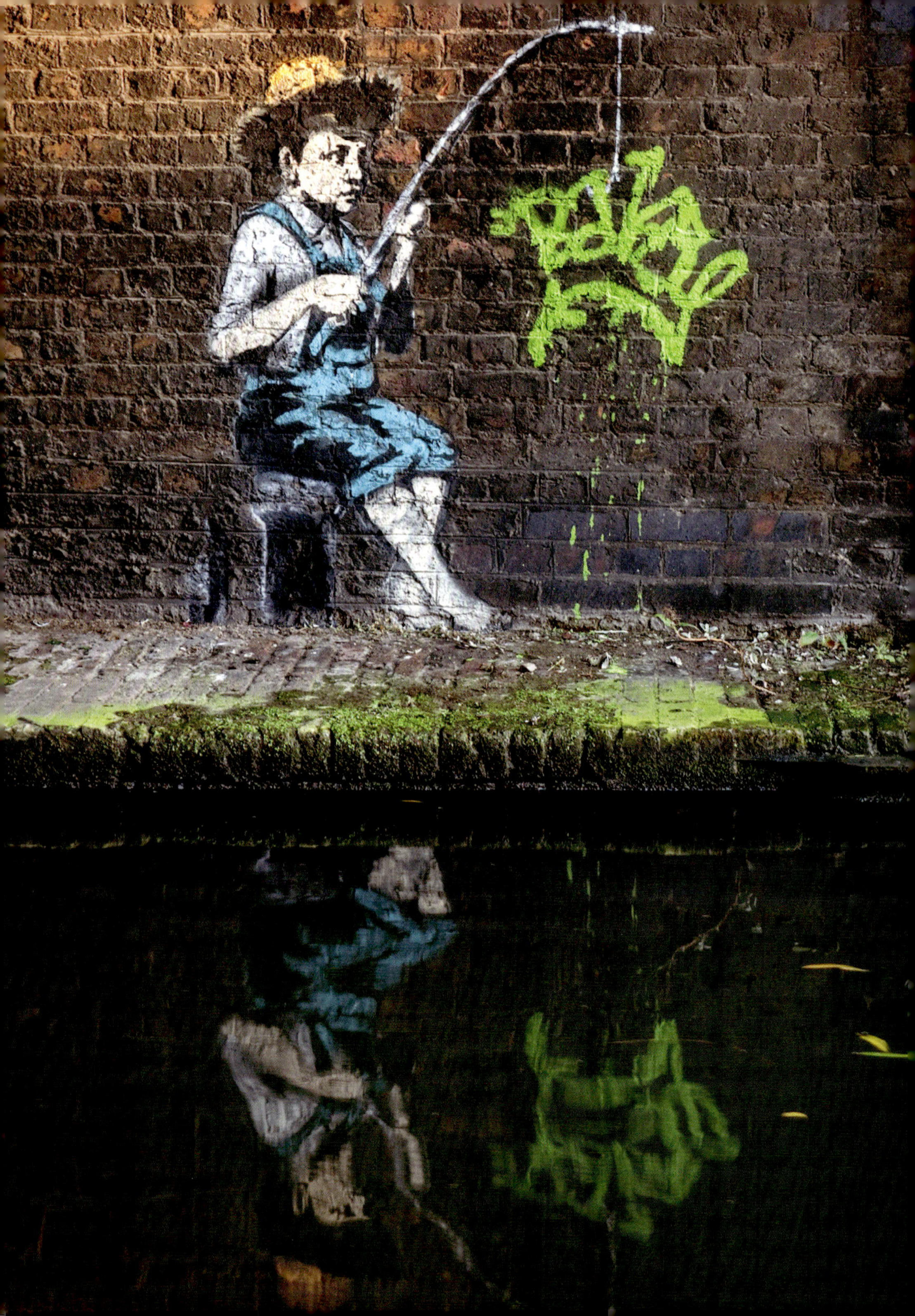

ALONG REGENT'S CANAL IN CAMDEN, LONDON, A YOUNG BOY HAS CAUGHT BANKSY'S TAG. THE FATE OF THIS GRAFFITI WORK IS TIED TO THE FAMOUS "WAR" AGAINST THE ROBBO TEAM, WHICH VANDALIZED THIS WORK BY COVERING IT WITH A PAINTED SIGN READING "STREET CRED."

92–93 THROUGH THE IMAGE OF A REFUGEE CHILD, BANKSY EXPRESSES THE POWER OF ART TO SURVIVE THE DESTRUCTIVE PHENOMENA OF CLIMATE CHANGE. HE ALSO AIMS AT RAISING AWARENESS ON THE LIVING CONDITIONS OF THE MOST DISADVANTAGED PEOPLE, OFTEN FORCED TO LEAVE THEIR HOMELAND TO SURVIVE.

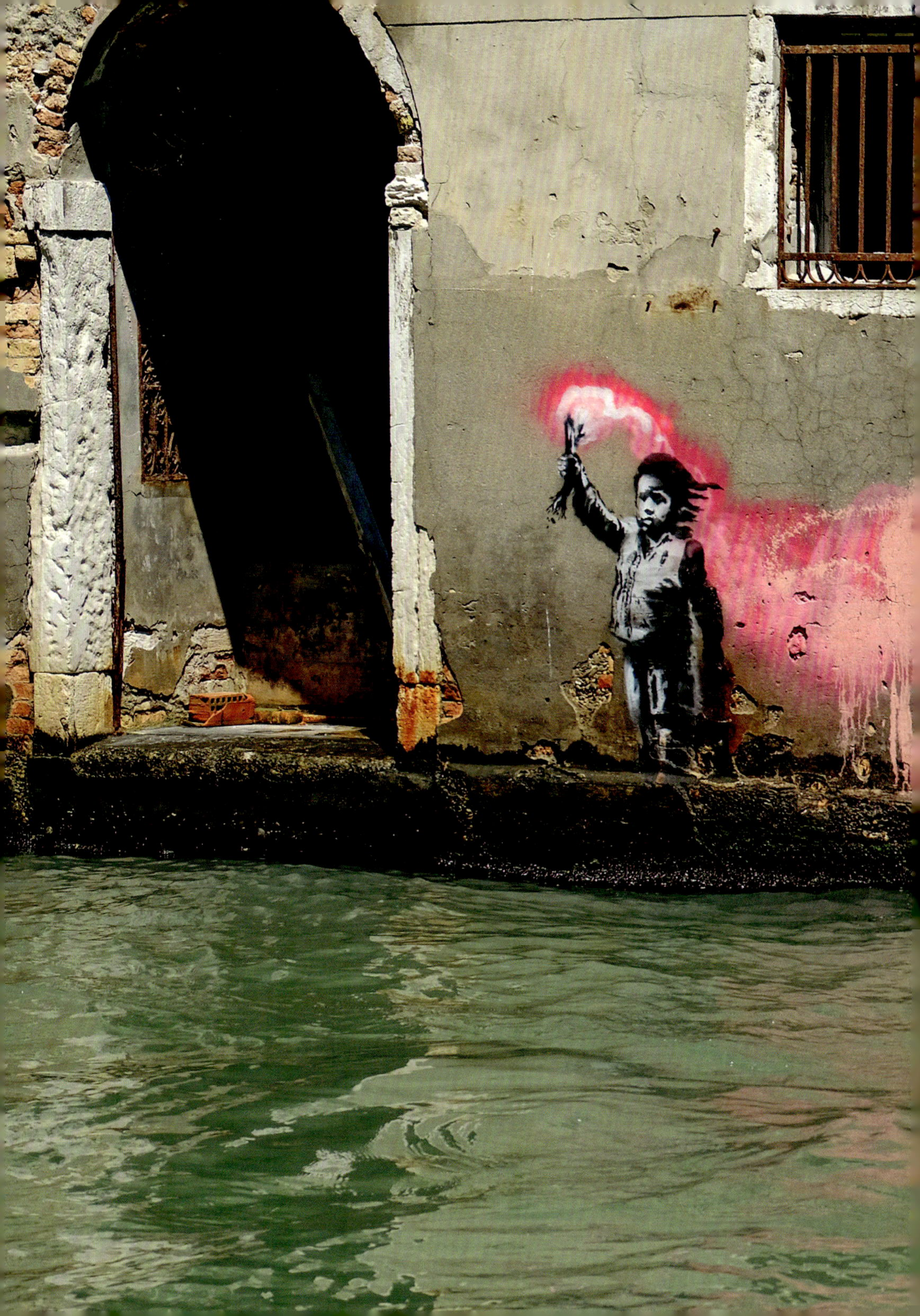

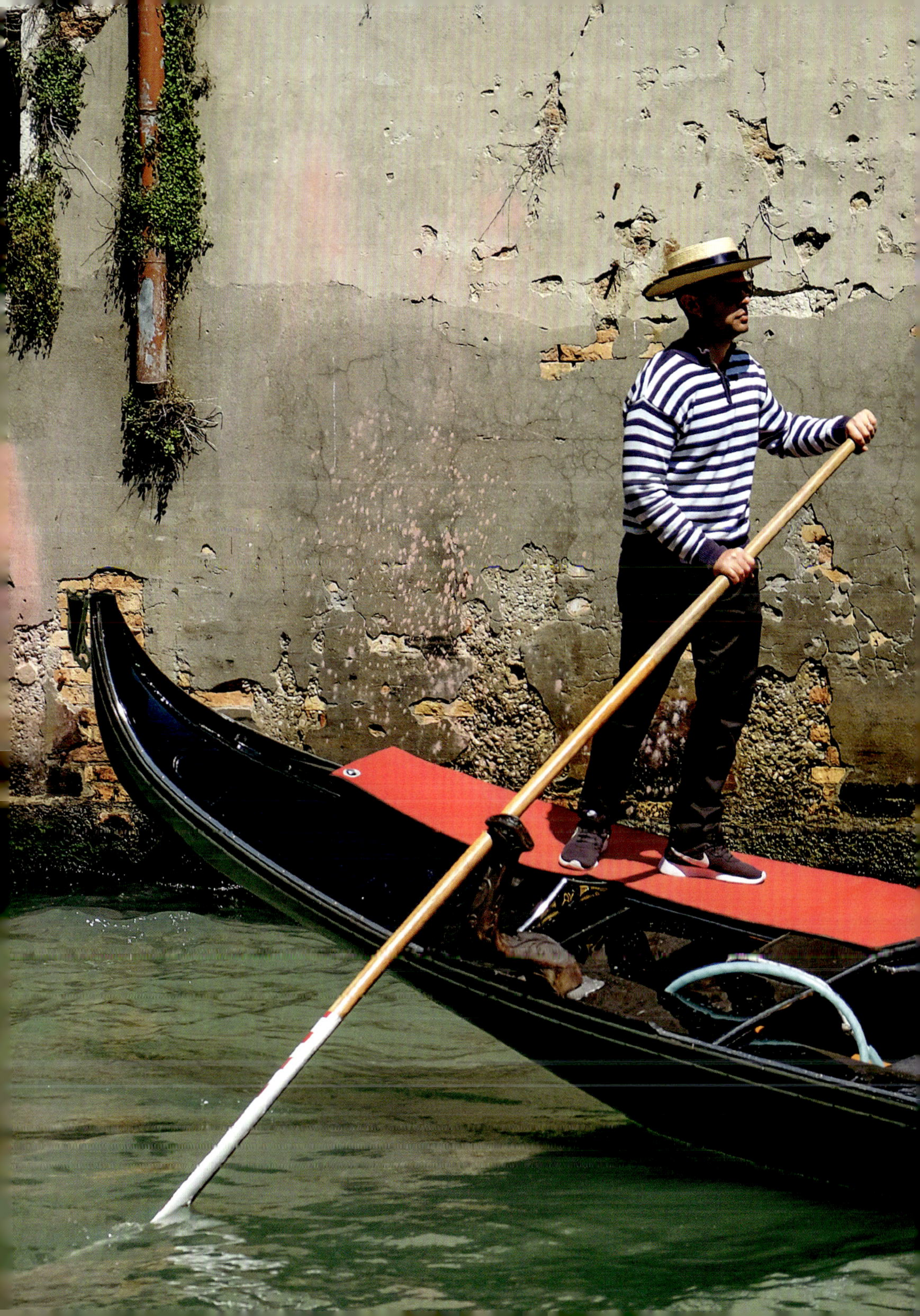

ABOUT THE AUTHOR

ALESSANDRA MATTANZA is a multi-award-winning writer and journalist, screenwriter, fine art photographer, and multimedia artist, and she lives between Munich, New York, San Francisco, Los Angeles, and Paris. She has collaborated with several magazines, including *Forbes, Vanity Fair, Elle, Cosmopolitan, How to Spend It, Icon, F,* and *Natural Style,* and she also writes novels and murder mysteries for several publishing houses. She won several awards for best articles and books at the Annual Southern California Journalism Awards and the SoCal Journalism Awards, in Los Angeles. Among the many awards she has received, she also won first prize in the nonfiction category for the books *C215 #christianguemy: Stencil Art* and the first *Banksy* book, and third prize for *Street Art: 20 Famous Artists Talk About Their Vision.* As an artist, she created the projects and media campaigns *www.newyorkblackandwhite.org,* exhibited at the Kunstlabor 2 museum, linked to the MUCA Museum in Munich, and *www.abetterplanetabetterworld.com,* presented in a major exhibition at the United Nations Headquarters of New York in 2023 and at the Italian Mission to the UN in New York until 2025. This last project for the environment was inspired by the book *SOS Planet Earth: Voices for a Better World,* published by National Geographic and White Star.

ABOUT THE CAPTIONS AUTHOR

LUCA GRECO is a copywriter, social media manager, and art blogger. After graduating in philosophy and completing a master's degree in marketing and communication from the IED in Turin, he collaborated with important communication agencies in Turin. An attentive observer of reality, Luca loves sharing his way of interpreting it by constantly experimenting with new forms of digital communication on his news and cultural study blog called "Fatti e Fabulae" (www.fattiefabulae.com). He is currently a copywriter and social media manager for a leading Italian digital experience company. Since 2022, he has been a social media management professor, teaching a course in Social Innovation, Communication, and New Technologies at the University of Turin.

PHOTO CREDITS

PAGE 1 Matthias Wehnert/Alamy Stock Photo

PAGES 2-3 Peter Harvie/Alamy Stock Photo

PAGE 5 PA Images/Alamy Stock Photo

PAGES 7, 9, 11 Marco Di Lauro/Getty Images

PAGES 12-13 Leigh Green/Alamy Stock Photo

PAGES 14-15 basphoto/123RF

PAGES 16-17 Ted Soqui Getty Images

PAGES 18-19 Ted Soqui/Getty Images

PAGES 20-21 Stefano Baldini/Alamy Stock Photo

PAGES 22-23 Marco Di Lauro/Getty Images

PAGES 24-25 Marco Di Lauro/Getty Images

PAGES 26-27 imageBROKER.com GmbH & Co. KG/ Alamy Stock Photo

PAGE 28 Julian Anderson/Alamy Stock Photo

PAGES 30-31 Julian Anderson Alamy Stock Photo

PAGE 32 Erik Pendzich Alamy Stock Photo

PAGES 34-35 Erik Pendzich/Alamy Stock Photo

PAGE 37 Rune Hellestad – Corbis/Getty Images

PAGES 38-39 Louis Berk/Alamy Stock Photo

PAGE 40 Coaster/Alamy Stock Photo

PAGES 42-43 Aflo Co. Ltd./Alamy Stock Photo

PAGES 44-45 Richard Levine/Alamy Stock Photo

PAGES 46-47 Philippe Lopez/Getty Images

PAGES 48-49 Phillip Roberts/Alamy Stock Photo

PAGES 50-51 Jamie Lorriman/Alamy Stock Photo

PAGES 52-53 Erik Pendzich/Alamy Stock Photo

PAGE 54 Erik Pendzich/Alamy Stock Photo

PAGE 55 Jan Fritz/Alamy Stock Photo

PAGES 56-57 Matthias Kestel/Alamy Stock Photo

PAGES 58-59 Dan De Kleined Alamy Stock Photo

PAGES 60-61 Gavin Rodgers/Alamy Stock Photo

PAGES 62-63 Graham Bridgeman-Clarke/Alamy Stock Photo

PAGES 64-65 PA Images/Alamy Stock Photo

PAGE 66 dpa picture alliance/Alamy Stock Photo

PAGE 68 Matthias Kestel/Alamy Stock Photo

PAGE 69 James Anderson/Alamy Stock Photo

PAGES 70-71 Matthias Kestel/Alamy Stock Photo

PAGES 72-73 Malcolm Park/Alamy Stock Photo

PAGE 73 LoremIpsumART/Shutterstock

PAGES 74-75 Matthias Kestel/Alamy Stock Photo

PAGES 76-77 Sipa USA/Alamy Stock Photo

PAGES 78-79 Carl Court/Getty Images

PAGE 80 Chris Wood/Alamy Stock Photo

PAGE 81 Mark Phillips/Alamy Stock Photo

PAGES 82-83 ukartpics/Alamy Stock Photo

PAGES 84-85 Frances Roberts/Alamy Stock Photo

PAGES 86-87 Justin Tallis/Getty Images

PAGES 88-89 Mondadori Portfolio/Getty Images

PAGE 90 Martyn Goddard/Alamy Stock Photo

PAGES 92-93 NurPhoto/Getty Images

SLIPCASE Michelle Hulmes - Art/Alamy Photo Stock

COVER MK Vienna/Alamy Photo Stock

BACK COVER Richard Levine/Alamy Photo Stock

Project Handling: Weiß-Freiburg GmbH – Grafik & Buchgestaltung
Translation: Carlotta Cappato
Editing: Abby Young
Editing and proofreading: John Stilwell
Editorial Direction at Prestel: Curt Holtz
Production at Prestel: Martina Effaga

Printed in China

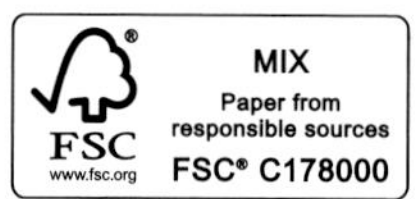

ISBN 978-3-7913-9309-4
www.prestel.com

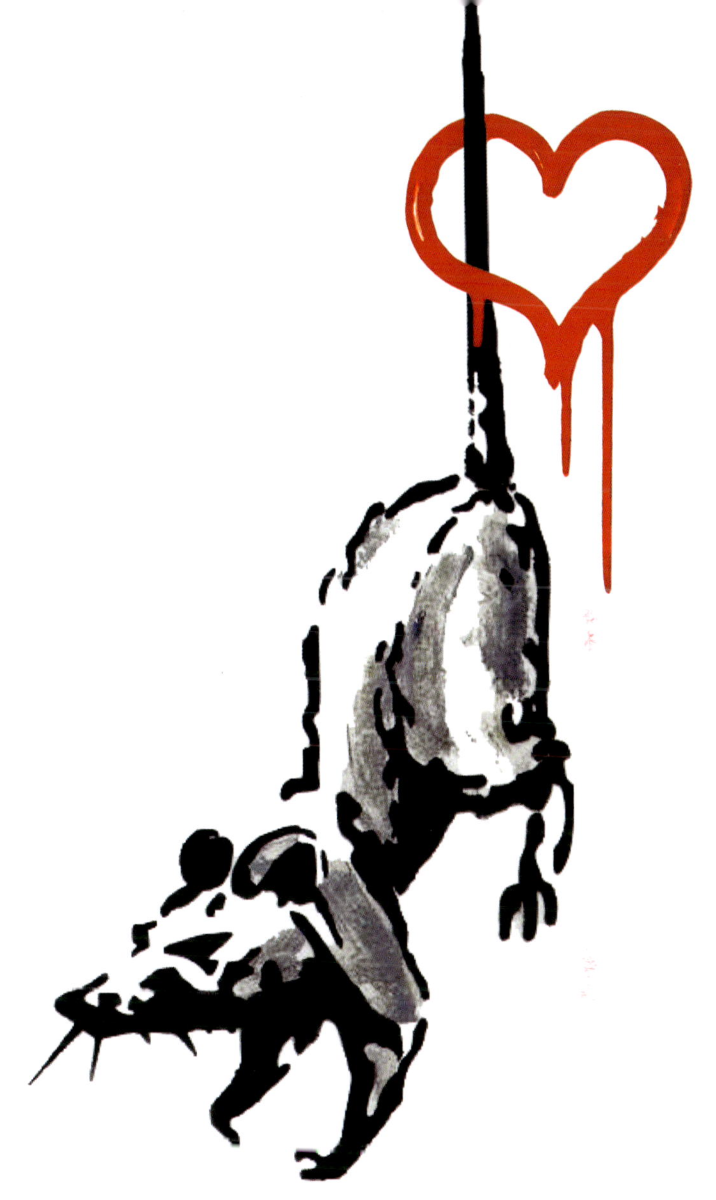

PRESTEL

MUNICH · LONDON · NEW YORK

RATS & MONKEYS

ALESSANDRA MATTANZA

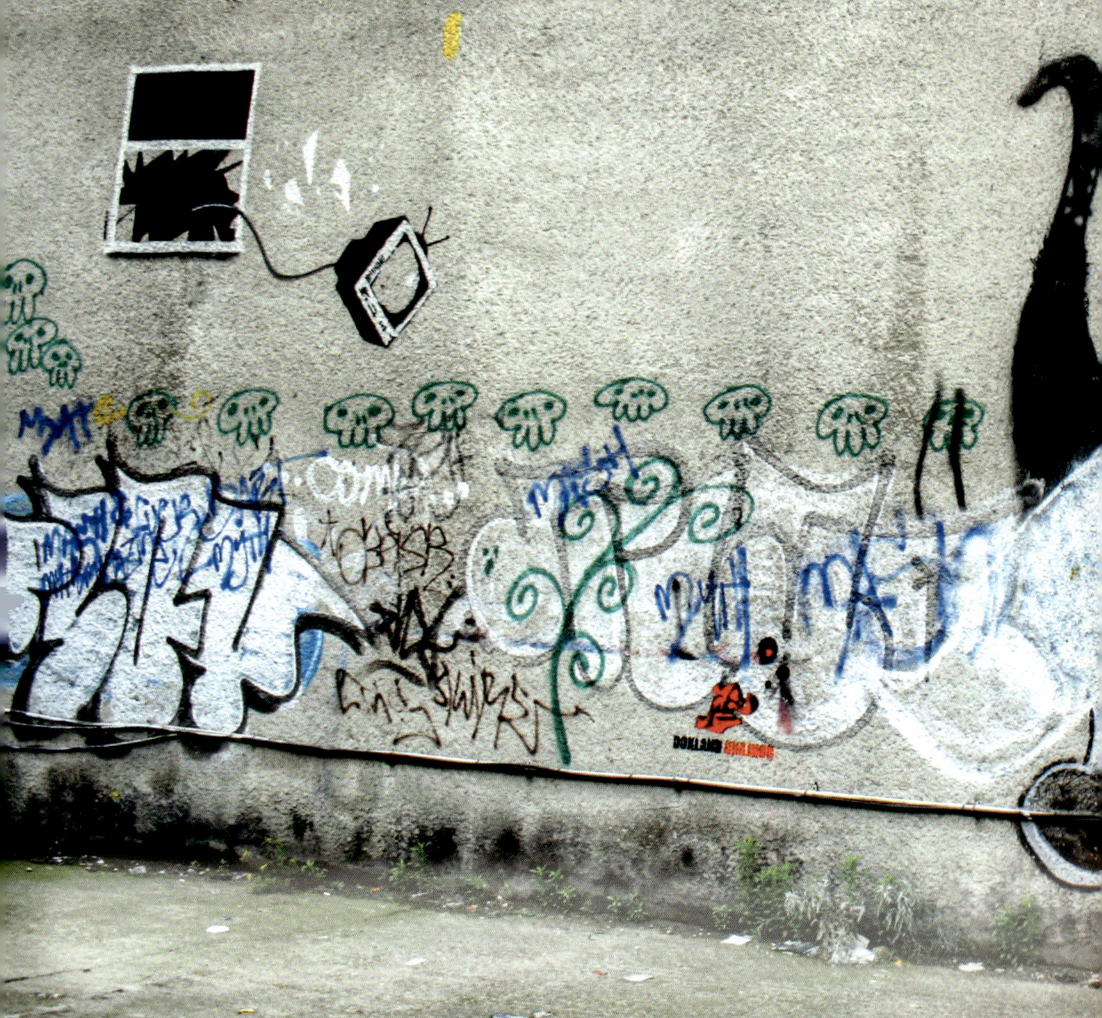

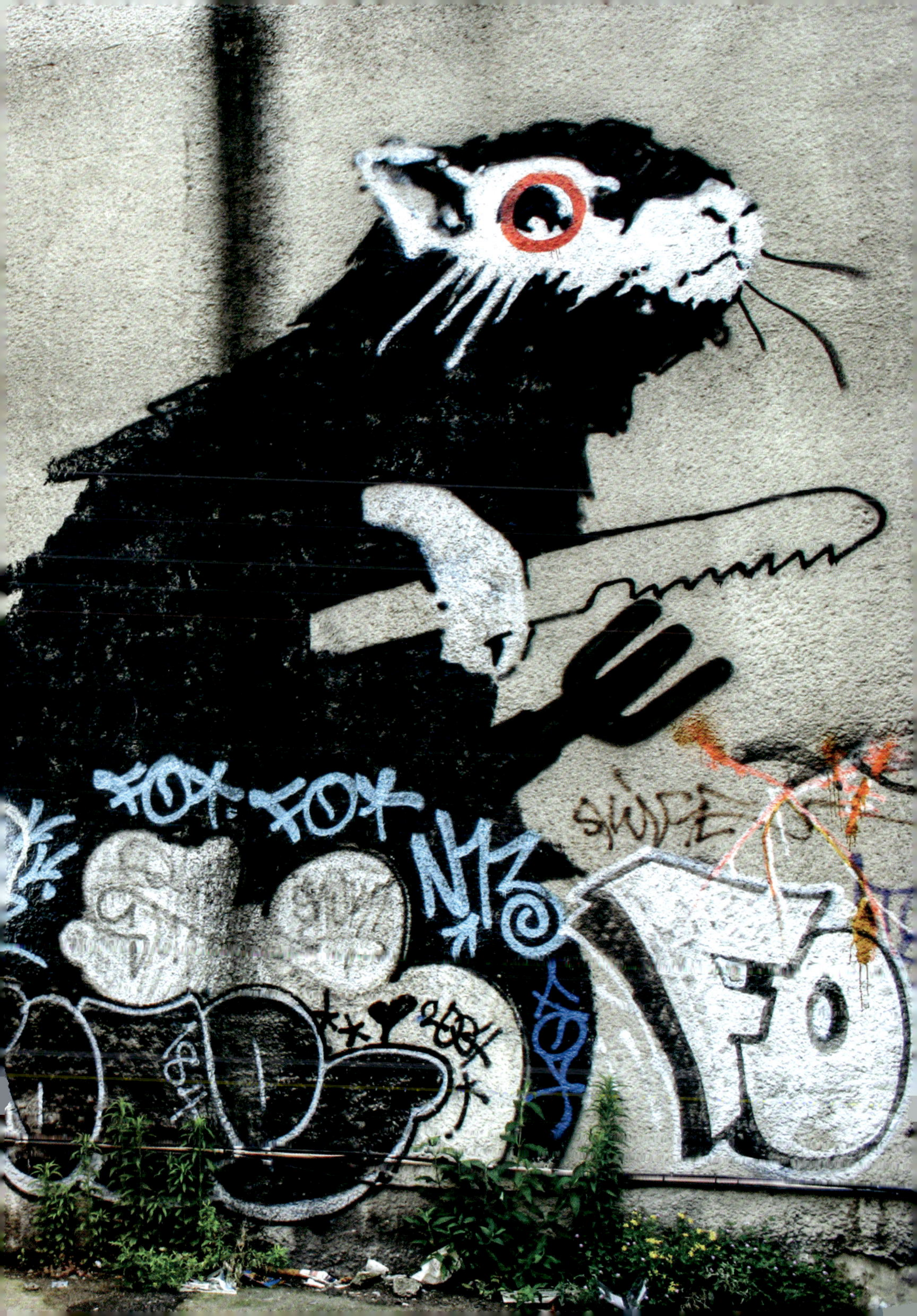

FOX FOX
SWIPE

THE ARMY OF THE INVISIBLES

"NOBODY NEAR ME HERE, BUT RATS, AND THEY ARE FINE STEALTHY SECRET FELLOWS."
CHARLES DICKENS

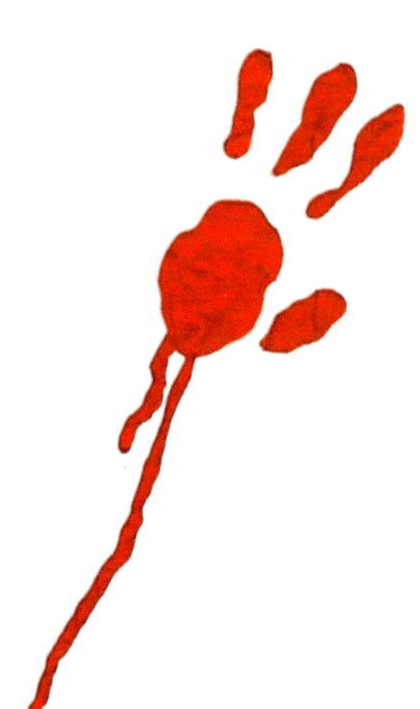

BANKSY HAS ALWAYS LOVED RATS. "RATS EXIST WITHOUT PERMISSION. THEY ARE HATED, HUNTED AND PERSECUTED. THEY LIVE IN QUIET DESPERATION AMONGST THE FILTH. AND YET THEY ARE CAPABLE OF BRINGING ENTIRE CIVILISATIONS TO THEIR KNEES," HE STRESSED. IT'S NO SURPRISE ANYWAY, BECAUSE, IF YOU DIG DEEP ENOUGH, YOU WILL FIND THAT BANKSY AND RATS HAVE A LOT IN COMMON.

Rats are shy, quiet, alert, and very intelligent. They move at night, while everyone else is sleeping. They hide in the walls, on street corners, underground—they can sneak into the smallest holes, taking advantage of the flexibility of their bodies. They can also blend in perfectly with their surroundings,

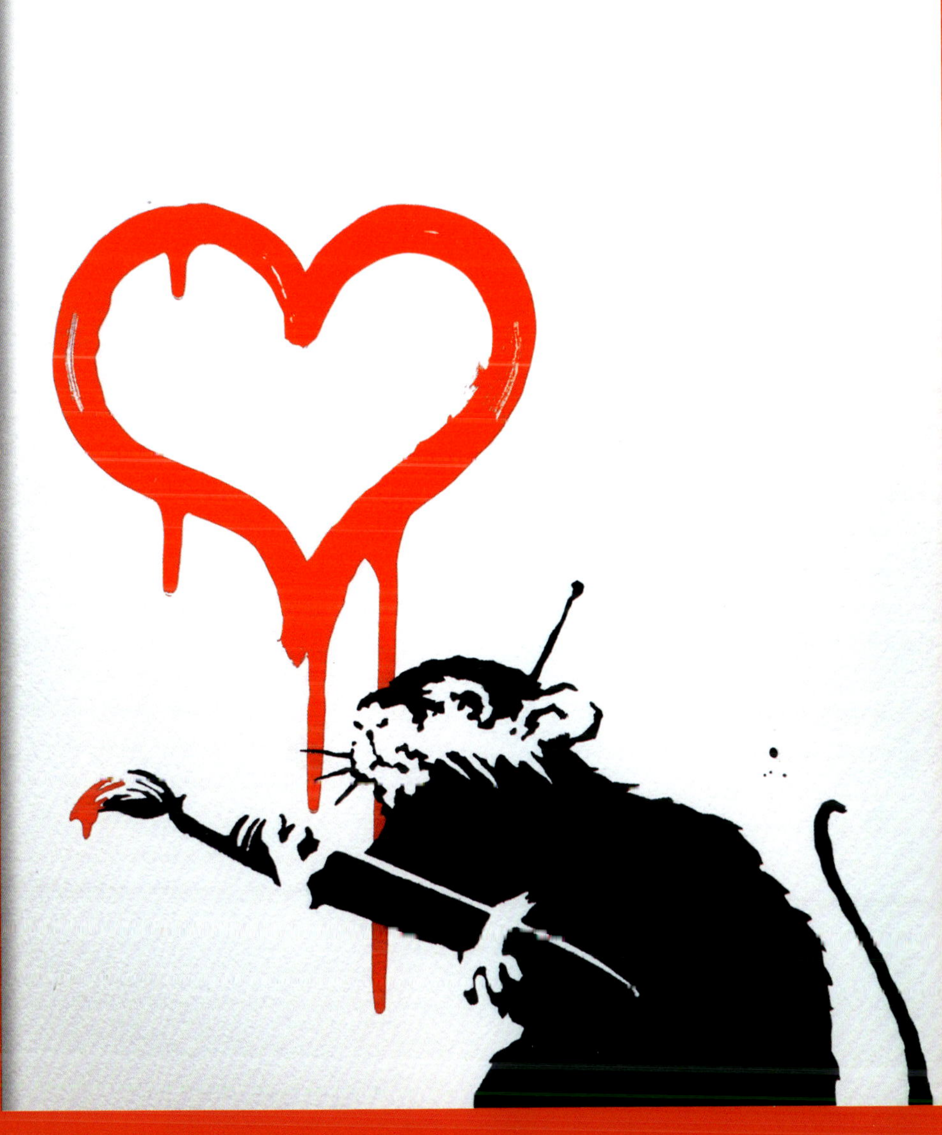

always cautious and careful not to get caught. They can run on the roofs as if they were flying; they know how to be silent when they have to; they attack at the right moment and have a high reproductive capacity. They love the metropolis as much as the countryside; they are endowed with an incredible instinct and an extraordinary ability to survive. They can adapt to any environment depending on the circumstances, but they are unpopular and despised almost everywhere.

Not surprisingly, Banksy said: "If you are dirty, insignificant and unloved then rats are the ultimate role model."

Strangely, RAT is an anagram of ART. Surely, Banksy didn't fail to notice this peculiarity, since he turned rats into one of his allegorical tools to reveal the vices and flaws of the human race and take a stand for those who suffer and fight in the darkness, who are ignored and misunderstood by the conformist society, and who too often become invisible. Rats are deeply connected to Banksy, as if they represented his alter ego. Hunted like graffiti artists sometimes still are, rats hide during the day and come out of their holes at night to move around in the darkness. Most people see rats as disgusting, annoying, and dangerous, and it is for this reason that they are persecuted and pursued, but, for Banksy, rats represent the

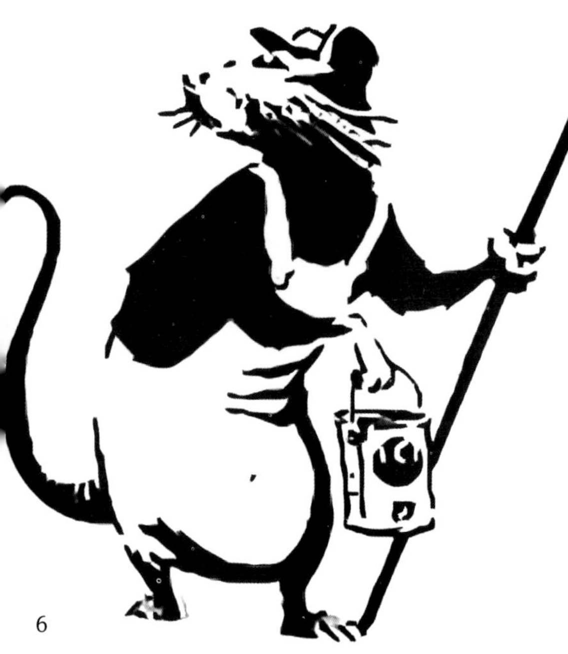

voice of the oppressed, of those who are too often defeated by unbridled consumerism and aggressive competition, by the corporate world, and by those who only care about their own profit and interests. That's why Banksy talks about the "rat race": the race of the invisibles and the downtrodden for survival.

Rats have also been appreciated and portrayed many times by another great artist, the French Xavier Prou, better known as Blek le Rat. "Every time I think I've painted something slightly original, I find out that Blek le Rat has done it as well, only twenty years earlier," admitted Banksy himself. Indeed, Blek le Rat was the first to use stencils in street art, of which he was one of the forerunners in Europe. As a matter of fact, he introduced street art to France in the '80s with the aim of creating artworks capable of awakening social conscience by bringing art to the streets and making it available

to everyone. He chose to paint rats because they are "the only free animals in the city" and they "spread the plague everywhere, just like street art." One of his favorite themes was the inhuman living conditions of the homeless. With his works, he wanted to get them out of darkness, make them visible to everyone, so that no one could make them disappear. He wanted to encourage people to reflect and not to simply look away. With his art and his way of facing even the most thorny issues straightforwardly, Blek le Rat has surely been a great source of inspiration for Banksy. Just like him, Blek le Rat managed to remain anonymous for a long time, until he was arrested and identified in 1991 while he was painting a replica of Caravaggio's *Madonna and Child*. Mindful of this episode, Banksy has become even more careful about hiding his identity, especially since his fame has grown exponentially worldwide.

The first rats Banksy painted had some truly unique characteristics despite showing simpler lines and perhaps less aggressive attitudes. Then as today, they speak through the walls and urge people to reflect on social injustice, illegality, and pointless cruelty. They often hold tools to saw, perforate, and cut in their little paws, and sometimes they are humanized, with some strengths and many weaknesses.

They can also be extremely mischievous in a joking, combative, violent, or subtle way, even when they wear a necklace with the symbol of peace. They certainly are icons of an alternative system. "Rats are called rats because they'll do anything to survive," said Banksy, and his voice seems to echo in the darkness behind each of them, just like in a Tim Burton movie, where creatures of darkness are monstruous but also capable of great empathy. Speaking of his army of rats, Banksy said: "Like most people, I have a fantasy that all the little powerless losers will gang up together. That all the vermin will get some good equipment and then the underground will go overground and tear this city apart."

In Banksy's vision, rats are portrayed in different images and styles, depending on the moment, the situation, and the purpose.

There's the Gangsta Rat, who appears to be the most well-off: he is well-groomed, confident, and fearless of the world he lives in. He is quite a hip rat, with a New York Mets baseball cap on his head; he carries a boombox and wears a showy chain necklace around his neck. Throughout Europe, especially in '80s and '90s England, this New York Underground style was greatly appreciated in the graffiti and street art world, which ist so close to hip-hop music and culture. It is no coincidence that this rat appeared during Banksy's so-called artistic residence in New York, Better Out Than In.

And then there's the *Placard Rat*, who, standing on his hind feet like a human being, holds up a placard in his paw, with a powerful message on it. There are many such rats who show their awareness and self-confidence, giving voice to clear and true words often written in red or pink. Some placards read "Welcome to Hell, Get Out While You Can," or just "Welcome to Hell," others "Because I'm Worthless" or "Get Out While You Can." This series of works was inspired by George Marshall's book *Get Out While You Can, Escape the Rat Race*, a title that appears on some of the placards as well. With his rats, Banksy wants to protest against capitalism, consumerism, militarism, and modern life in large cities, subject to an extreme surveillance system that limits the freedom of individuals. It is this last aspect that the *Radar Rat* wants to emphasize, with all his equipment to watch and listen to the world around him. There's also the *Paparazzi Rat*, equipped with a camera and in search of secrets and sensational gossip to uncover.

The list of Banksy's rats is very long...

There's the *Rat with Roller* holding a paint roller in his paw to remove graffiti

There's the *Racing Rat Clock*, running on a clock face as if he got stuck in a cog, trapped in what Banksy calls "the relentless and steady ticking towards the great unknown" that is "the endless rat race we find ourselves in."

And then, there's the *Rat Holding a Box Cutter*, which

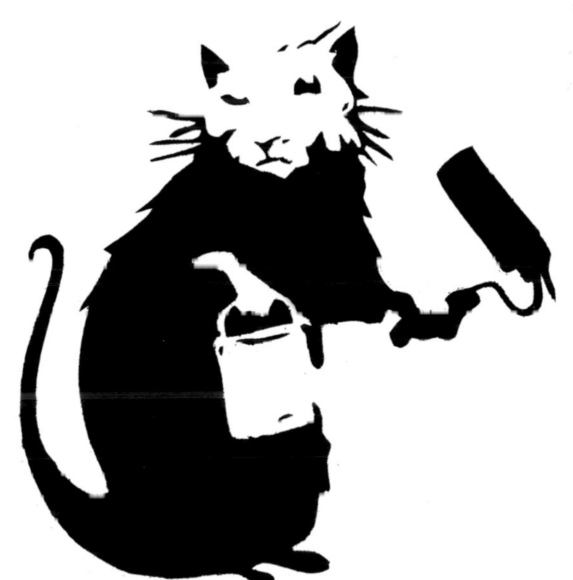

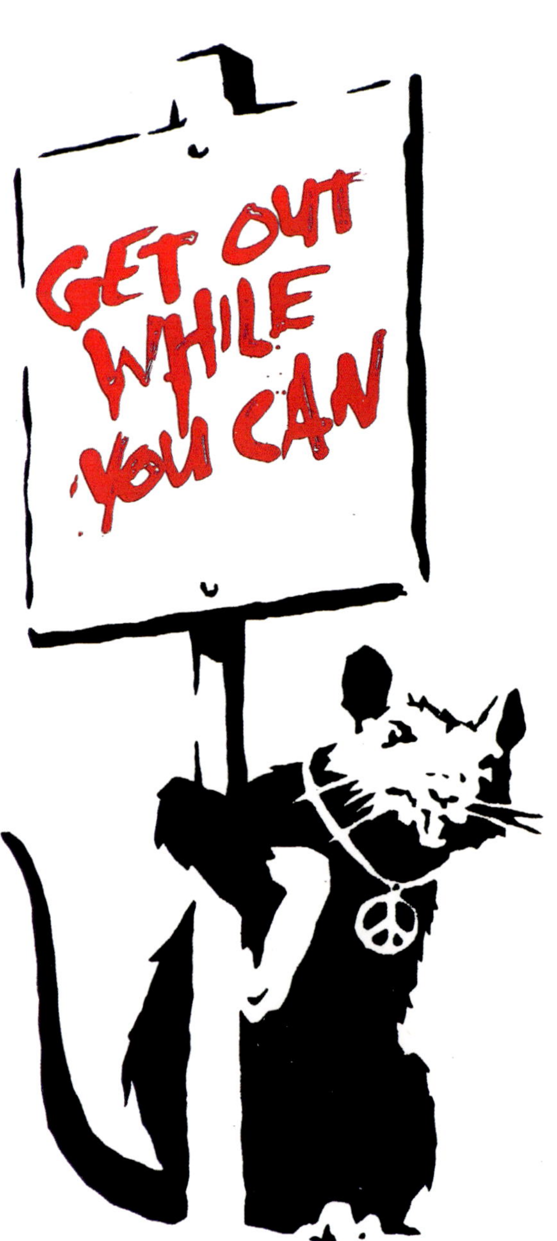

Banksy painted in Paris in June 2018. It is part of a series of rats painted on the walls of the French capital, especially in the Sorbonne University district, to commemorate the fiftieth anniversary of the students and workers uprisings of May 1968. To support these movements, Banksy said: "Fifty years since the uprising in Paris 1968. The birthplace of modern stencil art."

And then there are those rats expressing Banksy's most intimate side and his political views.

There's *Love Rat*, who might appear as a romantic at first sight but actually retains that sarcasm and harshness that characterize Banksy. The rat is portrayed while painting a heart with some red paint dripping from the wall. One may wonder: "Is a rat capable of love?" Some art critics suggest the red paint dripping down the wall might be blood and represent a wound caused by some pain of the heart. "It might be ideal for a cheating spouse," suggested

Banksy jokingly with a certain sarcasm. And yet, there's the couple of *Paris Rats* timidly looking at the Eiffel Tower together from a wall near the shore of the Seine, surrounded by a vintage and somewhat romantic spirit.

And then, there are the *COVID Rats*. These show how Banksy himself was affected by the 2020 pandemic, which limited his work by forcing him to stay home. In one of his works, which apparently Banksy created at his home, rats mischievously roam around his bathroom, arousing his wife's complaints, as the artist himself posted on Instagram: "My wife hates it when I work from home!" Other *COVID Rats*, with their face masks and hand sanitizers, are part of an artwork by Banksy and his "faithful squires" titled *London's Underground Undergoes Deep Clean*. Even in the toughest times, Banksy never lost his urge to "hit," and from Instagram he warned: "If you don't mask, you don't get."

We can hope that his rats will keep admonishing us from the city walls, urging us to reflect on the injustices of the society we live in, and awakening consciousnesses from a comfortable ignorance. We can hope that Banksy's fearless and biting spirit will keep speaking up through his artworks, but most of all we need to ensure that his works won't remain just words fading in the sun.

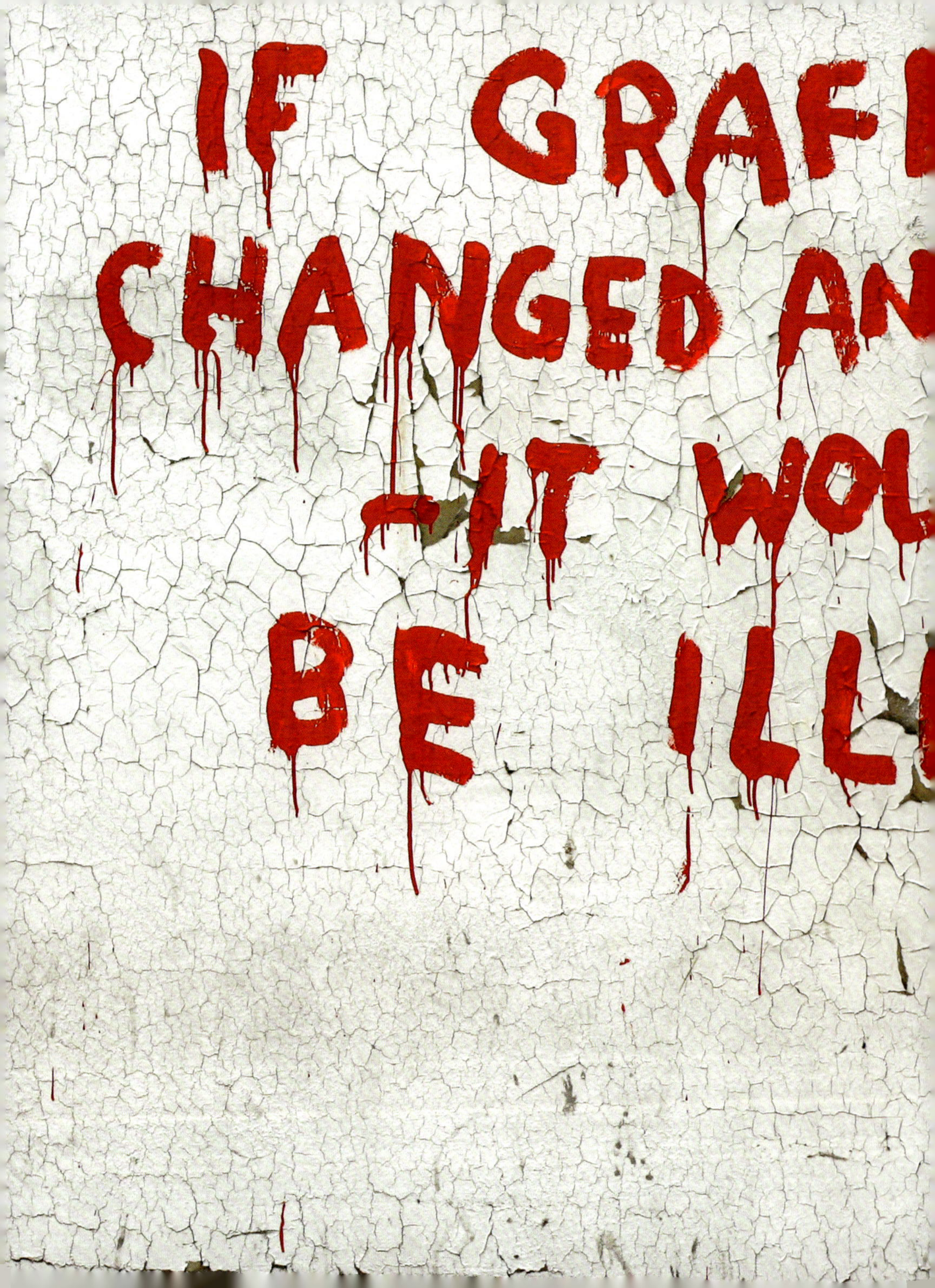

IF GRAFF
CHANGED AN
IT WOL
BE ILL

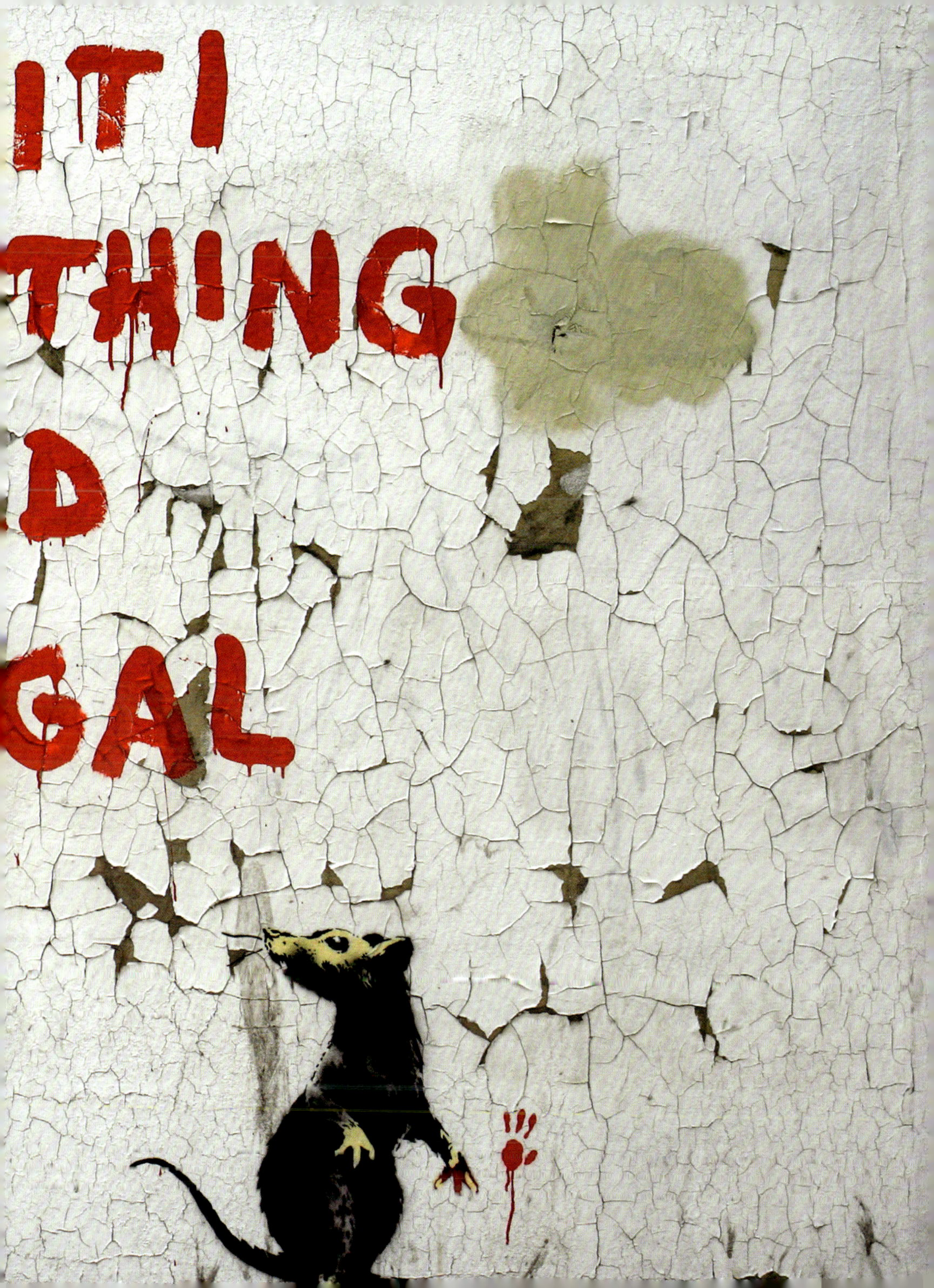

IT I
THING
D
GAL

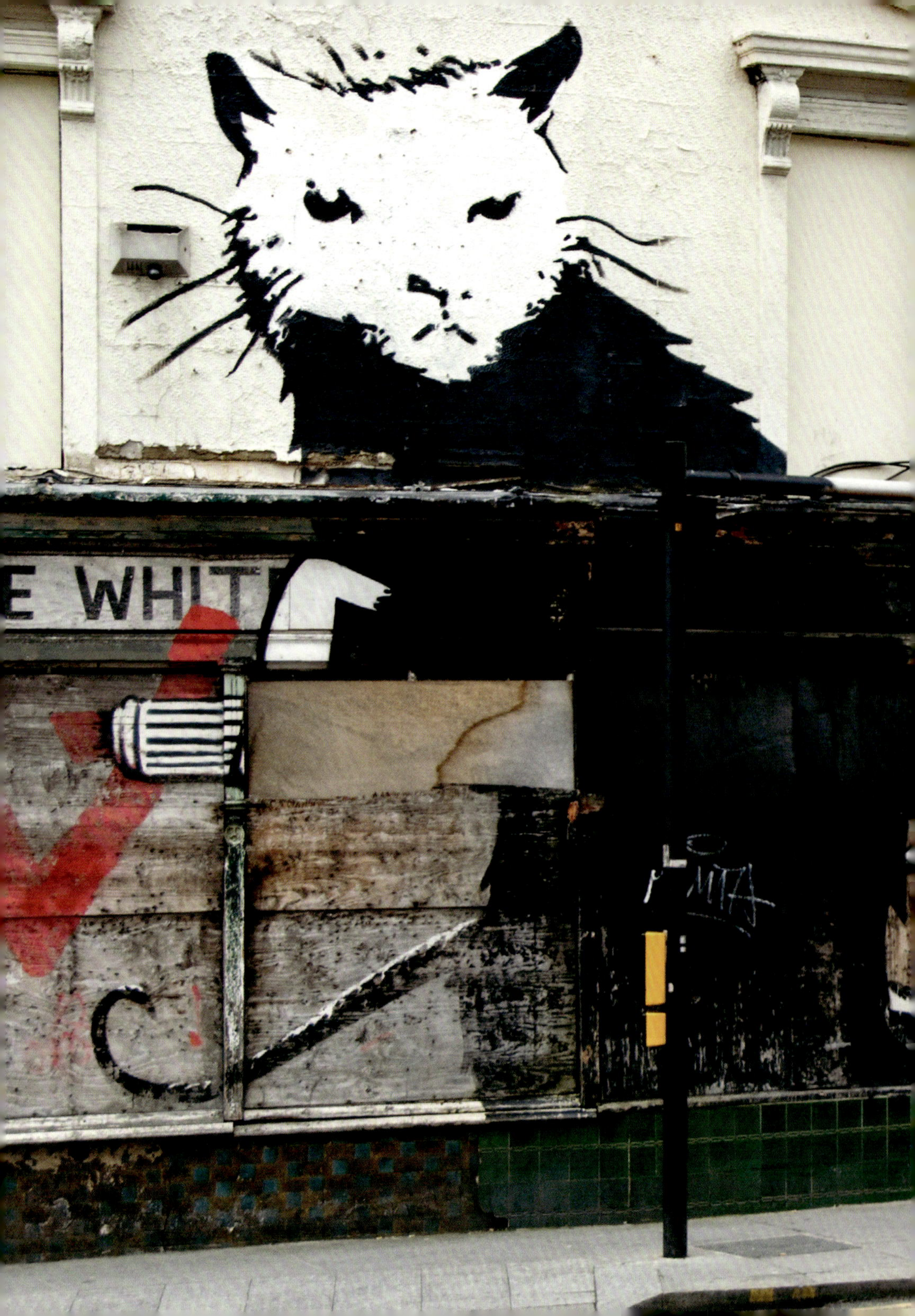

E WHIT
MTA

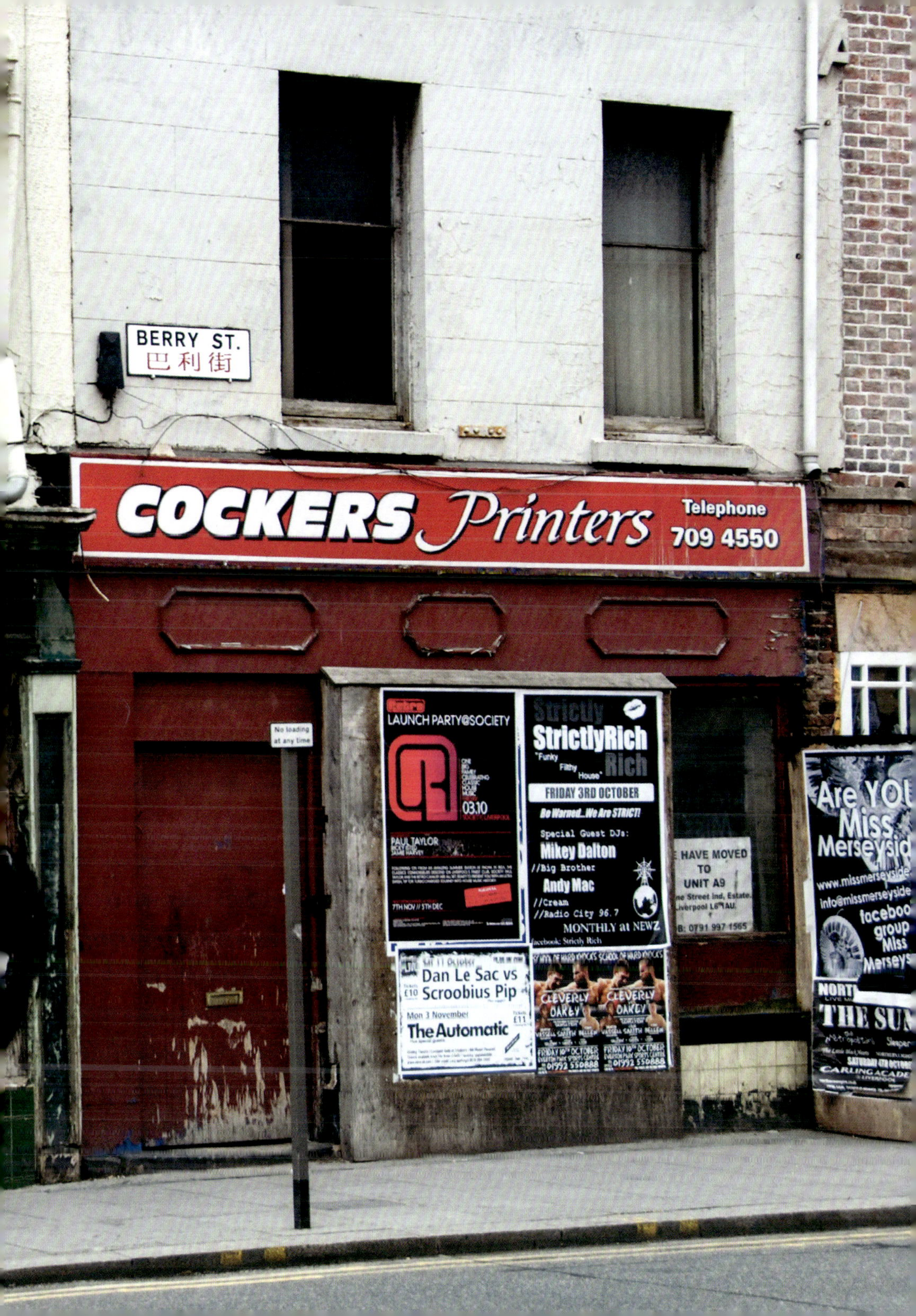

BERRY ST.
巴利街
COCKERS Printers
Telephone
709 4550
No loading
at any time
Retro
LAUNCH PARTY@SOCIETY
03.10
PAUL TAYLOR
7TH NOV / 5TH DEC
Strictly
StrictlyRich
Rich
"Funky
Filthy
House"
FRIDAY 3RD OCTOBER
Be Warned...We Are STRICT!
Special Guest DJs:
Mikey Dalton
//Big Brother
Andy Mac
//Cream
//Radio City 96.7
MONTHLY at NEWZ
facebook: Strictly Rich
WE HAVE MOVED
TO
UNIT A9
ne Street Ind. Estate,
Liverpool L6 1AU
B: 0791 997 1565
Dan Le Sac vs
Scroobius Pip
Mon 3 November
The Automatic
CLEVERLY
OAKEY
CLEVERLY
OAKEY
FRIDAY 10TH OCTOBER
01992 550888
FRIDAY 10TH OCTOBER
01992 550888
Are YOU
Miss
Merseysid
www.missmerseyside
info@missmerseyside
facebook
group
Miss
Merseys
NORT
THE SUN
CARLING ACADE

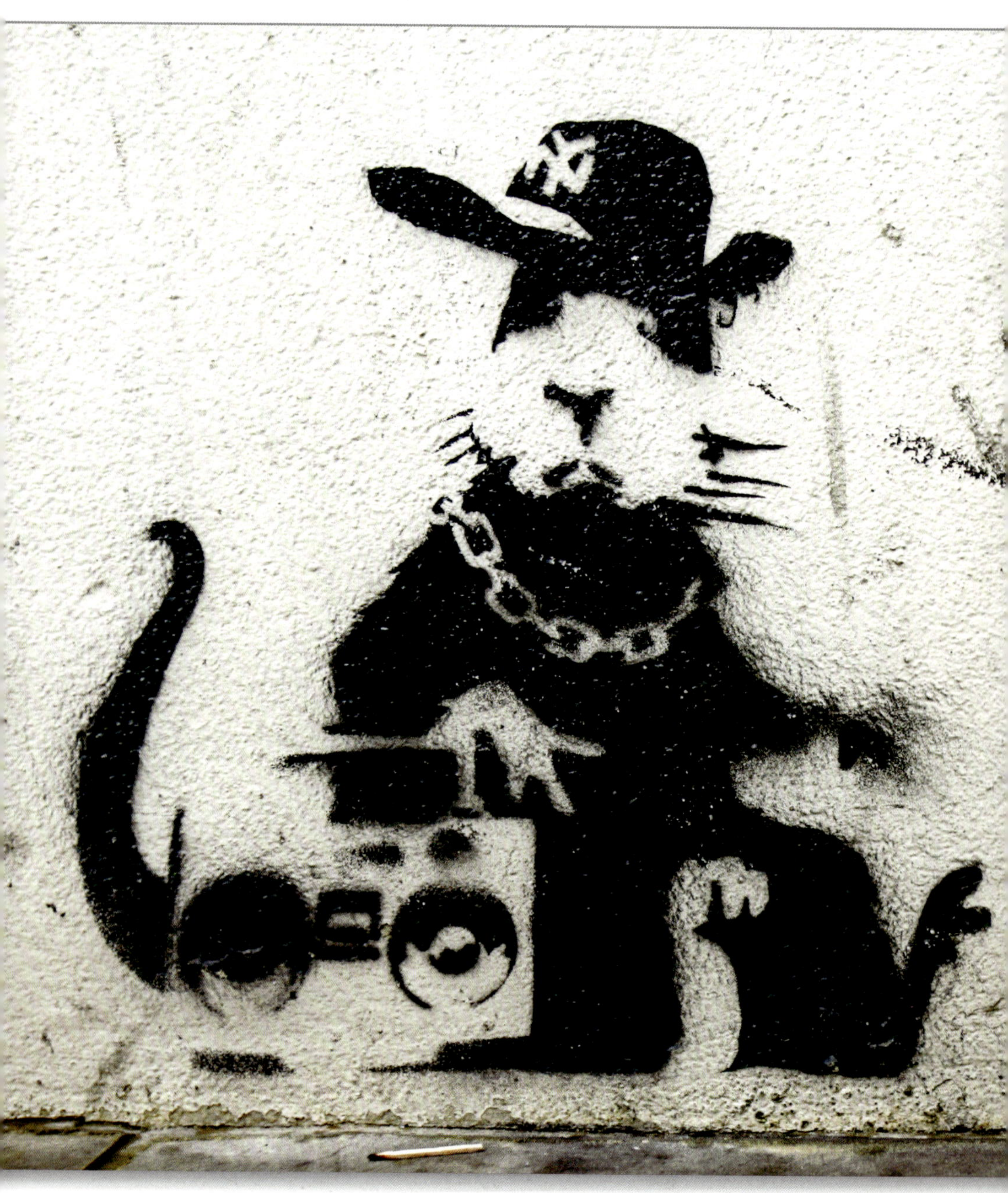

A BASEBALL CAP, A CHAIN NECKLACE, AND A BOOMBOX: ALL THE '90S NEW YORK UNDERGROUND STYLE ELEMENTS IN ONE WORK OF GRAFFITI.

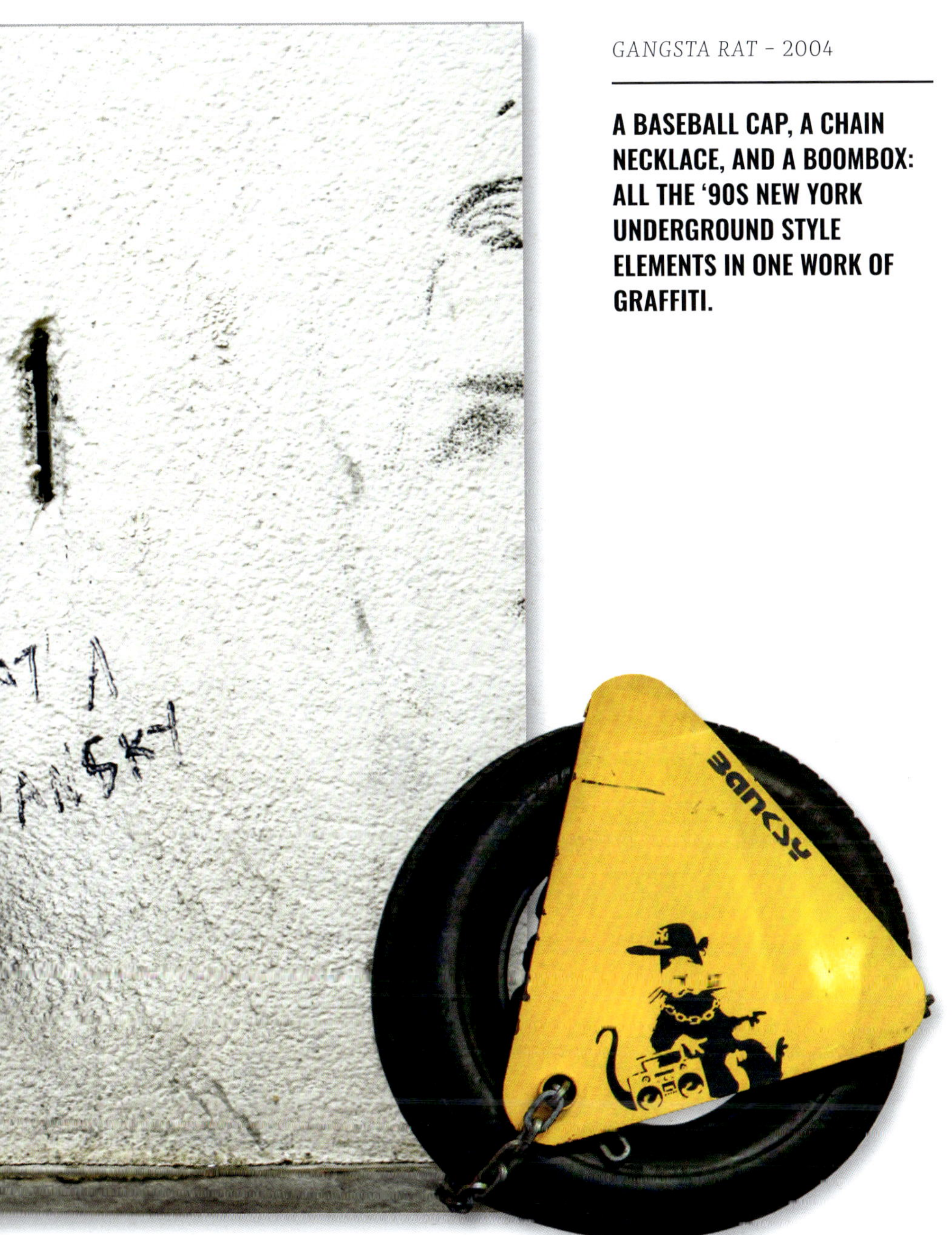

AS TALL AS A THREE-STORY BUILDING, THIS GRAFFITI WORK APPEARED ON THE FAÇADE OF THE COLOSSAL MEDIA BUILDING AT THE SAME TIME AS BANKSY'S EXHIBITION "THE VILLAGE PET STORE AND CHARCOAL GRILL," WHICH OPENED IN OCTOBER 2008 IN A SMALL SHOP IN GREENWICH VILLAGE.

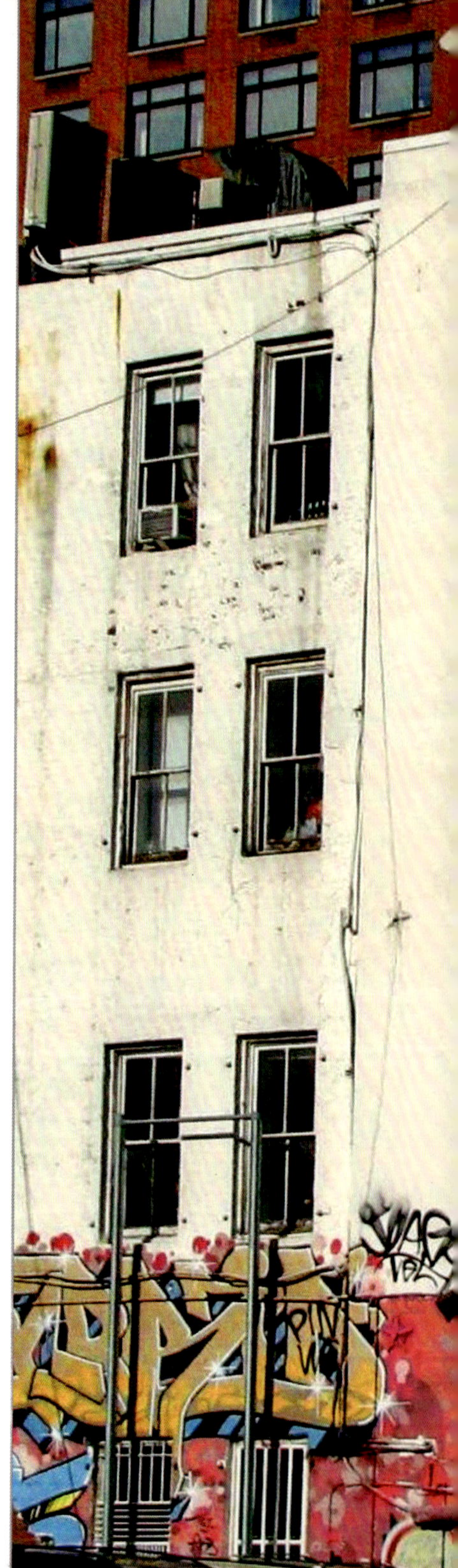

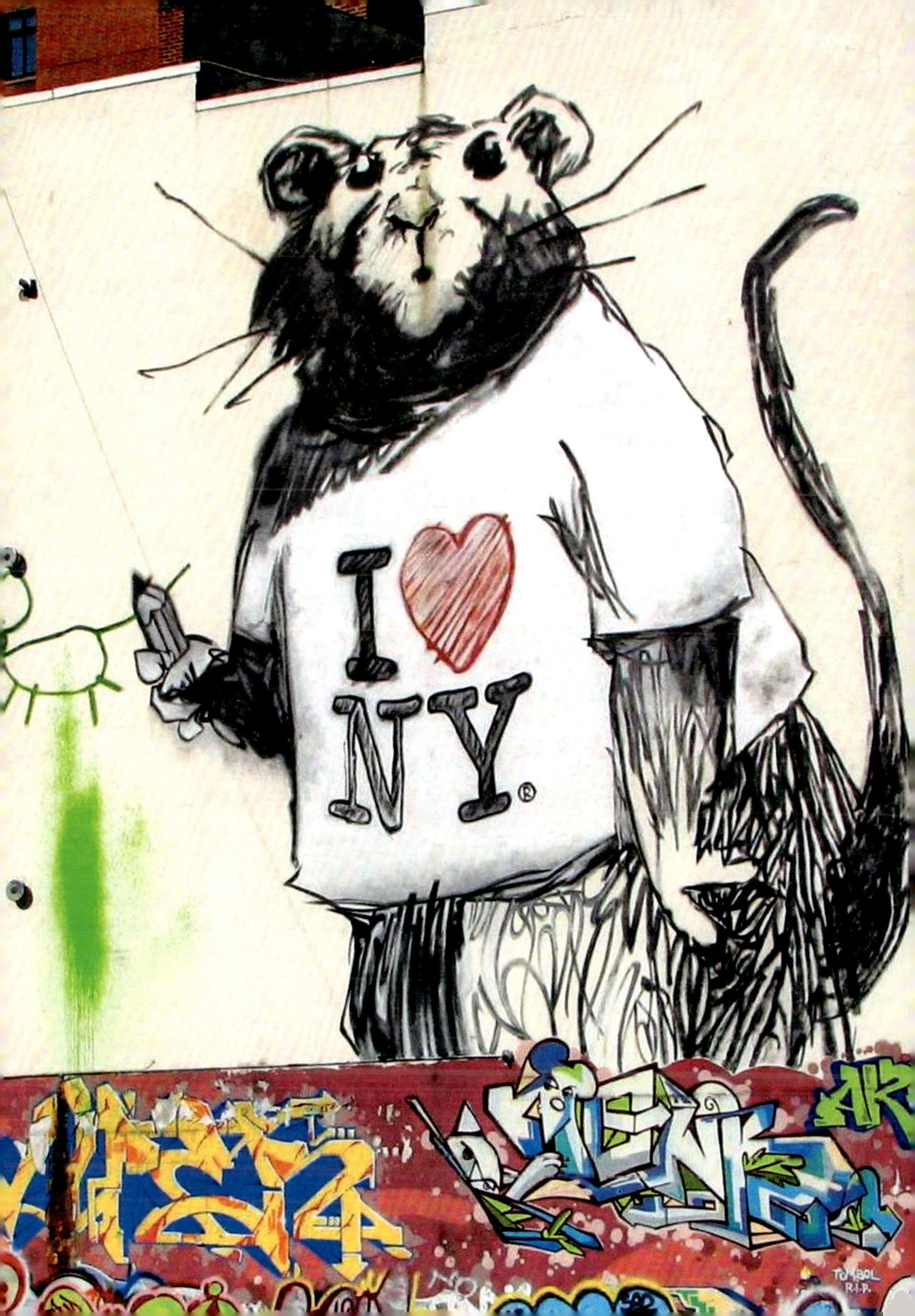

I ♥ NY

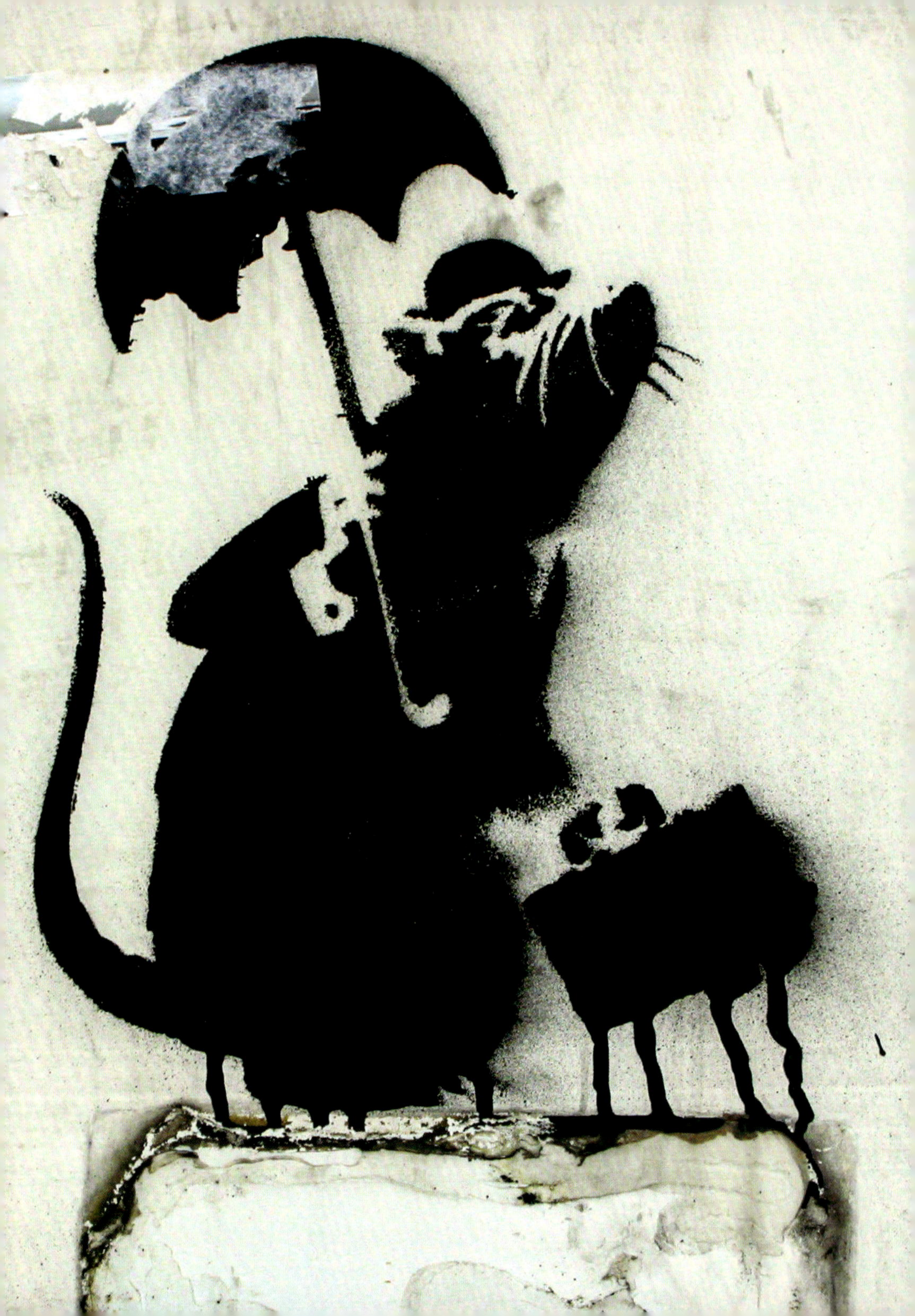

WHAT WILL BE THE NEXT DESTINATION FOR THIS ELEGANT RAT WITH AN UMBRELLA AND SUITCASE?

*RACING RAT CLOCK –
MANHATTAN, NEW YORK, 2018*

A RAT IS FRANTICALLY
RUNNING COUNTER-
CLOCKWISE BETWEEN
THE HANDS OF A CLOCK
ON THE FAÇADE OF A
BUILDING SCHEDULED
FOR DEMOLITION ON THE
CORNER OF 14TH STREET
AND SIXTH AVENUE,
MANHATTAN.

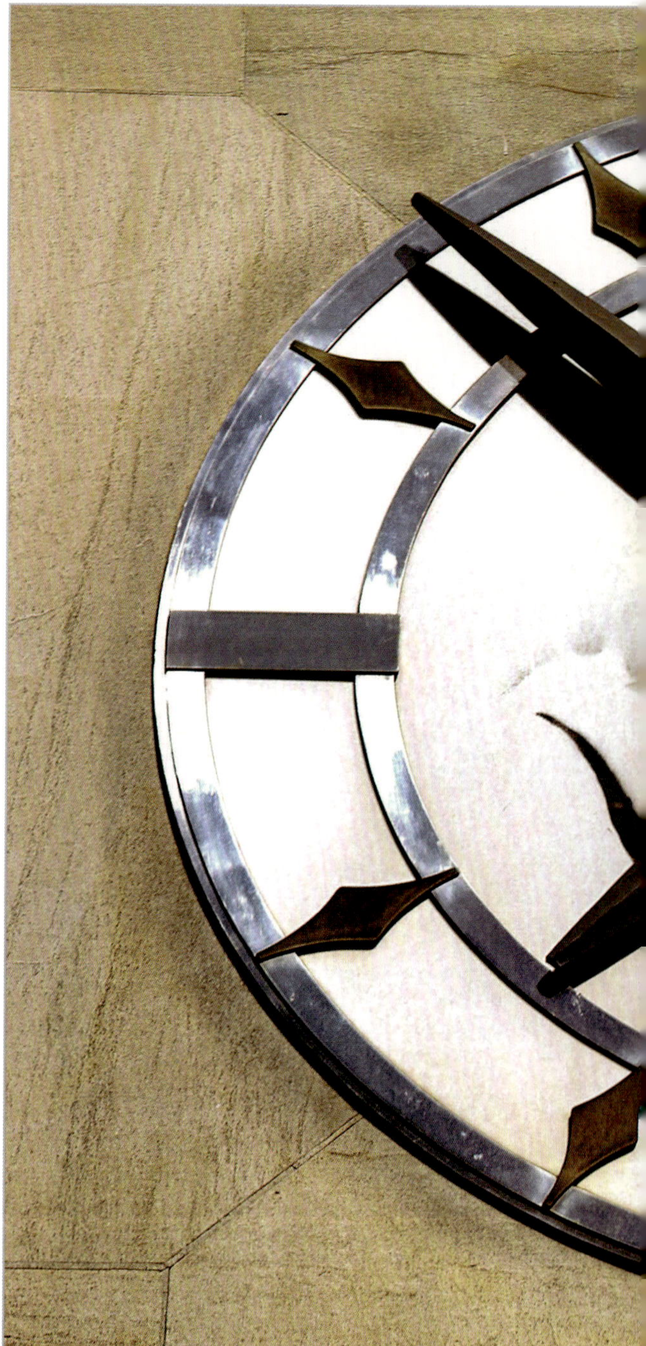

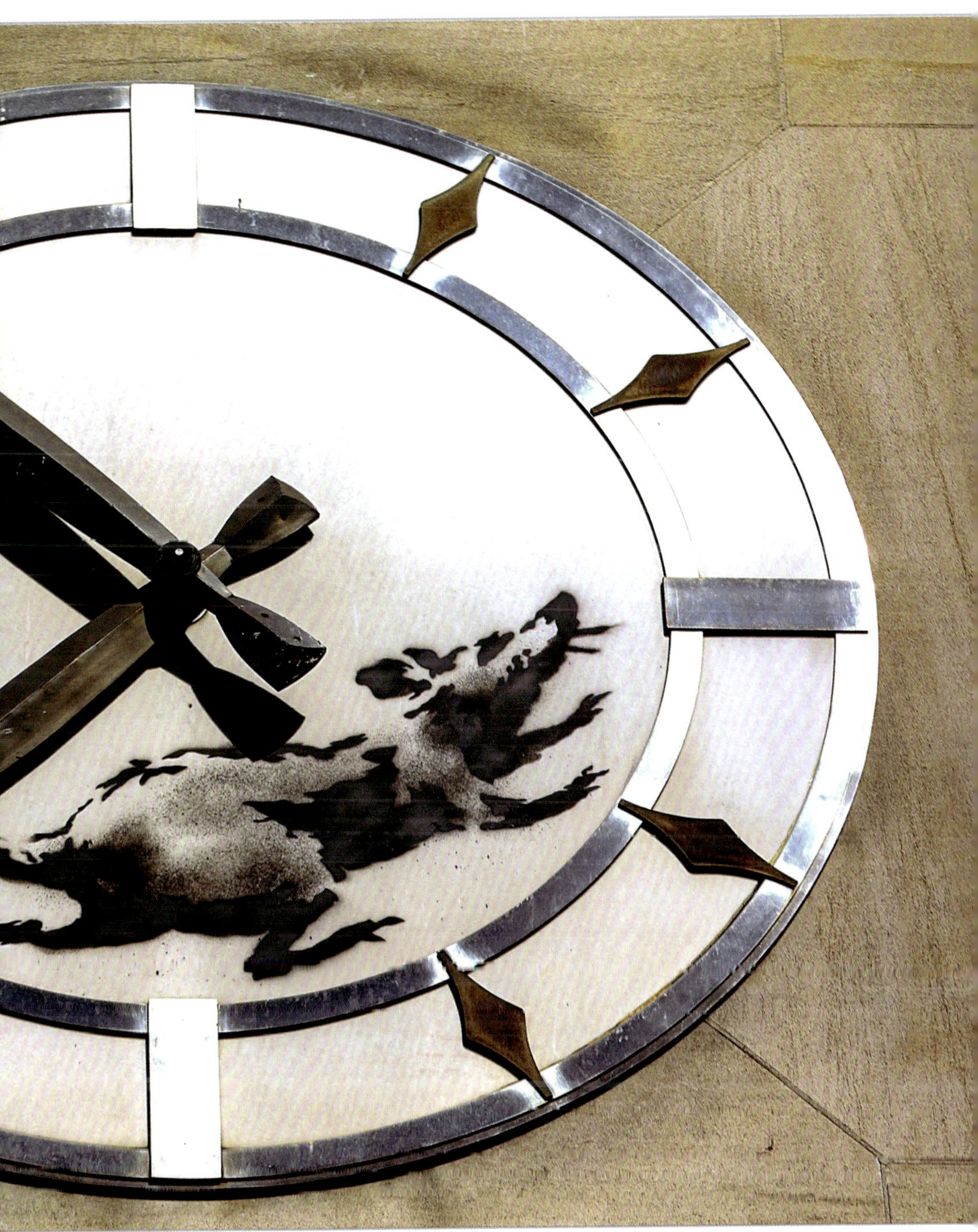

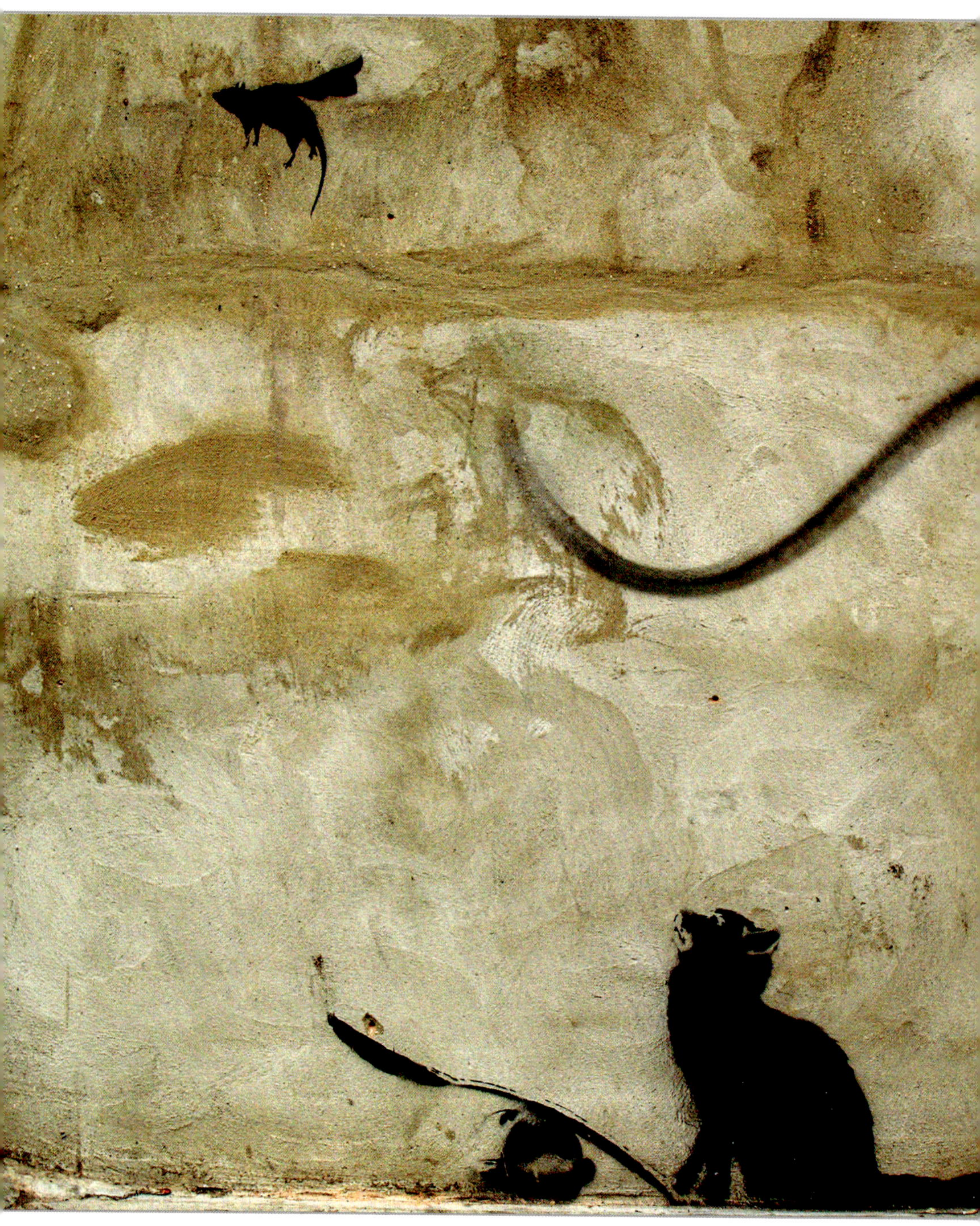

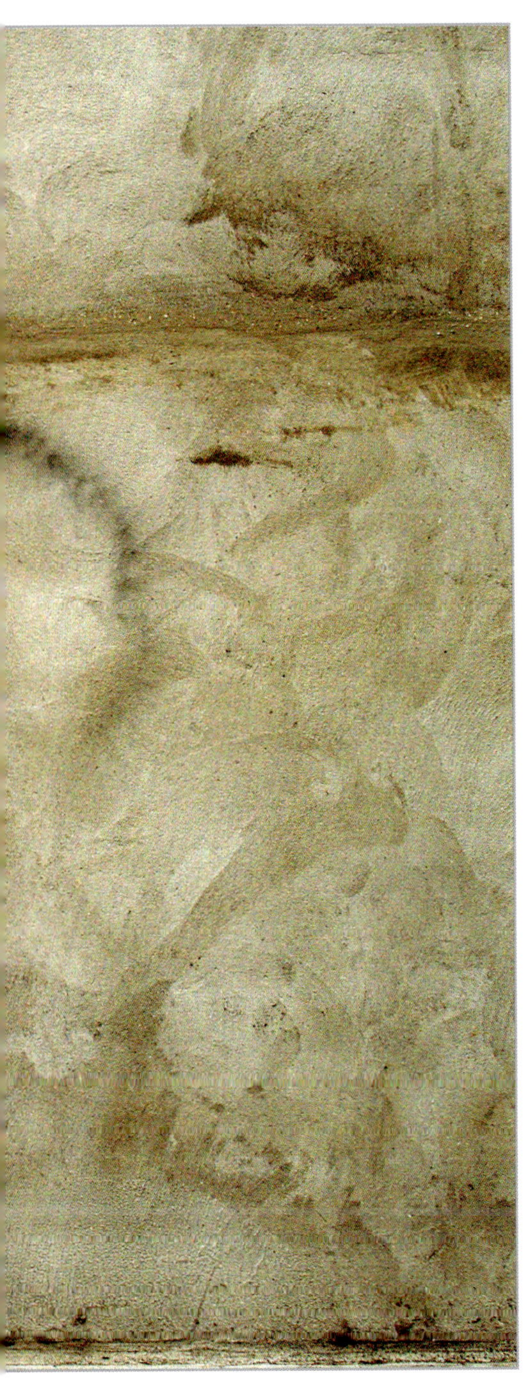

USING A SPOON AS A CATAPULT, A CAT THROWS A SUPERHERO RAT IN THE AIR.

26–27 TWO RATS WITH PROTECTIVE EYEWEAR, CROWBAR, AND CIRCULAR SAW ARE READY TO DISMANTLE THE SYSTEM IN ORDER TO CHANGE IT.

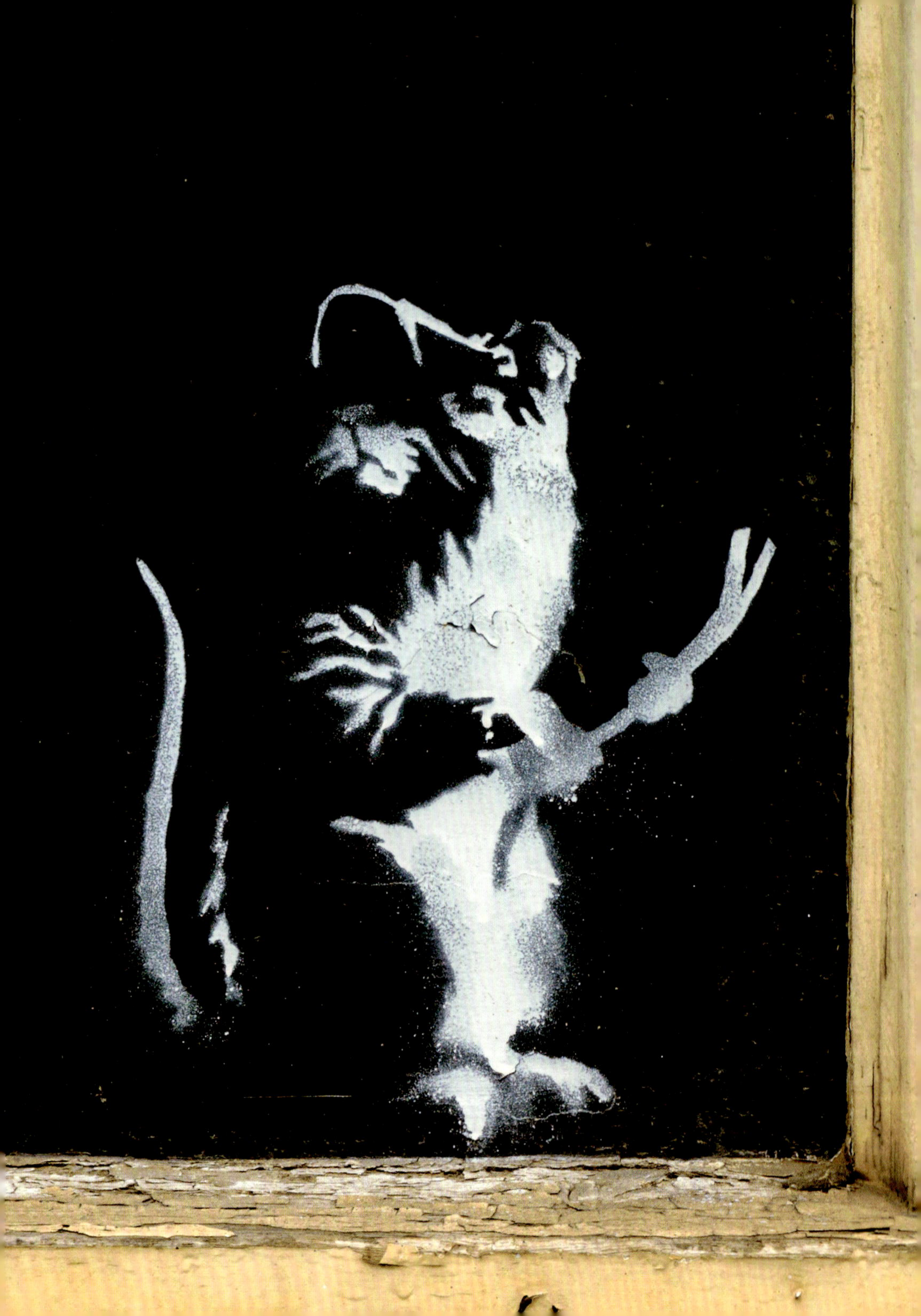

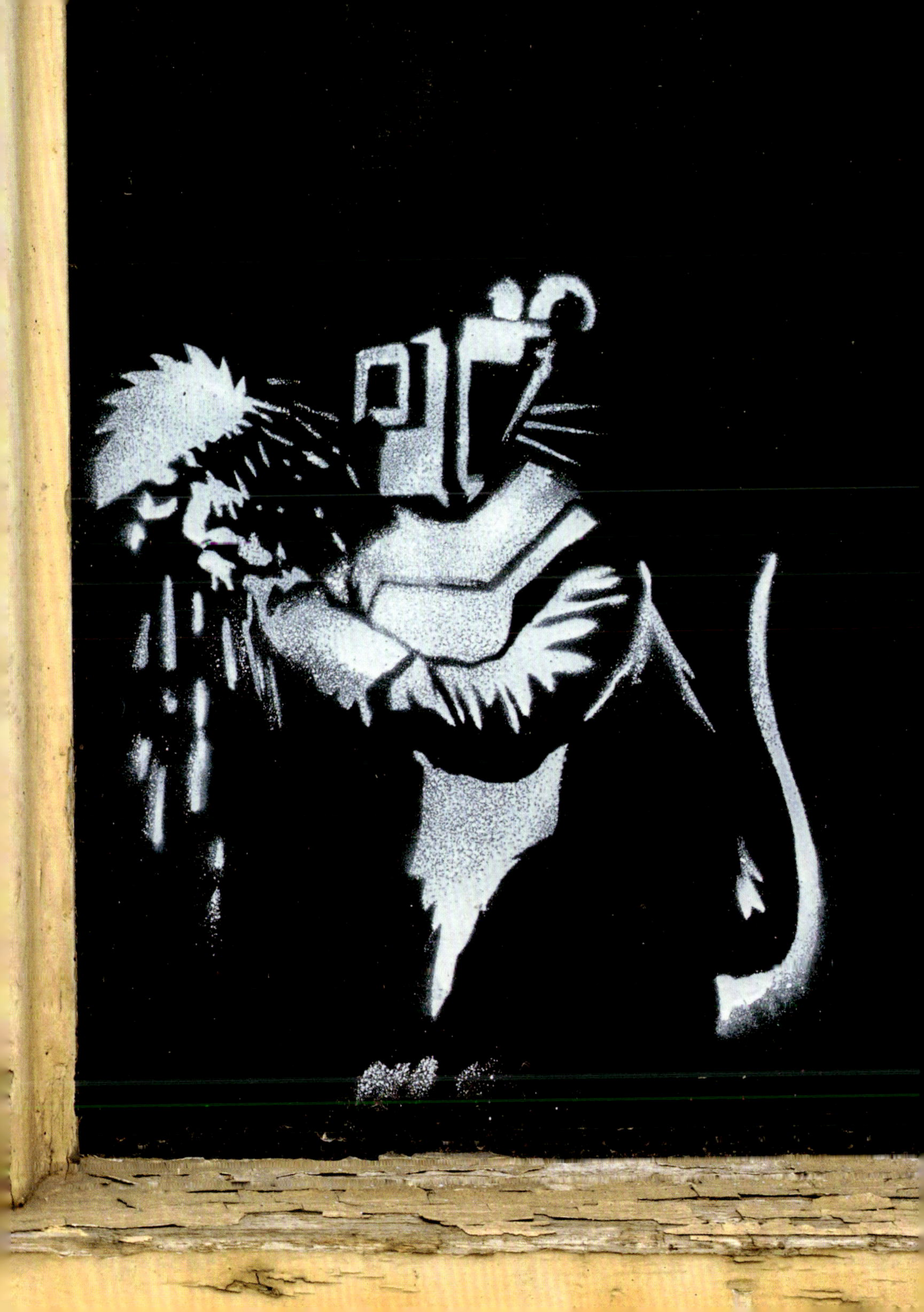

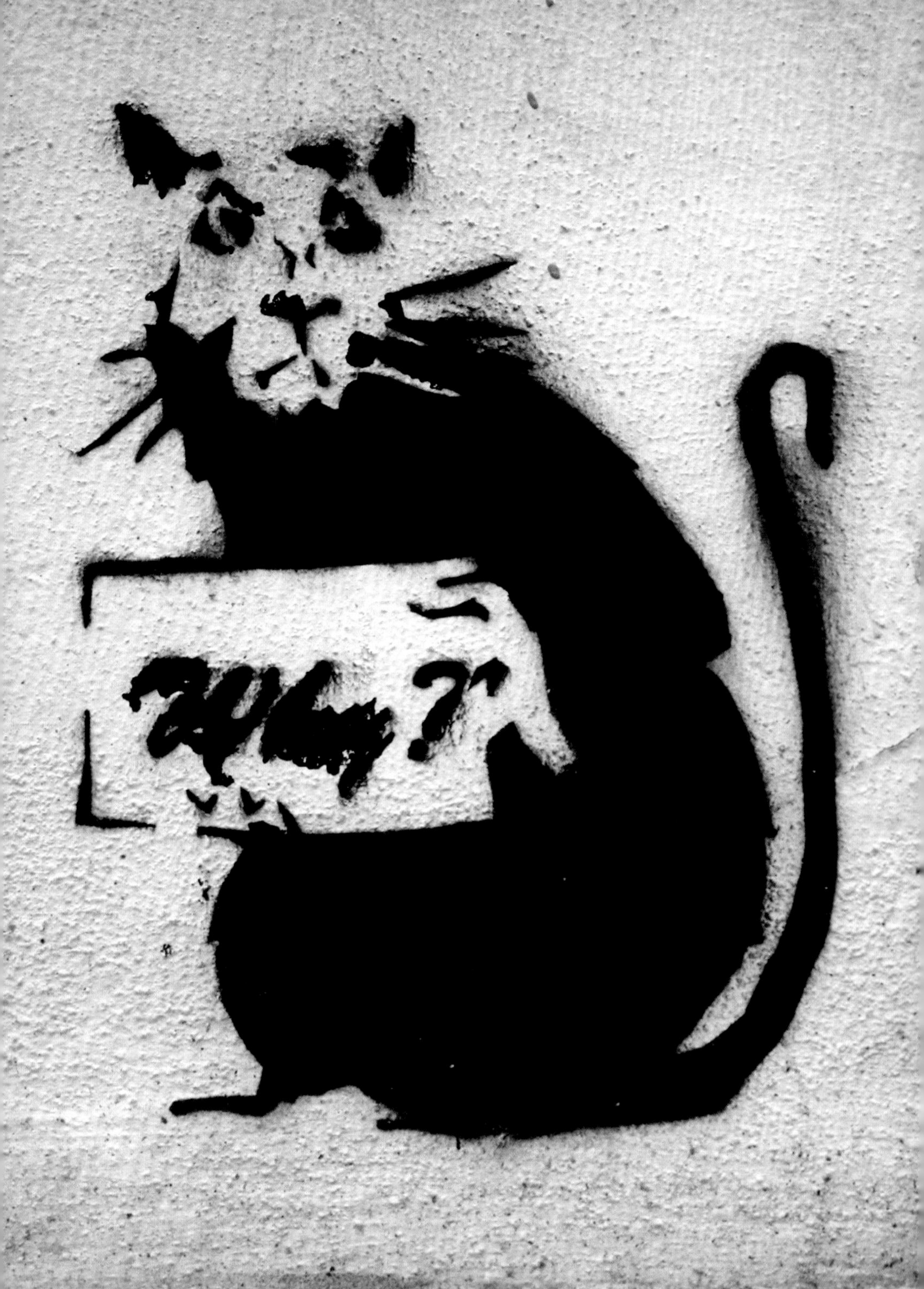
Why?

"THEY EXIST WITHOUT PERMISSION. THEY ARE HATED, HUNTED AND PERSECUTED." WITH THIS QUOTE FROM WALL AND PIECE, BANKSY DESCRIBES THE EXISTENTIAL CONDITION OF RATS (AND OF GRAFFITISTS AS WELL).

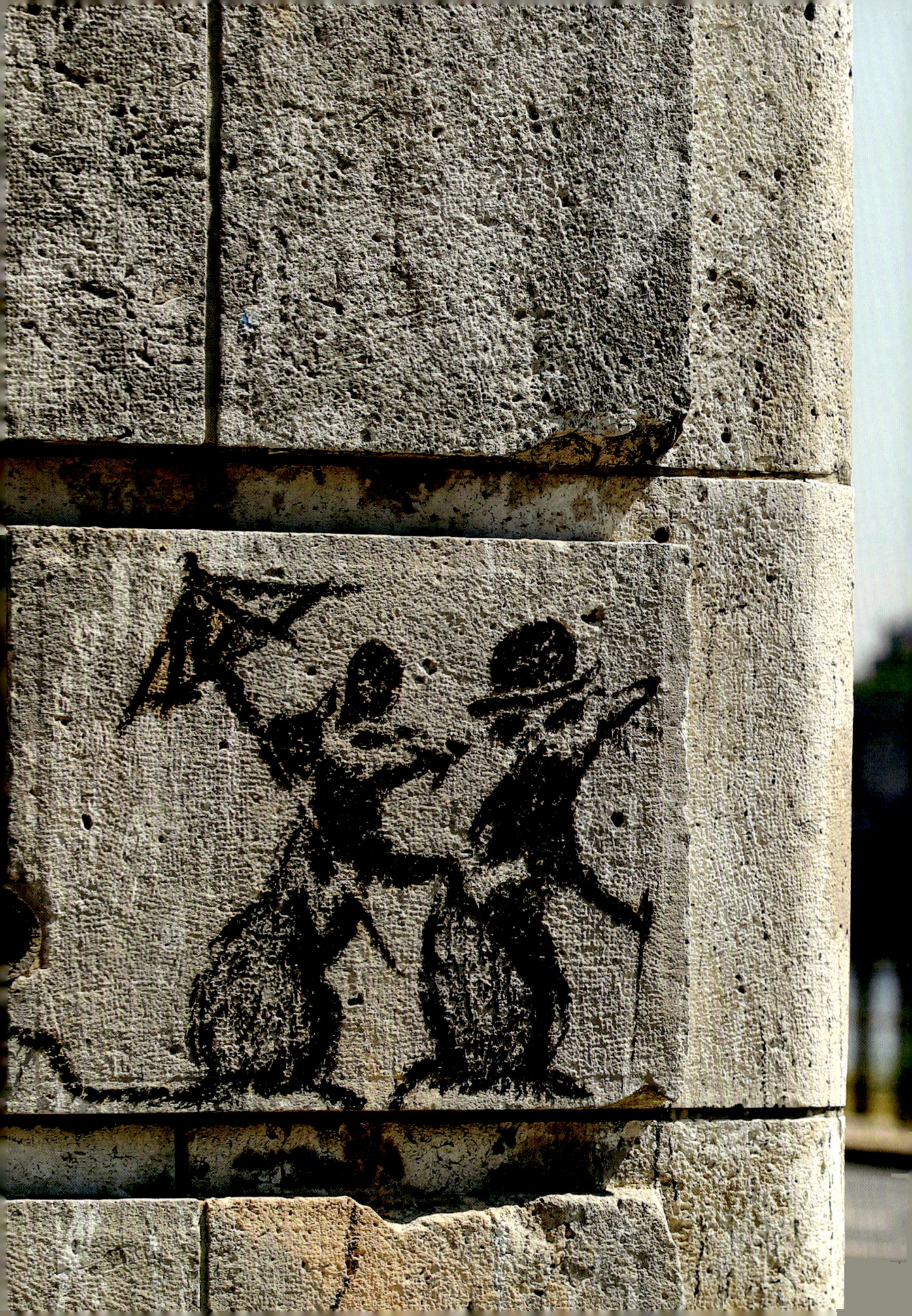

**AN ELEGANT COUPLE
OF RATS WITH HATS
AND AN UMBRELLA IS
HEADING TOWARD THE
EIFFEL TOWER.**

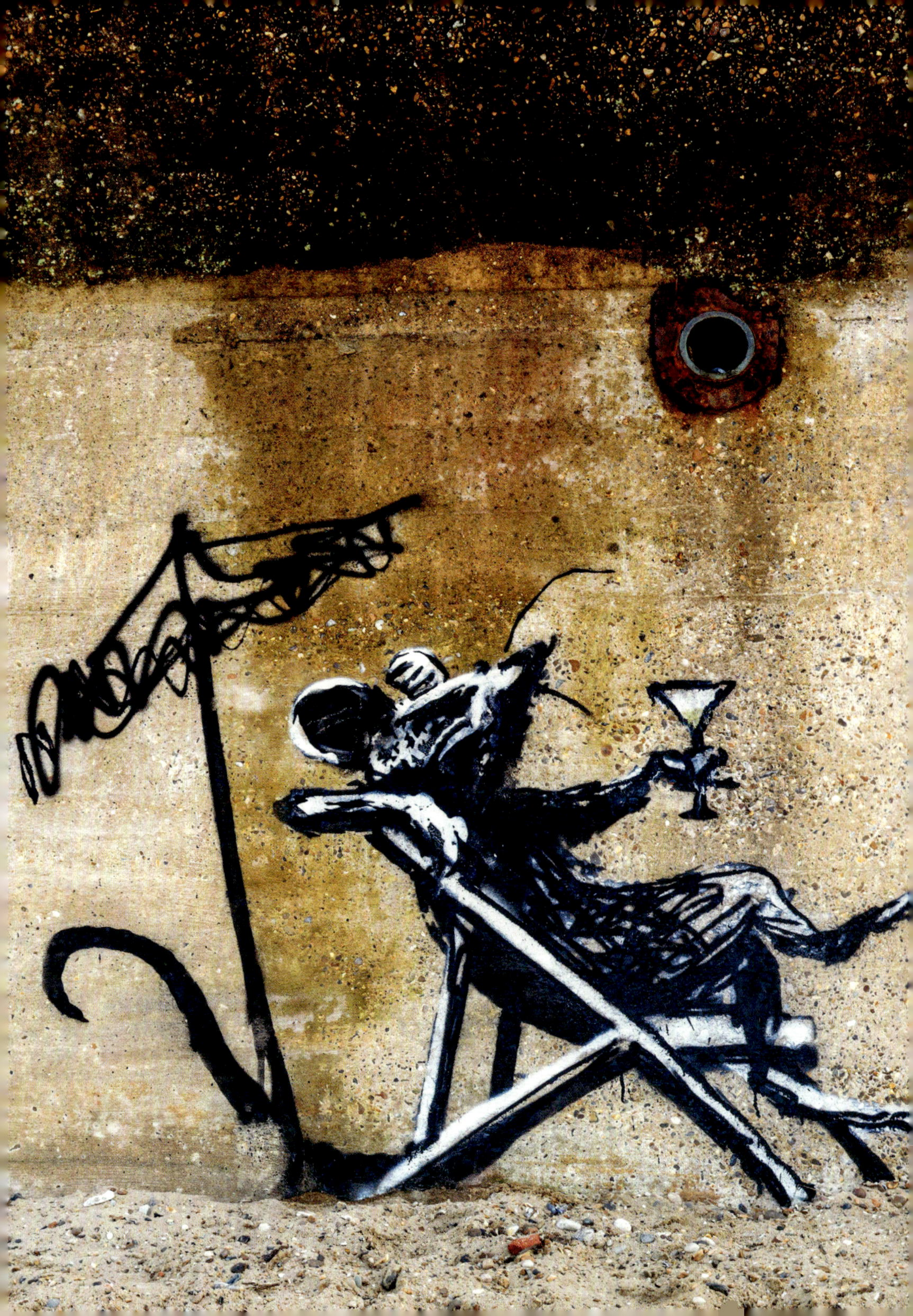

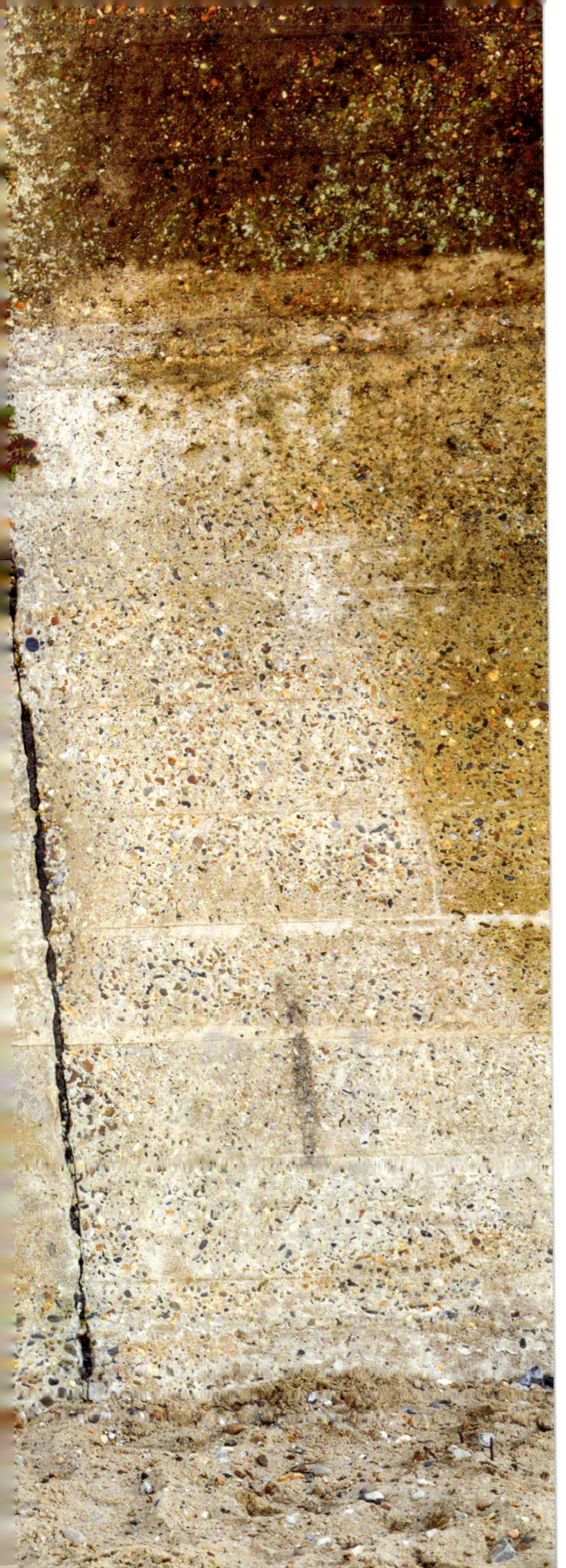

A GREAT BRITISH SPRAYCATION
– LINKS HILL, NORTH BEACH,
LOWESTOFT, ENGLAND, 2021

HAIGHT STREET RAT – SAN FRANCISCO, 2010

A RAT WITH A BERET AND A RED MARKER LEAVES A MESSAGE ON SAN FRANCISCO'S BUILDINGS.

RED CARPET RATS

36–37 BANKSY'S RATS: HONEST AMBASSADORS OF PROTEST MESSAGES.

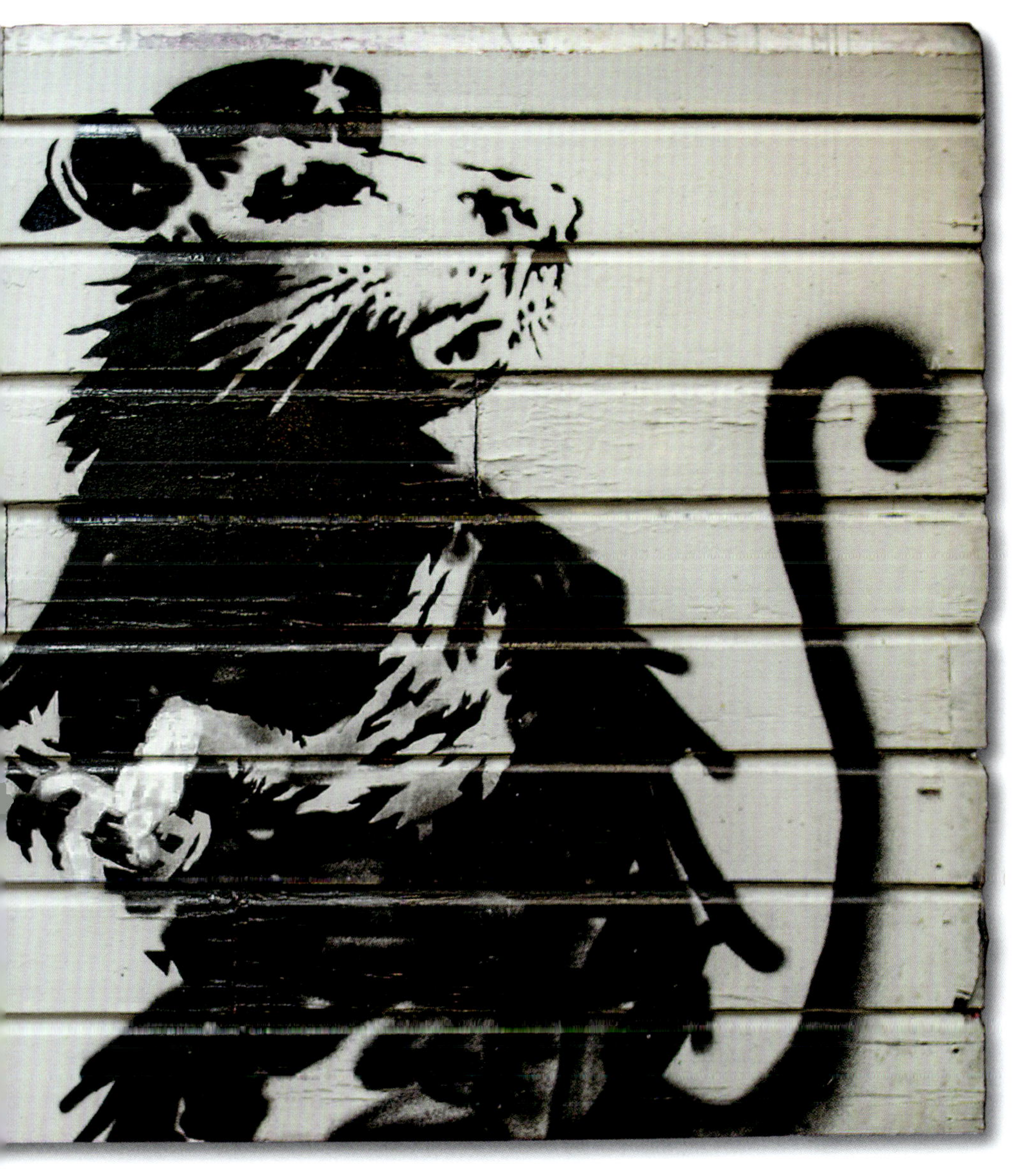

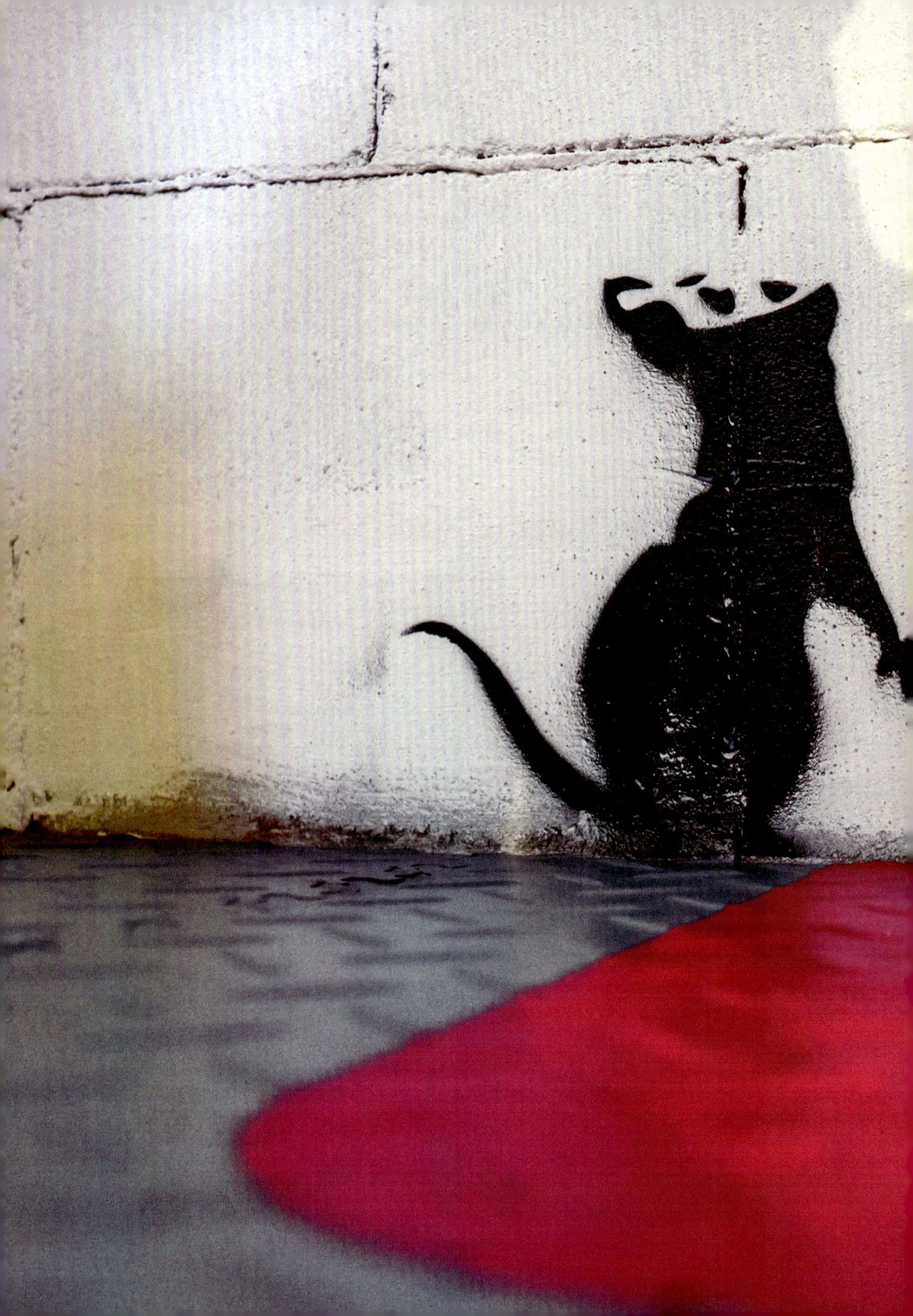

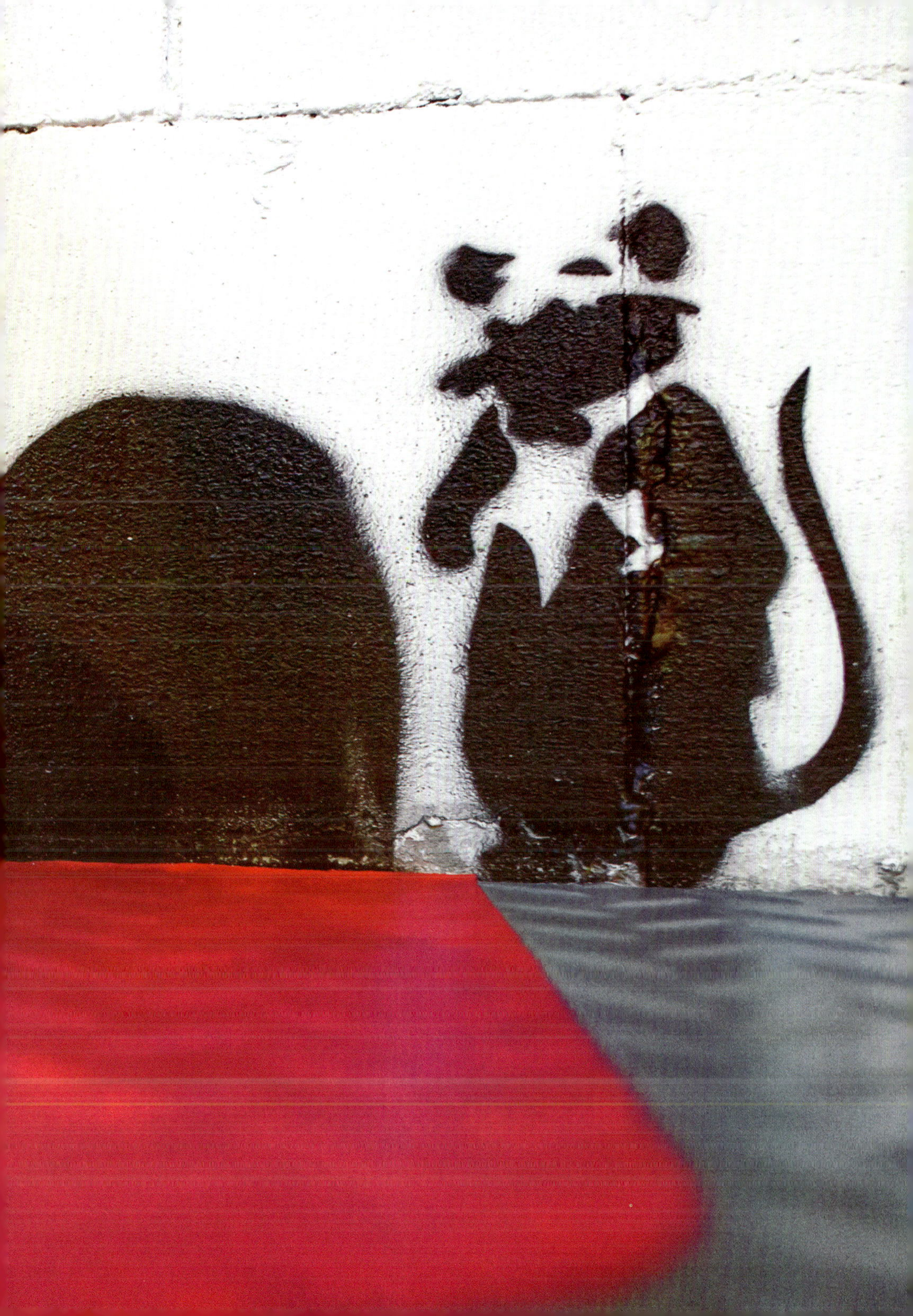

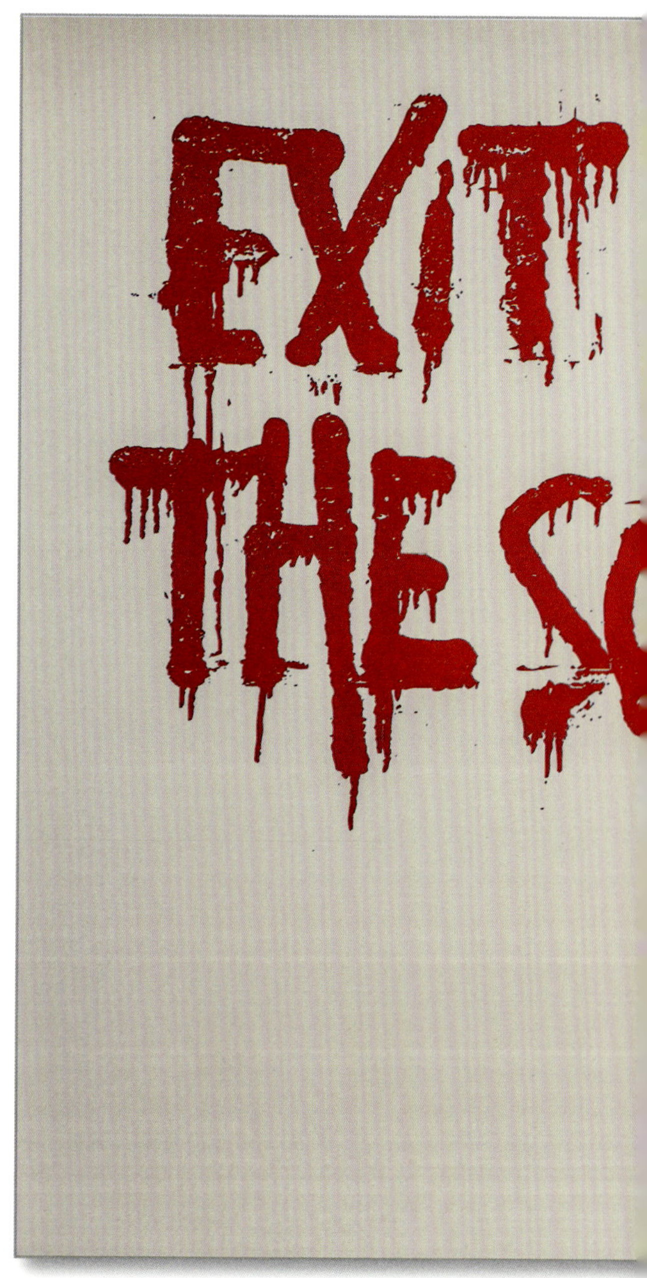

EXIT THROUGH THE SOHO GRIND – LONDON, 2014

HERE BANKSY PLAYS WITH THE FAMOUS TITLE OF HIS ONLY MOVIE AND REFERS TO A FAMOUS BAR ON BEAK STREET IN THE SOHO DISTRICT WHERE THE GRAFFITI WORK WAS PAINTED.

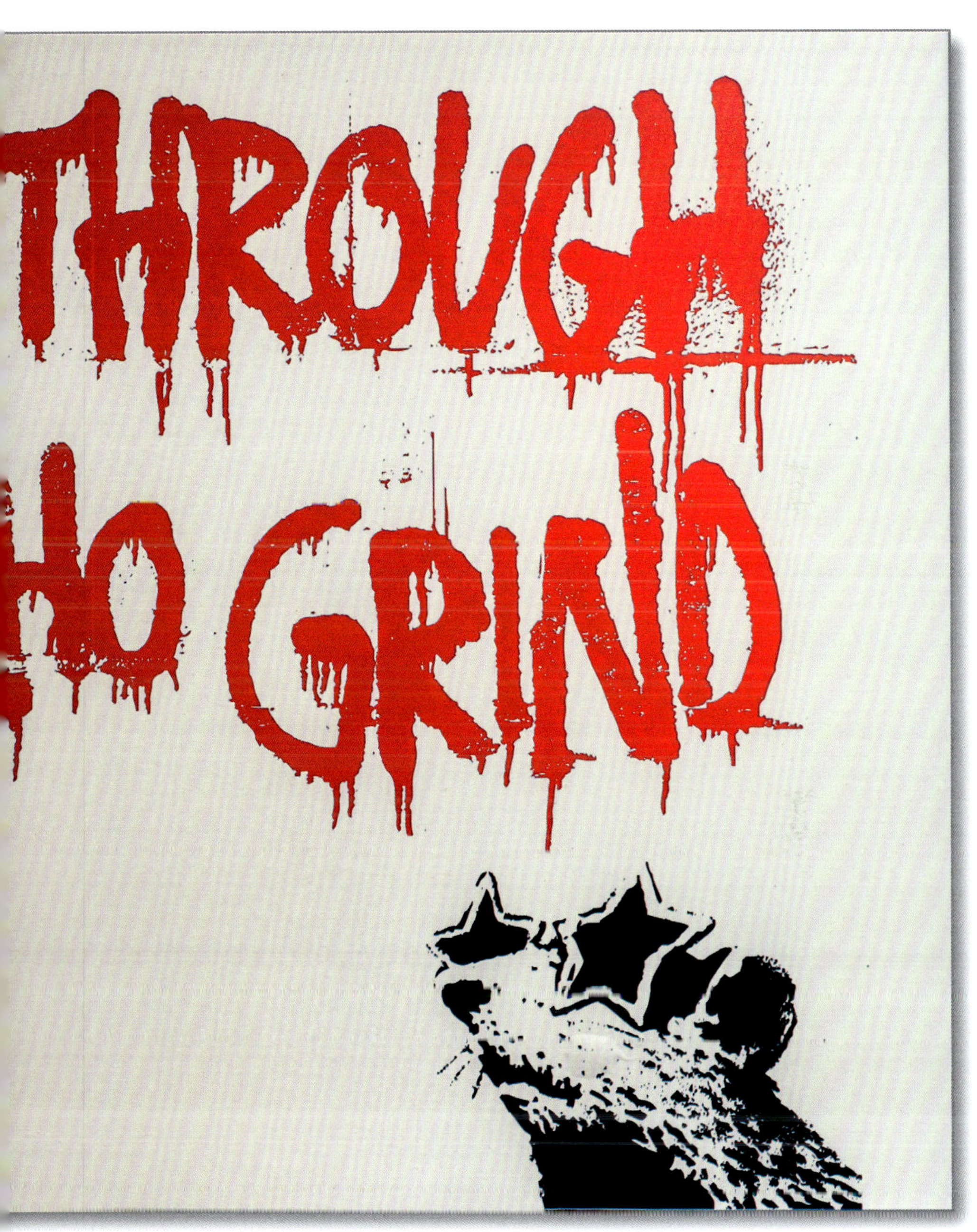
THROUGH
THO GRIND

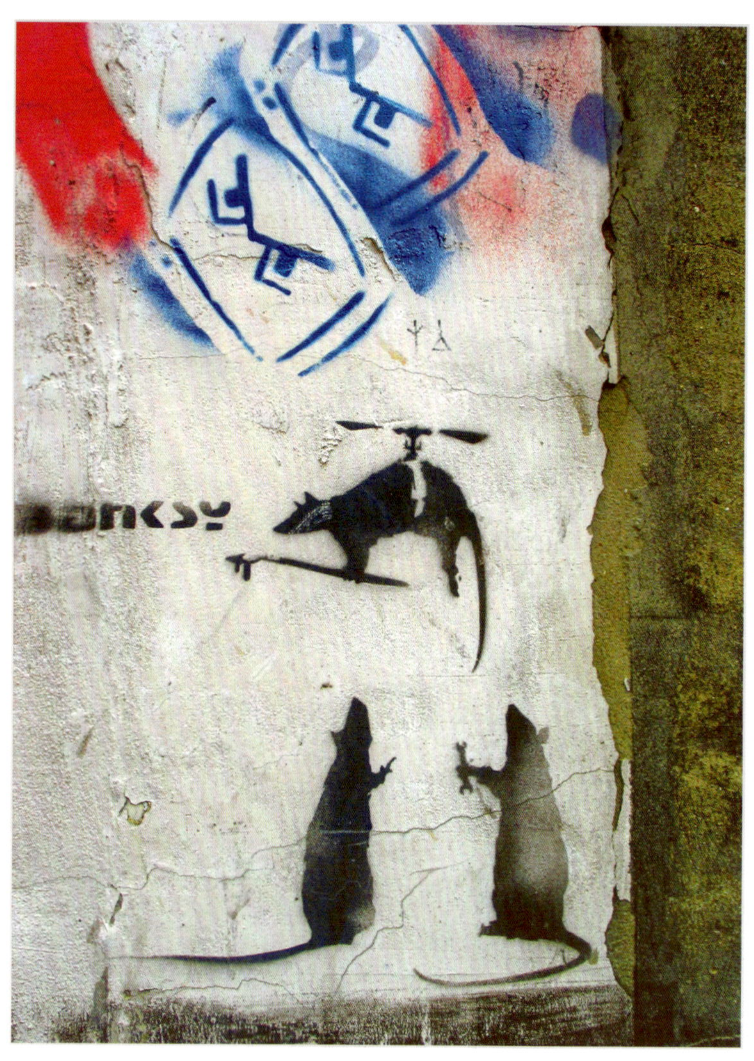

NO PLACE IN THE CITY IS SAFE ANYMORE. THE HELICOPTER RAT
WITH HIS BRUSH AND THE PARACHUTING RAT CAN GET ANYWHERE,
JUST LIKE GRAFFITISTS.

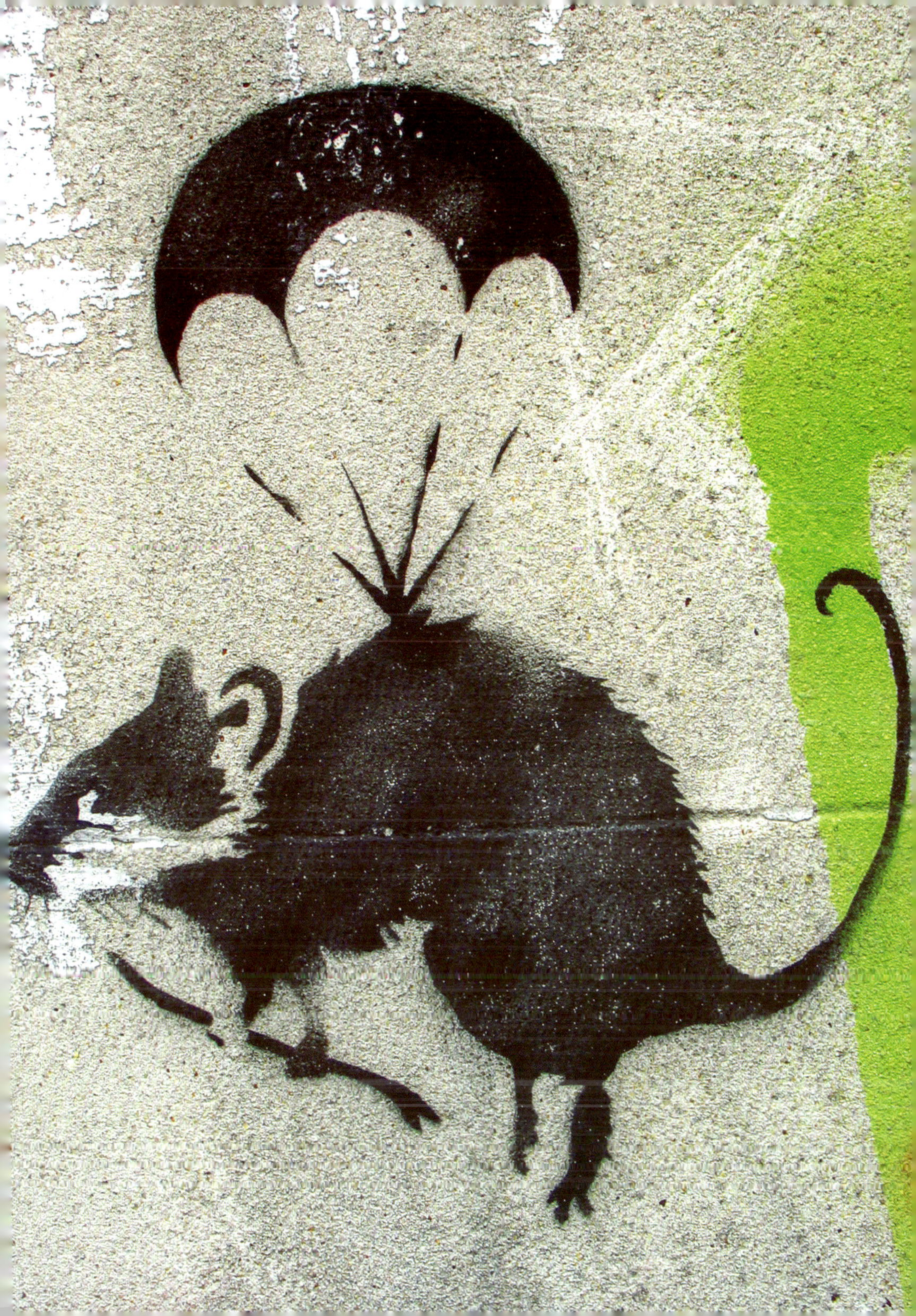

A RAT IN THE GUISE OF A BUSINESSMAN WITH HIS ID BADGE, A BRIEFCASE FULL OF MONEY, AND PAINT STILL ON HIS PAWS IS WALKING AWAY AFTER WRITING "LET THEM EAT CRACK" ON THE WALL, A REFERENCE TO THE FAMOUS QUOTE INCORRECTLY ATTRIBUTED TO MARIE ANTOINETTE, "LET THEM EAT CAKE," WHICH HAS BECOME A SYMBOL OF SOCIAL INEQUALITIES. THE REFERENCE TO THE SCOURGE OF DRUG ABUSE IS ALSO EVIDENT.

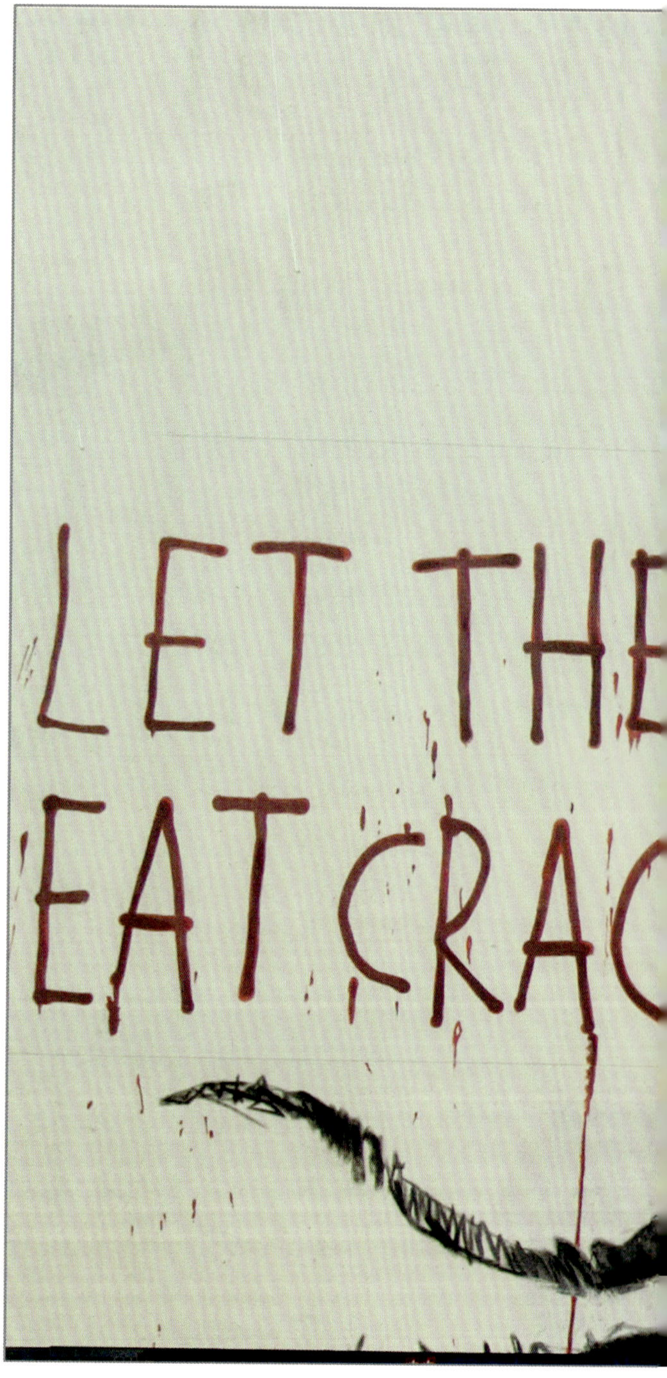

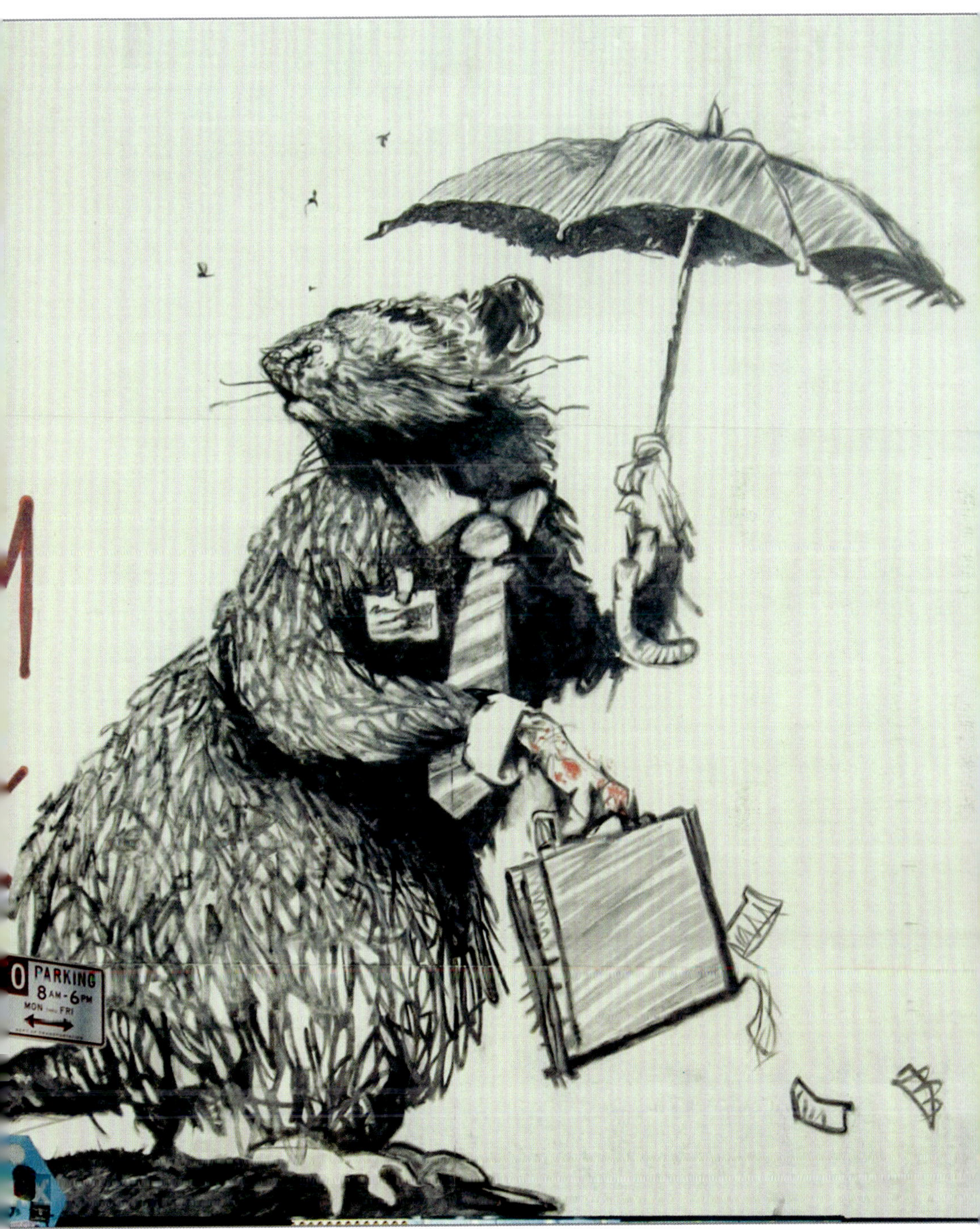
PARKING
8 AM - 6 PM
MON to FRI

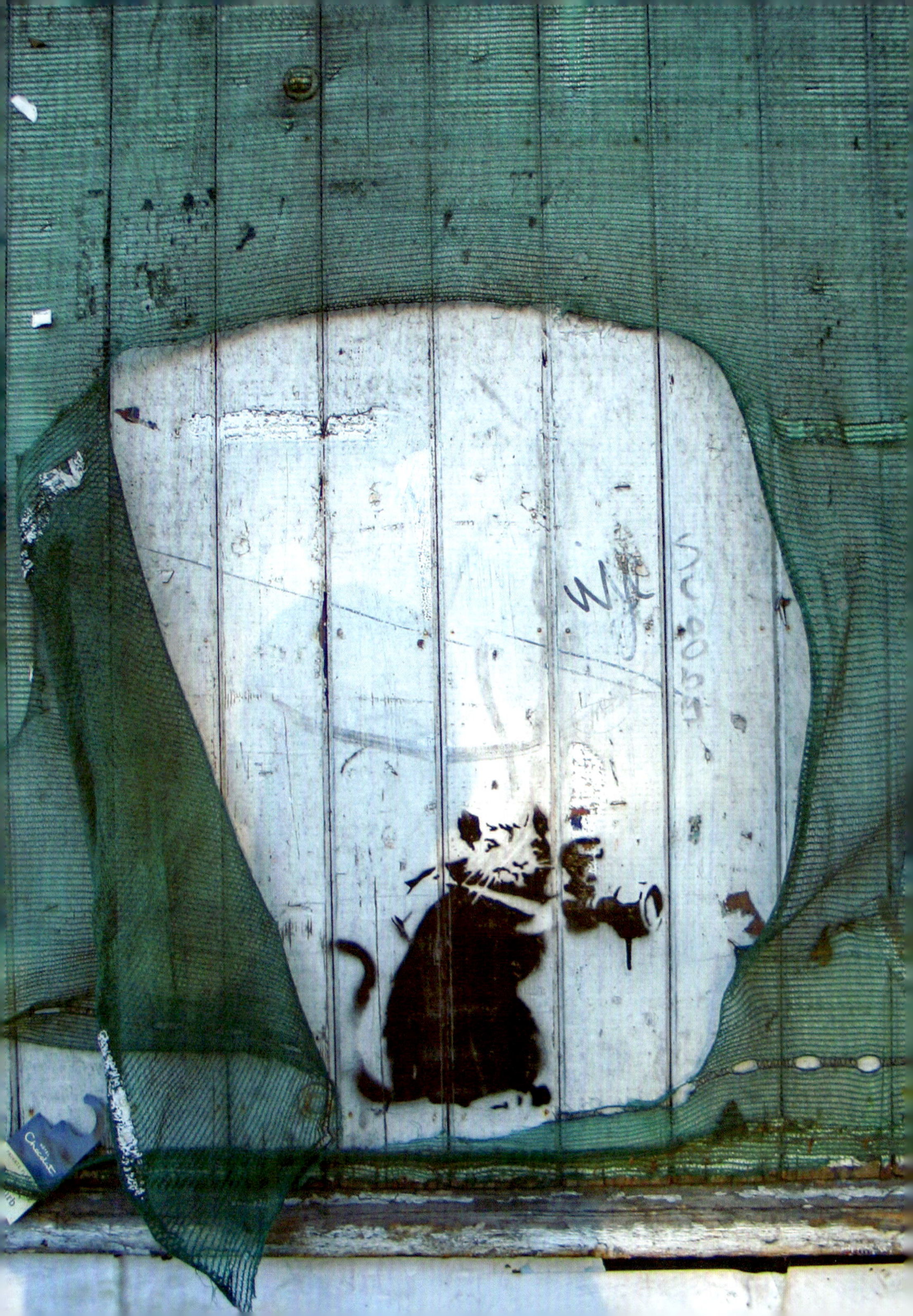

THIS RAT WITH CAMERA, SYMBOLIZING THE PAPARAZZI, WARNS AGAINST THE DANGER OF THE OBSESSIVE PURSUIT OF FAME.

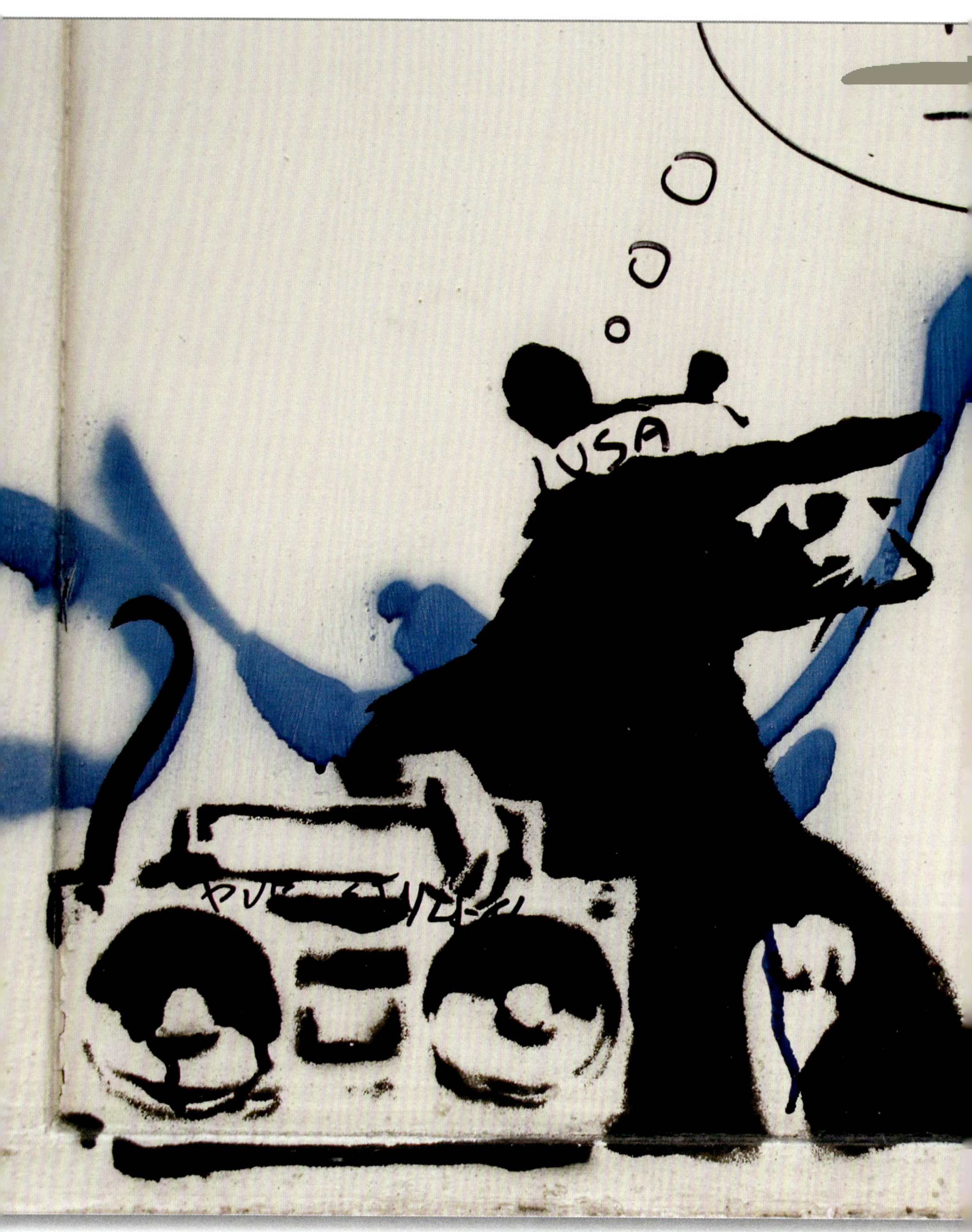
USA

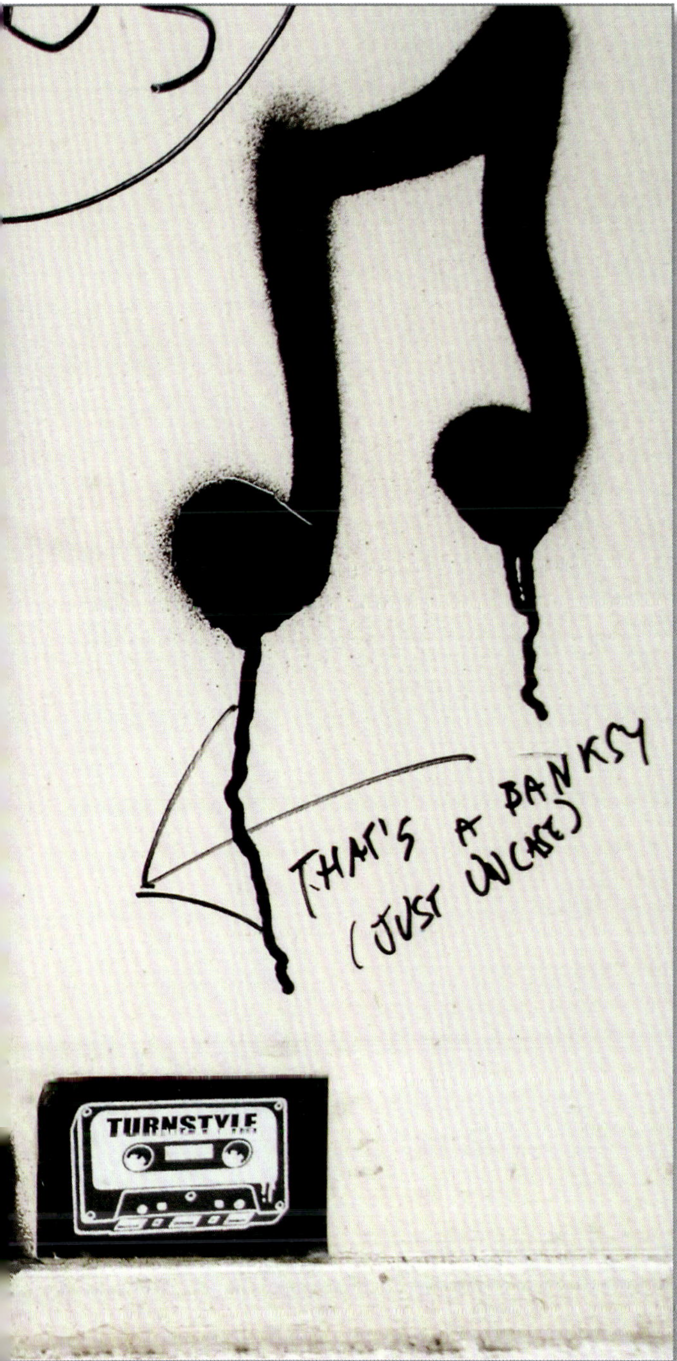

RAPPER RAT

THE POWER OF HIP-HOP MUSIC LIES IN ITS SENSE OF REBELLION AGAINST AUTHORITY, DISCRIMINATION, AND ANY FORM OF INJUSTICE.

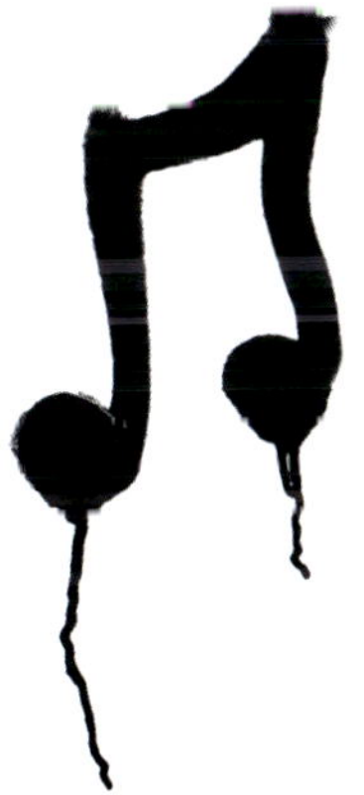

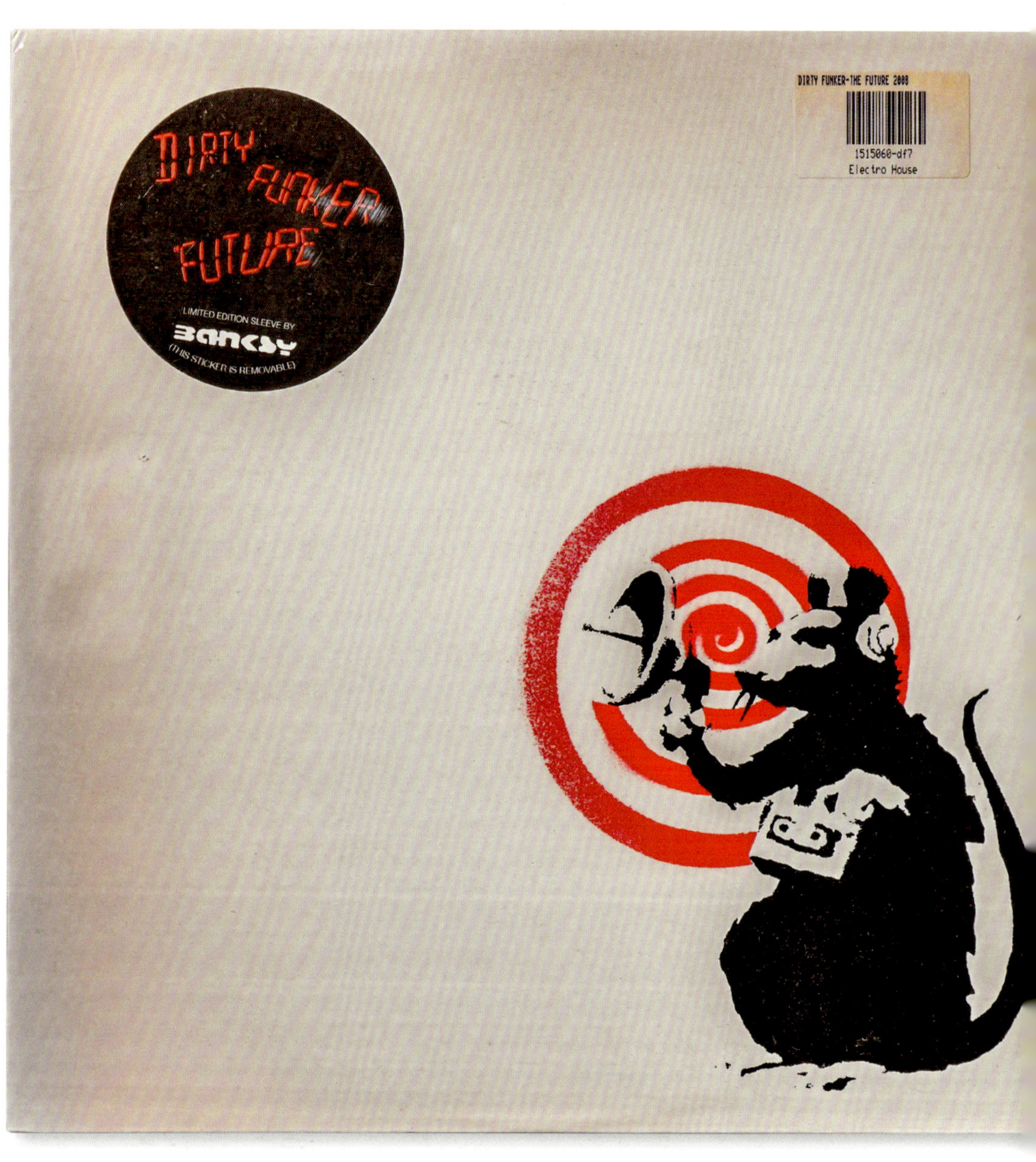
DIRTY FUNKER
"FUTURE"
LIMITED EDITION SLEEVE BY
BANKSY
(THIS STICKER IS REMOVABLE)
DIRTY FUNKER-THE FUTURE 2008
1515060-df7
Electro House

ON THIS COVER OF A DIRTY FUNKER ALBUM, A RAT ARMED WITH HEADPHONES AND SONIC RADAR IS TRYING TO DETECT SURVEILLANCE DEVICES IN THE CITY. BEHIND ITS BACK, A RED SPIRAL STANDS OUT.

WHAT IS A GUERRILLA RAT
DOING IN PARIS IN 2018?
THIS IS HOW BANKSY
CELEBRATED 50 YEARS OF
STENCILS RELATED TO THE
1968 UPRISINGS.

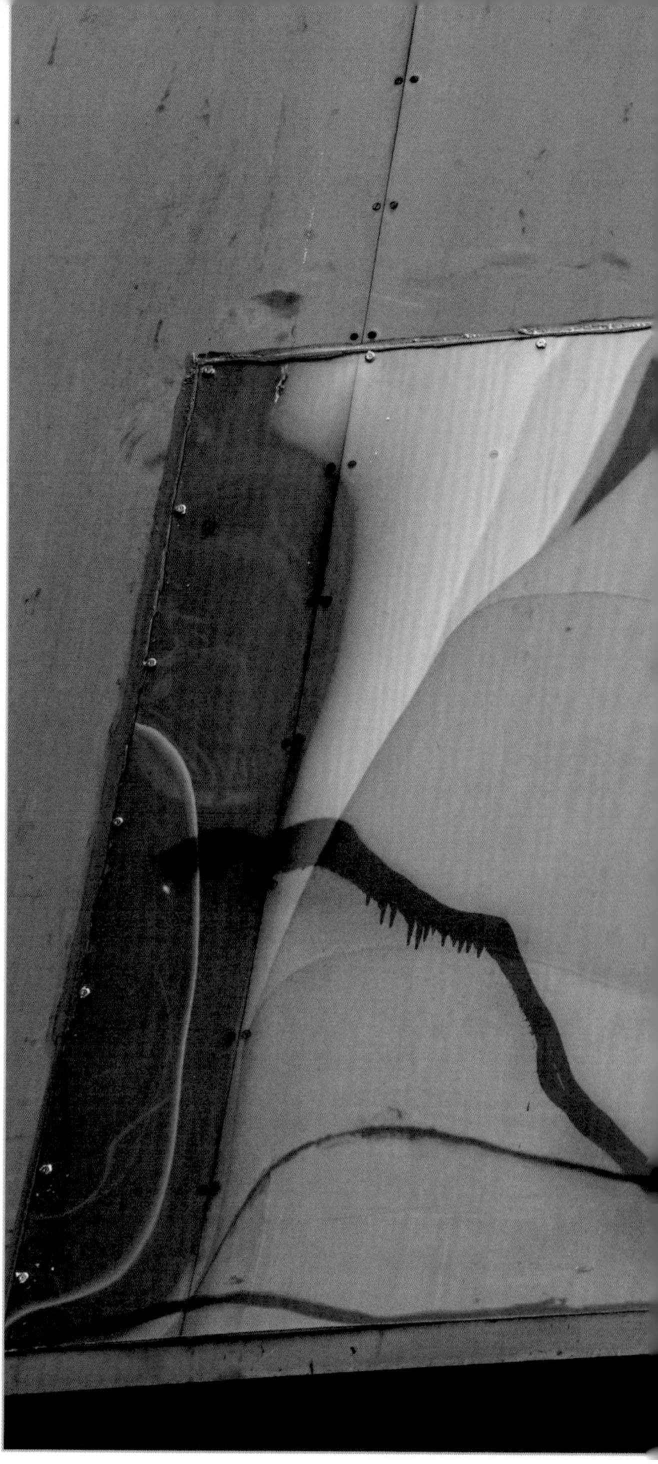

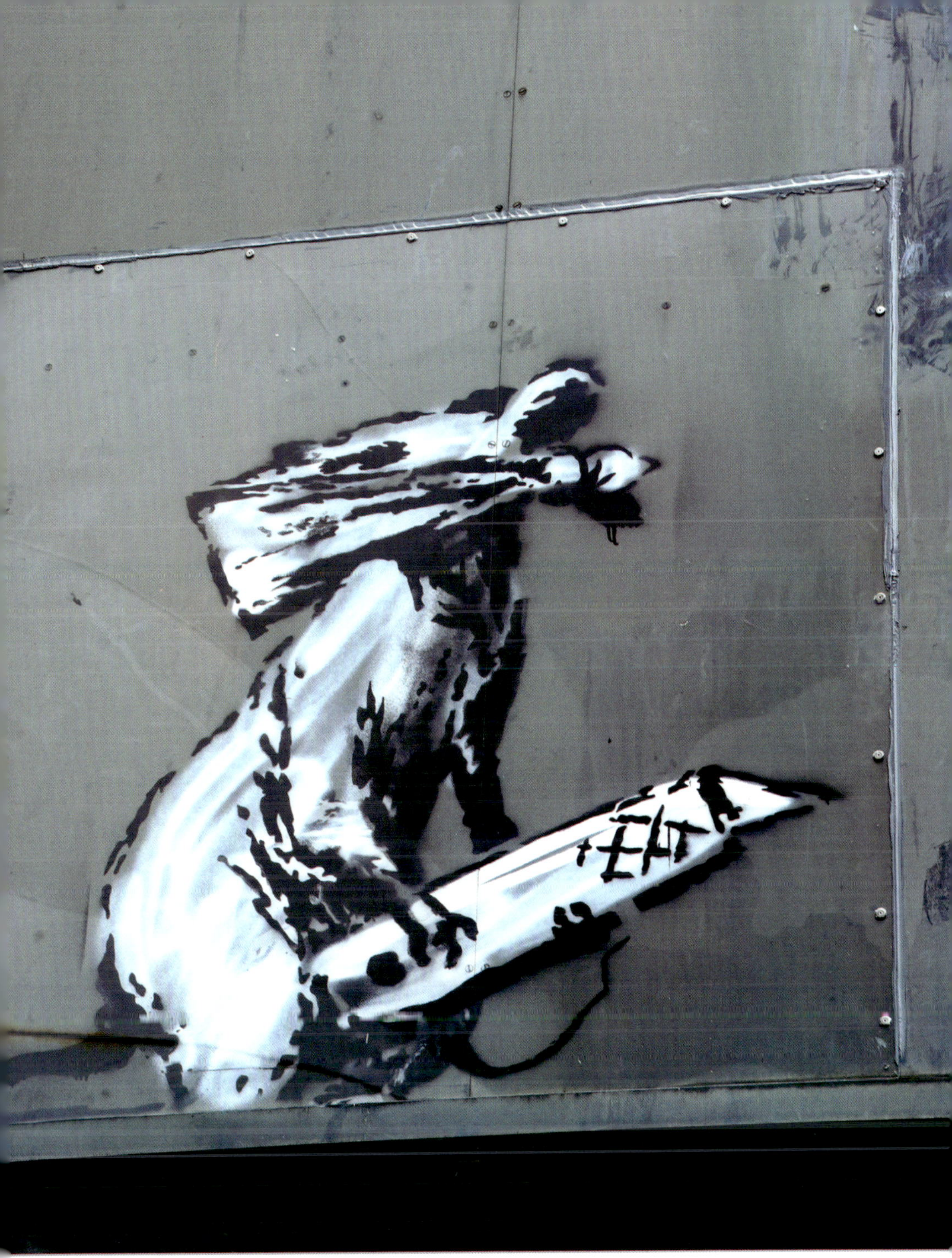
EAT

IN 2010, BANKSY
WAS IN TORONTO TO
PROMOTE THE MOVIE
EXIT THROUGH THE
GIFT SHOP. THIS IS
ONE OF THE SEVEN
GRAFFITI HE LEFT TO
THE CITY.

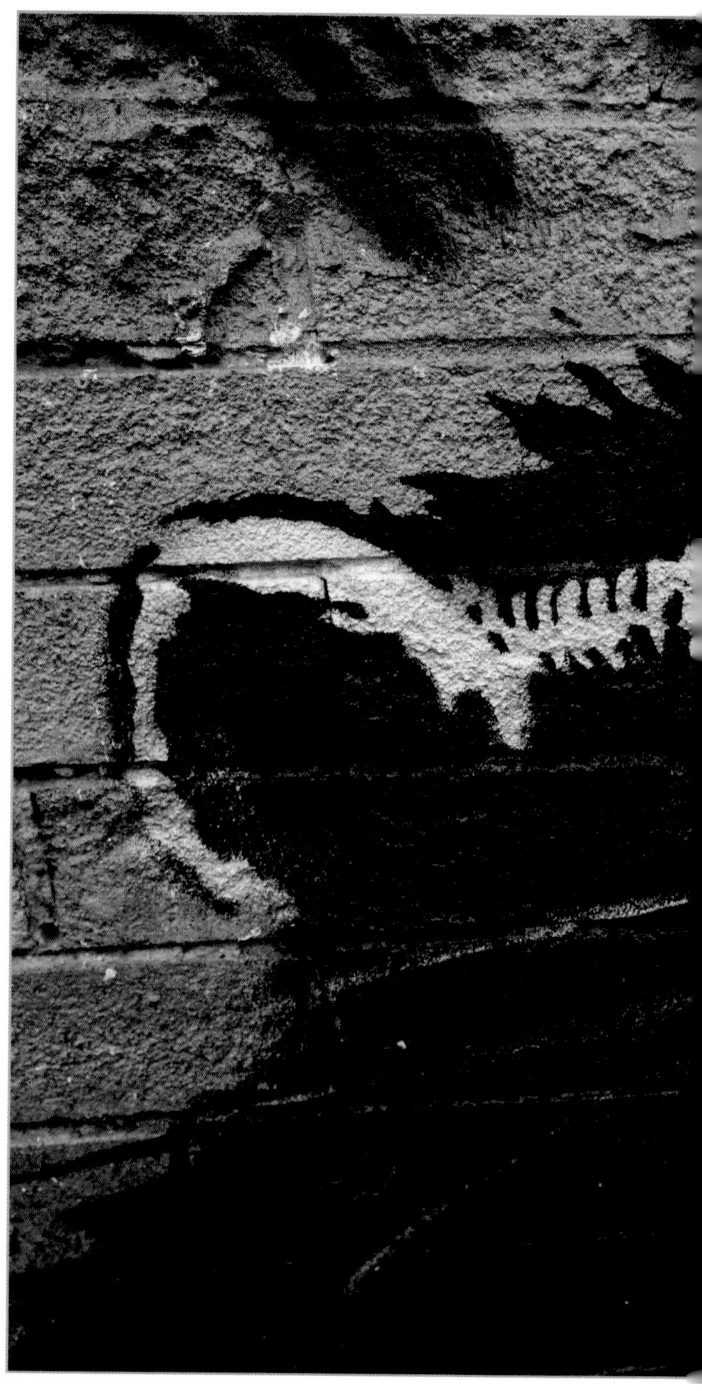

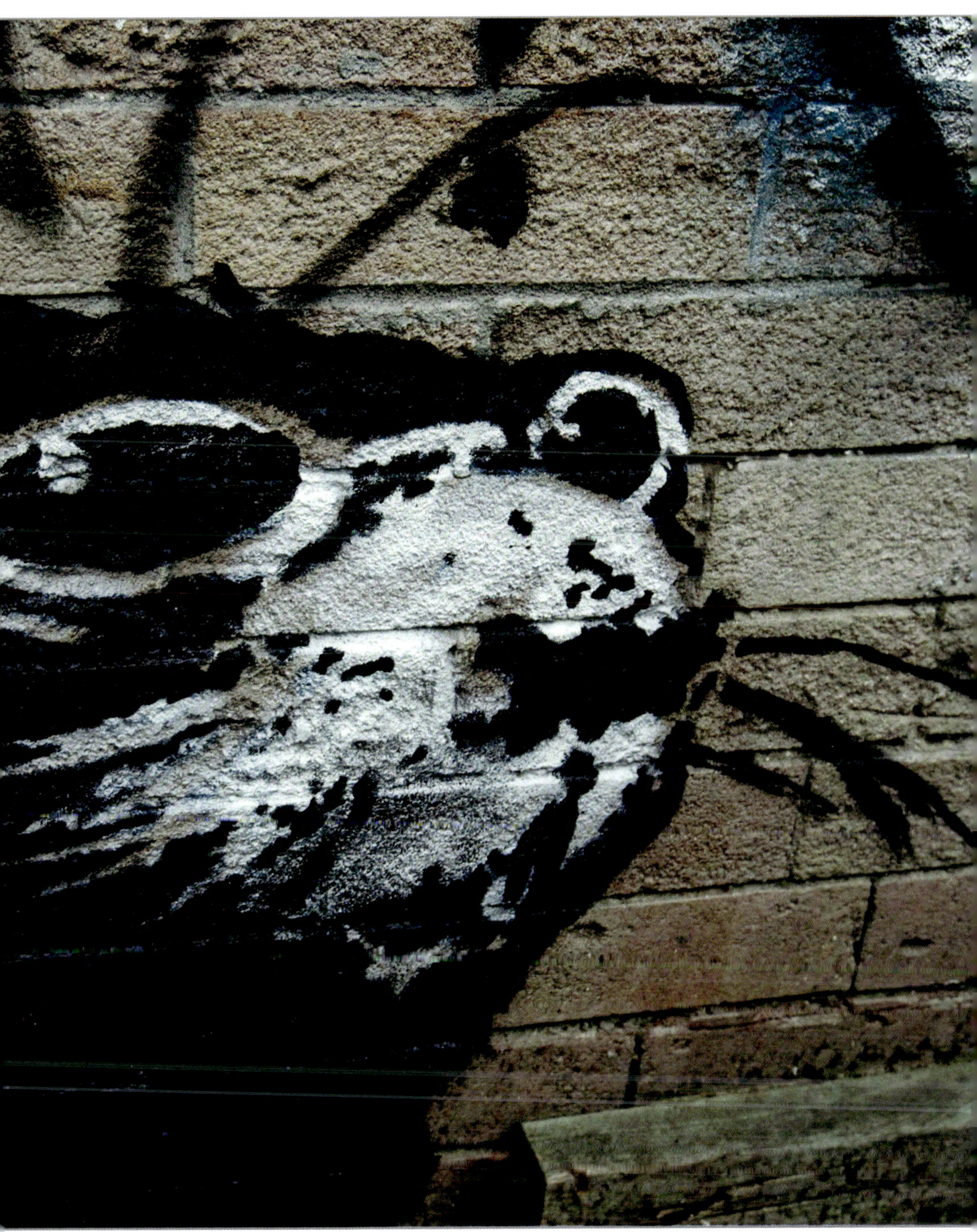

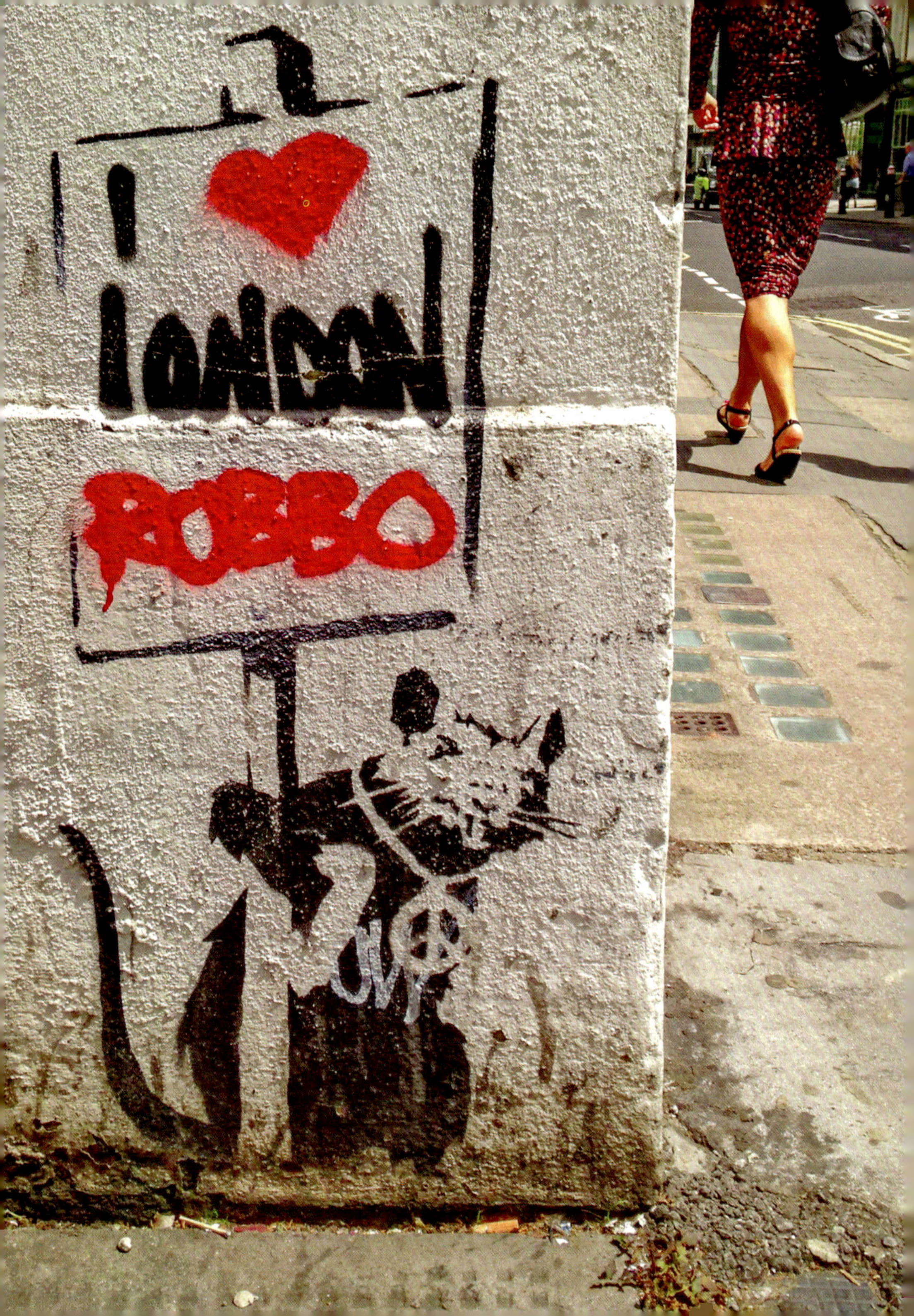

I ♥
LONDON
ROBBO

I LOVE LONDON, ROBBO IS ONE OF THE BEST GRAFFITI
THAT CAN STILL BE ADMIRED IN LONDON. IT TELLS THE
STORY OF BANKSY'S FAMOUS FEUD WITH THE STREET
ARTIST ROBBO. THE RAT WAS ORIGINALLY HOLDING UP A
PLACARD READING "LONDON DOESN'T WORK," BUT TEAM
ROBBO VANDALIZED THE PLACARD, REPLACING IT WITH
ANOTHER ONE READING "I LOVE LONDON, ROBBO."

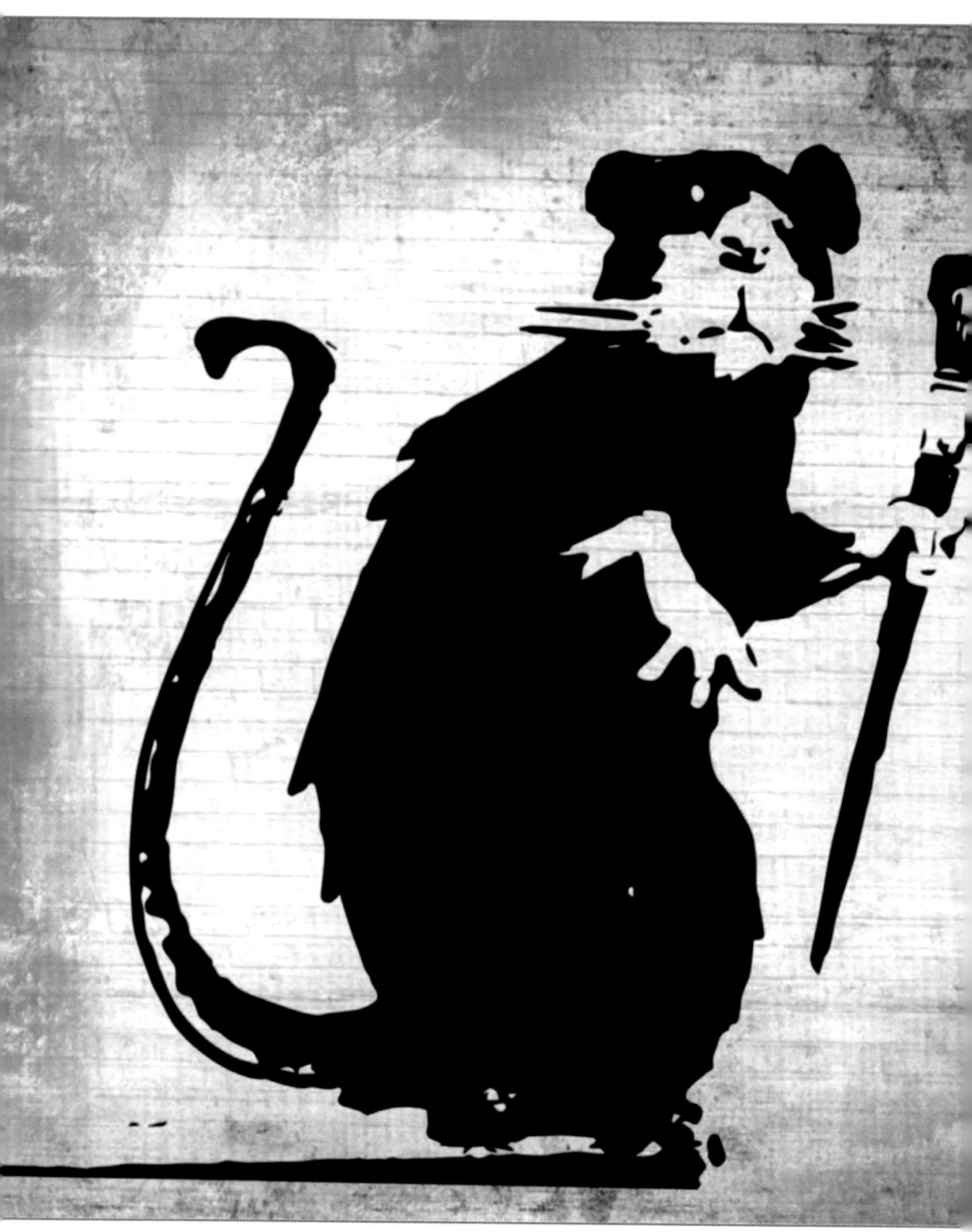

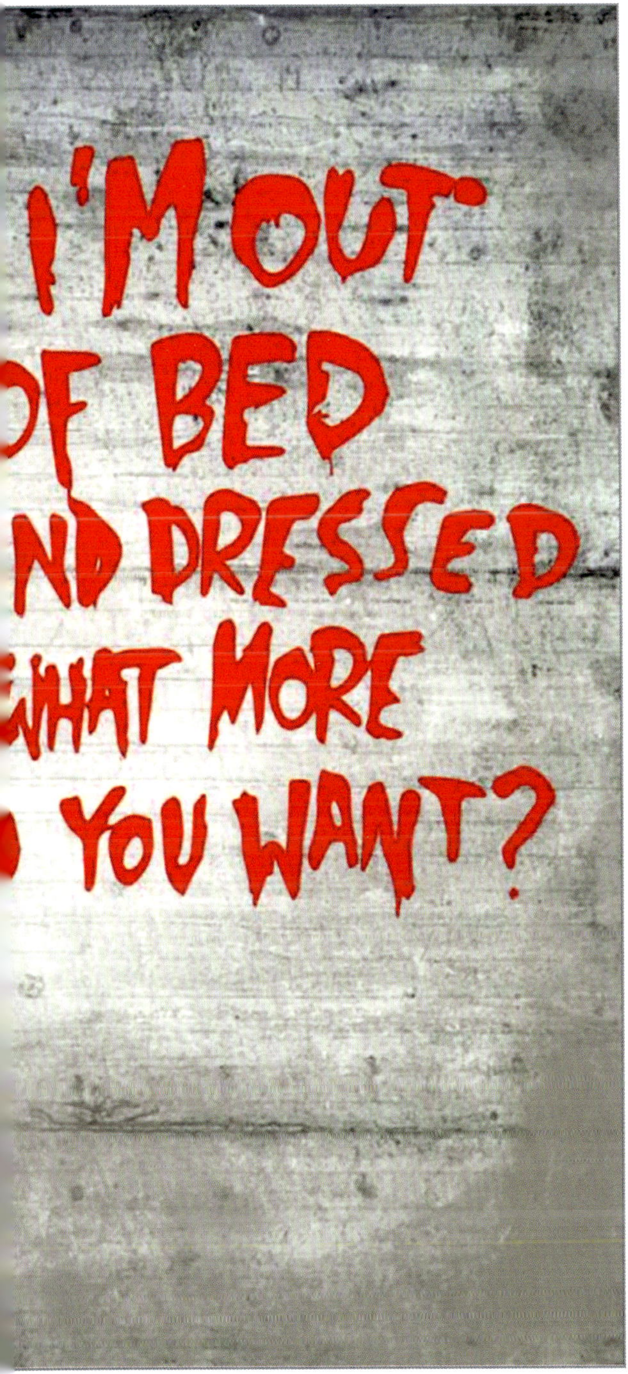

OUT OF BED RAT – LONDON, 2006

A RAT UNDER A HOUSE'S ROOF LAUNCHES A PROVOCATION: "I'M OUT OF BED AND DRESSED—WHAT MORE DO YOU WANT?"

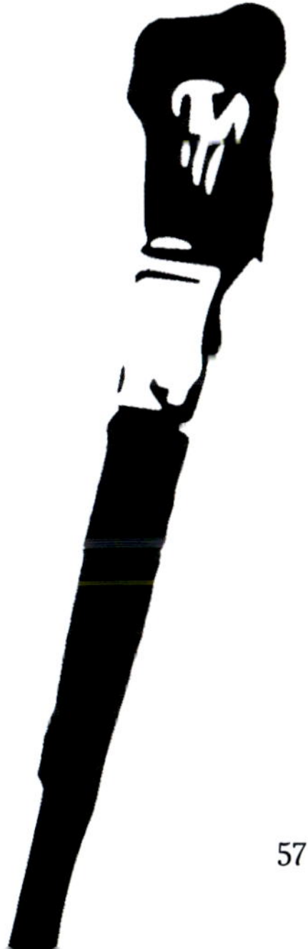

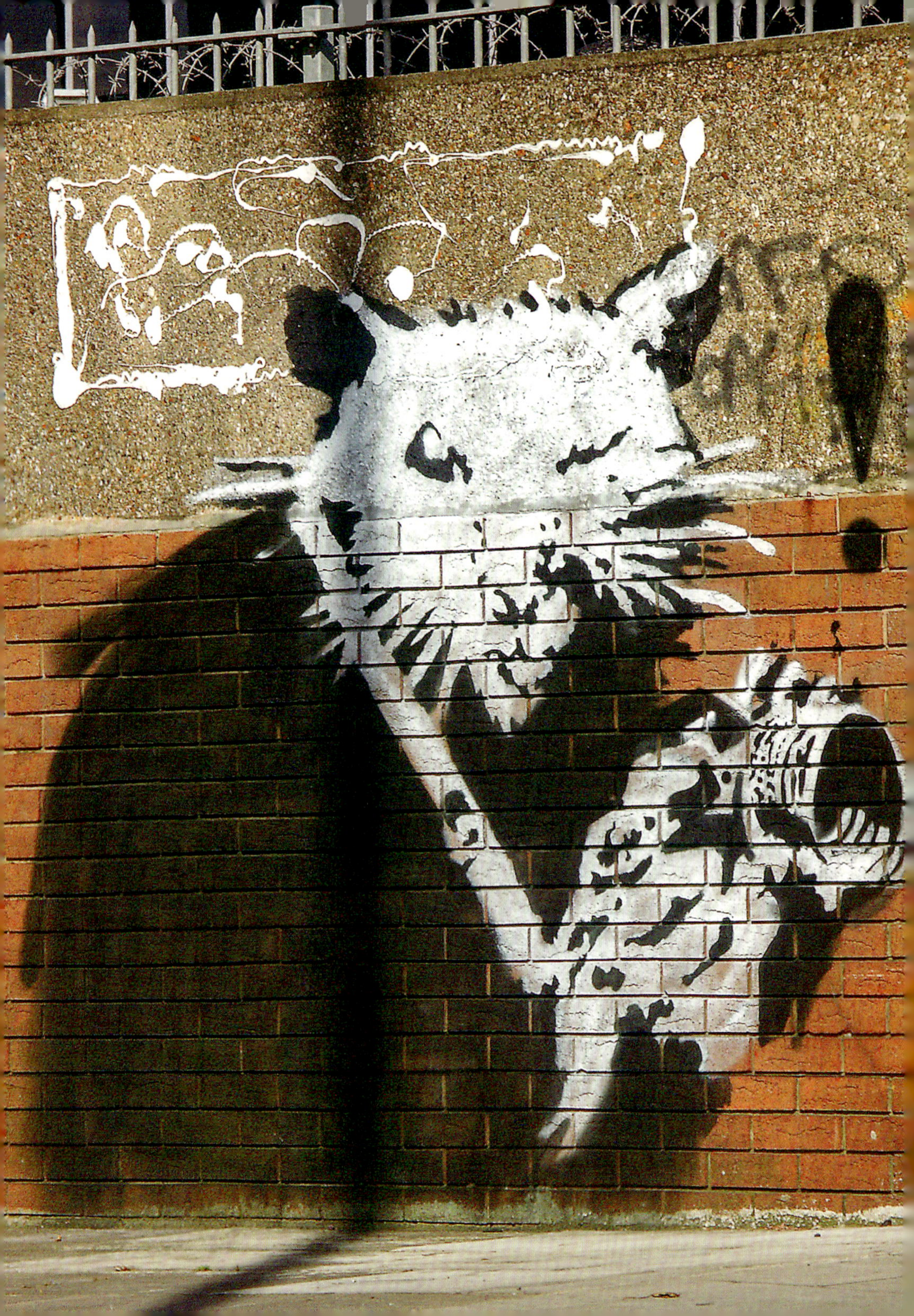

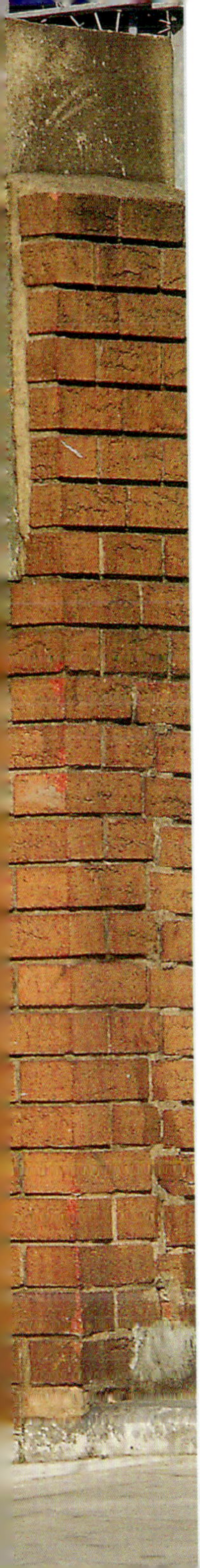

WHILE BANKSY USUALLY PORTRAYS RATS AS THOSE HAVING TO HIDE TO AVOID BEING CAUGHT, IN THIS GRAFFITI, RATS TAKE ON A NEW ROLE: OF PAPARAZZI, COMPLETELY REVERSING THE PERSPECTIVE: NOW IT IS RATS MONITORING WHAT'S GOING ON.

THE UPRISING OF NINE RATS IN THE BATHROOM. ONE OF THEM IS MARKING THE DAYS ON THE WALL, ANOTHER IS PLAYING WITH THE MIRROR. THERE'S A RAT UNROLLING TOILET PAPER, ANOTHER ONE SQUEEZING TOOTHPASTE, WHILE ANOTHER IS HANGING FROM THE BATHROOM EMERGENCY PULL CORD.

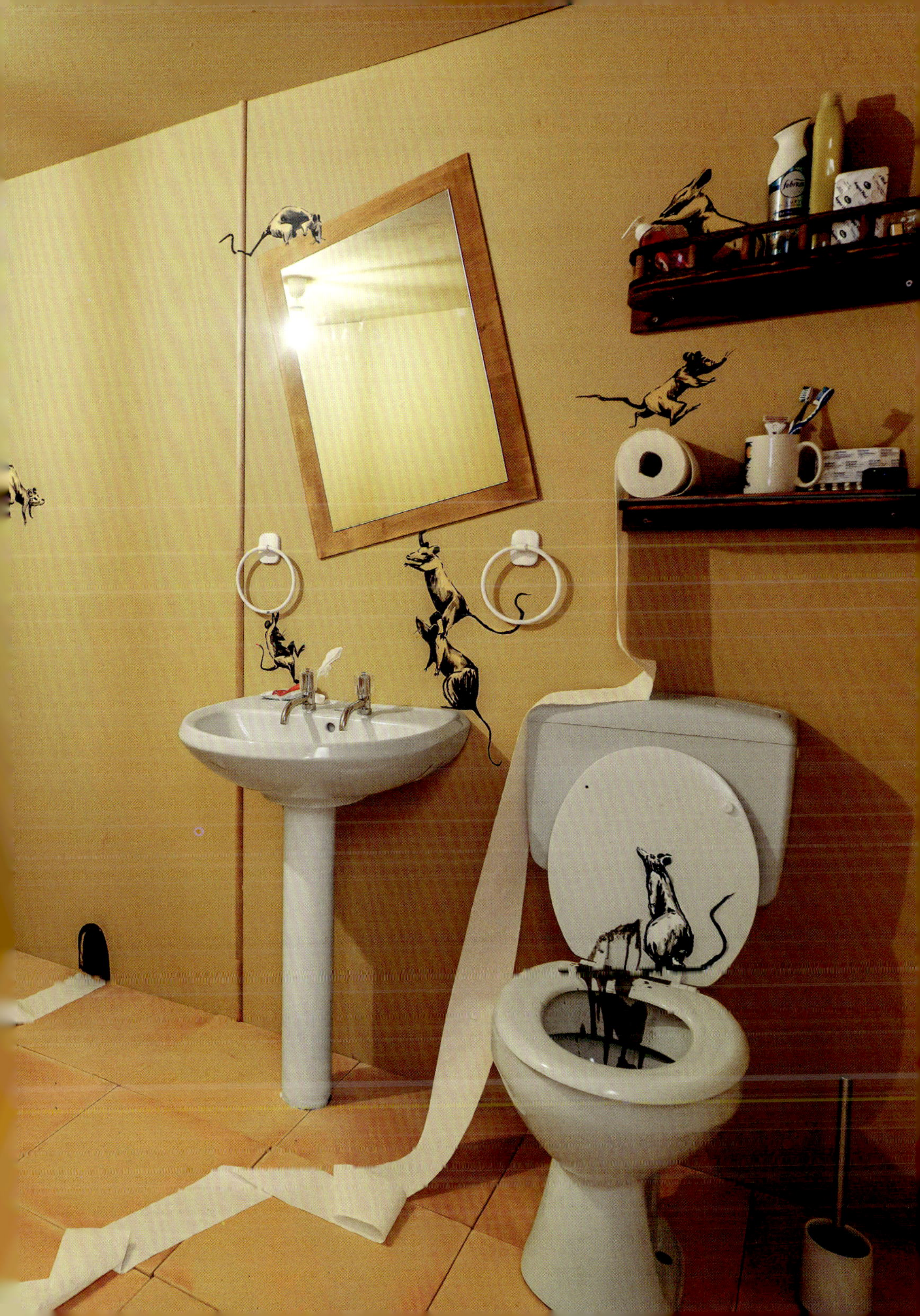

TOWARD THE PLANET OF THE APES

HONORIUS: TELL US, WHY ARE ALL APES CREATED EQUAL?
GEORGE TAYLOR: SOME APES, IT SEEMS, ARE MORE EQUAL THAN OTHERS."
THE PLANET OF THE APES, MOVIE, 1968

A WORLD POPULATED BY MONKEYS WHO CAN TALK AND WHO LIVE IN A HUMAN-LIKE SOCIETY: THIS IS WHAT THE 1968 SCI-FI MOVIE *PLANET OF THE APES* IS ABOUT. CHARLTON HESTON PLAYS THE ROLE OF GEORGE TAYLOR, AN ASTRONAUT IN HIBERNATION WHO, WITH HIS CREW, EMBARKS ON A LONG JOURNEY INTO SPACE AND WAKES UP BACK ON EARTH IN A DISTANT FUTURE, IN 3978.

Planet of the Apes is based on the 1963 novel of the same name by the French writer Pierre Boulle. George finds himself fighting for his own survival in a world unknown to him and dominated by monkeys who regard human beings as nothing more than

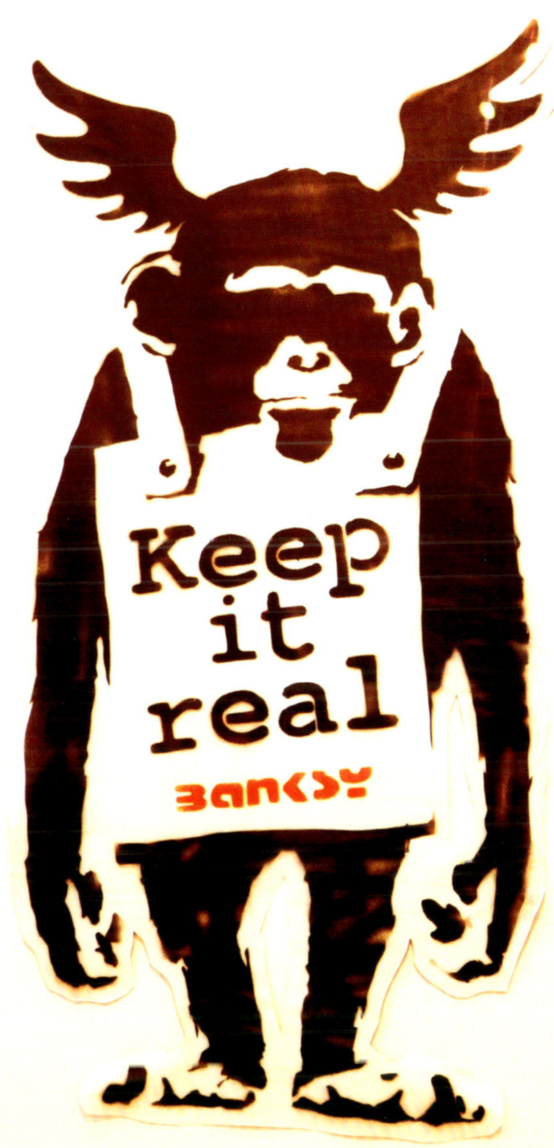

Keep
it
real
BANKSY

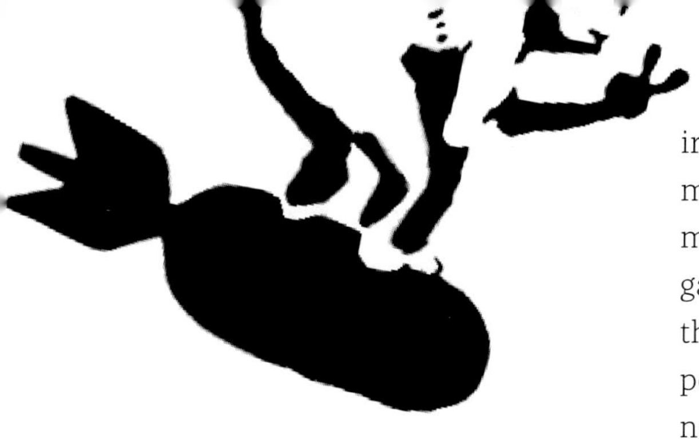

wild animals, only useful for scientific experiments. In this society, chimpanzees are scientists and intellectuals, gorillas are soldiers and members of the police force, and orangutans are administrators, priests, and politicians. George will find out that human civilization destroyed itself as a result of a devastating nuclear war. Decimated and deprived of all that progress had given them, human beings quickly regressed, while apes evolved significantly.

For Banksy, monkeys are extremely intelligent creatures often associated with the human figure. His monkeys are playful, revolutionary, irreverent, and expressive as much as humans are, and even more so. "They say that if you gave a thousand monkeys a thousand typewriters at some point you'd have yourself a novel. I was wondering if you gave a thousand monkeys a thousand sticks of dynamite how long would it take for them to make the city a more beautiful looking place," he reflects.

For Banksy, monkeys are also a tool to voice his contempt for the system, to encourage rebellion, and to criticize human actions. Even though monkeys are not as despised as rats, they certainly are creatures living on the margins of society, often exploited by humans for their own ends. We should not forget that monkeys are often used as test animals in scientific experiments; they are tortured, mistreated, and deprived of their freedom. In Banksy's artworks, monkeys are turned into heroic figures, engaged in a strenuous resistance against the system and the world's pitiless superficiality.

Banksy's monkeys look like a contemporary take on Singerie, a visual arts genre especially popular in France in the eighteenth century that depicted satirical scenes of monkeys dressed in human clothes. These representations targeted the weaknesses, injustice, and corruption of society at the time, just like Banksy's chimps do. A clear example is 2009's *Devolved Parliament,* where Banksy's satire is clear and fierce. In this monumental oil painting, Banksy portrayed the House of Commons (one of the two chambers of the United Kingdom's Parliament) with chimps sitting in the MPs' seats. The question arises: "Could they do better?" Banksy often humanizes monkeys to make his message more powerful and immediate. This is the case of the bellhop with his red uniform at the entrance of Banksy's *Walled Off Hotel,* overlooking the barrier separating Israel from the Palestinian territories.

In 2000, Banksy painted his self-portrait titled *Monkey Self-Portrait,* in which he is portrayed while spraying paint from two spray cans, but he replaced his head with that of a monkey.

Among the works that emphasize human arrogance, and humankind's habit of thinking it is above all other creatures, *Simple Intelligence Testing* is very significant. It is a series of five oil paintings that Banksy created in 2000, where the protagonist is a chimpanzee locked up in a laboratory undergoing an intelligence test that requires him to open three safes in order to find bananas. The test ends in quite an unexpected way: after eating the bananas, the chimp stacks all the safes on top of

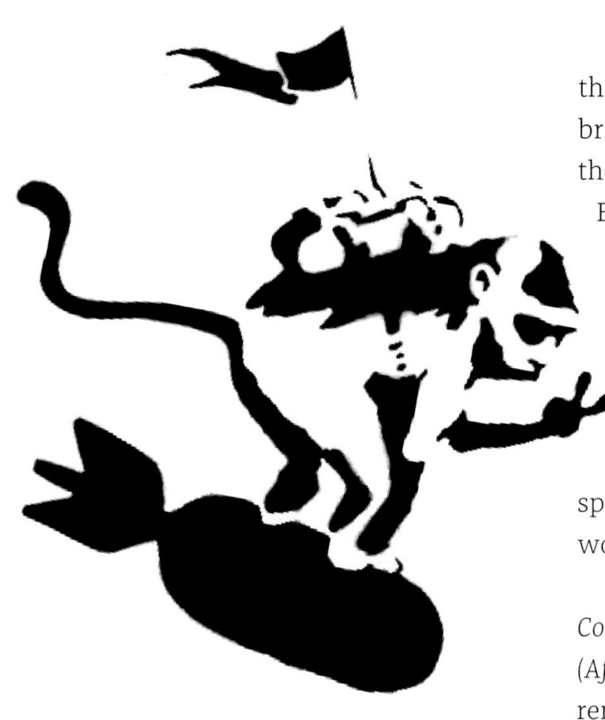

each other and uses them to escape the laboratory through an opening on the ceiling. For this work, Banksy was inspired by a comic strip, but his message goes far beyond the seemingly fun spirit of the scenes. The chimpanzee feels trapped and helpless, perhaps just like Banksy feels in a consumerist and manipulative society that aims at imposing values and lifestyles. This is once again about breaking the rules, evolving toward a brighter future and finding the way that leads to freedom. Banksy aims at goading those who just follow the rules, without reflecting, without asking themselves questions, and without making their own decisions independently, and he spares no one, not even Hollywood stars.

A clear example is *Original Concept for Barely Legal Poster (After Demi Moore)* — clearly reminiscent of the 1991 *Vanity Fair* cover — where heavily pregnant Demi Moore appears completely naked with the face of a monkey. This image was also used on the poster advertising Banksy's iconic *Barely Legal* exhibition, organized in Los Angeles in 2006. The choice of this city was not random, because Los Angeles was one of the most controversial metropolises in the world, where glamor, wealth, and the ephemeral universe of celebrities sharply contrasted with an impressive number of homeless people and just as many cases of extreme poverty and crime.

If it's true that Banksy spares no one, his criticism becomes particularly harsh when it comes to English nobility. How can we forget his *Monkey Queen* depicting Queen Elizabeth II in full regalia at the 2002 Golden Jubilee in the guise of a monkey? Queen Elizabeth II, who had already been a "victim" of the artist in some quite irreverent stencils, here becomes a perfect metaphor for a conservative, obsolete institution. Also very famous is Banksy's *Monkey Laugh Now*, which he presented in several different versions. It is a "sandwich monkey" with a slogan that sounds more like a warning, a threat, and reads "Laugh Now But One Day We'll Be In Charge." The chimp looks so sad, as if he felt oppressed and enslaved, but his message

immediately lets us understand that his condition is temporary, that he won't give up, and that it will soon be payback time. Banksy's message is clear: it is an exhortation to those in power to enjoy their undeserved privileges while they still can, because he believes that in the not-too-distant future his "army" of rats, monkeys, and street creatures will rise up, claiming their rights and dignity. Sooner or later a revolution will come. Banksy is sure about it, and he makes it clear with his *Monkey Detonator*, where a chimp jumps on a detonator in a decisive manner to ignite an explosion, his determination appearing to be unshakable. While the image might make us smile, it also makes us reflect on the socio-political implications a similar situation might generate, and the tragic consequences that such a violent gesture might provoke. Although Banksy fights against the system's injustices, he has always proclaimed his pacifism: "It takes a lot of guts to stand up anonymously in a western democracy and call for things no one else believes in—like peace and justice and freedom."

In his *Monkey Keep It Real*, Banksy reminds us of the importance of not losing the sense of reality and keep our feet firmly planted on the ground without being misled by false promises and easy gains. This is the philosophy that Banksy has definitely made his own. Despite his great fame, he is still the same person and artist, strongly defending his anonymity and private life. Despite millions of followers and all his fans, Banksy remains true to himself and the same values, passion, and ideals that have always inspired him from the very beginning.

Finally, it is worth mentioning *Monkey Poison*, which Banksy created in 2004 to denounce something so dear to him. This work, superimposed on the reproduction of an old painting, shows a monkey perched on a tree branch greedily drinking some gasoline from a carton, unaware that he is poisoning himself. It is a clear critique of capitalist logic, which will stop at nothing to pursue more profit, heedless of the irreparable harm caused to our planet and the creatures inhabiting it.

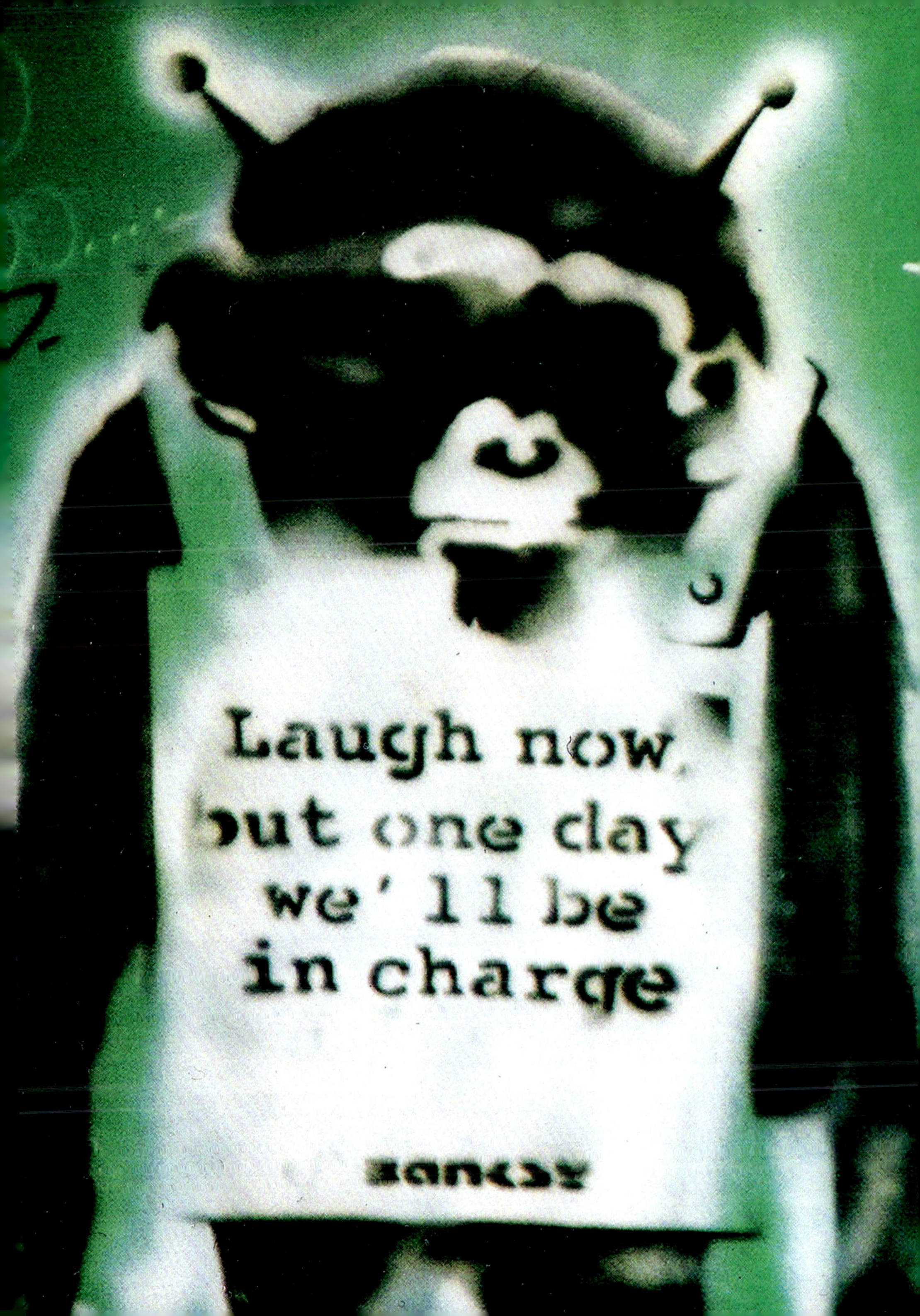

Laugh now.
but one day
we'll be
in charge
Banksy

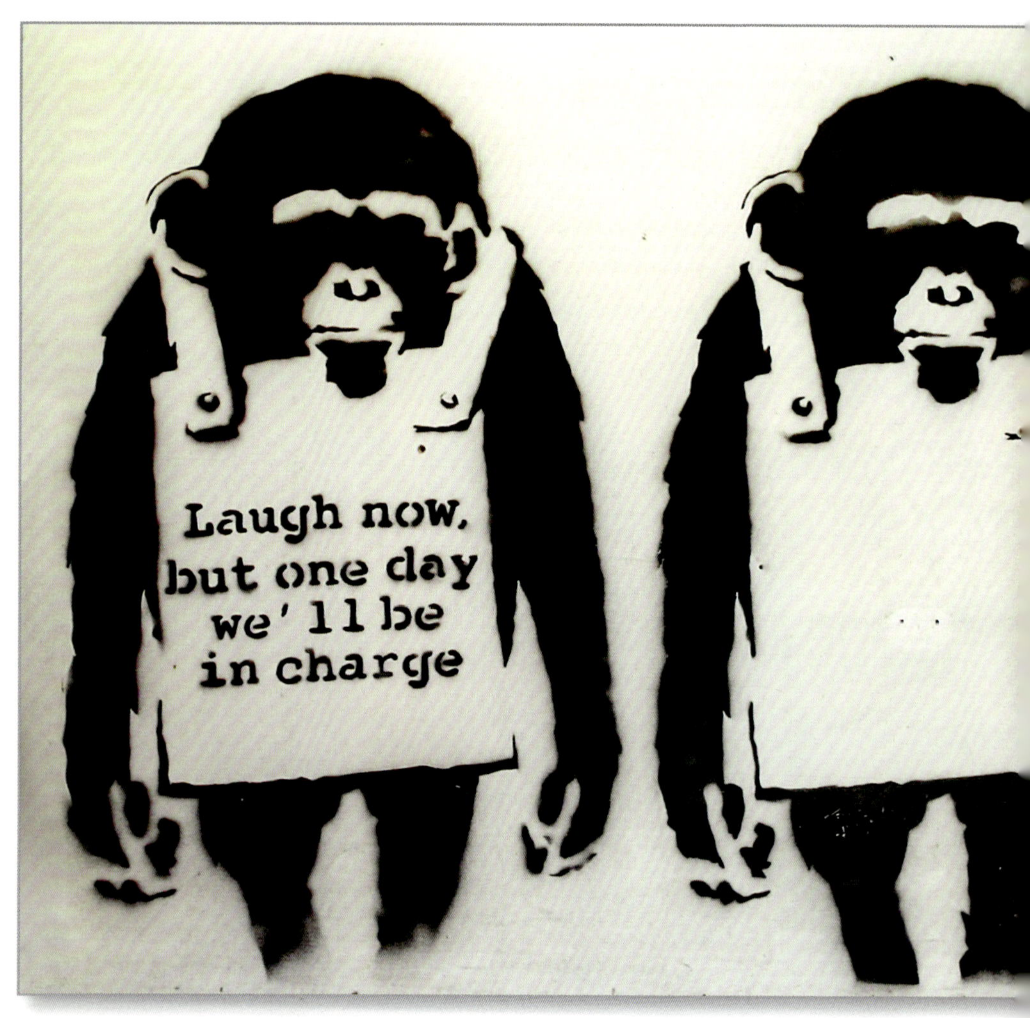

LAUGH NOW - 2002

(DETAIL)

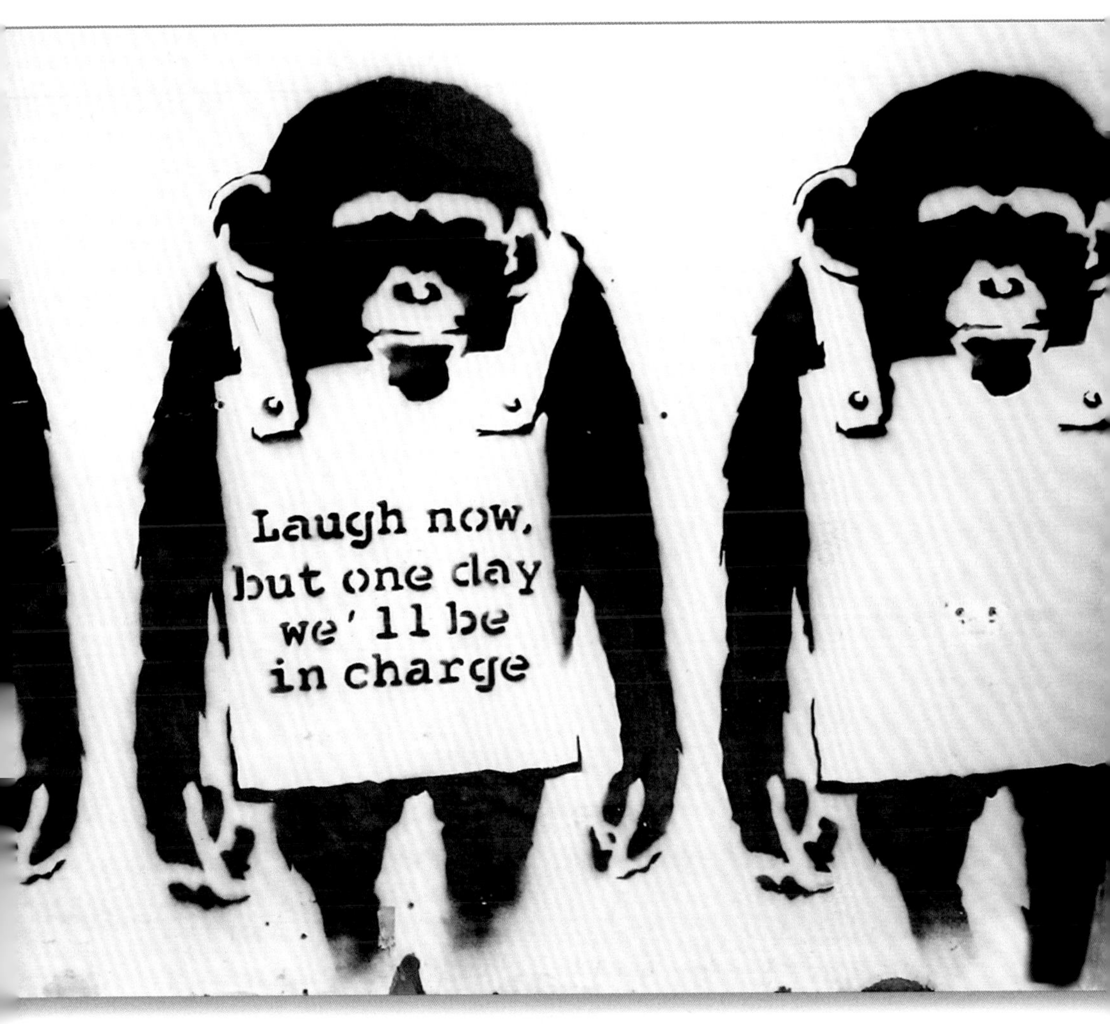

TEN MONKEYS PLACED NEXT TO EACH OTHER EMBODY THE POWER OF THE WORKING CLASS. IN LAUGH NOW, BANKSY EXPLOITS THE SERIAL NATURE OF COMMUNICATION, TYPICAL OF THE LOGICS OF CAPITALISM, TO AMPLIFY THE REVOLUTIONARY POWER OF THE MESSAGE WRITTEN ON THE SANDWICH BOARDS.

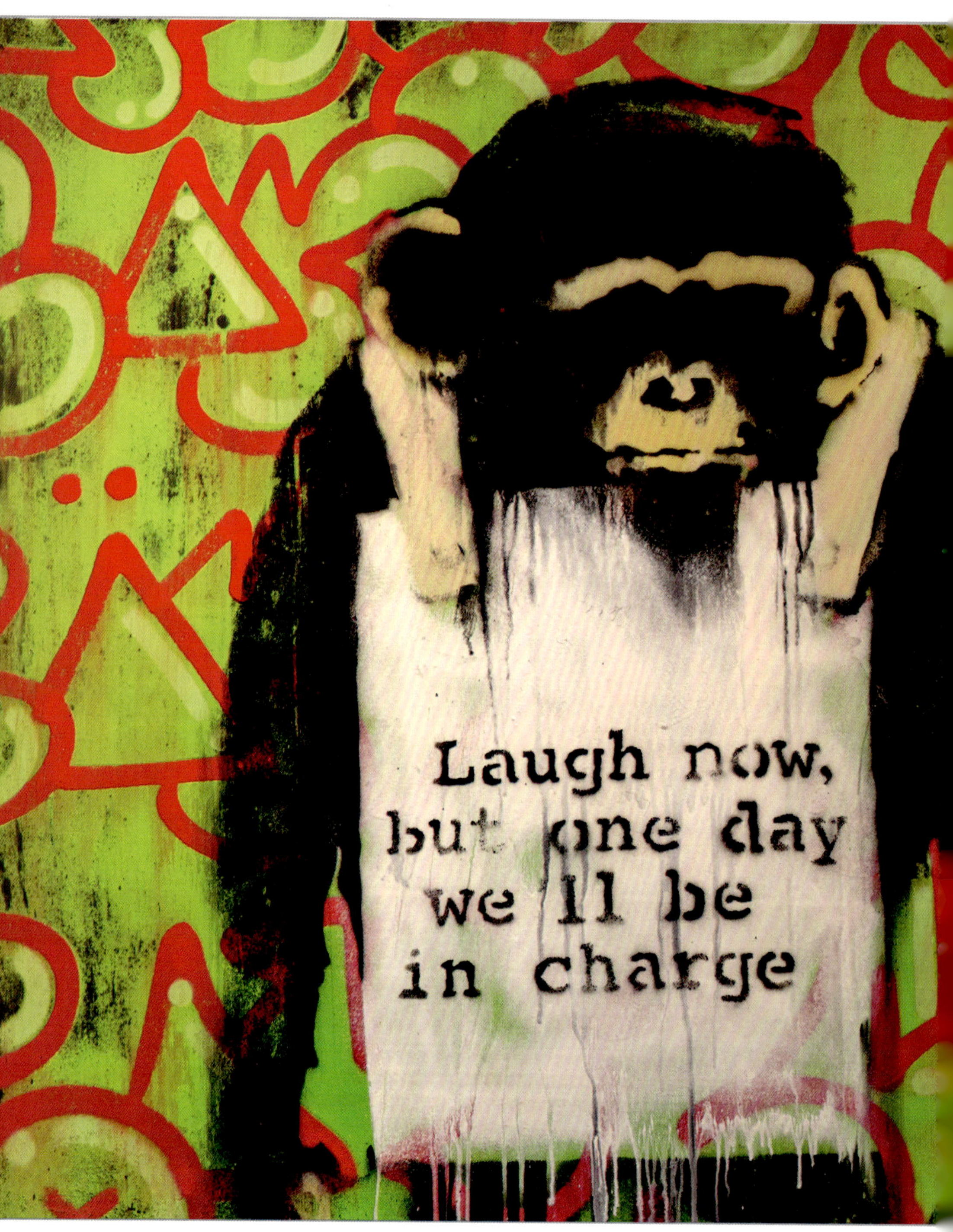

Laugh now,
but one day
we'll be
in charge

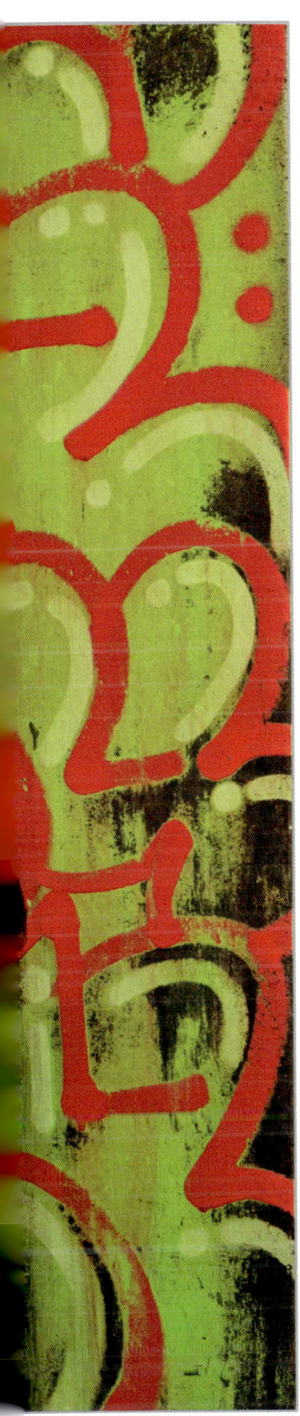

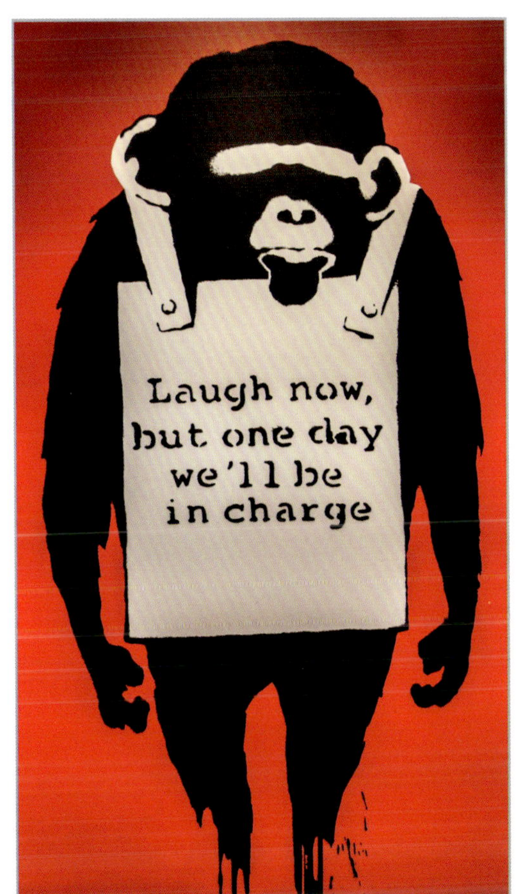

LEFT *LAUGH NOW BUT ONE DAY WE'LL BE IN CHARGE* – 2008
TOP *LAUGH NOW* – MÜLHEIM, GERMANY, 2003

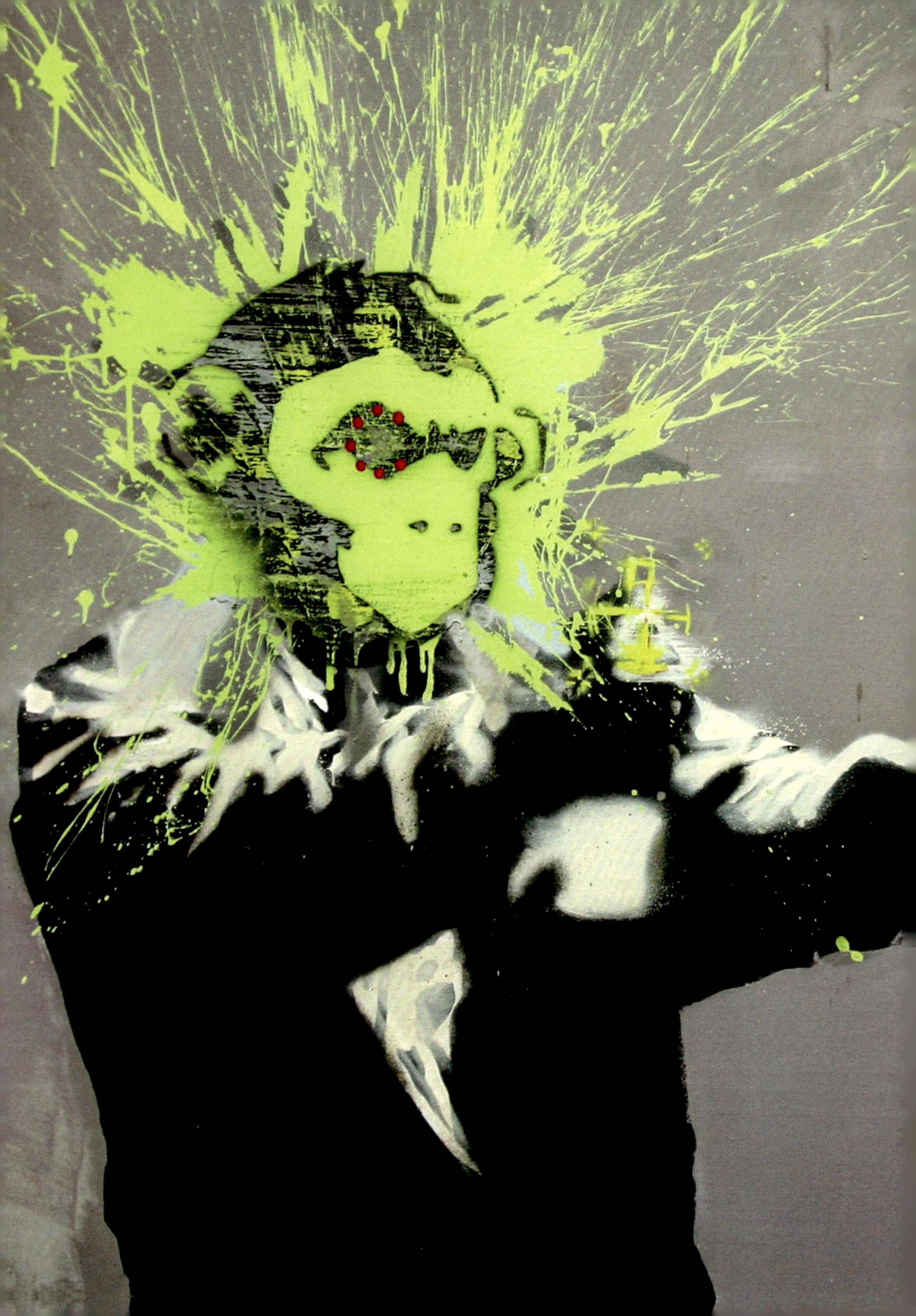

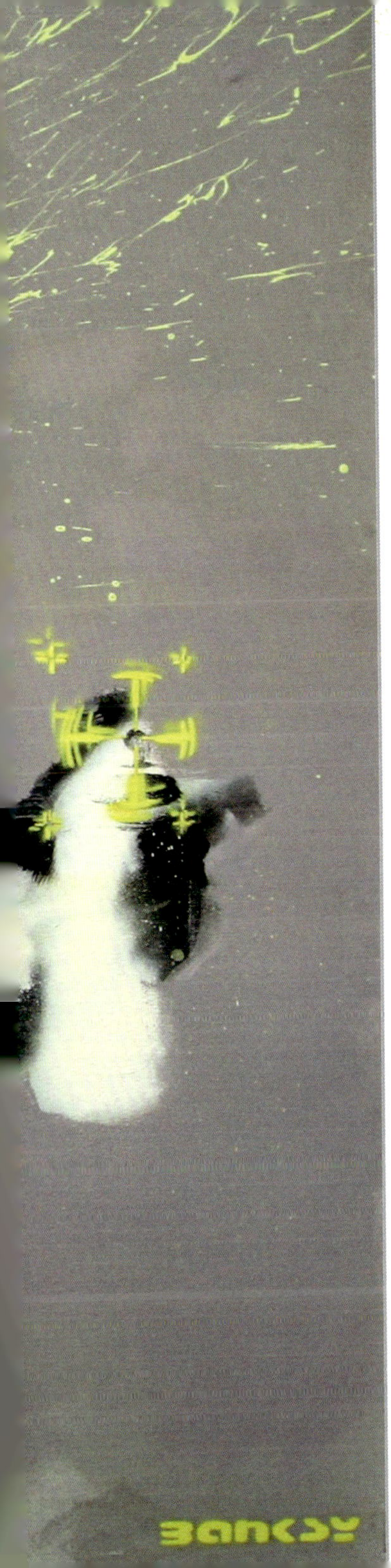

SELF-PORTRAIT – 2000

BANKSY PORTRAYS HIMSELF IN THE GUISE OF A MONKEY ARMED WITH SPRAY CANS AND SURROUNDED BY AN EXPLOSION OF YELLOW PAINT.

BANKSY TURNS THE IMAGE OF THE PREGNANT AND NAKED DEMI MOORE, CREATED BY ANNIE LEIBOWITZ FOR THE AUGUST 1991 COVER OF VANITY FAIR, INTO A MONKEY WITH A BLACK WIG AND A CIGARETTE BETWEEN HER LIPS, PARODYING AN EQUALLY PROVOCATIVE COVER.

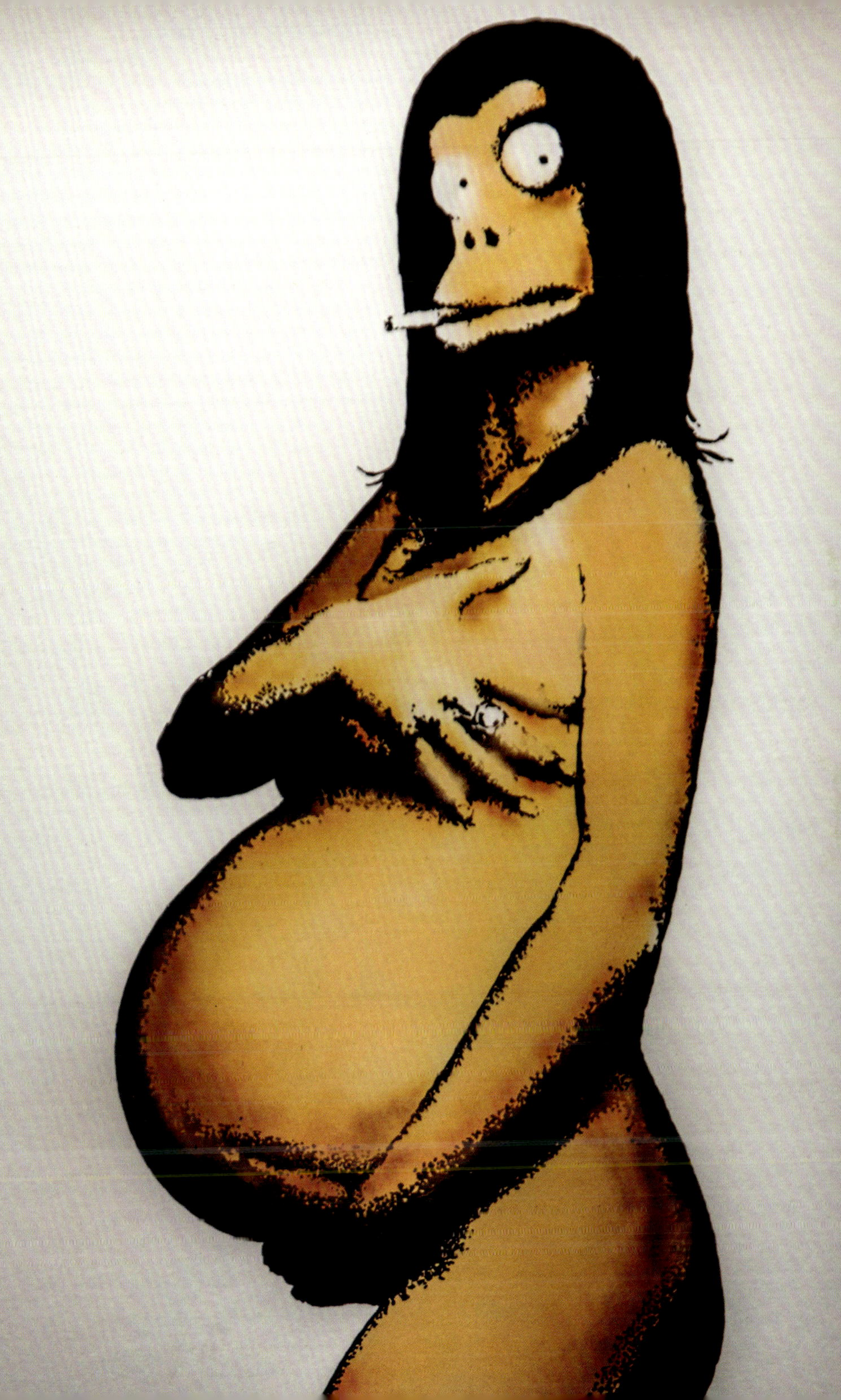

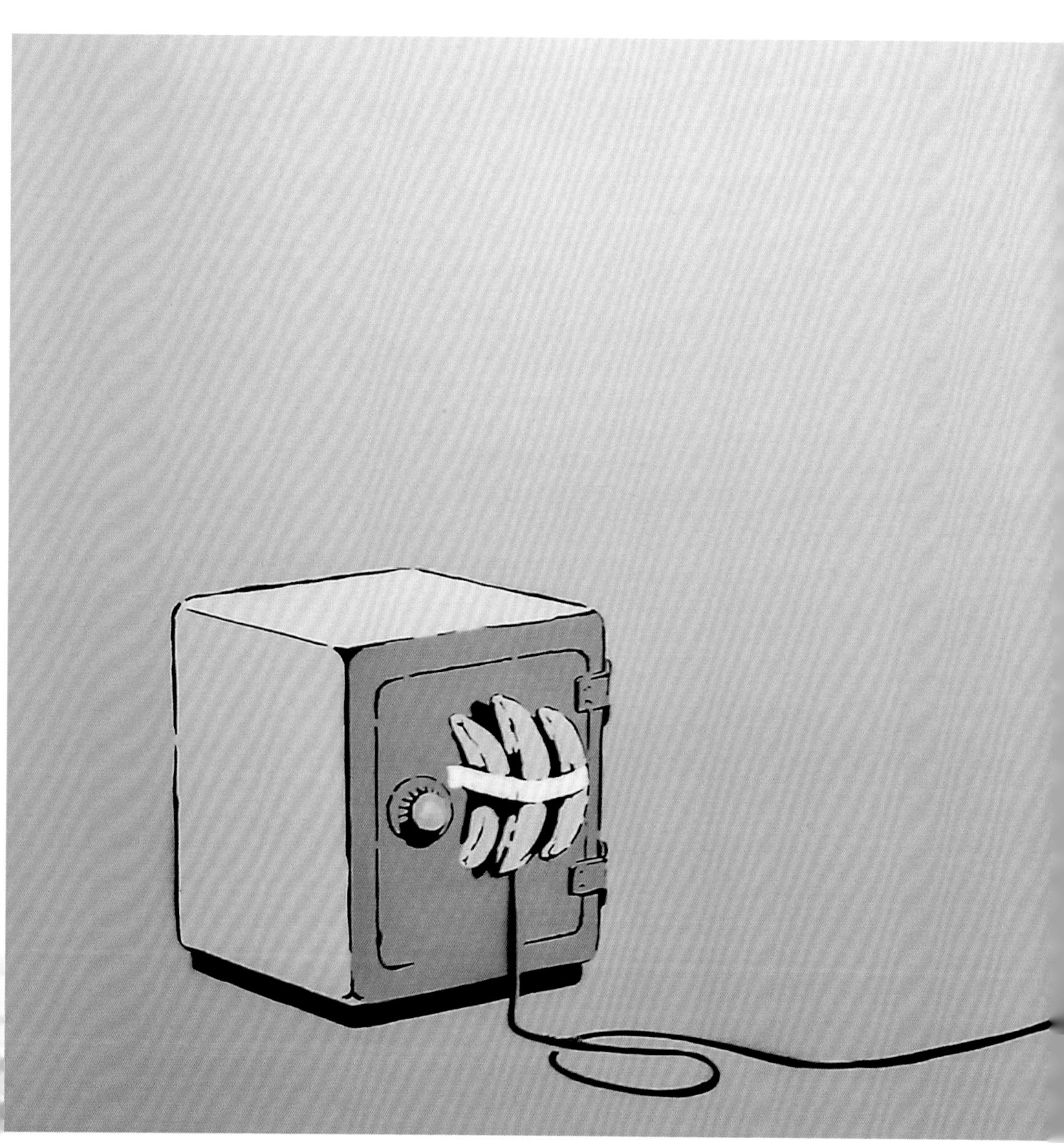

MONKEY DETONATOR – 2000

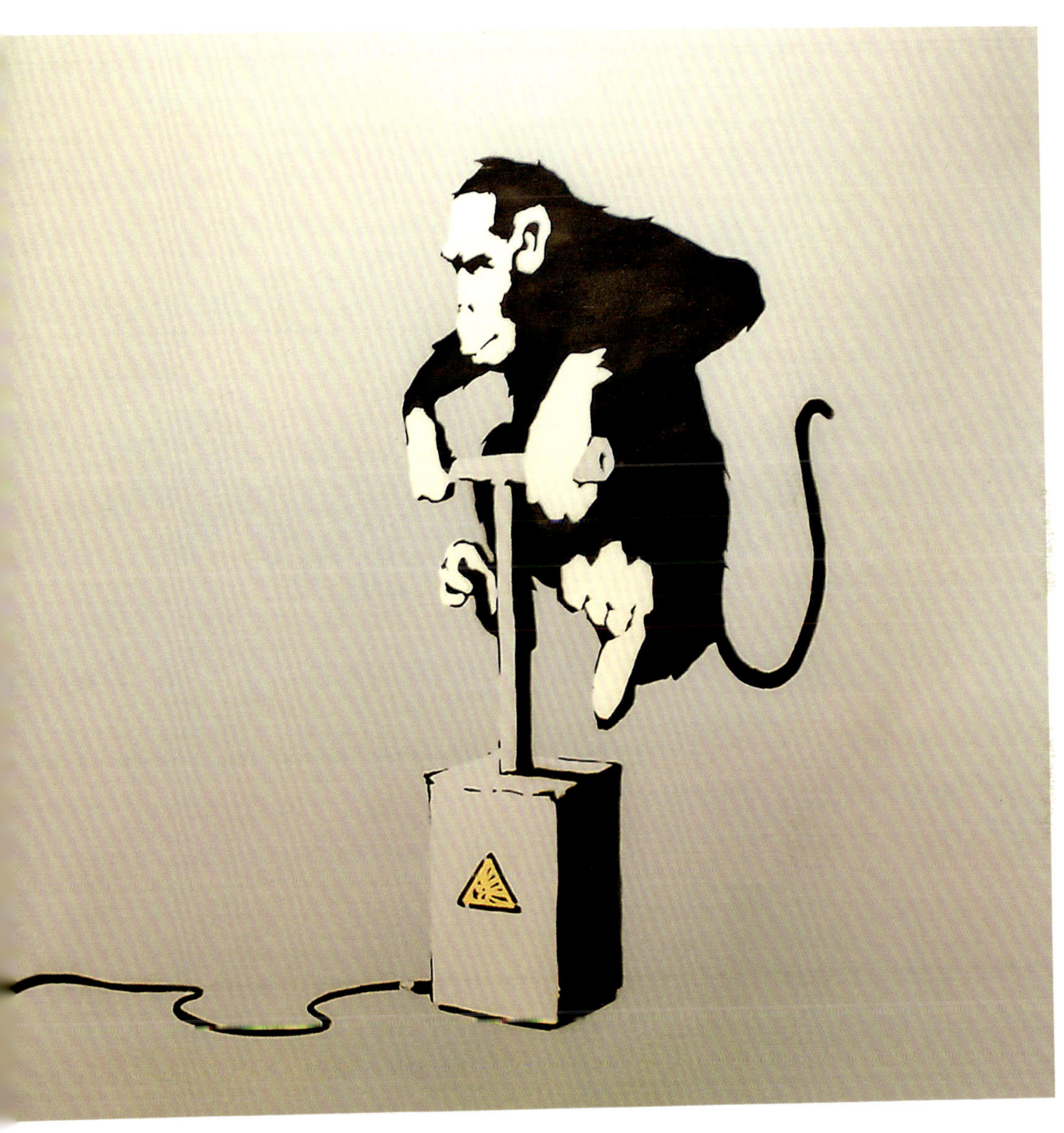

3, 2, 1... THE REVOLUTION HAS JUST BEGUN! A MONKEY IS
ABOUT TO TRIGGER AN EXPLOSION OF A BUNCH OF BANANAS.

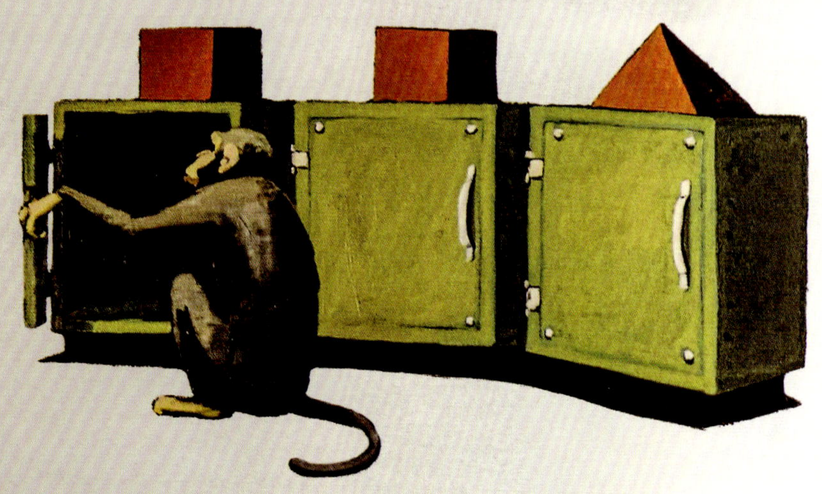

AFTER STACKING ALL THE SAFES ON TOP OF EACH OTHER, A CHIMPANZEE MANAGES TO ESCAPE FROM THE LABORATORY, THUS PASSING THE TEST BEYOND HUMANS' BEST EXPECTATIONS.

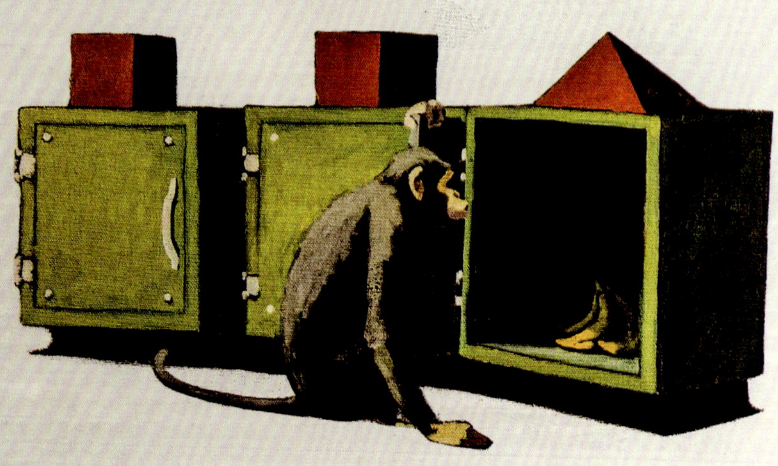

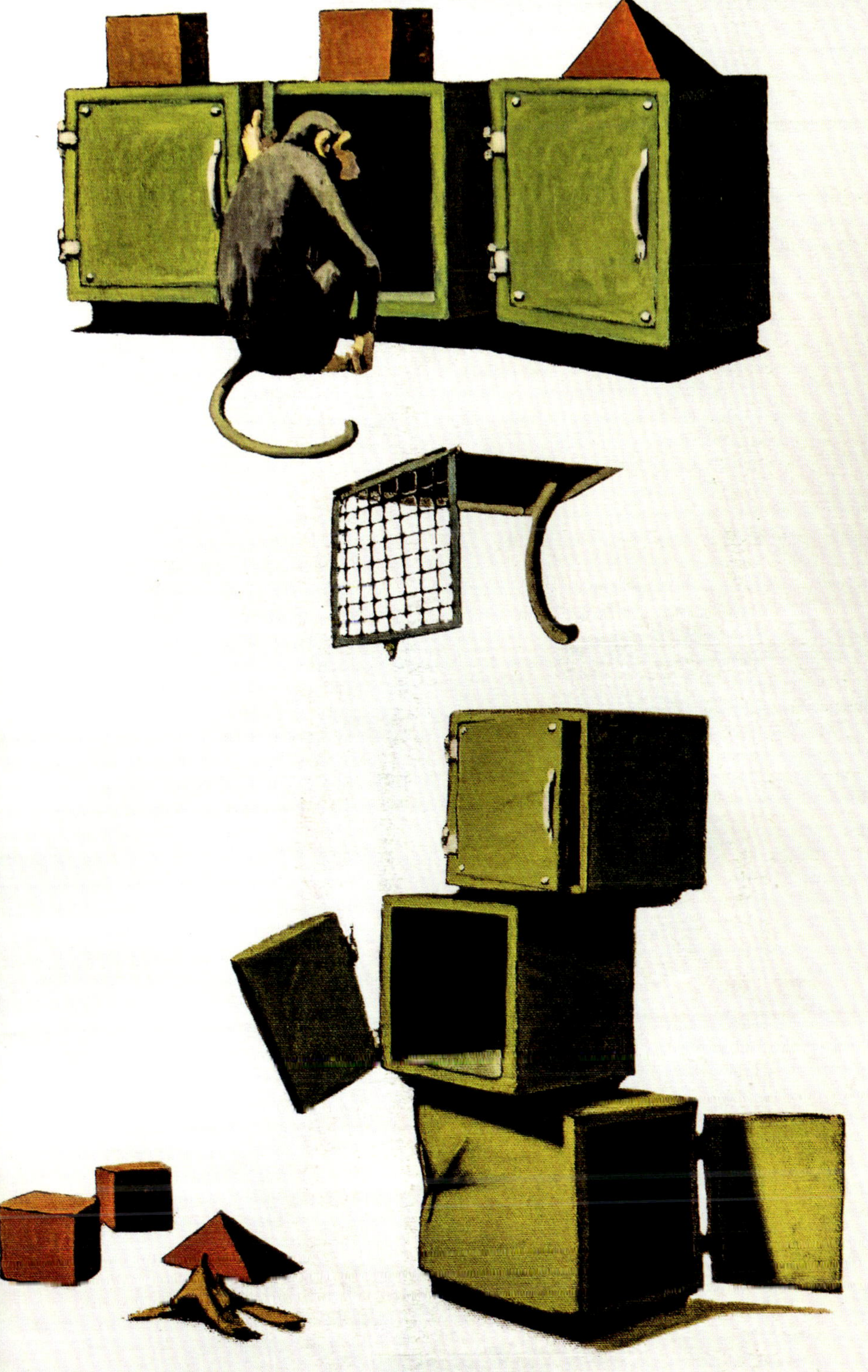

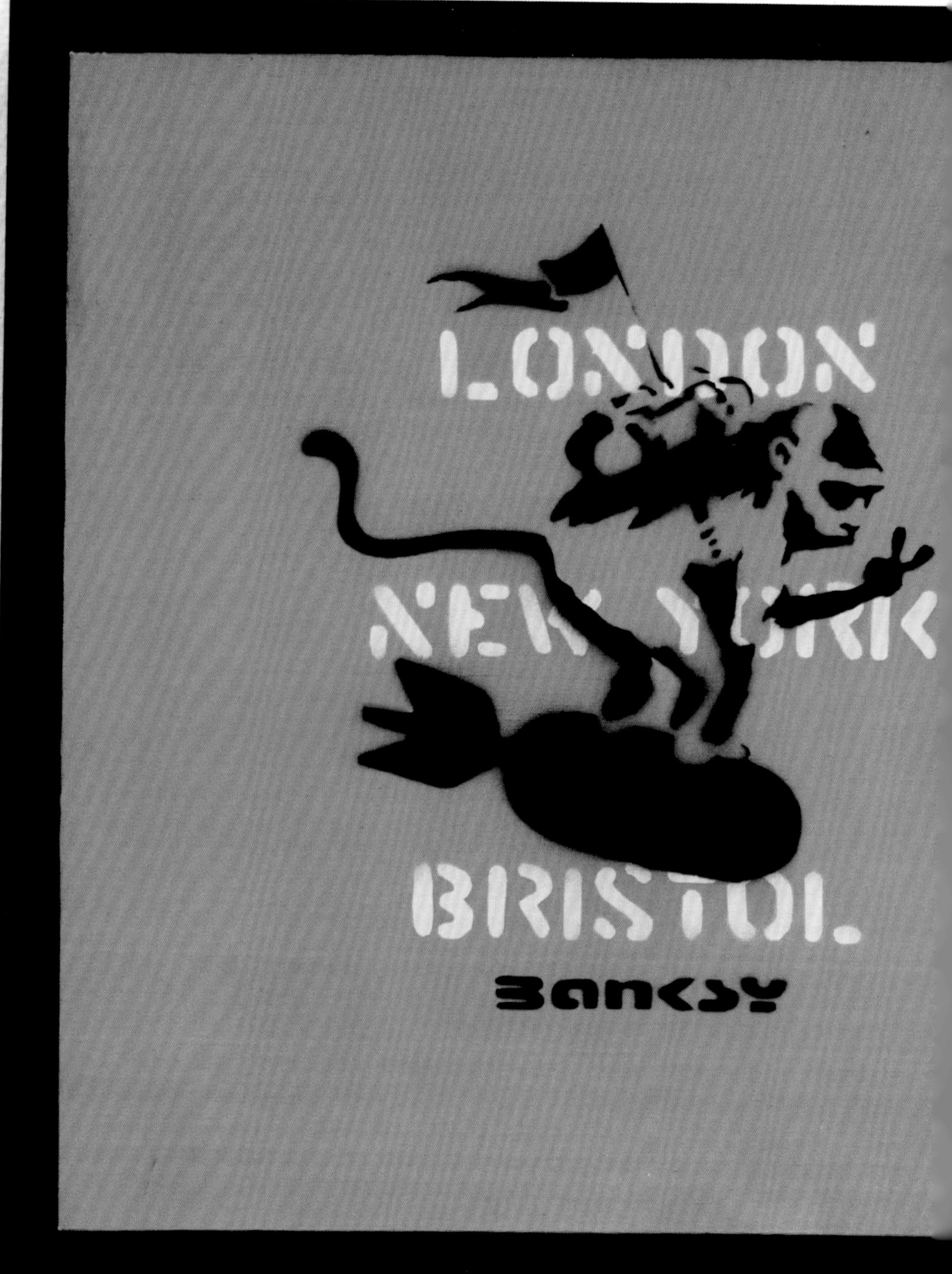
LONDON
NEW YORK
BRISTOL.
BANKSY

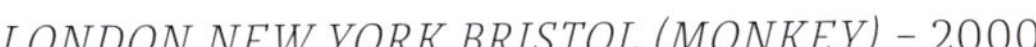

A MONKEY IS SURFING ON A BOMB AND FLASHING THE V SIGN. THE IMAGE IS A REFERENCE TO THE FAMOUS SCENE FROM THE NOIR COMEDY DR. STRANGELOVE OR: HOW I LEARNED TO STOP WORRYING AND LOVE THE BOMB, WHERE MAJOR KONG RIDES A BOMB UNTIL IT DETONATES.

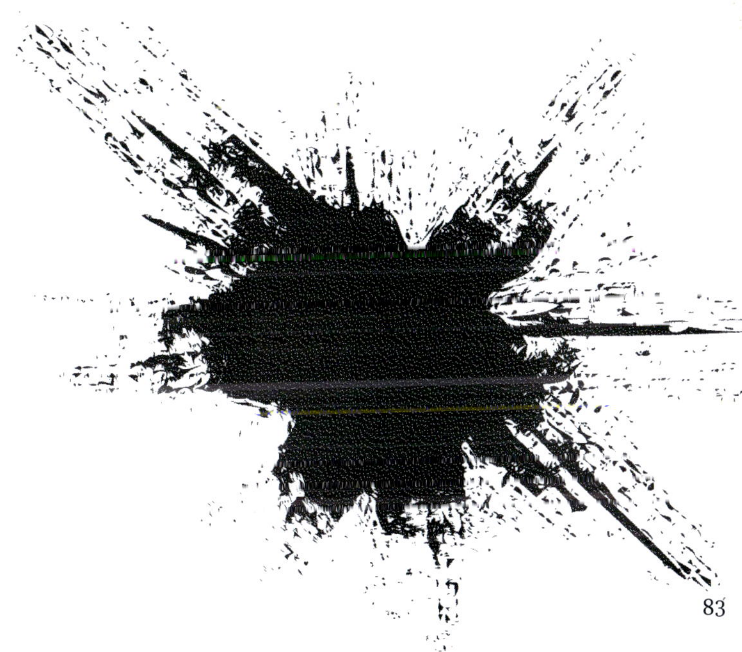

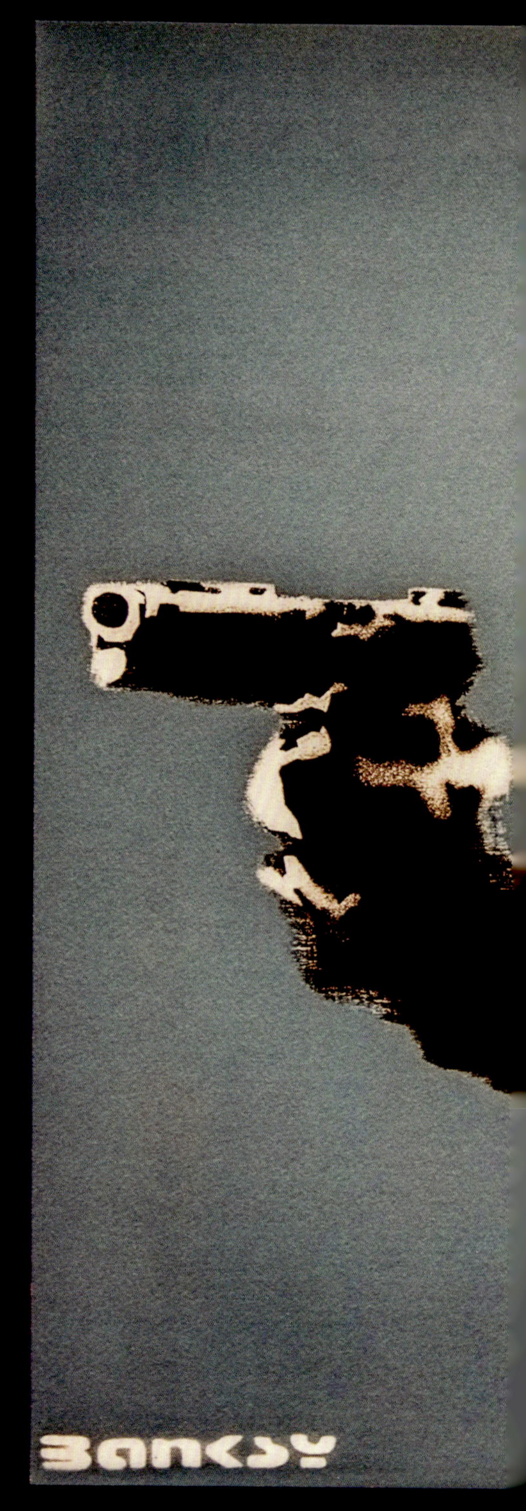

MONKEY GUNS – 2000

IN THIS WORK, BANKSY PORTRAYS A MONKEY FIRMLY POINTING TWO GUNS AT THE VIEWER.

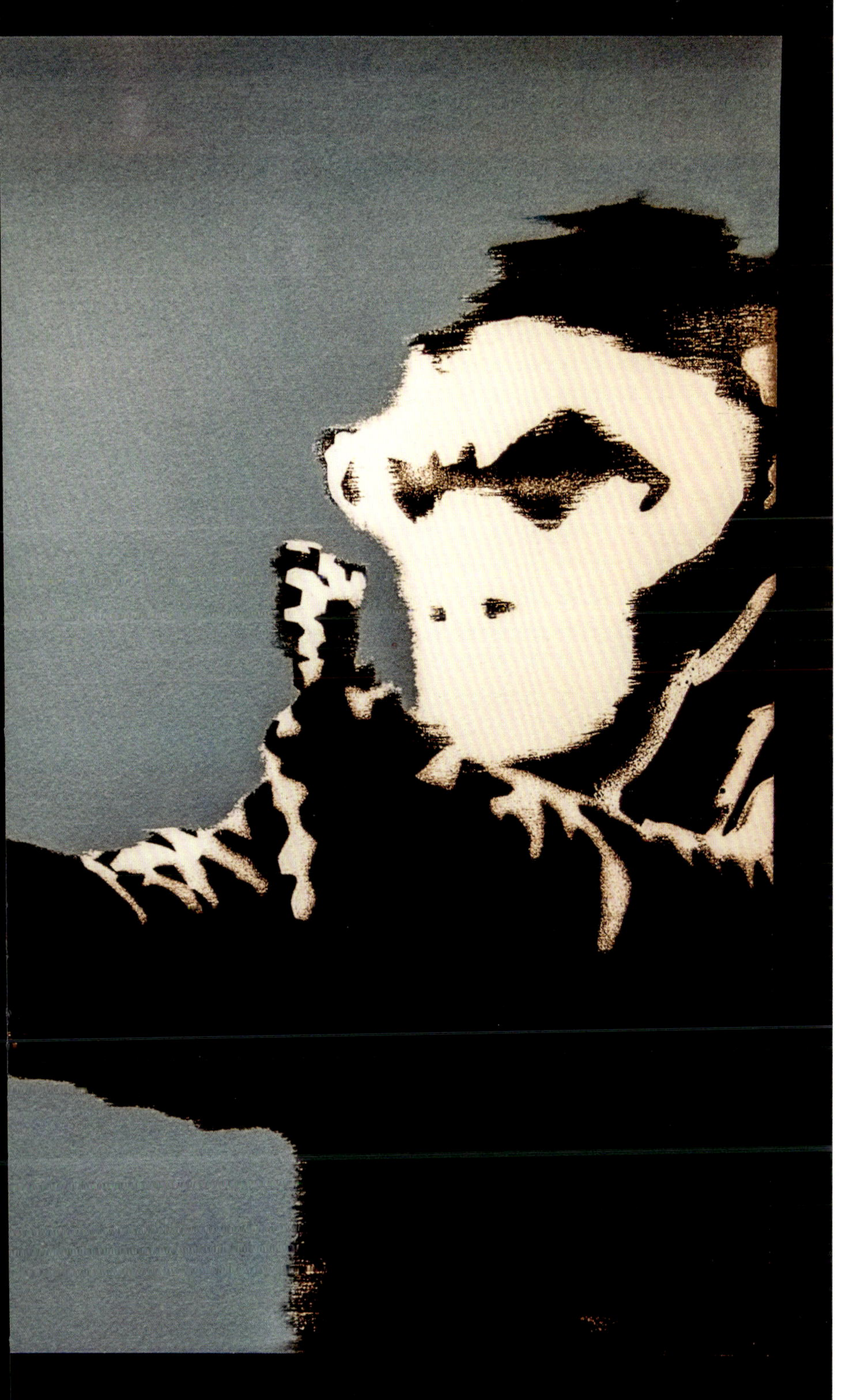

**IN THIS DOCUMENTARY,
BANKSY PERFECTLY CAPTURES
THE STREET ART SITUATION IN
THE LATE '90S.**

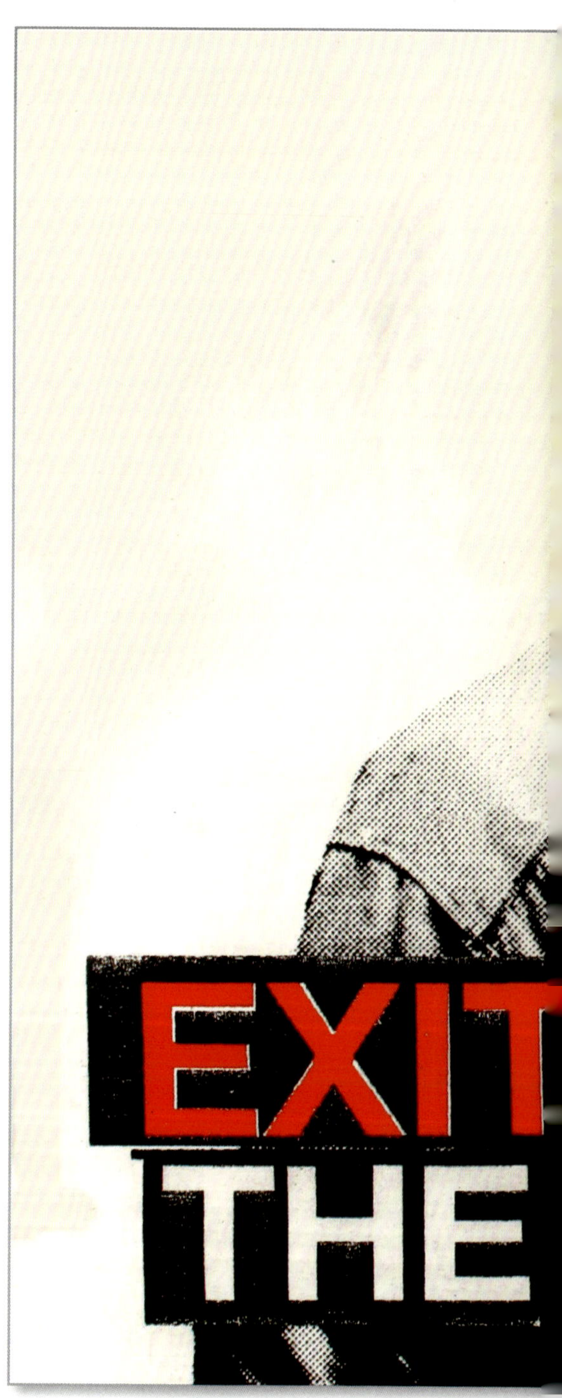

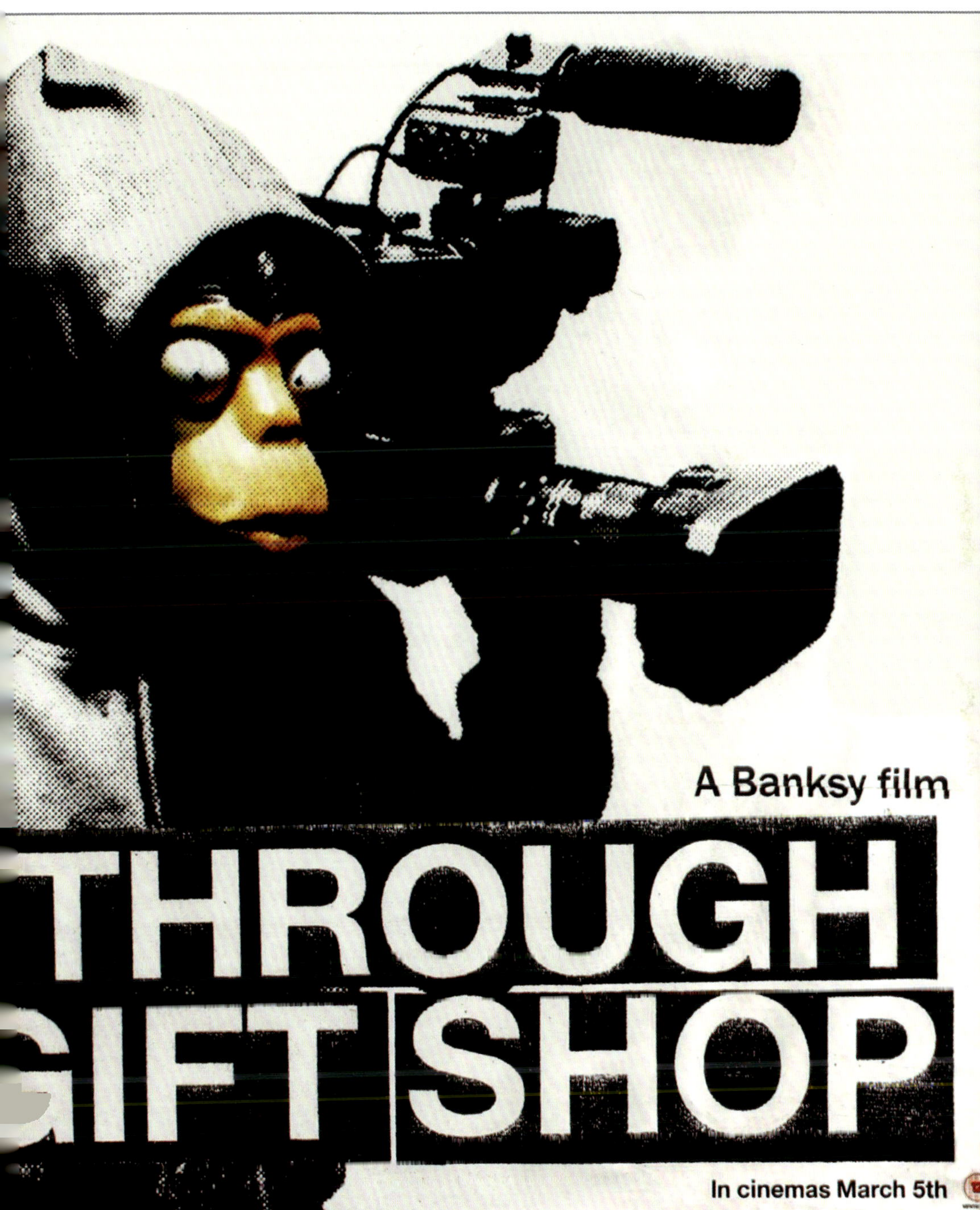

A Banksy film
THROUGH
GIFT SHOP
In cinemas March 5th

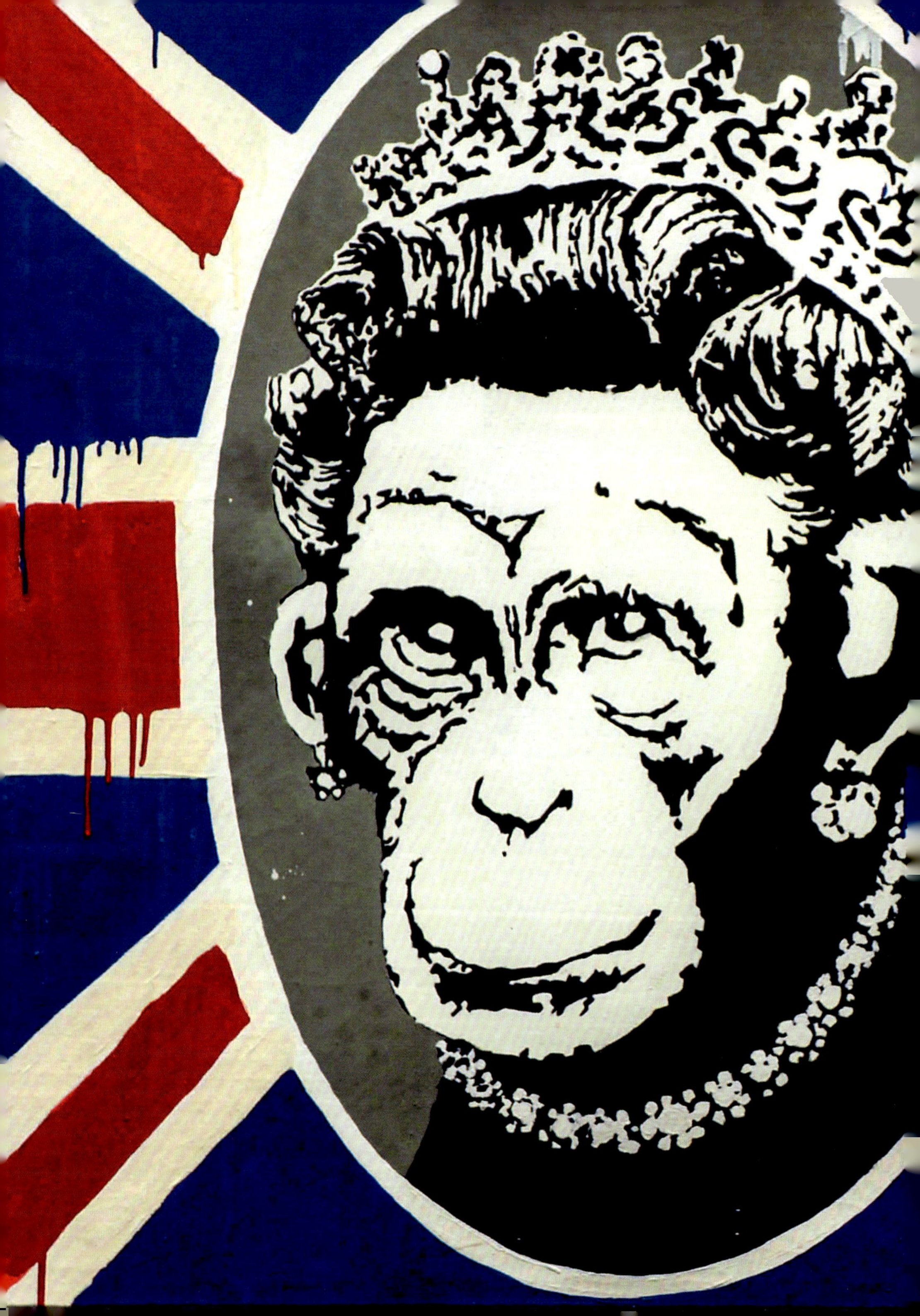

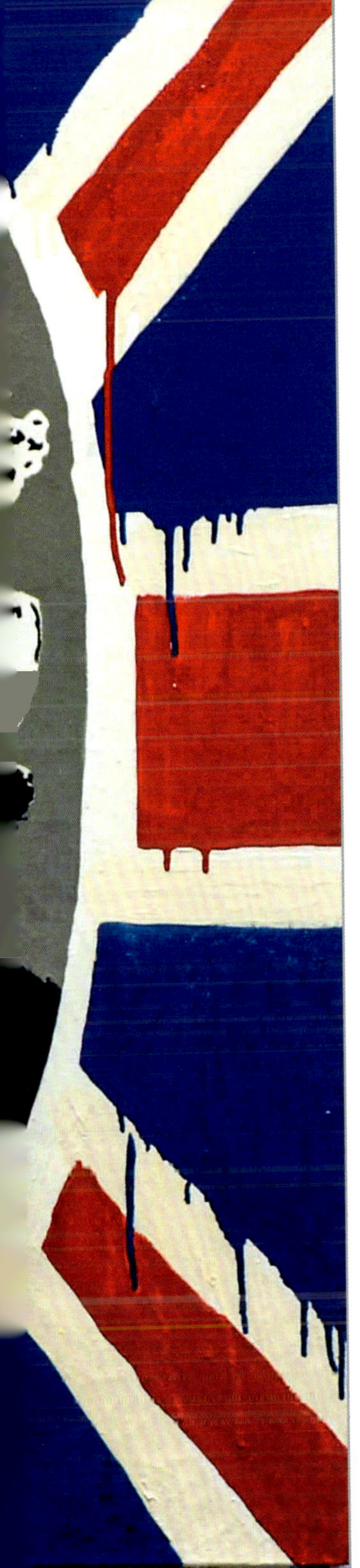

BANKSY CRITICIZES THE POWER OF THE BRITISH MONARCHY BY TURNING ONE OF THE MOST ICONIC PORTRAITS OF QUEEN ELIZABETH II INTO A MONKEY DECKED OUT IN THE ROYAL CROWN AND JEWELS.

DARWIN'S THEORY HAS DEFINITIVELY BEEN REFUTED HERE. MONKEYS SIT IN PARLIAMENT INSTEAD OF BRITISH POLITICIANS: A CLEAR SIGN OF BRITISH AND, MORE BROADLY, HUMAN "POLITICAL INVOLUTION."

92–93 A CARTOON-STYLE MONKEY AGAINST A BACKGROUND OF A CLASSIC PAINTING IS DRINKING FROM A GAS CAN. IT IS A CLEAR CRITIQUE AGAINST THE EXCESSIVE CONSUMPTION OF FOSSIL FUELS AND THE CRUELTY TO ANIMALS.

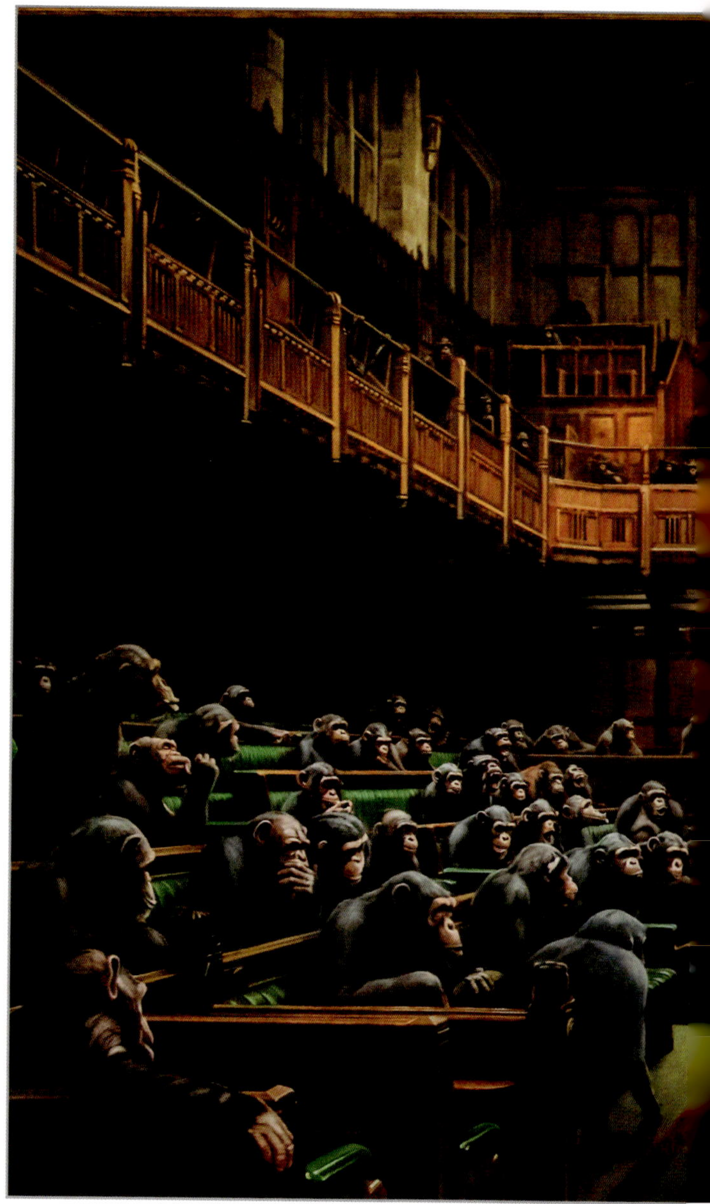

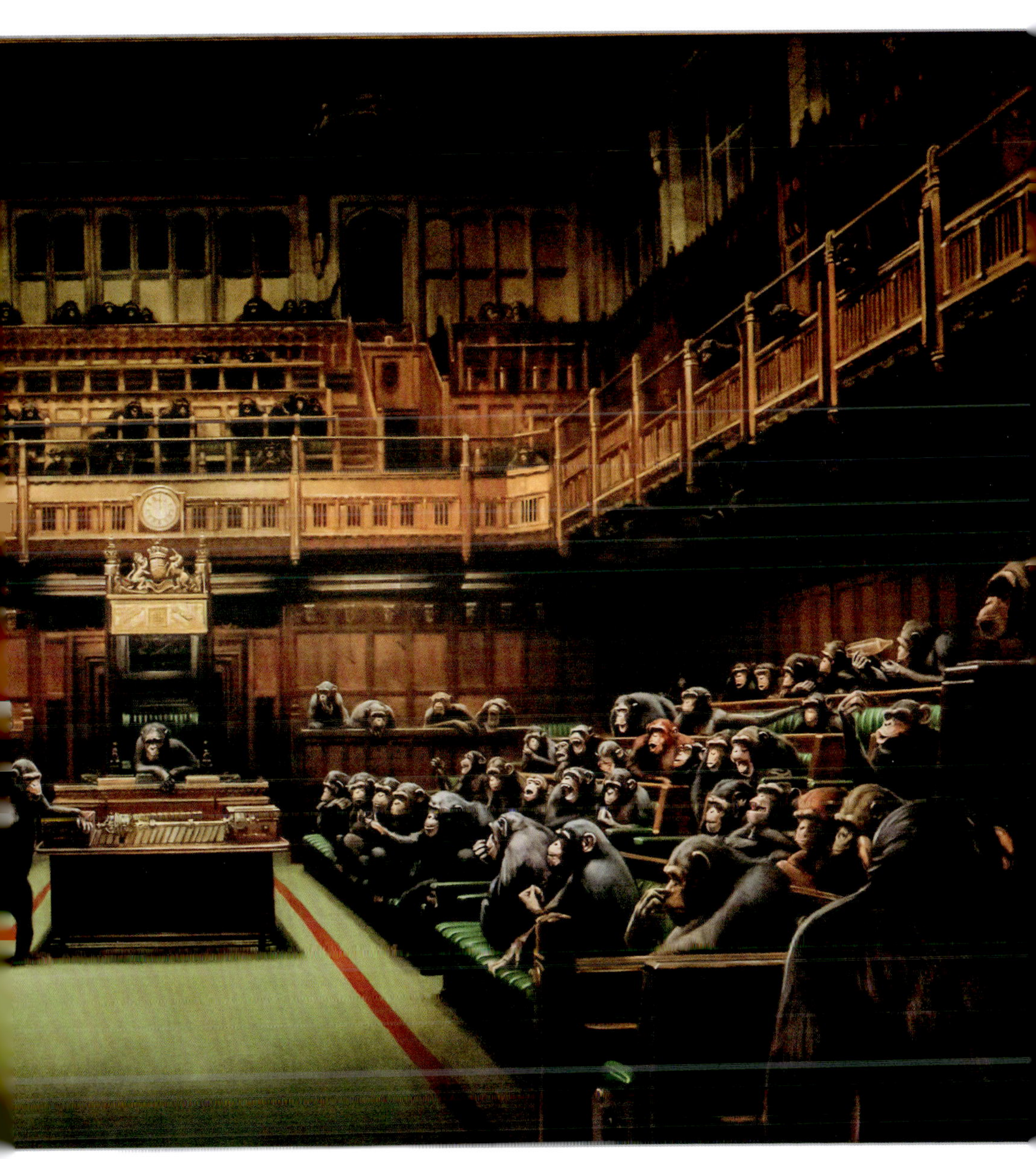

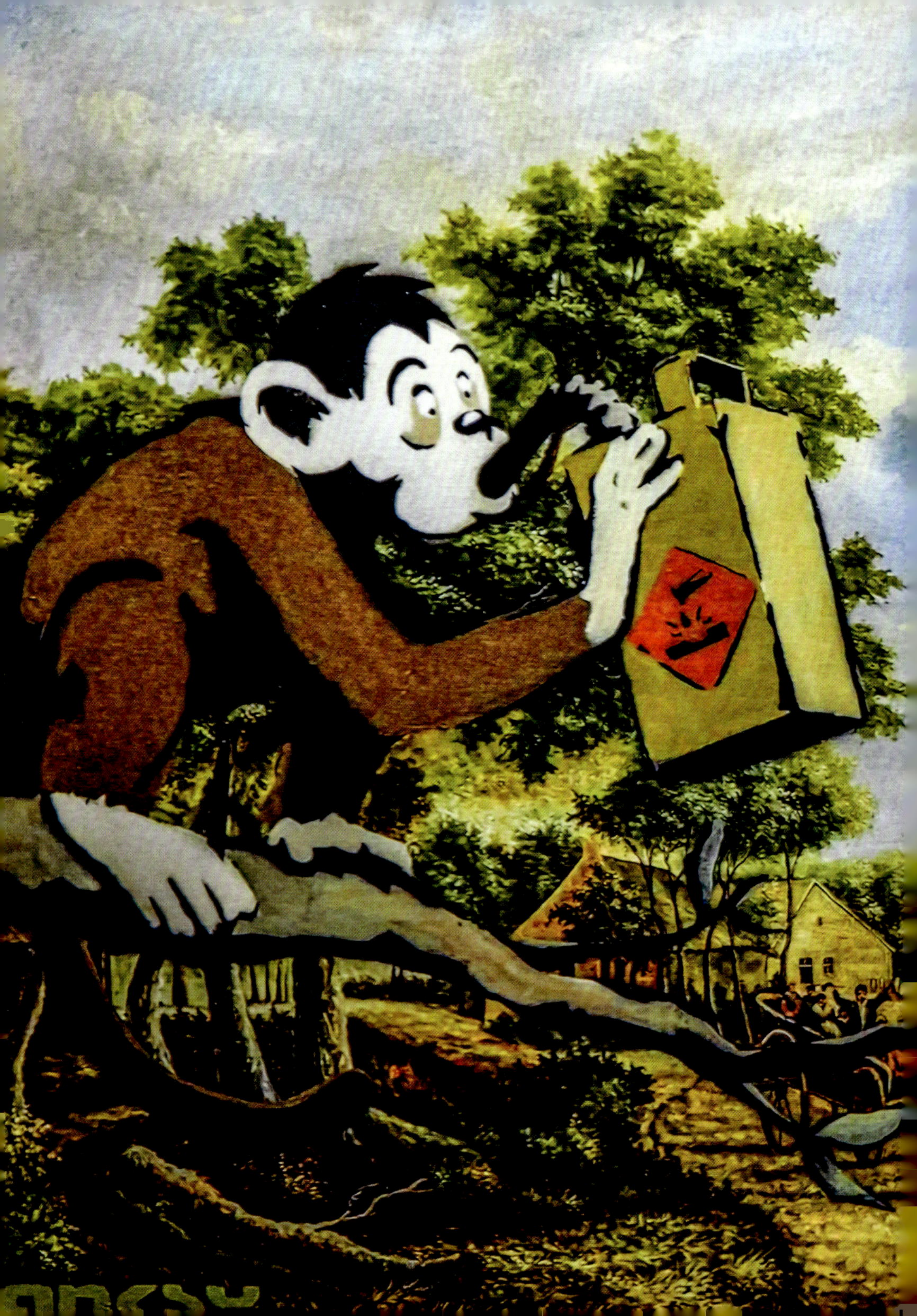

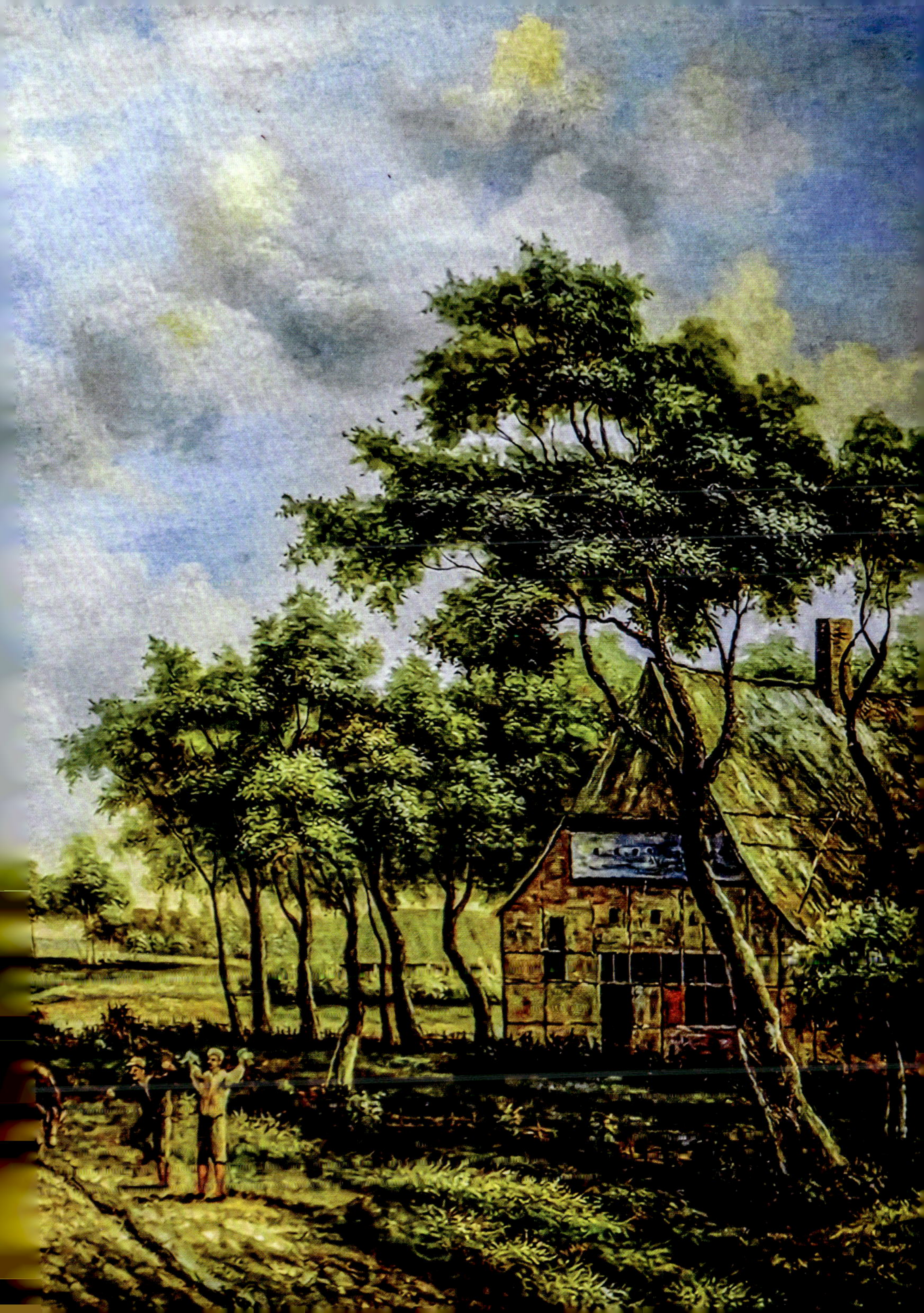

ABOUT THE AUTHOR

ALESSANDRA MATTANZA is a multi-award-winning writer and journalist, screenwriter, fine art photographer, and multimedia artist, and she lives between Munich, New York, San Francisco, Los Angeles, and Paris. She has collaborated with several magazines, including *Forbes, Vanity Fair, Elle, Cosmopolitan, How to Spend It, Icon, F,* and *Natural Style,* and she also writes novels and murder mysteries for several publishing houses. She won several awards for best articles and books at the Annual Southern California Journalism Awards and the SoCal Journalism Awards, in Los Angeles. Among the many awards she has received, she also won first prize in the nonfiction category for the books *C215 #christianguemy: Stencil Art* and the first *Banksy* book, and third prize for *Street Art: 20 Famous Artists Talk About Their Vision.* As an artist, she created the projects and media campaigns *www.newyorkblackandwhite. org,* exhibited at the Kunstlabor 2 museum, linked to the MUCA Museum in Munich, and *www.abetterplanetabetterworld.com,* presented in a major exhibition at the United Nations Headquarters of New York in 2023 and at the Italian Mission to the UN in New York until 2025. This last project for the environment was inspired by the book *SOS Planet Earth: Voices for a Better World,* published by National Geographic and White Star.

ABOUT THE CAPTIONS AUTHOR

LUCA GRECO is a copywriter, social media manager, and art blogger. After graduating in philosophy and completing a master's degree in marketing and communication from the IED in Turin, he collaborated with important communication agencies in Turin. An attentive observer of reality, Luca loves sharing his way of interpreting it by constantly experimenting with new forms of digital communication on his news and cultural study blog called "Fatti e Fabulae" (www.fattiefabulae.com). He is currently a copywriter and social media manager for a leading Italian digital experience company. Since 2022, he has been a social media management professor, teaching a course in Social Innovation, Communication, and New Technologies at the University of Turin.

PHOTO CREDITS

MIX
Paper from
responsible sources
FSC® C178000
FSC
www.fsc.org